AUTHOR'S PROFILE

Paul Baweja was born in Sydney, the Commonwealth of Australia. Paul Baweja was educated at LaSalle Catholic College (the City of Sydney, New South Wales), the College of the former Australian Prime Minister, the Right Honourable Paul John Keating of the Commonwealth of Australia (r. 1991-1996). In 2012, Paul Baweja earned the Bachelor of Commerce Degree from Macquarie University. Thereafter, in 2014, Paul attained the Graduate Diploma of Chartered Accounting from the Institute of Chartered Accountants Australia. Furthermore, Paul is the recipient of numerous academic awards, including the prestigious 'Golden Key International Honour Society' Award (Atlanta, Georgia, the United States of America).

In addition, Paul attended the Macquarie Business School (Macquarie University) to obtain the Master of Business Administration Degree in 2016. Paul further completed research-based postgraduate study at the Australian National University, graduating with the Master of Diplomacy (Advanced) Degree in 2018. Paul's Master's Degree Thesis was completed under the auspices of the ANU College of Asia and the Pacific. Paul's Thesis was titled 'International Conflict Mediation: A Diplomatic Analysis of the U.S. Camp David Talks (1978)'.

Paul Baweja is an Australian Author, Publisher, and Writer. Paul has previously written and published 'A Philosophical Treatise of Reality' in 2021, a 500,000-word four-volume treatise. Paul's fifth book, 'The Struggle of Women: Major Female Figures throughout World History' published in 2022 is 125,000 words in length. Furthermore, in 2022, Paul completed the Certificate of Catholic Theology at the Augustine Institute (Colorado, the United States of America). Last but not least, also in the year 2022, Paul attained the Certificate in Biblical Studies from the Biblical Training Institute (Camas, Washington, the United States of America).

THE STRUGGLE OF WOMEN

Major Female Figures throughout World History

PAUL BAWEJA

First published in Melbourne,

the Commonwealth of Australia, 2022.

Published by Paul Baweja

APTOR2021_enquiries@protonmail.com

ISBN: 978-0-6489818-0-0 (Hardcover Book)

Printed by Ingram Spark

I dedicate this book to the memory of Gentlelady Augusta Ada Lovelace (1815-1852). Lovelace was an English mathematician and writer, she made unprecedented progress in the field of Computing Science.

TIMELINE

1848 - The Women's Rights Convention (also known as the Seneca Falls Convention) is held in New York City, the United States of America

1848 - The Declaration of Sentiments is signed at the Seneca Falls Convention

1861 - The British Crown Colony of South Australia permits women who own real property and pay council rates the right to vote

1893 - New Zealand grants women the right to vote

1902 - Australia grants women who are British subjects the right to vote at elections for the Federal Parliament

1906 - The Grand Duchy of Finland grants women the right to vote and seek appointment to public office

1911 - First International Women's Day is held across Europe

1918 - Canada grants women over the age of twenty-one the right to vote

1918 - The United Kingdom grants women over the age of thirty, who satisfy a property qualification, the right to vote

1919 - The U.S. Congress passed the Nineteenth Amendment to the United States Constitution, granting American women the right to vote

1927 - The All-India Women's Conference is convened

1928 - The United Kingdom grants all British women over the age of twenty-one the right to vote (on equal terms with British men)

1946 - The United Nations Commission on the Status of Women is established

1960 - The United States Food and Drug Administration approves the first oral contraceptive pill (i.e., Enovid)

1960 - Sirimavo Bandaranaike becomes the modern world's first democratically elected Prime Minister of independent Ceylon

1974 - The United Nations General Assembly adopts The Declaration on the Protection of Women and Children in Emergency and Armed Conflict

1975 - The first United Nations World Conference on Women is held in Mexico City, Mexico

1975 - The United Nations celebrates International Women's Day

1979 - The United Nations General Assembly adopts The Convention on the Elimination of All Forms of Discrimination Against Women

1979 - Margaret Thatcher is elected as Prime Minister of the United Kingdom

1980 - The second United Nations World Conference on Women is held in Copenhagen, Denmark

1985 - The third United Nations World Conference on Women is held in Nairobi, Kenya

1995 - The fourth United Nations World Conference on Women is held in Beijing, China

2010 - The United Nations General Assembly establishes UN Women

2014 - Malala Yousafzai is the youngest ever recipient of the Nobel Peace Prize

2015 - Saudi Arabia grants women the right to vote and stand as candidates at its municipal elections

LIST OF
ABBREVIATIONS

A&A	Anaesthesia and Analgesia
AAC	Afro-American Council
AAGPBL	All-American Girls Professional Baseball League
AAS	American Astronomical Society
AASS	American Anti-Slavery Society
AAU	Amateur Athletic Union
ACBWA	All-Ceylon Buddhist Women's Association
ACLU	American Civil Liberties Union
ACS	American Cancer Society
ACT	Australian Capital Territory (Australia)
ACTH	Adrenocorticotropic hormone
AD	Anno Domini
ADA	American Diabetes Association
AERA	American Equal Rights Association
AFPA	American Free Produce Association
AGU	American Geophysical Union
AHA	American Heart Association
AHMA	American Holistic Medical Association

AIIMS	All-India Institute of Medical Science
AJDC	American Journal of Diseases of Children
AJOG	American Journal of Obstetrics and Gynaecology
AJP	American Journal of Physiology
AMA	American Medical Association
AMWA	American Medical Women's Association
AO	Australian Open
APA	American Philosophical Association
ARC	American Red Cross
ARI	Ayn Rand Institute
ATA	American Tennis Association
AUS	Australia
AWC	Association for Women in Computing
AWSA	American Woman Suffrage Association
BA	Bachelor of Arts
BA	British Airways
BAA	British Airports Authority
BAe	British Aerospace
BCC	British Coal Corporation
BCL	Bachelor of Civil Law
BCS	British Computer Society
BCURA	British Coal Utilisation Research Association
BEd	Bachelor of Education
BMJ	Buffalo Medical Journal
BOT	British Overseas Territories
BP	British Petroleum
BR	British Rail
BSc	Bachelor of Science
BT	British Telecommunications

CBE	Commander of the Order of the British Empire
CBWC	Cleveland Business Women's Club
CHD	Congenital Heart Disease
CHOGM	Commonwealth Heads of Government Meeting
CJ	Chief Justice
CLR	Columbia Law Review
CNZM	Companion of the New Zealand Order of Merit
CPC	Canada Post Corporation
CPGB	Communist Party of Great Britain
CSU	California State University
CTH	Commonwealth
CWC	Congress Working Committee
CWCC	Cleveland Women's City Club
CWL	Coloured Women's League
DBE	Dame Commander of the British Empire
DCL	Doctor of Civil Law
DNA	Decxyribonucleic Acid
DNZM	Dame Companion of the New Zealand Order of Merit
DSO	Distinguished Service Order
EBRI	European Brain Research Institute
EC	European Committee
ECIC	Employer's Casualty Insurance Company
ELS	English Law Society
ERA	Equal Rights Amendment
ERP	Equal Rights Party
FAMU	Florida Agricultural and Mechanical University
FRS	Fellow of the Royal Society
GB	Great Britain
GCSAA	Golf Course Superintendents Association of America

GFASHOF	Greater Flint Area Sports Hall of Fame
GSA	Genetics Society of America
GSK	GlaxoSmithKline
GWAA	Golf Writers Association of America
HCO	Harvard College Observatory
HCWSA	Henry County Woman Suffrage Association
HGH	Human Growth Hormone
HK	Hong Kong
HLR	Harvard Law Review
IAAF	International Association of Athletics Federation
IAW	International Alliance of Women
ICB	Institute of Cell Biology
ICW	International Council of Women
IGHOF	International Gymnastics Hall of Fame
INC	Indian National Congress
IOC	International Olympic Committee
IOWA	Iowa Organisation of Women Attorneys
ISHOF	International Swimming Hall of Fame
ISU	International Skating Union
IUCr	International Union of Crystallography
IUPAC	International Union of Pure and Applied Chemistry
IWSA	International Woman Suffrage Alliance
IWSHOF	International Women's Sports Hall of Fame
JAMA	Journal of the American Medical Association
JCEM	Journal of Clinical Endocrinology and Metabolism
JID	Journal of Infectious Diseases
JP	Justice of the Peace
KC	King's Counsel
LLB	Bachelor of Laws

LLD	Doctor of Laws
LOC	Library of Congress
LPGA	Ladies Professional Golf Association
LSS	Law Society of Scotland
LWC	Ladies World Championships
MA	Master of Arts
MBE	Member of the Order of the British Empire
MD	Doctor of Medicine
MP	Member of Parliament
MPP	Member of Provincial Parliament
MWSA	Montana Women's Suffrage Association
NACA	National Advisory Committee for Aeronautics
NACWC	National Association of Coloured Women's Clubs
NAM	Non-Aligned Movement
NAS	National Academy of Sciences
NASA	National Aeronautics and Space Administration
NAWL	National League of Women Lawyers
NAWSA	National American Woman Suffrage Association
NAZI	National Socialist German Workers' Party
NCAA	National Collegiate Athletic Association
NCL	National Consumers League
NCW	National Council of Women
NCWC	National Council of Women of Canada
NCWNZ	National Council of Women of New Zealand
NEJM	New England Journal of Medicine
NERL	National Equal Rights League
NGF	Nerve Growth Factor
NHL	National Historic Landmark
NHS	National Health Society

NLA	National Library of Australia
NMS	National Medal of Science
NPT	Treaty on the Non-Proliferation of Nuclear Weapons
NRHP	National Register of Historic Places
NSW	New South Wales (Australia)
NSWLSA	New South Wales Ladies Swimming Association
NWHF	National Women's Hall of Fame
NWP	National Woman's Party
NWSA	National Woman Suffrage Association
NYC	New York City
NYPAL	New York Police Athletic League
NYSTA	New York State Teachers' Association
NYU	New York University
NZ	New Zealand
NZWCTU	New Zealand Women's Christian Temperance Union
OHCHR	Office of the High Commissioner for Human Rights
OM	Order of Merit
OSHOF	Ontario Sports Hall of Fame
PAS	Pennsylvania Abolition Society
PhD	Doctor of Philosophy
PLC	Presbyterian Ladies' College
Po	Polonium (Chemical Element)
POW	Prisoner of War
PRC	People's Republic of China
QC	Queen's Counsel
Ra	Radium (Chemical Element)
RAF	Romanian Athletics Federation
RC	Red Cross
RCC	Roman Catholic Church

RDGI	Royal Danish Geodetic Institute
RIA	Radioimmunoassay
RNA	Ribonucleic Acid
ROC	Romanian Olympic Committee
RRC	Royal Red Cross
RVO	Royal Victorian Order
SCOTUS	Supreme Court of the United States
SLAS	Scottish Law Agents Society
SS	*Schutzstaffel* (Protective Echelon)
UCLA	University of California, Los Angeles
UDHR	Universal Declaration of Human Rights
U.K.	United Kingdom of Great Britain and Northern Ireland
UN	United Nations
UNFP	United National Front Party
UNP	United National Party
UNRRA	U. N. Relief and Rehabilitation Administration
UPU	Universal Peace Union
U.S.A.	United States of America
USAR	United States Army Reserve
USATF	United States Track and Field
USDoS	United States Department of State
USGA	United States Golf Association
USMC	United States Marine Corps
USPO	United States Patent Office
USPS	United States Postal Service
USSC	United States Sanitary Commission
U.S.S.R.	Union of Soviet Socialist Republics
USTA	United States Tennis Association
VAT	Value Added Tax

VC	Victoria Cross
WAGC	World Artistic Gymnastics Championships
WC	World Championships
WCRA	Women's Central Relief Association
WCTU	Women's Christian Temperance Union
WFL	Women's Franchise League
WILPF	Women's Int. League for Peace and Freedom
WPGB	Women's Party of Great Britain
WSA	Women's Swimming Association
WSPU	Women's Social and Political Union
WWI	World War 1 (1914-1918)
WWII	World War 2 (1939-1945)
YMCA	Young Men's Christian Association
YWCA	Young Women's Christian Association
YWHA	Young Women's Hebrew Association

KEYWORDS

American, Australian, Birth, Born, British, Brother, Canada, Catholic, Child, Childhood, Child prodigy, Death, Died, Discrimination, Divorce, Doctor, Education, Employment, England, Equality, Ethics, Ethnicity, Family, Father, Female, Feminism, Gender, Geography, History, Hospital, Human rights, International law, Ireland, Justice, King, Law, Male, Marriage, Medicine, Men, Morality, Mother, New York, New Zealand, Nurse, Parents, Parliament, Peace, Philosophy, Politics, Power, Queen, Race, Religion, Rights, School, Science, Scotland, Sex, Sexism, Sibling, Sister, Sovereign, Sport, Suffrage, Suffragettes, Teacher, United Kingdom, United States, University, Vote, War, and Women.

PREFACE

This book investigates *who* were the women that made a significant contribution to world history, and *what* was their unique contribution. In contemporary times, greater attention has been attributed to research and writing on women in scholarly literature and academic study. Undoubtedly, the increased attention and importance that recent scholars have attributed to women's role in society, education, work, culture, and politics was long overdue. Yet, much more remains to be examined about the women who have made modern history in their own capacity and right. The struggle of women in the world has been an unequal one, and regrettably, it still remains an unequal one.

This book examines the contribution of women from different walks of life. It considers women across multiple nation-states, various eras and epochs, women in slavery, poverty, and aristocracy. Furthermore, this book identifies the invaluable contribution of saintly and secular women alike, it also cuts across the variations of gender, race, colour, social class, ethnicity, private wealth, education, socio-economic status, vocation, and marital status.

Last but not least, this book will illuminate and underscore the importance of women in shaping the modern world. More importantly, this book serves as newfound impetus for the modern society to devote greater attention and awareness to the indispensable role of women in society, culture, and politics.

Paul Baweja

Australian Author and Writer

the Commonwealth of Australia

April 2022

1INTRODUCTION

The Women's Strugg.e for equality, liberty, justice, citizenship, and enfranchisement has been (and in many respects, continues to be) an unequal one. This book highlights some of the major female figures who have made profound contributions to the universal cause of women in the world. From the onset it is essential to delineate the contours of this book's grand objective. This book identifies select women who have made history in different spheres and dimensions of the world. It is an impossible endeavour for one book to describe and detail the countless women who have made both ancient and modern history. Needless to say, there are many important women who are not included in this concise historical account, as scope does not permit examination. This does not infer, that certain unexamined women's contributions are insignificant or inconsequential.

This book intends to achieve two aims. First, identify the major female figures who have made extraordinary contributions throughout world history. Second, describe the life and experiences of those select women. In achieving these two aims, this book examines the accomplishments of women across a multitude of domains. This book is organised across seven distinct chapters, namely:

1. Women in Philosophy
2. Women in Religion
3. Women in Science
4. Women in Medicine
5. Women in Politics
6. Women in Law
7. Women in Sport

This book provides the reader with an outline of women's contribution to the human civilisation. The author trusts it will serve as foundational intellectual stimulus to the interested reader. The author encourages the reader to undertake a further critical examination of the enduring struggle of women in the modern world.

CONTENTS

CHAPTER ONE

WOMEN IN PHILOSOPHY

'Life is growth, and the more we travel, the more truth we can understand. Understanding the things that surround us is the best preparation to understand the things that lie beyond.'

Hypatia of Alexandria

The intrinsic purpose of philosophy is to question, inquire, and examine into the human perception of reality. By definition, philosophy ought to commence such an honourable undertaking without the express limitation of prejudices, assumptions, systematic bias, or partiality. Notwithstanding, the pursuit of such a noble and lofty aspiration, for much of human history, philosophical thoughts, ideas, concepts, doctrines, principles, assumptions, and narratives have been predominantly debated, delineated, and defined by learned men. Among other significant barriers, most notably, it was by the discrimination of sex, that women were not afforded equal participation, in conjunction with the lack of equal education opportunities, to develop their intellectual faculties and become comprehensively immersed in the pre-modern philosophical discourse.

Historically speaking, when women were involved in the sphere of philosophy, it was usually on the margins and fringes of the pre-modern society. However, women have always made seminal contributions to the field of philosophy, serving to enrich the field with diverse, complementary, and competing perspectives on a wide variety of subject matters, including aesthetics, logic, metaphysics, phenomenology, history, the classics, ethics, anthropology, epistemology, political theory, religion, mind, and science. From ancient times to modern times, from the Old World into the passage of the New World, one will find a number of female philosophers scattered across the scholarly literature. In fact, in contemporary times, women have made great contributions to the discipline of philosophy. For example, consider the original works and writings of political philosopher, Hannah Arendt (1906-1975), existential philosopher, Simone de Beauvoir (1908-1986), English writer and philosopher, Mary Wollstonecraft (1759-1797), and Russian-born American writer, Ayn Rand (1905-1982).

This chapter explores several women who have made lasting and monumental impressions in the field of philosophy. It will examine the lives and ideas of Hypatia, Héloïse d'Argenteuil, Tullia d'Aragona, Edith Stein, Ayn Rand, Hannah Arendt, Simone de Beauvoir, and Iris Murdoch. All these female philosophers, and many more, have made seminal contributions to the literature on philosophy. Indeed, women's contribution to philosophy has served to advance human knowledge and create a more diverse array of views on the subjective discourse encompassing the existential reality of being and the human condition.

Hypatia (ca. 360 AD - 415 AD)

Hypatia was born in the year 360 AD in the great City of Alexandria in Egypt. Hypatia was the daughter of Theon of Alexandria, one of the most educated gentlemen in Alexandria at the time. Hypatia's father, Theon of Alexandria, was an astronomer, scholar, and professor of mathematics at the world-renowned University of Alexandria. The details regarding Hypatia's biological mother have been forever lost to history. With the guidance, wisdom, and instruction of her father, from a very young age Hypatia was immersed in a world of learning and education. Hypatia's formal studies included astrology, astronomy, mathematics, and philosophy.

Hypatia followed in the footsteps of her scholarly father, and she became an academic and intellectual figure. Hypatia wrote extensive commentaries on some of the most authoritative texts of her time, including Diophantus' *Arithmetica* and Ptolemy's *Almagest*. In addition, Hypatia also edited Apollonius' *On the Conics*. Arguably, Hypatia is the most distinguished Egyptian female philosopher of the ancient world. Most notably, Hypatia made original contributions to the fields of algebra, arithmetic, astronomy, geometry, and mathematics.

Furthermore, Hypatia was appointed Head of the Platonist School of Alexandria in ca. 400 AD. This was a remarkable and unprecedent achievement for a female philosopher at the time. Hypatia was a talented philosopher in her own right, and she even wore the traditionally male apparel, known as the *tribon* (i.e., the robes of a learned intellectual and scholar). Symbolism mattered, and the *tribon* served to demonstrate Hypatia's influence, prestige, education, and scholarly accomplishments. Not to mention, Hypatia frequently presented public lectures and captivating speeches to those people willing to listen to her intellectual discourses on Aristotle and Plato.

In addition, Hypatia become a Professor of Philosophy at the University of Alexandria in Egypt. Hypatia taught, wrote, and lectured on the Neoplatonist branch of Western philosophy. As an academic, Hypatia had virtually unimpeded access to the Great Library of Alexandria which held some 500,000 books in its main building, and many thousands more that were stored in its adjacent annex. Hypatia's unrivalled access to such a grand storehouse of advanced writings and seminal texts, made possible her invaluable contributions to scholarship and learning in Alexandria, albeit most of her original writings have been lost to history.

Hypatia practiced what she preached. The Egyptian philosopher never married, and more likely than not, she led a celibate and chaste life. Hypatia was a gifted orator, and her philosophical discourses earnt her the admiration and praise of Alexandria's Governor, Orestes. Unfortunately, Hypatia was a convenient political target in turbulent times. Not only was Hypatia a woman who engaged in public speaking in civil society, she was also a Pagan, and she did not believe in Christianity. Furthermore, Hypatia also preached the principles, doctrines, theories, and ideas of Neoplatonism, which espoused non-Christian philosophy and secular thought. In Hypatia's teachings, she espoused predominantly Platonist philosophical ideas, such as the Oneness of all Reality, the Doctrine of Platonic Forms, the abstraction of reality beyond the material world, the ideal concepts of Transcendentals (i.e., truth, beauty, and goodness), and meditative contemplation on the Soul.

Regrettably, Hypatia's life ended in utter tragedy in the year 415 AD. Hypatia was an innocent victim of mob violence by select Christian monks that were directed by Peter the Lector. During this time in the great ancient City of Alexandria, religious tolerance was diminishing. Christianity was starting to dominate other religions and public life in the City. Consequently, public riots and sporadic violence often broke out between groups of Egyptian people with competing beliefs, values, idols, Gods, and ideologies. For example, consider the distinct presence of Christians, Jews, and Pagans in the City of Alexandria, which made preserving the peace an uneasy task, if not a problematic one.

Through the insights of history, it is widely understood that Cyril, the Christian Archbishop of Alexandria, an influential leader among the Christians, and Orestes, the Civil Governor / Prefect of Alexandria, who was a Pagan, both vehemently detested each other. Hypatia was a staunch supporter of Orestes, and therefore, Cyril fabricated unfounded accusations against Hypatia, which ultimately resulted in a violent mob attack on her by a number of Christian monks. One day on Hypatia's way home from the University of Alexandria, she was forced out of the chariot that she was travelling in. Hypatia was then dragged through the streets of Alexandria, taken into a local Church, where she was stripped naked, viciously beaten, and stoned with pottery and other items of clay, before being burned to her most violent death.

The end of Hypatia's life was a turning point in the history of Alexandria, but it also marked a significant moment in time for the Western world. For the death of Hypatia came to represent the end of the Classical Era, and the beginning of the end of Paganism. Thereafter, Christianity began to flourish throughout the City of Alexandria, and the land of Egypt, until the 7th century advent of Islam and the arrival of the Muslim people, which is altogether another fascinating story of medieval history.

Héloïse d'Argenteuil (ca. 1098 -1164)

The profound story of *Héloïse* is one intertwined with love, philosophy, faith, romance, writing, and education. The exact details surrounding *Héloïse's* father and mother have been lost to history, more likely than not she was an orphan. Notwithstanding the scant details of *Héloïse's* parentage, she did have extended family who were involved in her early life. Most importantly, *Héloïse* was the niece of Canon Fulbert, who was one of the influential figures in her early life. From a young age *Héloïse* displayed a remarkable ability to read, write, and learn. Not to mention, *Héloïse* was taught several languages, including Greek, Hebrew, and Latin. *Héloïse's* early education was completed at the Convent of Argenteuil, where she was educated by French nuns.

In 12th century French society, by the hallmarks and dictates of medieval custom, women were not permitted to receive a university level education. Thus, formal study to obtain a university degree was not a plausible option for *Héloïse*. Consequently, Canon Fulbert arranged for *Héloïse* to be entrusted to the learned company of French theologian, poet, and philosopher, Peter Abelard (1079-1142), who was responsible for her further education. In his own right, Peter was a first-rate university scholar. In fact, Peter was one of the greatest French philosophers of the 12th century. *Héloïse* went on to learn philosophy and medicine in the company of Peter Abelard.

Although Peter was a celibate and demonstrated negligible sexual interest in women, during the time *Héloïse* was in the company of Peter, the two fell in love. Peter found a strong desire and newfound sexual interest to be with *Héloïse*. More importantly, *Héloïse* and Peter were more than just intimate lovers, with both parties sharing a mutually satisfying friendship and genuine passion for learning. Peter admired *Héloïse* for both her sharp intellect and captivating beauty, however, he was quick to emphasise that he courted *Héloïse* for her brilliant mind and remarkable literary ability, in particular, her thoughtfully written letters. Peter was a learned man, and he did not wish to portray his relationship with *Héloïse,* purely on the illegitimate grounds of concupiscence. On this occasion, both the material form and intangible substance of their relationship mattered.

During the course of their intimate relationship *Héloïse* became pregnant and she gave birth to their illegitimate son (i.e., Astrolabe). This secret romantic union and unexpected offspring outraged *Héloïse's* extended family members. Consequently, the two lovers got married as a means to make amends for their questionable actions. Their marriage was not without considerable controversy. Initially, *Héloïse* was totally against the marriage proposal, being a free-willed and fiercely independent woman, she did not wish to enter into the ancient institution of marriage. *Héloïse* even went so far to claim that she would proudly be Peter's concubine. However, the social expectations of women in the medieval French society, coupled with Peter's more conservative and traditional world perception, made such ongoing informal sexual relations problematic between the two lovers. In the irrational course of reasoning out passion, *Héloïse* eventually acquiesced to the marriage proposal, albeit reluctantly. In reality, this civil union was more a matter of social expediency for Peter's distinguished academic career and the preservation of his stellar reputation, or at least what was left of it.

Héloïse's relative, Canon Fulbert remained furious at the immoral actions of Peter Abelard. Canon felt that Peter had personally betrayed his trust and taken sexual advantage of *Héloïse.* In so far as their marriage was concerned, in the eyes of Canon Fulbert, it did little to make amends for Peter's self-interested actions. In response, Canon Fulbert took matters into his own hands and sought out retribution against Peter. Canon devised a plan for the physical assault of Peter at his home, where he was forcefully castrated. This traumatic act of involuntary sterilisation that was performed upon Peter was without the use or benefit of proper medical procedures found in modern surgery. Nonetheless, Peter survived this devastating physical assault on his bodily integrity. Thereafter, Peter became a Benedictine monk at the Royal Abbey of Saint Denis located near the City of Paris.

Following the intense love ordeal and forced castration, Peter was plagued by jealousy, resentment, and bitterness. Not to mention, *Héloïse* now sincerely desired to become his wife, however, Peter felt that the 'sexual' dimension of their relationship was so strong, that she would eventually seek out another lover to engage in extramarital sexual intercourse, in an attempt to fulfil her desires, that he was no longer physically capable of satisfying. As a result, Peter ultimately convinced *Héloïse* to become a nun, and she eventually went on to become a high-ranking abbess in the Catholic Church.

Héloïse and Peter exchanged multiple letters throughout their lifetime. Not to mention, the two individuals made original contributions to French thought, philosophy, and literature. Some of *Héloïse* and Peter's writings include the four *Personal Letters* and the three *Letters of Direction.* *Héloïse's* thought was influenced by a number of prominent

Western philosophers and Catholic theologians, including Marcus Tullius Cicero, Marcus Annaeus Lucanus, Tertullian, Saint Augustine, Benedict of Nursia, and Saint Jerome. *Héloïse's* original writings were impressive, and they included the timeless topics of friendship, love, ethics, romance, theology, feminism, sex, morals, marriage, childbearing, and concupiscence. Furthermore, *Héloïse's* thought and writing influenced many great thinkers that came after her, such as Italian poet, Francesco Petrarca, Genevan philosopher, Jean-Jacques Rousseau, French philosopher, S mone Adolphine Well, Saint Thomas Aquinas, and French Enlightenment writer, François-Marie Arouet (also known as Voltaire).

On 21 April 1163 *Héloïse* passed away. *Héloïse* was approximately 66 years old at the time of her death. Both *Héloïse* and Peter have a tombstone dedicated to them at the *Père Lachaise* Cemetery in Paris, France. *Héloïse* is remembered as the 'Woman of Letters' and her writings remain just as relevant today, as they were when she wrote them, which was over 800 years ago.

Tullia d'Aragona (1510-1556)

Tullia d'Aragona was born in Rome, Italy, and she was educated by the Italian Roman Catholic Cardinal, Luigi d'Aragona (1474-1519). Tullia's biological father is not confirmed. As a result, there exist claims that Tullia is the daughter from an extramarital affair between Giulia Ferrarese and Costanzo Palmieri d'Aragona from Naples, however, there are also competing claims that her father was Cardinal Luigi d'Aragona. In the year 1519, Tullia left Rome, and over the course of the next several years, she travelled extensively throughout the cultural centres and major cities of Italy, including Ferrara, Florence, Siena, and Venice, before she returned to her home City of Rome in the year 1526. Upon Tullia's return to her birth place, she ultimately decided to follow in the direction of her mother, Giulia Ferrarese, and became an upper-class Italian courtesan. Tullia's vocation as a courtesan was far more diverse and encompassing than the insipid intimacy of sensual pleasure. As a courtesan, Tullia engaged in travel, social entertainment, profound conversations with learned people, and the company of notable elite men with power, influence, reputation, prestige, and wealth.

As a young, intelligent, learned, and beautiful courtesan, Tullia entertained an independent and lavish lifestyle. This vocation gave Tullia greater freedom and unprecedented autonomy in the organisation of her personal affairs, a far-fetched world reality for the common Italian woman in the 16th century Italy. As a result, Tullia was able to experience a life which was usually restricted for the elite Italian women of nobility, private wealth, affluence, upper social class, prestige, or political power. As a courtesan, Tullia not only enjoyed social independence, which was beyond the economic means of the majority of Italian women in the 16th century Italian society, however, she was also able to commit time and resources to her writing endeavours, and thereby, more fully develop her intellectual abilities.

During Tullia's lifetime, she engaged in a string of high-profile romantic affairs, including with a Florentine banking elite named Filippo Strozzi, a descendant of an influential Roman family named Emilio Orsini, and the renowned Italian courtier and poet named Bernardo Tasso. In addition,

Tullia was an artistic inspiration to a number of significant European people, including French composer, Philippe Verdelot, Italian humanist and dramatist, Sperone Speroni, Italian author, Girolamo Muzio, Italian painter, Sebastiano del Piombo, and Italian humanist, historian, and poet, Benedetto Varchi.

Tullia went on to become a Venetian writer, poet, intellectual, and philosopher. One of Tullia's major writings is the *Dialogue on the Infinity of Love* (1547). This thoughtful Neoplatonic philosophical discourse discusses Tullia's intimate perceptions on a woman's need for sexual freedom and emotional autonomy in relationships. This was a unique publication for its time, as it was a woman and not a man, who was writing about a woman's perspective and experiences on sexual relations and the intimacy of love. In addition, Tullia also wrote a series of epic and heroic poems which were collated and published in the text *Rime della Signora Tullia d' Aragona et di diversi a lei* (Poems by Tullia di Aragona and by Others to Her) (1547). Last but not least, one of Tullia's many poems, namely *Il Meschino, altramente detto il Guerrino* (The Wretch, Otherwise Known as Guerrino) was published posthumously in the year 1560. Unfortunately, most of Tullia's profound writings on philosophy, love, sexuality, and romance have been lost to history.

The fine details of Tullia's marriage life are scant, however, there are claims that in 1543 she married a gentleman by the name of Silvestro Guiccardi of Ferrara, and that she also birthed a son who was named Celio. Thereafter, Tullia became a member of the Florentine Court of Duke *Cosimo de' Medici*. Despite Tullia's marriage and privileged membership to the Florentine Court, she was not a conformist, but rather a true feminist. Tullia defiantly challenged the Italian conventions, customs, traditions, and norms that were expected of and imposed upon Italian women of her time. For example, Tullia constantly violated the dress codes expected of an Italian courtesan. In the high ideal of preserving her liberty, Tullia constantly moved from city to city in order to escape the stringent social requirements imposed upon Italian women during her lifetime. Above all, Tullia's noble desire for liberty and freedom was married with the pursuit to reach the highest potential of her intellectual abilities.

During the high period of *the Renaissance*, Tullia was one exceptional Italian woman who made monumental contributions to philosophy, romanticism, and feminism. At a time in European history, when women were considered intellectually inferior, Tullia demonstrated an astounding intellectual capacity that could rival any learned European man in the classics, philosophy, literature, poetry, and the humanities. Tullia defied the rigid gender roles, stereotypes, dress codes, and social norms that were expected of an Italian woman during her lifetime in the Italian society. Tullia socialised with influential people, she was an intellectual giant capable of original thought, a prolific writer, and she lived a truly distinctive life. In the final analysis, Tullia became an accomplished woman of letters, love, and literacy.

Edith Stein (1891-1942)

Edith Stein was born on 12 October 1891 in Breslau, Germany (present day Wrocław, Poland). Edith came from a German-Jewish family of eleven children. Edith was the youngest child of eleven in her family. According to Jewish tradition, Edith was born on the annual Day of

Atonement, a time when the *Yom Kippur* festival is held, it is one of the holiest dates in the Jewish calendar. Edith's father, Siegfried Stein was involved in the timber business, and he tragically passed away when Edith was approximately two years old. Edith's widowed mother, Auguste Courant Stein was left to raise the family of several children, and also continue the family lumberyard business. Notwithstanding the onset of such privations, Auguste remained committed to her children receiving a quality education at the start of their life.

Edith was a gifted and inquisitive child; she was able to learn how to read and write at a young age. Edith attended the Victoria Gymnasium School in Breslau, she completed her school studies with commendable results in the year 1911. Thereafter, Edith matriculated at the University of Breslau, where she studied the German language and history, however, her real interests resided in contemporary women's issues and the study of philosophy. During Edith's time at university, she became a member of *the Prussian Society for Women's Franchise* to associate with like-minded people on advancing the just cause of Women's Suffrage.

In 1913, Edith transferred to the University of Göttingen to study philosophy under the tutelage of German philosopher and mathematician, Edmund Gustav Albrecht Husserl (1859-1938). Ultimately, Edith decided to complete a Doctoral Degree in Philosophy with Edmund Husserl as her academic advisor. Edith's Ph.D. thesis was related to the subject matter of 'empathy'. However, the onset of *World War I (1914-1918)* caused considerable disruption to Edith's doctoral studies. During the course of *the Great War*, Edith served as a Red Cross Volunteer Nurse in 1915. The following year, Edith relocated to the University of Freiburg to complete her Ph.D. thesis on empathy. Edith's 1916 doctoral thesis was titled 'the Empathy Problem as it is Developed Historically and Considered Phenomenologically'.

In the year 1919, the University of Göttingen rejected Edith's habilitation thesis on the grounds of her sex. The fact that Edith was a woman failed to qualify her for the entry-level office of a teacher in a prestigious public German university. Notwithstanding the vast disparities and inequalities of sex in modern Europe, Edith published widely in the field of philosophy. Some of Edith's original works include: *On the Problem of Empathy*, *Finite and Eternal Being: An Attempt at an Ascent to the Meaning of Being-*, *Philosophy of Psychology and the Humanities*, *Knowledge and Faith-*, *An Investigation Concerning the State*, *The Hidden Life: Hagiographic Essays, Meditations, and Spiritual Texts*, *Essays on Woman*, *Potency and Act: Studies Toward a Philosophy of Being*, and *The Science of the Cross*.

In the year 1933, Edith joined the Discalced Carmelite monastery *St. Maria vom Frieden* (Our Lady of Peace) located in the City of Cologne, Germany. It was at this sacred institution that Edith adopted the religious name Teresa Benedicta of the Cross. Yet the greater social and political environment was extremely disturbing, given the rise of Nazism and anti-Semitism across modern Germany. As a result, Edith relocated to the Discalced Carmelite monastery located in the City of Echt, the Netherlands. Regrettably, Edith was arrested by the NAZI SS (*Schutzstaffel*) in August of 1942. Edith was then incarcerated at the *Amersfoort* and *Westerbork* Concentration Camps, prior to her inhumane execution in a gas chamber at the infamous *Auschwitz* Concentration Camp.

On 1 May 1987, Edith's memory and legacy was forever enshrined in the Roman Catholic faith when Pope John Paul II (r. 1978-2005) beatified her as a martyr of the faith under the name Teresa Benedicta of the Cross. Several years later, on 11 October 1998, Pope John Paul II canonised Teresa Benedicta of the Cross. Teresa Benedicta of the Cross is one of the six Patron Saints of European origin, and her annual Feast Day is commemorated on 9 August. Teresa Benedicta is the Patron Saint of Europe, converted Jewish people, martyrs, and orphans.

The truly remarkable story of Edith Stein is one of sainthood, service, and scholarship. In Saint Teresa Benedicta of the Cross' honour, there are a number of memorials dedicated to her, including one at the Stella Maris Monastery located in the City of Haifa, Israel, one at the City of Prague in the Czech Republic, and another one in the Church of Our Lady in Wittenberg, Germany. Furthermore, a bronze bust of Edith Stein is situated outside the building of the Federal Ministry of the Interior in Berlin, Germany. Last but not least, in Edith's memory there is a sculpture erected at the Catholic church where she was formally baptised.

Saint Teresa Benedicta of the Cross was more than just a philosopher, writer, and nun. Saint Teresa's unique life story and virtuous path to sainthood demonstrates how to lead a good and honourable life, regardless of one's privations, circumstances, and worldly suffering. Many factors were beyond the control of Saint Teresa during her lifetime. Indeed, the force of circumstance often dictated Edith's movements and her place of residence. Not to mention, Edith lived with the constant terror and horror of ethnic persecution at the hands of the NAZI German state. Yet, when all is said and done, Saint Teresa kept the faith. Blessed is She.

Ayn Rand (1905-1982)

Ayn Rand (Alisa Zinovyevna Rosenbaum) was born on 2 February 1905 in Saint Petersburg, Russia. Ayn's father, Zinovy Zakharovich Rosenbaum was university educated and an affluent pharmacist. In fact, Zinovy operated his own pharmacy business. Ayn's mother, Anna Borisovna was a language teacher, and she also operated a private hair salon at home. Ayn came from a cultured and upper-middle class Jewish-Russian family. Furthermore, Ayn was the eldest of three daughters in her family.

In the earlier years of Ayn's life, *the February Revolution of 1917* and *the October Revolution of 1917* created political, social, and economic instability across Russia. In fact, the latter Russian Revolution, also known as *the Bolshevik Revolution of 1917*, resulted in Ayn's immediate family briefly departing Saint Petersburg for the Crimean Peninsula. During Ayn's school years she read the influential works of a number of great novelists, poets, essayists, playwrights, and dramatists, including Fyodor Mikhailovich Dostoevsky (1821-1881), Victor Hugo (1802-1885), Edmond Eugène Alexis Rostand (1868-1918), and Johann Christoph Friedrich von Schiller (1759-1805).

Following *the Russian Revolution of 1917*, Ayn returned to Saint Petersburg (which was now officially renamed Petrograd). Thereafter, Ayn enrolled at the Petrograd State University, with her university studies focusing on the field of social pedagogy, she majored in the field of history. During Ayn's time at university, she also studied the philosophical writings of some of the greatest ancient and modern European philosophers, including Aristotle, Plato, and Nietzsche. In 1924, Ayn graduated from the Petrograd State University with a Diploma in History. The great Russian City of Petrograd was later renamed to Leningrad in 1924. Thus, Ayn's university was renamed the Leningrad State University (now known as the Saint Petersburg State University). After Ayn received her university diploma, she enrolled at the State Institute for Cinematography in the Union of Soviet Socialist Republics (USSR), where she intended to acquire the specialist knowledge and technical skills to become a professional screenwriter.

Following the receipt and exchange of written correspondence with Ayn's extended family in the United States of America, in 1926, Ayn decided to travel to the United States. Ayn visited New York City and Hollywood in the City of Los Angeles, California. Ayn witnessed first-hand the immense potential and newfound opportunities in the United States, career opportunities that were likely not available to her in the Soviet Union. As a result, Ayn was determined to make a professional career for herself in the United States' lucrative film industry, and concurrently, as an American author and prolific writer. It was during Ayn's visit to Hollywood that she had a chance encounter with renowned American film director, producer, and actor, Cecil Blount DeMille. Subsequently, Cecil secured Ayn temporary work in his upcoming film *the King of Kings* (which was officially released in 1927).

Furthermore, it was during Ayn's time in Hollywood, while she worked as a background actor in *the King of Kings* (she later secured work as a junior screenwriter), that she met American actor, Frank O'Connor. Arguably, Ayn and Frank's chance encounter is a romantic story in and of itself, a true story of 'love at first sight' on the film production studio. Ayn and Frank entered into a romantic relationship, and they subsequently got married on 15 April 1929. Once Ayn had established her new life in the United States of America, she secured Permanent American Resident status in July of 1929. Thereafter, Ayn became a United States citizen on 3 March 1931. Once Ayn was a citizen of the United States, she made a number of attempts to secure approval for her parents and sisters to immigrate to the United States of America, however, the Soviet Union did not grant the necessary approval.

Throughout Ayn's impressive career, she wrote several major screenplays, captivating scripts for dramas, scholarly and original essays, and influential (not to mention, often controversial) fiction and non-fiction novels. Some of Ayn's major writings and notable works include: *For the New Intellectual, The Virtue of Selfishness, Capitalism: The Unknown Ideal, The Romantic Manifesto: A Philosophy of Literature, The New Left: The Anti-Industrial Revolution, We the Living, Anthem, Night of January 16th, The Fountainhead, Atlas Shrugged, The Unconquered*, and *Introduction to Objectivist Epistemology*. Ayn's systematic philosophy centred around Objectivism, and her original philosophy made seminal contributions to ethics, metaphysics, political philosophy, epistemology, and aesthetics. Following Ayn Rand's death, notable posthumous publications attributed to her include: *Ideal, Letters of Ayn Rand, Philosophy: Who Needs It,* and *Journals of Ayn Rand*.

Ayn's philosophical views promoted the ideologies of liberalism, materialism, egoism, the pursuit of rational self-interest, individual rights, capitalism, and private property rights. In particular, Ayn made significant contributions to the discourse and debate on American libertarianism. During Ayn's later years, she lectured at a number of top-ranking U.S. universities, including Columbia University, Harvard University, the Massachusetts Institute of Technology, Princeton University, and Yale University.

On 6 March 1982, Ayn passed away due to heart failure in New York City, the United States. Ayn was 77 years old at the time of her death. Ayn was buried at the Kensico Cemetery in Valhalla, New York. During and beyond Ayn's lifetime, her work and writing has attracted considerable attention and honour. Not to mention, Ayn was awarded the prestigious

Prometheus Hall of Fame Award for two of her many brilliant novels, namely, *Atlas Shrugged* (1983) and *Anthem* (1987). In addition, *the Ayn Rand Institute* (ARI) was established in 1985 to promote greater global awareness and understanding of Ayn's writings and philosophy. Last but not least, in Ayn's honour and memory, several distinguished American philosophers founded *the Ayn Rand Society* in 1987. The *Ayn Rand Society* is affiliated with the American Philosophical Association (APA).

Hannah Arendt (1906-1975)

Hannah Arendt (Johanna Arendt) was born on 14 October 1906 in Linden, the City of Hanover, Germany. Hannah came from an influential and affluent Jewish-German family. Hannah's father, Paul Arendt was an engineer and intellectual with a strong love of classical studies. Hannah's mother, Martha Cohn Arendt was a talented musician. Hannah was the only child in her family. Furthermore, Hannah was raised in a politically progressive household, and her family embodied a secular worldview. That is to say, the Arendt family did not strictly practice the Jewish faith.

In August of 1913, Hannah commenced attending *the Hufen-Oberlyzeum*, a girls' gymnasium located in *Königsberg*, Germany. Shortly thereafter, on 30 October 1913, Hannah's father passed away, she was only seven years old at the time of his death. Regrettably, the force of circumstances continued to prove most unfavourable to Hannah in her early life. Following the devastating loss of her father, subsequently, the outbreak of *World War I (1914-1918)* meant that Hannah and her mother had to relocate to the City of Berlin in 1914. Hannah and her mother resided with Hannah's mother's younger sister, *Margarethe Fürst*, and Hannah attended a local girls' lyceum to continue her early school studies.

After the passage of a few uncertain months, when Hannah's home town of *Königsberg* appeared to be safe again, Hannah and her mother returned to their former place of residence. Hannah excelled in her studies at school, she learnt ancient Greek, poetry, widely read French and German literature, and she also studied modern philosophy. In so far as it concerns the subject of philosophy, during Hannah's teenage years, she read the notable works of Danish theologian and philosopher, *Søren* Aabye Kierkegaard (1813-1855), German psychiatrist and philosopher, Karl Theodor Jaspers (1883-1969), and German philosopher, Immanuel Kant (1724-1804). Hannah's secondary school education was completed at the *Königin-Luise-Schule*, which was also situated in the town of *Königsberg*.

From 1922 to 1923, Hannah matriculated at the University of Berlin, where she studied Christian theology and classical studies under the direction of German Catholic priest, author, and academic, Romano Guardini (1885-1968). Thereafter, Hannah succeeded in the university entrance exam required for her to enrol at the University of Marburg in Hesse, Germany. Hannah's university studies in philosophy and theology involved engagement with some of the best and brightest minds of the twentieth century Europe. Having successfully completed the required university entrance exam, from 1924 to 1926, Hannah intently studied philosophy at the University of Marburg under the supervision of the renowned German philosopher, Martin Heidegger (1889-1976).

During Hannah's tenure at the University of Marburg, she engaged in a short-lived affair with Martin Heidegger. In the year 1926, Hannah went on to complete her doctoral studies in the field of philosophy at the University of Heidelberg, with her Ph.D. supervisor being the German psychiatrist and existential philosopher, Karl Theodor Jaspers (1883-1969). In accordance with Hannah's earlier university studies on Christian theology, her Ph.D. thesis was on the theme of 'love'. Hannah's thesis examined the authoritative writings of Algerian-Roman theologian and philosopher, Saint Augustine of Hippo (354AD - 430AD). Hannah's Ph.D. thesis was titled 'On the Concept of Love in the Thought of Saint Augustine: Attempt at a Philosophical Interpretation'. Hannah completed her doctoral dissertation in the year 1929.

Due to the rise of radical NAZI ideology and anti-Jewish sentiment, Hannah was arrested and imprisoned in 1933. Upon Hannah's release from prison, she left the NAZI Germany and moved across Europe, she lived in Czechoslovakia, Paris, and Switzerland. Finally, Hannah settled in New York City, the United States of America, where she remained for the rest of her life. With respect to Hannah's personal life, she was married to German poet, journalist, and philosopher, *Günther* Anders in 1929, however, the couple divorced in 1937. Hannah later re-married to German poet and philosopher, Heinrich Friedrich Ernst *Blücher* in the year 1940.

Hannah was a prolific writer, philosopher, and editor. Hannah's major works include *The Origins of Totalitarianism*, *On Violence*, *Eichmann in Jerusalem: A Report on the Banality of Evil*, *The Human Condition*, *On Revolution*, *Between Past and Future*, *Men in Dark Times*, and *Crises of the Republic*. Hannah's last major work *The Life of the Mind* was unfinished due to her untimely and sudden death from a heart attack in 1975. *The Life of the Mind* was a brilliant multi-volume work of philosophy, which intended to articulate the three mental faculties of thinking, willing, and judging, however, due to Hannah's death, only two volumes were completed, namely, Volume One of thinking, and Volume Two on willing.

On 4 December 1975, Hannah tragically passed away from a heart attack in Manhattan, New York City, the United States of America. Hannah was 69 years old at the time of her death. Hannah's ashes were buried alongside those of her late husband, Heinrich *Blücher* at the Bard College Cemetery in Annandale-on-Hudson, New York. The loss of Hannah was mourned and deeply felt by the academic community of philosophers across the United States of America.

Hannah's invaluable writings and her profound scholarly contribution to the field of philosophy covered major themes which include moral philosophy, political power, intellectual history, the nature of evil, the human condition, political ideologies, the power and structure of the nation-state, theory of modernity, philosophy of history, matters concerning ontology, theory of totalitarianism, and the philosophy of mind.

Without question, Hannah is one of the greatest philosophers of the twentieth century. Not to mention, Hannah's invaluable scholarly work has influenced many twentieth and twenty-first century political theorists. Hannah's greatest contribution to philosophy is that she was an original humanist thinker. Hannah contributed to many important debates and discourses of prime importance of the twentieth century. Debates and discourses that are just as, if not more, relevant in the present twenty-first century.

Based on Hannah's life experiences and observations, she earnestly attempted to answer the social, political, ethical, and moral questions concerning the power dynamics and political structure of the state. Furthermore, Hannah explored the fundamental essence of the mind, the newfound existential reality of human life in the age of modernity, the political and social dimensions of citizenship, the nature of human judgement and thought, the properties of human action, the value of human interaction in the public sphere, and the idea of a collective identity. Indeed, Hannah's profound writings and her insightful philosophy will remain relevant for many centuries to come.

Simone de Beauvoir (1908-1986)

Simone de Beauvoir (Simone-Ernestine-Lucie-Marie Bertrand de Beauvoir) was born on 9 January 1908 in Paris, France. Simone's father, Georges Bertrand de Beauvoir was a lawyer, and her mother, Françoise Beauvoir was the daughter of a wealthy banker. In addition, Simone's mother was a devout Catholic by faith. Thus, Simone was raised in a Catholic household, and she was deeply religious as a child, however, during her teenage years, she abandoned her faith. In Simone's world view there was no basis for the existence of God, and she decided to remain an atheist from the age of fourteen until her death.

While Simone's mother exerted a profound religious influence upon her daughter, it was Simone's father who developed her intellectual love for literature, philosophy, and the arts. In many respects, Simone was a child prodigy, she was immensely curious about the world and possessed a gifted intellect. Through the encouragement of her father, Simone learnt to read and write at a young age. Furthermore, Simone was also introduced to a number of carefully selected literary works by her father to stimulate her early intellectual development and thinking.

Simone attended *the Institut Adeline Désir*, a private Catholic School for girls, where she studied until the age of seventeen. In 1925, Simone passed her *Baccalauréat* exams in the subjects of mathematics and philosophy. Thereafter, Simone attended the *Institut Catholique de Paris* to study mathematics. Subsequently, Simone studied literature and languages at the *Institut Sainte-Marie*. In 1926, Simone completed her Certificate of Higher Studies in French literature and Latin.

In the year 1927, Simone commenced her formal studies in the field of philosophy at *the Sorbonne* (the University of Paris). Simone's graduate dissertation was on 'the Concept in Leibniz'. Of great importance here, early in Simone's adult life, she formed strong working relationships with several notable and distinguished French philosophers, including Jean-Paul Sartre (1905-1980), Paul Nizan (1905-1940), and René Gabriel Eugene Maheu (1905-1975). These noteworthy relationships proved instrumental in Simone joining influential academic circles, participating in intellectual discourses, and even shaping her own philosophical writings, both as an academic, novelist, essayist, and prolific writer.

Simone's liberal love life was just as prolific and intense as her academic publications and philosophical writings. While Simone was in a long-term and open relationship with Jean-Paul Sartre, she was against the traditional and normative ideals expected of a woman in the twentieth century modern society, namely that of marriage and producing children. In fact, Simone entertained several affairs and romantic relationships throughout her lifetime, including with American writer, Nelson Algren, and French filmmaker, Claude Lanzmann. Simone also unapologetically explored her sexuality with other women, including, French writer, Bianca Lamblin. On one occasion, Simone also engaged in a promiscuous sexual encounter with a 17-year-old girl named Natalie Sorokine.

Simone's notable publications, both during her lifetime and those published posthumously, include *She Came to Stay*, *The Blood of Others*, *The Ethics of Ambiguity*, *The Second Sex*, *All Men are Mortal*, *Adieux: A Farewell to Sartre*, *All Said and Done*, *America Day by Day*, *The Coming of Age*, *Force of Circumstance*, *Letters to Sartre*, *The Long March*, *Memoirs of a Dutiful Daughter*, *The Prime of Life*, *Must We Burn Sade?*, *She Came to Stay*, *A Transatlantic Love Affair: Letters to Nelson Algren*, *A Very Easy Death*, *When Things of the Spirit Come First*, *Who Shall Die?*, *The Woman Destroyed*, *The Mandarins*, and *Les Inséparables*.

Undoubtedly, Simone made significant contributions to the modern Feminist Movement. In addition, Simone also influenced the thoughts of a number of notable female writers, activists, and intellectuals that came after her, including American feminist writer, Katherine Murray Millett, Canadian-American feminist writer and activist, Shulamith Firestone, Australian writer and public intellectual, Germaine Greer, British psychoanalyst and author, Juliet Mitchell, and British sociologist and writer, Ann Rosamund Oakley. Most notably, Simone had a profound impact on American writer, Betty Friedan (1921-2006), who regarded Simone as a political and intellectual giant of her time. Simone's seminal publication *The Second Sex* also shaped Betty's thinking, and it proved original stimulus for her own 1963 book titled *The Feminine Mystique*.

On 14 April 1986, Simone passed away from pneumonia in Paris, France. Simone was 78 years old at the time of her death. Simone was buried next to French literary critic, playwright, and philosopher, Jean-Paul Sartre at the *Cimetière du Montparnasse* (the Montparnasse Cemetery) in Paris. Simone was much more than just a philosopher, she was a writer, intellectual, social theorist, academic, novelist, scholar, activist, and feminist.

During the long twentieth century, Simone challenged both the old and new ideas relating to sex, gender, politics, ethics, the subjectivity of human experience, and the reality of the human condition. Simone's seminal writings made original and scholarly contributions to several important areas of philosophy, including continental philosophy, existentialism, feminism, Marxism, and existential phenomenology. Some of Simone's greatest ideas include feminist ethics, existential feminism, and the ethics of ambiguity.

Iris Murdoch (1919-1999)

Iris Murdoch was born on 15 July 1919 in Phibsborough, Dublin, Ireland. Iris' father, Wills John Hughes Murdoch was a British civil servant, and her mother, Irene Alice Richardson Murdoch was an aspiring singer, however, the conventional reality of married life resulted in Irene's desired singing career remaining unfulfilled. The Murdoch family relocated to London before Iris was one year old. Not to mention, Iris was the sole child in her family. Iris was raised in Chiswick, a district of West London, and she attended the Froebel Demonstration School in London, later followed by the Badminton School in Bristol.

Once Iris finished her school studies, she matriculated at Somerville College at the University of Oxford in Oxford, England where she studied the humanities, the classics, ancient history, and philosophy. From 1942 to 1944, Iris worked at the British Treasury (formally known as Her Majesty's

Treasury). Thereafter, Iris was employed as an 'Administrative Officer' with *the United Nations Relief and Rehabilitation Administration* (UNRRA). Initially, Iris worked at the UN agency's London Office, however, her brief tenure with the UNRRA also included foreign postings to the European cities of Brussels, Graz, and Innsbruck. In the year 1946, Iris left the UNRRA, and she returned to university life for further study, and the unfettered pursuit of scholarly and academic endeavours.

Thus, after several years in the workforce, Iris returned to her lifelong passion, namely, the study of the arts, the classics, literature, and philosophy. From 1947 to 1948, Iris was a postgraduate student at the Newnham College at the University of Cambridge in Cambridge, England where she studied graduate level philosophy. While Iris was at Newnham College, she met the renowned Austrian-British philosopher and logician, Ludwig Josef Johann Wittgenstein (1889-1951), however, she never attended his distinguished lectures on philosophy. In 1948, Iris was appointed a fellow at St. Anne's College in Oxford, where she taught philosophy until the year 1963.

Iris' political views were to the left of the political spectrum. In Iris' earlier years, she was a committed socialist and communist. Not to mention, from 1938 to 1942, Iris was a member of the Communist Party of Great Britain (CPGB). Iris resigned from the Communist Party membership to work at the British Treasury, however, she remained left of the political spectrum for most of her life. In fact, Iris only renounced her long-held communist political beliefs in the last ten years of her life.

In 1990, Iris denounced Marxism, however, at that time, the Union of Soviet Socialist Republics (USSR) was on the brink of its disintegration, and several popular anti-communist revolutions had already swept across Europe. For example, consider *the Hungarian Revolution of 1956*, *the Prague Spring of 1968*, *the Romanian Revolution of 1989*, and *the Velvet*

Revolution of 1989. Indeed, *the Cold War* (1947-1991) was coming to its decisive conclusion. Now the high hopes and empty theoretical promises of Marxism and Communism were rapidly approaching their fruitless end.

In the year 1956, Iris married British academic, literary critic, and writer, John Oliver Bayley (1925-2015). Iris and John did not have any children during their more than forty years of marriage. However, Iris entertained a number of extramarital affairs with both men and women. Throughout Iris' academic and writing career, she published a variety of notable works, such as novels, short stories, dramas, philosophical texts, plays, and poems. Some of Iris' many writings include *Sartre, Romantic Rationalist*, *The Nice and the Good*, *Under the Net*, *The Sea, The Sea*, *The Flight from the Enchanter*, *The Bell*, *The Time of the Angels*, *A Severed Head*, *The Italian Girl*, *The Sandcastle*, *The Red and the Green*, *A Fairly Honourable Defeat*, *Jackson's Dilemma*, *The Message to the Planet*, *The Black Prince*, and *The Unicorn*.

Iris's outstanding achievements in the fields of philosophy and literature have been widely recognised. In 1976, Iris was bestowed the title of Commander of the Order of the British Empire (CBE). In addition, Iris' most brilliant novel *The Sea, The Sea* made her a recipient of the prestigious and world-renowned Booker Prize in 1978. Furthermore, in 1987, Iris was appointed as a Dame Commander of the Order of the British Empire (DBE). Iris was also the recipient of numerous honorary degrees awarded by the University of Cambridge, Kingston University, and the University of Bath. Not to mention, in 1982, the American Academy of Arts and Sciences (AAA&S) recognised Iris's grand contribution to philosophy, and she was admitted as a Foreign Honorary Member of the aforesaid prestigious academy. Last but not least, in 1997, Iris was awarded the Golden PEN Award by English PEN for her immense contribution and lifetime of service to literature.

In the later years of her life, Iris was diagnosed with Alzheimer's disease. Unfortunately, Iris struggled in the final years of her life. In particular, the quality of Iris' life markedly deteriorated due to her medical condition notably worsening. On 8 February 1999, Iris passed away in Oxford, the United Kingdom. Iris was 79 years old at the time of her death. Iris' original writings have made lasting contributions to the fields of moral philosophy, Western philosophy, analytical philosophy, virtue ethics, modern Platonism, and contemporary philosophy. Two of Iris' most notable ideas in philosophy include the 'Idea of Perfection' and 'Sovereignty of the Good'.

There is no doubt that Iris's novels, poems, plays, and short stories have considerably enriched the vast collection of English literature and philosophy. Iris's voluminous writings represent some of the best contribution to the twentieth century English literature. Not to mention, Iris' writing is comparable to the highly acclaimed and accomplished English writers, including Samuel Richardson (1689-1761), William Makepeace Thackeray (1811-1863), Charles Dickens (1812-1870), Ford Madox Ford (1873-1939), Virginia Woolf (1882-1941), George Orwell (1903-1950), and Jane Austen (1775-1817). In Iris' cherished memory, a bench is dedicated to her on the scenic grounds of Lady Margaret Hall at the University of Oxford in Oxford, England.

Chapter Two

WOMEN IN RELIGION

'For prayer is nothing else than being on terms of friendship with God.'

Saint Teresa of Ávila

The ancient institution of religion has been shaped and influenced by women from all walks of life. While this chapter will exclusively focus on the Catholic faith, it acknowledges that there are countless women who have made pivotal contributions across the many faiths that are present across the numerous continents, countries, and cultures of the world. Within the purview of the Catholic faith, women have made seminal contributions to the religious order, including the Roman Catholic Church's Doctrine, Biblical Hermeneutics, the establishment of monastic orders for monks and nuns, alleviation of the untold suffering of the countless sick and poor people of the world, leading by example on renunciation of the material world, the embodiment of a pious life, and writing original texts and insightful commentary concerning matters of theology and religious studies.

As noted earlier, this chapter examines select women who have made significant contributions to the Catholic faith. The chapter bridges geographical, racial, cultural, linguistic, national, theological, and historical divides to present a broad perspective of women in Catholicism. It examines the lives, doctrines, teachings, principles, writings, and ideas of Saint Cecilia, Saint Agatha of Sicily, Saint Brigid of Kildare, Saint Hildegard of Bingen, Saint Bridget of Sweden, Saint Catherine of Siena, Saint Rita of Cascia, Saint Catherine of Genoa, Saint Teresa of Ávila, Saint Rose of Lima, Saint Virginia Centurione Bracelli, Saint Thérèse of Lisieux, and Mother Mary Teresa (also known as Saint Teresa of Calcutta).

While the historical record vividly demonstrates that the role of women within the sphere of religion and the Roman Catholic Church is defined by the ideological forces of tradition, decrees of the Ecumenical Councils, religious custom, Papal Bull, Canon Law, Papal Supremacy, and Church Doctrine, women have an equally important role to perform in matters of faith. This chapter will shine light on the courage, conviction, and credence of saintly women, who have set a fine example of living a life marked by the moral principles of integrity, duty, honour, wisdom, service, and justice.

Saint Cecilia (ca. 200AD - ca. 235AD)

Saint Cecilia was a noble Roman who originated from a wealthy and prosperous family, she was deeply pious as a child. In Cecilia's childhood years, she made a faithful vow of virginity to God and she did not wish to seek matrimony, however, by her parents' wishes, she was married against her will to a Roman Pagan nobleman by the name of Valerian. According to the old stories of tradition, while several musicians performed at Cecilia's wedding, she heard heavenly music in her heart, a most divine melodic discourse with the Lord.

The immense religious and spiritual influence of Saint Cecilia upon Valerian, later on witnessed her beloved spouse convert to Christianity, and himself be martyred for his newfound belief in Jesus Christ. Not to mention, Valerian was subsequently canonised as a saint of the Catholic faith. As demonstrable signs of Cecilia's steadfast conviction to the Catholic faith, she often fasted, performed acts of penance, and earnestly prayed to God that her honourable promise of virginity be preserved. Saint Cecilia was a blessed and holy person of musical instruments and songs, to the present time she symbolises the pivotal function of music in liturgy. In fact, Saint Cecilia is often depicted playing musical instruments, such as the viola, harpsichord, pipe organ, violin, harp, and flute. Not to mention, Saint Cecilia is commonly referred to as the 'Patroness of Musicians'.

According to legend, in spite of Cecilia's marriage to Valerian, an angel appeared before her and counselled her to remain a virgin. As Cecilia had been married to Valerian against her will, she shared with her spouse this sacred revelation of the faith, so that she may uphold her sacred vow of virginity to God. Valerian agreed to respect Cecilia's wishes as long as he was able to bear witness to this angel. Cecilia instructed Valerian that he may witness the angel only if he were baptised. Valerian agreed to Cecilia's proposal, and he travelled to the third milestone on the Via Appia (also known as the Appian Way), where he was baptised by Pope Urbanus. Following Valerian's conversion to the Catholic faith and return to his wife, he witnessed first-hand an angel standing beside Cecilia, and crowning her with roses and lilies.

Valerian's brother, Tiburtius, visited the blessed couple, and he also converted to Christianity. The two brothers, Tiburtius and Valerian began to preach throughout the vast territory of the Roman Empire, and they gave generous donations and alms to the countless poor people. Furthermore, the aforesaid brothers also buried Christian martyrs, a Christian religious practice that was strictly forbidden at the time by the Roman authorities. In addition, Cecilia also preached the Divine Word of God, and she converted hundreds of Roman Pagans to Christianity. However, the questionable religious activities of all three Christians came to the attention of Roman Prefect, Turcius Almachius. Consequently, Turcius condemned the three Christians to death.

First, it was Cecilia's spouse, Valerian and her brother-in-law, Tiburtius that were martyred for their strong belief and unwavering faith in the Lord. Subsequently, a number of attempts were made by the Roman authorities on the life of Cecilia. Initially, Cecilia was arrested and imprisoned for the widespread propagation of her religious beliefs and Christian values in the Roman Empire, however, Cecilia refused to renounce her faith. Shortly thereafter, Cecilia was condemned to her death by suffocation. Cecilia was locked in a bathhouse with raging fires, however, after the passage of one day and night, surrounded by the immense heat of burning flames, the Blessed Cecilia remained unaffected by the destructive physical environment in which she was condemned to her death.

Following this miracle, the Roman Prefect, Turcius Almachius, ordered Cecilia be immediately beheaded. Cecilia's executioner used his sword to strike her neck three times, however, on all three attempts, her executioner was unable to totally sever Cecilia's head from her body. Subsequently, Cecilia was left to die from her violent bodily injuries, during this grief-stricken time, a countless number of Roman people, including Roman Pagans, came to visit her, in order to seek her blessings and pay their respects. In the midst of Cecilia's severe suffering and life-threatening injuries, with total disregard for her personal welfare, Cecilia continued to preach the Divine Message of God and convert such people to Christianity. Three days after the failed execution by beheading attempt on Cecilia's life, she went to be with the Lord. Cecilia was not only a Catholic martyr; she also served her local community with a sense of duty, integrity, and honour.

Cecilia's life narrative all too vividly demonstrates that calamites and tribulations will arise during one's finite time on Earth. Notwithstanding the many struggles Cecilia encountered, it was the boundless grace and love with which Cecilia confronted her opponents and often formidable catastrophes, that allowed her to conquer the greatest of threats. Not to mention, Cecilia managed to achieve such victory in the many significant challenges that she confronted, with a profound sense of equanimity and inner peace.

Upon Cecilia's passing to the Heavenly Kingdom of God, she was buried next to the papal crypt in the Catacombs of Saint Callixtus. In Saint Cecilia's lasting memory and honour, the Basilica of Santa Cecilia was erected in Trastevere, Rome, Italy. Saint Cecilia is the Patron Saint of the blind, bodily purity, poets, hymns, pipe organs, singers, France, composers, music, and musicians. Saint Cecilia's annual Feast Day is commemorated on 22 November. Blessed is She.

Saint Agatha of Sicily (ca. 231AD - 251AD)

Saint Agatha came from a prosperous and noble Roman family. In the early years of Agatha's life, she made a vow of virginity to God. The Roman Prefect, Quintianus desired marriage with Agatha of Sicily, however, she steadfast refused his intimate advances. Quintianus showed no mercy, honour, justice, or dignity to Agatha of Sicily in the face of his rejection. The Roman Prefect was adamant he could influence Agatha to reject her vow of virginity, and accept his marriage proposal. Quintianus was uncontrollably impressed by Agatha's beauty, social status, and wealth, and he continued his endless pursuit of her, without any sense of civility, decency, or moral restraint.

Quintianus knew that Agatha was a Christian, and he utilised Agatha's faith against her. For this was a troubled time in the Roman Empire's history, when the Christian people were being persecuted for their faith under the autocratic rule of the Roman Emperor, Decius. Taking full advantage of the winds of fortune and currents of time, Quintianus reported Agatha to the local authorities, and had her sent to Aphrodisia, the keeper of a brothel, where Agatha was unjustly incarcerated. This act was done in the vain hope that Agatha may turn against God and desire to accept the alternative - a married life with Quintianus. Agatha's unfavourable time in the brothel was kept occupied in sincere prayer and solemn reflection upon God. Agatha's thoughts were sincere, and she overcame the many worldly temptations and sensual desires of her immediate environment.

The Roman Prefect, Quintianus yielded significant power in Sicily, he was also a Roman Judge and the Governor of Sicily. Quintianus was prepared to utilise all the necessary and available means at his disposal to enforce his malignant will upon Agatha, albeit, his unworthy endeavour was in vain, and ultimately to no avail. Following the unjust incarceration of Agatha, Quintianus had her reappear before a judge. Once again, Quintianus threatened Agatha with further suffering and pain, if she did not renounce her vow of virginity, and accept him as her legitimate husband. Agatha affirmed that the Lord was her only Saviour, and her true freedom resided in being a faithful servant of Jesus Christ. To Agatha, bodily integrity and individual sovereignty were secondary matters, and she did not fear the repercussions of her independent decision to openly defy Quintianus' unwanted sexual advances and marriage proposals.

Quintianus was unable to convince Agatha to repent and voluntarily turn towards him. Thus, Quintianus had Agatha imprisoned a second time. On this occasion, Agatha was physically tortured and brutally beaten by the prison guards. Agatha's body was burnt and whipped; her flesh was torn with iron hooks while she was stretched on a wooden rack. Not to mention, Agatha's mammary glands were subject to excision with pincers. This brutal treatment of Agatha only served to strengthen her faith and belief in God. Agatha categorically refused to surrender herself to the venereal demands of Quintianus.

In the end, Quintianus determined that Agatha was to be burnt at the stake for her Christian beliefs, however, an earthquake deterred this terrible evil event from transpiring in the world. Thus, Agatha was returned to prison, where she was denied food and medical attention. During Agatha's hour of duress, the boundless grace and mercy of the Lord provided for her physical sustenance and spiritual needs. While Agatha was confined in prison, she had a mystical vision of Saint Peter the Apostle, who appeared to her, and He miraculously healed her wounds through the supernatural power of His prayers. After the passage of several days, Quintianus resumed his evil acts of torture against Agatha. This time Quintianus had Agatha stripped naked and her body burnt over hot coals.

Following this most terrible punishment, Agatha was returned to prison, where she earnestly prayed that the Lord receive her soul. Showing no sign of disavowing her faith, Agatha of Sicily went to be with the Lord in the year 251AD.

The life story of Saint Agatha illustrates an unwavering trust and profound belief in the Lord. Agatha was repeatedly subject to torture, duress, physical punishments, denial of medical treatment, denial of food, intimidation, threats, incarceration, and torment, however, no matter the pain and suffering of each and every ordeal that she confronted, she kept the faith. Blessed is She. Saint Agatha understood the profound meaning of the scripture verse found in the Holy Bible at John 16:33 'I have told you these things, so that in me you may have peace. In this world you will have trouble. But take heart! I have overcome the world'. In the final analysis, Saint Agatha fought the good fight, she overcame the many dark desires and terrible temptations of this world, she secured her ultimate destiny, namely, the Heavenly Kingdom of God.

Saint Agatha is the Patron Saint of rape victims, breast cancer patients, bellfounders, bell ringers, fire, fire services, earthquakes, volcanic eruptions, natural disasters, torture victims, wet nurses, Malta, San Marino, Sicily, Spain, and martyrs. Saint Agatha is one of several virgin martyrs who are commemorated by name in the Canon of the Roman Mass. Saint Agatha's annual Feast Day is commemorated on 5 February. In addition, the Festival of Saint Agatha in Catania, Sicily, which commemorates Saint Agatha is also held every year in February. Blessed is She.

Saint Brigid of Kildare (ca. 451AD - 525AD)

Brigid was born in Faughart, County Louth, Ireland in the year 451 AD. Brigid was born of a noble Pagan Chieftain of the Leinster Clan, namely Dubhthach. Brigid had a slave mother who was a Christian, originally from Portugal, namely Bricicsech. In the early years of Brigid's life, she was sold as a slave to a learned member of the ancient Celts, that is to say, an aristocratic Druid landlord. During Brigid's early childhood years in slavery, she worked tirelessly on a farm. The early life experience that Brigid acquired working on a farm, witnessed her involved in many farm and dairy-related activities throughout the course of her life, including milking cows, taking care of flocks of sheep, brewing ale, churning milk, making butter, and assisting with the harvest.

Brigid successfully converted her master to Christianity, and in due course she was emancipated from the institution of slavery. Upon securing her newfound freedom, Brigid decided to return to her father. Brigid's father, Dubhthach did not understand his daughter's charitable and generous nature, and he was often frustrated at her frequent donation of personal property and perishable food items, such as flour, butter, and milk to the underprivileged people in the Irish society. There exist unsubstantiated historical accounts that Brigid's father attempted to arrange her marriage with the King of Ulster, and failing that endeavour, sell her to the aforesaid King. According to legend, while Brigid's father, Dubhthach was in conversation with the King of Ulster, Brigid donated her father's prized sword to a beggar, so that the beggar could exchange the said item of property for food. While Brigid's father was disappointed with her immediate actions, instead the King was most impressed by her considerable merit and act of piety. Consequently, the King of Ulster granted Brigid freedom from parental control.

Brigid had an unrelenting charitable nature which was witnessed by her boundless virtuous acts of kindness, generosity, compassion, prayer, community service, faith, equality, justice, and environmental concern. On numerous occasions, Brigid donated food and other material goods that belonged to her family to the poor people of Ireland. Throughout Brigid's lifetime, she had very few personal possessions or property of her own.

According to tradition, Brigid requested the Christian King of Leinster grant her a parcel of land to establish a Christian monastery. Initially, the King denied Brigid's noble-minded request. Brigid prayed to God to soften the King's heart, and then she returned to him. This time Brigid requested the King provide her with only as much land as the surface of her cloak could cover. Upon witnessing the apparently small size of Brigid's cloak, the King readily agreed to her newfound proposal. Brigid, with the assistance of a few righteous people, stretched her cloak from all four of its corners, and it covered a sizeable portion of land. The King soon realised that Brigid was blessed by God, and he granted Brigid's noble request.

In addition, to the generous land donation by the King of Leinster, Brigid was endowed with money, food, and other necessary supplies to organise a Christian monastery. Thus, Brigid became the founder of a monastery at County Kildare for both monks and nuns (also known as *the Church of the Oak Tree*). Brigid's newfound monastery became a learning centre for religious instruction, art, prayer, and theological writing. During Brigid's lifetime, she became an ordained Bishop, this was an unprecedented leadership position for a religious woman in the fifth century Ireland.

Furthermore, Brigid performed several miracles during the course of her lifetime. On one occasion, she healed a gentleman that was afflicted by leprosy. Brigid blessed a mug of water, and she instructed one of the sisters in her monastery to assist the sick gentleman to utilise the blessed water to wash the surface of his infected skin. As a result, the gentleman's skin was purified and healed of leprosy. On another occasion, Brigid touched and blessed a cow that had already been milked. The cow was then able to produce ten times as much milk that was needed to satisfy the numerous undernourished people in Ireland.

Last but not least, Brigid is credited with restoring the eye sight of Dara, a blind nun. Brigid prayed to God for the restoration of Dara's sight, and her sincere prayer was granted. In addition, Saint Brigid is widely acknowledged and referenced in theological literature. For example, consider the following publications, *the Book of Lismore*, *the Bethada Náem n-Érenn*, and *the Breviarium Aberdonense*, all of which make reference to Brigid. Furthermore, Western history records Brigid of Kildare as a major force in the 'Christianisation' of Ireland. Brigid's many good works, establishment of double monasteries providing for both monks and nuns, service to the poor and sick people of Ireland, and performance of countless virtuous acts, have all made a positive contribution to Ireland, and the world, at large.

Brigid's life story is an inspiration to all the people of the world. Brigid's life narrative personifies the time-tested principle, that it is not where you start in life that matters, but where you finish. In the particular case of Brigid, she went from slavery to sainthood. Brigid did not let the circumstances of her life, nor the lack of privilege of her birth, determine the course and destiny of her life. Brigid was true to herself and she kept her faith in the Lord. Brigid's charitable nature and unceasing concern for the welfare of her community members serve as a universal and timely lesson in the contemporary world on how to promote the ideal principles of peace, equality, justice, faith, compassion, love, service, harmony, and charity.

On 1 February 525AD, Brigid went to be with the Lord. Saint Brigid's last rites were performed by Saint Ninnidh of the Pure Hand. Brigid is honoured as one of the Patron Saints of Ireland; she is also known as the 'Mary of Ireland'. In addition, Brigid is the Patron Saint of children whose parents are not married (i.e., illegitimate children), dairy workers, sailors, midwives, poets, dairy farmers, scholars, travellers, nuns, and children born into abusive unions, among her many other categories. Last but not least, Brigid's Feast Day (also known as Saint Brigid's Day) is held on the 1st of February each year, and it is celebrated well beyond the borders of Ireland, in countries as far away as Australia, New Zealand, and the United States of America. Furthermore, Saint Bride's Church located on Fleet Street in London, England is dedicated to Saint Brigid. Blessed is She.

Saint Hildegard of Bingen (1098-1179)

Hildegard was born in the year 1098 in Bermersheim, Germany. Hildegard came from an affluent and noble German family. Hildegard's father was Hildebert of Bermersheim, and her mother was Mechtilde of Marxheim-Nahet. Both of Hildegard's parents were faithful and practicing Christians. Hildegard was the youngest of several children in her family. When Hildegard was born, her parents tithed a portion of their private wealth to the Church, and she was also promised to the Church. Hildegard's religious parents, and her early childhood development in a strong religious sphere, ultimately shaped Hildegard's life, and positioned her on the path to realising her God-given destiny.

From the early age of five, Hildegard started to receive ecstatic and mystical visions. Both of Hildegard's parents were supportive of her piety and religious world perspective. When Hildegard was eight years old, her parents offered her as an oblate to the Church. Thus, Hildegard entered into the Benedictine Convent at Disibodenberg. During Hildegard's earlier years in the Benedictine Convent, she was taught how to read and write by the religious recluse and the daughter of Count Stephen of Sponheim, Abbess Jutta von Sponheim (also known as Jutta of Disibodenberg). The Blessed Jutta also instructed Hildegard in Latin, religious study, the Christian faith, music, theology, the interpretation of Scripture, and the Lord's Prayer. The two forged a very close friendship, and Jutta had an immense impact on Hildegard's personal development and religious devotion.

In addition, Hildegard received important religious teaching and instruction from the Venerable Monk, Volmar of Disibodenberg. Volmar later succeeded in persuading and encouraging Hildegard to detail an account about her profound ecstatic visions. Volmar was much more than just a religious teacher to Hildegard. In fact, Volmar acted as Hildegard's spiritual guide, confessor, and personal scribe, until he went to be with the Lord in the year 1173. At the age of fourteen, Hildegard was admitted to the Benedictine Sisters at the Monastery at Disibodenberg. When Blessed Jutta went to be with the Lord, Hildegard, at the age of 38, was chosen as Jutta's next successor. Thus, Hildegard was confirmed as the *magistra* (spiritual teacher), and as the next Abbess of the Convent at Disibodenberg.

At the age of 42, Hildegard finally began to write about her religious visions and metaphysical experiences in a book titled *Scito vias Domini* (Know the Way of the Lord). It took Hildegard approximately ten years to write about her supernatural visions. Hildegard's finished work which detailed her visions consists of twenty-six prophetic and apocalyptic visions. In addition, Hildegard's *Scito vias Domini* addresses a number of important topics on Catholic theology, including the especial relationship between God and humanity, the Roman Catholic Church, redemption, and salvation.

Most notably, Pope Eugene III (r. 1145-1153) examined Hildegard's abovementioned work, and the Pope encouraged her further scholarly pursuit and writing on matters concerning Catholic theology. Notwithstanding Hildegard's considerable contribution to the field of theology, the *Scito vias Domini* remains Hildegard's most influential work, and in it she reveals that she is God's beloved messenger. Hildegard also makes the claim that she had received mystical visions prior to her birth, when she was still subject to gestation in her mother's womb. Hildegard credits God with ordering her to write about the Holy Secrets that God had directly revealed to her.

In the later years of Hildegard's life, she established the Convent of Rupertsberg, with the assistance and company of several nuns. Beyond the domains of Catholic theology, liturgy, religious study, natural history, cosmology, medieval literature, and Western philosophy, Hildegard also wrote extensively on the natural sciences, botany, physiology, medicine, and surgery. Among Hildegard's influential writings on the latter topics was *the Liber Subtilatum* (the Book of Subtleties of the Diverse Qualities of Created Things). By any standard of measurement, Hildegard was an accomplished writer, polymath, philosopher, theologian, and intellectual.

In addition, Hildegard is credited with the unique invention of her own language, known as *Lingua Ignota*, a philological construct of twenty-three letters! Furthermore, Hildegard also composed unique plays and musicals on the human body, soul, spirit, vice, and virtue, namely *Ordo Virtutum* (the Order of the Virtues) and *Liber Vitae Meritorum* (the Book of Life's Merits). Another one of Hildegard's great works on Catholic theology is *Liber Divinorum Operum* (the Book of Divine Works).

In the historical context of Hildegard's lifetime, she was an extremely influential leader in the Roman Catholic tradition. Hildegard managed to independently organise the affairs of nuns in the convent under her stewardship. In addition, Hildegard was not only a competent religious leader, she was a nun, poet, author, Christian mystic, Benedictine abbess, and composer. By all accounts, Hildegard was a cultivated, learned, and cultured German woman, one that was not afraid to openly challenge the male authority figures of her time. In fact, Hildegard corresponded with influential men and women during her time, and she also wrote extensively on religious and secular topics alike.

Hildegard is credited with writing some 300 letters to bishops, kings, popes, and queens during her lifetime, often containing prophecies and revelations that were directly communicated to her by the Holy Spirit. Furthermore, Hildegard was not afraid to call into question the privileged authority and standing of men in the Church. For example, consider the occasion Hildegard rebuked the Holy Roman Emperor, Frederick Barbarossa in relation to the unfortunate events concerning *the German Papal Schism*. No doubt Hildegard's prestige and influence were aided with the support of Pope Eugenius III (r. 1145-1153), who had officially proclaimed Hildegard as a Divine Messenger of God.

In the year 2012, Pope Benedict XVI (r. 2005-2013) applied the Principle of 'Equivalent Canonisation' to Saint Hildegard, thereby, extending her veneration to the entire Roman Catholic Church. Later on in the same year, Saint Hildegard was bestowed with the title of 'Doctor of the Church' by the aforesaid Pope. At the time of writing this book, Saint Hildegard is only one of four female saints to be granted the honourable title of 'Doctor of the Church'. Saint Hildegard is the Patron Saint of musicians and writers, and her annual Feast Day is commemorated on 17 September. Blessed is She.

Saint Bridget of Sweden (ca. 1303-1373)

Bridget of Sweden (Birgitta Birgersdotter) was born in the year 1303 in Uppland, Sweden. Bridget came from a distinguished and aristocratic family. Bridget's father, Sir Birger Persson of Finsta was a law speaker, landlord, and Governor of Uppland, and her mother was Lady Ingeborg Bengtsdotter. Furthermore, Bridget came from a pious and religious family. Not to mention, Bridget's father often attended Church services, regularly participated in Confessions, and he also made Holy Pilgrimages during his lifetime. Through Bridget's mother's side, she had royal blood, as she was related to the Swedish Kings of her era. From the age of ten, Bridget witnessed mystical visions of Jesus Christ crucified upon the Cross. This religious vision made a profound impression on Bridget's subconsciousness, and she continued to have mystical visions later on in her life, including a vision of *the Nativity of Jesus*.

At the age of fourteen, Bridget married the Lord of Närke, Ulf Gudmarsson. Bridget's husband treated her well, and she also taught him how to read. During the first two years of Bridget and Ulf's marriage, they lived as brothers and sisters, however, later on Bridget bore eight children, four daughters and four sons. Unfortunately, only six of Bridget's eight children survived infancy. According to legend, in the earlier years of Bridget's marriage she desired a fine bed that ought to be constructed for the married couple, however, she was sternly rebuked in a religious vision of Jesus Christ. The *Messiah* reminded Bridget that this world was full of empty sensual pleasures and material comforts.

In the year 1344, Bridget's husband, Ulf passed away at the Cistercian Alvastra Abbey in Östergötland, he went to be with the Lord. Following this tragic event, Bridget joined the Third Order of Saint Francis, where she devoted the rest of her life to sincere prayer, the performance of acts of penance, worship to God, and caring for the many poor and sick people of Sweden. During Bridget's lifetime, she rescued prostitutes, gave dowries to poor girls, and she also introduced her children to the Christian faith.

In addition, Bridget also spent a considerable amount of her time in quiet reflection and sincere prayer on the Son of the Lord, including her solemn reflection on *the Passion of Christ*. At one point, Bridget earnestly prayed to know the exact number of strikes Jesus Christ had suffered to His Body, and her prayer was answered. The *Messiah* appeared to Bridget in a mystical vision, and He advised her that the exact number of bodily strikes He had received was 5,480 and that if she intended to honour Him, then she ought to recite 'Our Father' and 'Hail Mary', coupled with select prayers over the course of one year, after which she would have honoured each and every one of His bodily wounds.

During Bridget's tenure at the Third Order of Saint Francis, she contemplated the establishment of a new monastery. In the year 1344,

Bridget founded the Order of the Most Holy Saviour (also known as the Bridgettines). This newfound religious Order catered to both nuns and monks. For this most charitable and religious mission, the newly established Order received an endowment from the King of Sweden, His Majesty Magnus IV (r. 1319-1364). Furthermore, in the year 1370, Pope Urban V (r. 1362-1370) approved the Rule of the Order.

Beyond the establishment of monasteries, Bridget also made original contributions to Catholic theology. Bridget wrote about her mystical visions and spiritual thoughts in the *Revelaciones* (the Revelations). Bridget's important work on Catholic theology contains sanctions, threats, and punishments that await sinners; however, it is also complemented by beautiful hymns of love for the Blessed Virgin Mary. *The Revelations* is one of the most significant theological works written by a religious Swedish woman in the fourteenth century, that has survived in the contemporary world. Much like *the Book of Revelation* which contains religious allegories and parables, Bridget's insightful writing in *the Revelations* is full of nuance, and requires much finesse to comprehend its true meaning. However, not of all Bridget's work was met with approval and endorsement. For example, the 16th century German priest, author, religious reformer, and theologian, Martin Luther (1483-1546) was highly critical of Bridget's theological writings, and he disavowed most of them.

Bridget was also a vocal advocate for an official end to *the Avignon Papacy*. As a matter of fact, *the Avignon Papacy* was institutionalised during a period of time in the 14th century history of the Roman Catholic Church, and it lasted in excess of six decades. From the 1300's through to the late 1370's, the Office of the Pope was domiciled in the French City of Avignon, rather than the Italian City of Rome. Notwithstanding Bridget's tireless work as an advocate of the Catholic faith, the all-important return of the Papacy to Rome was beyond her immediate lifetime.

Through Bridget's generosity, charitable nature, performance of good works, righteous practice of the Catholic faith, and community service, Bridget earnt herself an honourable reputation in the City of Rome. Not to mention, throughout Bridget's later years, she also encouraged the pursuit of sensible ecclesiastical reforms in the Roman Catholic Church. Last but not least, during Bridget's lifetime, she travelled extensively, including Holy Pilgrimages to Bethlehem, Jerusalem, and Rome.

On 23 July 1373, Bridget went to be with the Lord. On 7 October 1391, Bridget was officially canonised by Pope Boniface IX (r. 1389-1404). Bridget's canonisation was effectuated in a remarkably brief period of time after her passing to the Kingdom of Heaven, which all too vividly demonstrates the wide-ranging influence and impact of her religious work and community service during her lifetime. Furthermore, on 1 October 1999, Pope John Paul II (r 1978-2005) declared Saint Bridget a Patron Saint of Europe. In fact, Bridget is one of the six Patron Saints of Europe, and she is also the Patron Saint of Sweden and widows. Saint Bridget's annual Feast Day is commemorated on 23 July. In addition, one of Bridget's daughters was subsequently blessed to become Saint Catherine of Sweden (ca. 1332-1381). Blessed is She.

Saint Catherine of Siena (1347-1380)

Catherine (Caterina Ben ncasa) was born on 25 March 1347 in the City of Siena, the Republic of Siena (now part of Italy). Catherine was born to a middle-class family of twenty-five children, although approximately half of her siblings did not survive infancy. Catherine's father was Giacomo di Benincasa, a gentleman who was an entrepreneur that carried on a cloth dyer business. Catherine's mother was Lapa Piagenti. Around the young age of six, Catherine had her first mystical vision, she witnessed *Christ in Majesty* (also referred to as *Christ in Glory*), alongside the Apostles John, Paul, and Peter. Thereafter, at the age of seven, Catherine determinedly resolved to devote her entire life to God.

To Catherine's dismay, disappointment, and displeasure, her parents envisioned alternative plans for her life. That is to say, Catherine's parents intended a worldly life for their beloved daughter, one that included the traditional institutions of marriage and motherhood. When Catherine was sixteen years of age, her older sister, Bonaventura died during the process of childbirth. Following this exceedingly tragic and traumatic event, Catherine's parents desired that Catherine marry the late Bonaventura's widower. Catherine vehemently opposed this marriage proposal; she went as far as to commence fasting and also cut her hair to a short length in protest. Although Catherine was not fond of her parent's endless marriage proposals, Catherine's life philosophy was to treat her family members with devotion and respect. Catherine perceived her father in the divine image of Jesus Christ, her mother in the divine image of the Blessed Virgin Mary, and her several brothers in the divine image of the Apostles.

Beyond any doubt, Catherine was a deeply pious and religious woman. As a result, Catherine's parents were ultimately unsuccessful in convincing her to accept a married life. Thus, Catherine became a tertiary of a religious society, namely the Third Order of Saint Dominic. For Catherine, being a member of a monastic Third Order meant that she was able to take religious vows and concurrently remain situated outside the parameters of a convent or monastery. This newfound arrangement allowed Catherine to live with her immediate family, while she focused her endeavours on Mystical Union with God. Much to the displeasure of her mother, Catherine's father agreed to leave Catherine to pursue a religious life. Not to mention, in the furtherance of this spiritual endeavour, Catherine's father provided her with a separate room for quiet prayer, contemplation, reflection, and religious meditation.

Beyond the confines of a reflective life, Catherine was generous in her local community. Catherine often donated her family's food and personal belongings to the people most in need. Furthermore, Catherine's fellow Dominican Sisters at the Third Order of Saint Dominic assisted her to become literate, learning to read and write was a skill that proved most essential in Catherine realising her destiny. During Catherine's first few years as a member of the aforesaid Order, she spent most of her time in prayer, seclusion, and austerity. Catherine also had a mystical vision of the Castilian Catholic priest and founder of the Dominican Order, Saint Dominic (1170-1221). The vision of Saint Dominic provided Catherine with inner strength and a profound sense of peace during her many years spent in seclusion.

At twenty-one years of age, Catherine experienced another ecstatic vision. On this occasion, Catherine's unique experience of religious mysticism was of her 'Mystical Marriage to Christ'. Catherine also claimed to have received an invisible ring with Christ's foreskin (i.e., *the Holy Foreskin*), however, this claim remains somewhat contested and subject to debate. Following Catherine's 'Mystical Marriage', she became more involved in public life, and also an active member of the civil society, where she assisted the countless poor and sick people of Siena. Catherine also propagated the Catholic faith, and she even engaged in politics, making her personal contribution to the all-important questions of war and peace vis-à-vis diplomacy.

Throughout the later years of Catherine's life, she was actively and deeply involved in the internal affairs of the Roman Catholic Church. Most notably, Catherine promoted peace between the Italian city-states, republics, and principalities, and she also encouraged their unwavering loyalty to the Pope. Not to mention, Catherine also encouraged the Pope to reform the Roman Catholic Church, and she promoted her message of unconditional love to God. In addition, Catherine successfully formed an effective and influential working relationship with Pope Gregory XI (r. 1370-1378) and Pope Urban VI (r. 1378-1389). In fact, Catherine was instrumental in negotiating peace terms between Florence and Rome. In addition, Catherine's diplomatic efforts made possible Pope Gregory XI's departure from Avignon and return to Rome. Concurrently, the Papal Court was also relocated to the City of Rome.

Catherine's political and diplomatic activities meant that she travelled widely across Europe, including to Avignon, Florence, Pisa, Rome, and Tuscany. In addition, Catherine also influenced the affairs of state in Lucca and her home City of Siena. During the Middle Ages, when the traditional role of Italian women was restricted to the private sphere of the household, and was mostly confined to the institution of marriage and child-rearing, Catherine's extensive involvement in the affairs of the Roman Catholic Church, her personal interactions with two Popes, and her influential involvement in the politics of several Italian city-states and republics was most impressive. Catherine's many noteworthy accomplishments wholly justify and merit her deserving place in medieval history, as one of the greatest religious Italian women of her time.

Furthermore, Catherine made a profound contribution to Catholic theology. Catherine left behind many influential writings and intellectual works, such as *The Dialogue of Divine Providence*, an important work of

Catholic theology that engages in a religious discourse between a soul that desires spiritual elevation and Divine Union with God. Catherine's vast publication record includes approximately 380 letters, twenty-six prayers, and four treatises. Furthermore, Catherine is the Patron Saint of fire prevention, the United States of America, Europe, nurses, sick people, sexual temptation, miscarriages, bodily ills, the Philippines, and Italy. On 29 April 1380, at the young age of thirty-three, Catherine went to be with the Lord.

Catherine's towering legacy has been forever enshrined in the profound history of the Roman Catholic Church. In the year 1461, Catherine was canonised by Pope Pius II (r. 1458-1464). Thereafter, in 1866, Pope Pius IX (r. 1846-1878) declared Catherine a co-Patroness of Rome. Furthermore, in the year 1939, Pope Pius XII (r. 1939-1958) named Catherine a joint Patron Saint of Italy. Not to mention, in 1970, Pope Paul VI (r. 1963-1978) recognised Saint Catherine as a 'Doctor of the Church'. Last but not least, in 1999, Pope John Paul II (r. 1978-2005) proclaimed Catherine as one of Europe's Patron Saints. Saint Catherine's annual Feast Day is commemorated on 29 April. Blessed is She.

Saint Rita of Cascia (1381-1457)

Rita of Cascia (Margherita Lotti) was born in the year 1381 in the City of Roccaporena, Italy. Rita came from a noble and well-respected Christian family. Rita's father was Antonio Lotti and her mother was Amata Ferri.

Both of Rita's parents were honourable members of the *Conciliatore di Cristo* (the Peacemakers of Christ). Furthermore, Rita's parents performed service in their local community through their many charitable works.

As a young child, Rita wished to join the convent of the Augustinian Nuns in Cascia, where she frequently visited. Unfortunately, Rita's parents did not agree to her becoming a nun, for they had alternative plans for her life. At the age of twelve, upon the desire and wishes of her parents, Rita was given in an arranged marriage to Paolo Mancini, a man who had a violent temper and poor character. Rita's husband was also of immoral conduct, and he had several protracted family feuds to contend with. With respect to the arranged marriage proposal, Rita's parents were of the perspective that Paolo was a wealthy man, and that he was also able to provide for the security and safety of their beloved daughter. Against Rita's own wishes, she accepted the will of her parents as the sovereign will of God, and she affirmed her marriage with dignity, grace, reverence, and humility.

Rita was not well respected in her marriage with Paolo. On many occasions, Rita's husband, Paolo entertained numerous extramarital affairs and physically abused his wife. Notwithstanding Rita's ill-treatment at the hands of her husband, she worked tirelessly to reform him into a morally righteous person. Rita succeeded to some extent in moulding Paolo into a decent person. By Rita's grace, kindness, patience, and influence, Paolo became more favourable to Christian views and leading a life of peace and improved moral conduct. In addition, Paolo Mancini even renounced a long-standing family feud, between the Chiqui and Mancini families.

In spite of Paolo's genuine efforts at personal reform, however, the long history of his previous involvement in such deep-rooted family feuds, did not completely escape him. Ultimately, Paolo became a victim of unending family rivalries. Paolo and Rita's marriage lasted eighteen years, until her husband was murdered due to a protracted family feud. Rita publicly pardoned her husband's murderers at Paolo's funeral. During the course of Rita and Paolo's marriage, Rita had twin sons, namely, Giovanni Antonio and Paulo Maria. Both of Rita's and Paolo's sons were raised in the Christian faith and in accordance with Christian values.

Due to the malignant influence of Paolo's brother, Bernardo, Rita's two sons, Giovanni and Paulo wished to avenge the cold-blooded murder of their father. Bernardo began to increasingly exert his personal influence and autocratic leadership upon Rita's son's character and sway their thoughts towards seeking revenge. Rita earnestly attempted to dissuade her two sons from seeking revenge and following the bitter path proposed by their uncle, however, she was unable to convince them otherwise.

Subsequently, Rita prayed to God that her sons do not commit mortal sin, specifically, the immoral act of murder. God answered Rita's prayer, and both her sons died within a year due to dysentery. Thus, Rita's two sons were prevented from committing mortal sin, and saved from the otherwise forthcoming punishment of the depths and despair of hell. Rita deeply loved both of her sons, and although she was saddened at the personal loss of her beloved children, she was thankful and grateful to God that her son's souls were not tainted with mortal sins.

Having lost her husband and two sons, Rita was now a childless widow. Thereupon, Rita returned her life solely to faith. Rita became involved in prayer, the performance of penance, charity, community service, and acts of sincere love towards God. At the age of thirty-six, Rita joined the monastery of Saint Mary Magdalene. During the arduous journey of her life Rita endured multiple privations, and she held many roles throughout her life, including wife, widow, mother, and nun.

Some of Rita's greatest sacrifices were voluntary and representative of her personal devotion to God. For example, consider that according to legend, once Rita prayed before an image of *Jesus Christ on the Cross*, and a partial Stigmata became visible on her forehead, being a thorn from the Crown that was positioned upon Jesus Christ's Head, which penetrated her material body. This physical sign of Mystical Union with the Son of God, remained upon Rita's body until her passage into the Heavenly Kingdom of God, and it also remained on her body thereafter.

On 22 May 1457, Rita went to be with the Lord. Subsequently, Rita was beatified on 19 October 1626 by Pope Urban VIII (r. 1623-1644). Thereafter, on 24 May 1900, Rita was canonised by Pope Leo XIII (r. 1878-1903). Saint Rita is the Patron Saint of lost and impossible causes, heartbroken women, victims of abuse, marriage difficulties, wounds, sickness, mothers, parenthood, and widows.

The life story of Saint Rita is an endless source of inspiration and wisdom to countless people around the world. Saint Rita experienced much sorrow, loss, and grief during her lifetime; however, she did not let her personal circumstances define her life. Instead, Saint Rita continued to confront and surpass the many challenges on her worldly and spiritual journey. Not to mention, on each and every occasion Saint Rita rose up to become a visionary leader and role model, for men and women to emulate. In many respects, Saint Rita's life is an ideal and living testimony of the scripture verse attributed to Saint Paul that is found in *The Holy Bible* (New International Version) at *2 Timothy 4:7*, that is to say, 'I have fought the good fight, I have finished the race, I have kept the faith'. Saint Rita's annual Feast Day is commemorated on 22 May. Blessed is She.

Saint Catherine of Genoa (1447-1510)

Catherine (Caterina Fieschi Adorno) was born the year 1447 in Genoa, the Republic of Genoa. Catherine's father, Jacopo Fieschi was the former Viceroy of the Kingdom of Naples, and her mother was Francesca di Negro. Catherine was the youngest of five children in her family, she had one older sister and three elder brothers. Catherine came from an affluent, influential, and well-respected family. In fact, the Fieschi family line was associated with two former Popes, namely Pope Innocent IV (r. 1243-1254) and Pope Adrian V (r. 1276). Not to mention, the Fieschi family was a staunch supporter of the Papacy. During Catherine's childhood years, she received a first-rate education. As a child, Catherine was most interested in leading a spiritual and religious life centered around her Catholic faith and values.

In Catherine's earlier years, her older sister, Limbania Fieschi was a strong influence on Catherine's development and thought. Furthermore, Limbania had joined the Convent of Santa Maria Delle Grazie, and become an Augustinian nun. In 1460, at the age of thirteen, Catherine strongly desired to formally adopt the religious life of a nun. Following in the footsteps of her older sister, Catherine also wished to join the Convent of Santa Maria Delle Grazie, however, Catherine was refused admission due to her young age. After being denied membership to the aforesaid Convent, Catherine did not provision further thought to such an idea, even in the later years of her life.

In the year 1463, Catherine's father passed away. Thereafter, at the age of sixteen, Catherine was married to a Genoese nobleman by the name of

Giuliano Adorno. Giuliano was a young man who had traversed the Middle East, and he had been involved in the affairs of state concerning trade and military. Regrettably, Giuliano's temperament, personality, and character were not favourable for a blessed marriage. Unfortunately, Catherine had no self-determination in her marriage, and given that her father had passed away, it was her eldest brother that determined her future spouse.

Catherine was a beautiful and lettered gentlelady, who came from a noble family. There was definitely no shortage of potential suitors for her marriage, however, Catherine's hand was given to Giuliano, in order to resolve a long-standing dispute between two powerful and influential families. The mending of fences might have been a positive objective for the Adorno and Fieschi families, however, Catherine personally suffered in her marriage life for almost a decade, before her profound and life-changing conversion.

Catherine's arranged marriage turned out to be most unfortunate, for it was childless and Catherine's husband was violent, unfaithful, and obnoxious in his behaviour. Not to mention, Giuliano was most reckless with the family's assets and wealth. In addition, Giuliano entertained an extramarital affair with a mistress, and he even fathered an illegitimate child out of wedlock. For Catherine's part, she attempted to find meaning and solace in a life of seclusion in the first few years of her marriage. Thereafter, Catherine turned to indulgence and sensual pleasures (albeit, without her spouse), however, such worldly endeavours that were entertained by Catherine were ultimately in vain, and to no satisfactory avail.

In the year 1473, ten years into Catherine's difficult marriage with Giuliano, she had a mystical religious experience. Catherine's life changing experience occurred during Confession on the 22nd of March 1473, the Feast Day of Saint Benedict, and it led to her conversion. Thereafter,

Catherine devoted her life to prayer, charity, and community service to the poor and sick people of Italy. Catherine worked tirelessly at the Great Pammatone Hospital in Genoa to care for the many sick, poor, and vulnerable patients. In addition, Catherine was also entrusted with managerial and treasury duties during her tenure at the aforesaid hospital. The receipt of further good news followed Catherine's endeavours, for her husband, Giuliano Adorno, also had a change of heart. Giuliano converted to Christianity, and he became a lay member, that is to say, a tertiary of the Franciscan Order. Thereafter, Giuliano joined his wife in the honourable service of the countless sick and poor patients at the Pammatone Hospital in Genoa.

In 1479, both Catherine and Giuliano resided at the Great Pammatone Hospital, where they worked without the benefit of monetary compensation, dedicating their noble efforts to charitable service. In addition, from 1490 to 1496, Catherine served as Director of the Great Pammatone Hospital, however, in 1496, Catherine's health deteriorated. Consequently, Catherine had to briefly withdraw from her work duties at the Pammatone Hospital, however, she went on to make a full recovery. Shortly thereafter, in the year 1497, Catherine's husband, Giuliano passed away.

Beyond Catherine's many years of generous service to the destitute and disadvantaged people of her community, Catherine also made significant original contributions to Catholic theology.

In this respect, Catherine was responsible for the ideas and thoughts contained within two important theological texts. The first was the Trattato del Purgatorio (the Treatise on Purgatory). The aforesaid treatise dealt with spiritual matters, and it is a collection of Catherine's teachings and thoughts on the subject matter of purgation and purgatory.

Catherine's second important theological text was *the Dialogo* (the Dialogue of the Soul and Body), and it details Catherine's personal experience of inner conflict. *The Dialogue* demonstrates Catherine's psychology of a protracted battle between the human body and the soul, a grand contest between worldly matter and Godly Spirit. Furthermore, *the Dialogue* narrates the challenges and contradictions of the pursuit of lofty spiritual goals against the countless number of worldly desires. In essence, this text of Christian theology prescribes the end goal of life being steady progress towards Divine Union with God.

While Catherine's authorship of the aforesaid theological works remains somewhat contested, much of the writing contained within the two abovementioned texts is attributed to Catherine. Furthermore, the Austrian writer, theologian, Christian apologist, and Roman Catholic layperson, Friedrich von Hügel (1852-1925) explores the many significant ideas and substantial thoughts of Catherine, in his seminal work *the Mystical Element of Religion* which was first published in the year 1908.

On 15 September 1510, Catherine went to be with the Lord. In the year 1675, Catherine was beatified by Pope Clement X (r. 1670-1676). Thereafter, on 18 May 1737, Catherine was canonised by Pope Clement XII (r. 1730-1740). Furthermore, Pope Pius XII (r. 1939-1958) recognised Catherine as the Patroness of hospitals in Italy. Saint Catherine's annual Feast Day is commemorated on 15 September. Catherine is the Patron Saint of childless people, victims of unfaithfulness, difficult marriages, brides, temptations, widows, and victims of adultery. Blessed is She.

Saint Teresa of Ávila (1515-1582)

Teresa of Ávila (Teresa Sánchez de Capeda y Ahumada) was born on 28 March 1515 in Ávila, Spain. Teresa's father, Alonso Sánchez de Cepeda, was a wool merchant and a wealthy gentleman. Teresa's mother, Beatriz de Ahumada y Cuevas, raised her daughter as a faithful Christian. Teresa's father and mother had very different personalities, temperaments, interests, and traits. Teresa's father was disciplined, pious, and strict, he taught Teresa to never lie and always be honest. Whereas Teresa's mother had an interest in romance books and fictional love stories, something that Teresa's father objected to. As a child, Teresa felt that no matter what she did, in the end, she was likely to do something wrong, and consequently, displease at least one of her parents.

At the age of seven, Teresa devised a mischievous plan to leave home, and she escaped with her older brother. As a child, Teresa was inspired by the many accounts and fascinating stories of the Great Saints of Old, and she intended to seek martyrdom by fighting against the Moors. This was Teresa's brave and youthful expression of sacrifice, her then understanding of living a life in an honourable manner. Before Teresa and her brother escaped beyond the parameters of the city, the two children were located by their uncle, and they were later returned to their home.

As a young child, Teresa was playful and somewhat troublesome, however, with the passing away of her mother at the age of eleven, she turned to the Blessed Virgin Mary as her spiritual mother and guide. The death of Teresa's biological mother turned Teresa more towards a life of prayer and reflection. Teresa was quite close to her mother, and the affection she received from her greatly assisted Teresa in countering the strictness and discipline of her father. At the age of sixteen, Teresa's father sent her to a convent. This was Teresa's first experience in such a deeply religious and pious environment.

At the age of twenty, Teresa entered the Carmelite Convent of the Incarnation in Ávila, Spain. Over the course of Teresa's tenure at the Carmelite Convent of the Incarnation, she did not find solace, nor the inner sanctity of peace that she was earnestly seeking. With the generous assistance of Teresa's spiritual advisor, Franciscan Priest, Peter of Alcantara, and a gentlelady of considerable wealth and her good friend, Guimara de Ulloa, Teresa proceeded to establish a new convent, namely *the Convent of Saint Joseph* (est. 1562). The aforesaid convent of Discalced Carmelite nuns also had a church erected in the year 1607.

In the later years of Teresa's life, she became a dedicated monastic reformer. In the 1560's and 1570's, Teresa established several monasteries, and she founded numerous convents for both monks and nuns situated throughout the various cities and towns of Spain. For example, in the year 1567, when Teresa travelled to *Medina del Campo* in Spain, she came in contact with the Spanish Carmelite Priest, *Juan de Yepes* (later known as *Saint John of the Cross*). The two devout religious leaders came into agreement that Juan ought to lead the Carmelite Reform Movement for devout men. Within the period of one year, Juan went on to establish a monastery for monks, known as the Carmelite Primitive Rule located in Duruelo, Spain.

Teresa also made significant original contributions to the promotion and further understanding of religious doctrine and Catholic theology. In this respect, one of Teresa's greatest contributions is the 'Doctrine of the Four Stages of the Ascent of the Soul to God'. The first stage is 'Devotion of the Heart' which consists of mental prayer and contemplation. The second stage is known as 'Devotion of Peace' where the individual human will is unconditionally surrendered to God's supreme will. The third stage is 'Devotion of Union' where one seeks absorption with God. The fourth and final stage is 'Devotion of Ecstasy' where one's sensory facilities cease, and the instruments of memory and imagination are wholly absorbed in God.

Teresa expounded the notion that it is only by setting aside one's finite intellect, and placing one's total confidence and complete trust in God, that such a transcendental faith-based experience can be ascertained in this very lifetime. As a prolific spiritual author, Teresa wrote extensively throughout her lifetime. Some of Teresa's most influential works include: *Camino de Perfeccion* (the Way of Perfection), *the Castillo Interior* (the Interior Castle), *Libro de las Fundaciones* (the Book of Foundations), *the Life of the Holy Mother Teresa of Jesus*, *Spiritual Relations*, *Exclamations of the Soul to God*, and *Conceptions on the Love of God*.

On 15 October of 1582, Teresa of Ávila went to be with the Lord. Thereafter, on 24 April 1614, Teresa was beatified by Pope Paul V (r. 1605-1621). Subsequently, on 12 March 1622, Teresa was canonised by Pope Gregory XV (r. 1621-1623). In addition, Saint Teresa's annual Feast Day is commemorated on 15 October. Saint Teresa Ávila (also known as Saint Teresa of Jesus) is the Patron Saint of sick people, Croatia, Spain, the City of Talisay, lacemakers, and people in religious orders. Last but not least, in the year 1970, Pope Paul VI (r. 1963-1978) proclaimed Saint Teresa (along with Saint Catherine of Siena) as the first two of the four female Saints, thus far, to be affirmed as a 'Doctor of the Church'. Blessed is She.

Saint Rose of Lima (1586-1617)

Rose (Isabel Flores de Oliva) was born on 20 April 1586 in Lima, the Viceroyalty of Peru. Rose's father, Gaspar Flores served in the Imperial Spanish Army. Rose's mother was a Creole native of Lima named Maria de Oliva y Herrera. According to legend, Isabel was initially named after her maternal grandmother, Isabel de Herrera. While Isabel was in the care of an Indian maidservant in the Flores family household by the name of Mariana, the aforesaid servant commented that the newborn baby girl was extremely beautiful. Mariana noted that Isabel's facial complexion resembled that of an European flower, and thus, named her Rose. The newfound name found much approval amongst the members of the Flores household, and stayed with Rose for the rest of her life.

During Rose's memorable childhood years, she was an admirer of the notable tertiary of the Dominican Order, namely Catherine of Siena, and Rose often emulated her noble conduct. Not to mention, Catherine of Siena had an immense impact on Rose's life, values, actions, beliefs, and thoughts. In fact, Rose devoted significant time to the performance of prayer, fasting, community service, and acts of penance. In addition, Rose spent countless hours contemplating the Most Blessed Sacrament on a daily basis, and she also regularly took Holy Communion. Rose's natural and youthful beauty began to attract the unwanted attention of many suitors in the local community. In response, Rose cut her hair to a noticeably short length, and she applied hot peppers to her face, to make her facial skin blister and her appearance most unattractive. Rose adamantly rejected all admirers, much to the dismay of her family and friends.

Rose's parents were opposed to her taking the vow of virginity. Gaspar and Maria wanted their daughter to get married, however, Rose adamantly refused. Ultimately, Rose's father accepted her will to dedicate her life to God, and he allowed Rose to practice a life of austerity, reflection, and penance from home. Rose maintained her determination to take a vow of virginity, and she served the elderly, poor, hungry, homeless, and sick people of her local community. Not to mention, Rose often brought the many disadvantaged and sick people to her home, and she wholeheartedly took care of them. In the furtherance of assisting the many poor and sick people, Rose established a small infirmary in her parent's house. Within the parameters of her home-made infirmary, Rose attended to the needs of the poor and sick people, and she provided in as much medical treatment as her abilities, knowledge, and resources permitted.

In addition, during Rose's younger years, she grew flowers at her home, and she also completed fine needlework, sewing, and embroidery, selling such home-made items at the local market place. Subsequently, Rose utilised the sale proceeds from her work to promote charitable causes in her home City of Lima, and to financially assist her family at home. Apart from the performance of community service and worship at Church, Rose spent the majority of her time in seclusion.

Rose wanted to become a nun; however, her father was strongly opposed to the decision, and her parents did not permit Rose to enter a monastery or convent. Thus, at the age of twenty, in a compromise, Rose joined the Third Order of Saint Dominic as a tertiary, and she took her vow of perpetual virginity. This arrangement allowed Rose to live a life of solitude and penance at home with her parents, while she devoted her time, energy, and resources to a religious life of community service, penance, devotion, and prayer. Rose only slept two hours a night, in order to devote additional time in sincere prayer to God.

Rose earnestly emulated the sacrifices and life of Jesus Christ in all aspects of her life. Rose even wore a crown of pewter with spikes in it, thereby, depicting the Crown of Thorns that was worn by the *Messiah* at His *Crucifixion on the Cross*. The crown of pewter on Rose's head made incisions on the surface of her skin, thus, causing her to bleed, yet, Rose covered such a painful condition, by positioning a number of roses on her crown. For Rose, hiding her pain and suffering was an honourable mark of subduing her pride. On one occasion, Rose also burned her hands, as a self-imposed act of penance. Rose continued to impose several strict acts of penance upon herself, in sincere emulation of the pain and suffering of *Jesus Christ on the Cross*. For the remainder of Rose's life, she lived in strict seclusion, practicing a reflective life of austerity and asceticism.

The general populace of Lima was becoming increasingly aware of Rose's good works, charitable service to society, and religious life of austerity. As a result, the many residents of Lima visited Rose to seek her association and favour. Indeed, several Lima residents of wealth and fame sought Rose's company, including the royal accountant and his wife, Gonzalo de la Maza and María de Uzátegui, respectively. In addition, the wife of one of the viceroys, the marquise of Montes Claros befriended Lima. Rose was grateful for such friendship and good company; however, Rose was conscious of reality, that a life of luxury, power, and wealth was not compatible with her values of meekness, austerity, and humility.

On 25 August 1617, Rose's natural life came to its demise, and she went to be with the Lord. Rose was only thirty-one years old at the time of her ascent into the Heavenly Kingdom of God. According to legend, Rose had accurately predicted the date that she was destined to depart this world, for the Heavenly Kingdom of God. Thereafter, on 10 May 1667, Pope

Clement IX (r. 1667-1669) beatified Rose of Lima. Subsequently, on 12 April 1671, Rose was canonised by Pope Clement X (r. 1670-1676). Saint Rose of Lima's annual Feast Day is commemorated on 23 August.

Furthermore, Saint Rose is the Patron Saint of gardeners, Indigenous people of the Americas, embroiderers, people who are harassed for their piety, lacemakers, Peru, South America, the Indies, Lima, the Royal Chartered Borough of Arima, the Philippines, florists, and people who suffer from family problems. Rose of Lima was the first Catholic woman in the Americas to be declared a saint. Blessed is She.

Saint Virginia Centurione Bracelli (1587-1651)

Virginia was born on 2 April 1587 in Genoa, Italy. Virginia was a woman of noble status. Virginia's father, Giorgio Centurione was the Doge of the Republic of Genoa, and her mother was Lelia Spinola. As a young girl, Virginia never desired the traditional institution of marriage, however, her parents thought otherwise. On 10 December 1602, upon the unrelenting insistence of Virginia's parents, at the young age of fifteen, she was obliged to wedlock with Gaspare Grimaldi Bracelli. Virginia had two legitimate daughters during her marriage, namely Lelia and Isabella. Regrettably, Virginia's husband was an alcoholic and gambler.

Virginia's difficult marriage with Gaspare was short-lived. In 1607, Virginia's husband passed away, only after five years of them being together. Thus, Virginia became a widow, she was twenty years of age at the time, with the added responsibility of raising two young children. Virginia's father attempted to persuade Virginia into a second marriage, however, she altogether refused to consider the prospect of a new spouse. It was at this pivotal point in Virginia's life, that she undertook a vow to live a chaste life. Virginia committed herself to higher ideals, including charity, poverty alleviation, and assisting the poor and sick people in her home City of Genoa. In the interim, Virginia resided with her in-laws, who generously assisted in raising her two young daughters.

Once Virginia's daughters were grown up and married, she dedicated her life to community service, prayer, and charity. With the onset of war in her immediate region, from 1624 to 1625, there were countless orphans that required care and attention. Thus, in the year 1625, Virginia went on to establish *the Cento Signore della Misericordia Protettrici dei Poveri di Gesù* (the Hundred Ladies of Mercy, Protectors of the Poor of Jesus Christ). In many respects this institution was an infirmary that also served as a refuge for the many poor and sick people in Virginia's local community. The later outbreak of *the Italian Plague (1629-1630)*, coupled with the devastating effects of a famine across Italy, made public health matters much worse. This newfound dismal reality inevitably led to an increasing influx of sick children, the elderly, and poor people requiring medical attention and treatment in Genoa.

The aforementioned infirmary was no longer able to support the needs of hundreds of vulnerable, sick, and poor people in Genoa. Consequently, Virginia rented the Monte Calvario Convent in order to accommodate the increasing number of people that were requiring care. By the year 1635, the aforesaid convent was providing medical care for hundreds of patients. Furthermore, the aforesaid institution was also afforded official recognition as a hospital from the government of the Kingdom of Sardinia.

Most unfortunately, in the year 1647, the Monte Calvario Convent had its special government recognition as a hospital withdrawn. This unfortunate and disappointing outcome was partially due to the declining receipt of donations and the insufficient giving of charitable funds by the affluent and privileged people of Virginia's home city to keep the centre operable as a hospital. Despite Virginia's best intentions, the high operating expenses of the hospital had made it an unviable operation, coupled with its over-reliance on charitable funds and sporadic donations, meant that its operating expenses could no longer be sufficiently covered.

Virginia subsequently arranged for the construction of a church dedicated to Our Lady of Refuge in Genoa. Furthermore, Virginia organised the numerous sisters who worked with her into two separate congregations, namely, *Suore di Nostra Signora del Rifugio di Monte Calvario* (the Sisters of Our Lady of Refuge in Mount Calvary) and *Figlie di Nostra Signora al Monte Calvario* (the Daughters of Our Lady on Mount Calvary). This organisational structure permitted Virginia to provide much needed treatment and support to the sick, poor, and underprivileged people on a much larger scale and capacity in the Italian City of Genoa.

The two aforesaid institutions also catered for the religious instruction, learning, training, and education of the underprivileged people in Virginia's local community. In Virginia's later years, she retired from the management and administration of the religious orders and institutions that she was associated with. Thereafter, Virginia begged for alms, completed chores in her local community, and she also worked as a peacemaker between noble houses. Furthermore, Virginia promoted sincere efforts towards reconciliation between the Church and Republic authorities in her home city.

On 15 December 1651, Virginia went to be with the Lord. Virginia was 64 years old at the time of her ascent into the Heavenly Kingdom of

God. Thereafter, on 22 September 1985, Virginia was beatified by Pope John Paul II (r. 1978-2005). Subsequently, on 18 May 2003, Virginia was canonised also by Pope John Paul II. The life narrative of Virginia contains important lessons and principles which can be learnt by people of all faiths, ethnicities, and cultural backgrounds.

Virginia's moral responsibility, charity, sense of duty, untiring commitment to the most disadvantaged people of her home city, boundless generosity, and promotion of peace, are noble virtues that are universally applicable. Saint Virginia's annual Feast Day is commemorated on 15 December. Saint Virginia is the Patron Saint of the Sisters of Our Lady of Refuge in Mount Calvary. Blessed is She.

Saint Thérèse of Lisieux (1873-1897)

Thérèse (Marie Françoise-Thérèse Martin) was born on 2 January 1873 in Alençon, France. Thérèse's father was a jeweller and fine watchmaker by the name of Louis Martin. Thérèse's mother was Marie-Azélie Guérin. Both of Thérèse's parents were dedicated Catholics. Thérèse came from a family of nine children, and she was the youngest child in her family. In addition to Thérèse, only four of her older siblings survived childhood, all four siblings were sisters.

During the first several months of Thérèse's infancy, she was entrusted to the care of a wet nurse by the name of Rose Taillé. Rose had previously cared for two of Thérèse's older siblings. On 2 April 1874,

Thérèse was returned to the affectionate care of her biological parents. Unfortunately, on 28 August 1877, Thérèse's mother passed away at the age of forty-five due to complications arising from breast cancer. Thérèse was approximately four and a half years old at the time of her mother's death. Following this devastating family loss, Thérèse and the family moved to the French City of Lisieux.

After Thérèse's loss of her mother, she became withdrawn and despondent. As a child, Thérèse demonstrated strong emotions, and she was often nervous and sensitive, otherwise she was a happy and cheerful child. Regrettably, Thérèse was a victim of bullying and harassment during her school years, and she grew up preferring an existence of solitude, prayer, and reflection. When Thérèse was nine years old, her sister Pauline joined the Carmelite Convent located at Lisieux. Thérèse was left heartbroken by Pauline's departure from home, as Pauline had acted in the informal capacity of a 'second mother' to her. The emergent void in Thérèse's life was difficult to accept, however, Thérèse continued on her path to being the best person that she could be.

Initially, Thérèse was unable to join Pauline and enter the aforesaid convent herself due to her young age. When Thérèse was denied permission to join the Carmelite Convent, it only served to strengthen her faith and determination to join the religious order. In fact, all four of Thérèse's older sisters had become nuns. No doubt, Thérèse's family environment, and her older sister's decision to pursue a religious life, strongly influenced young Thérèse. For Thérèse had now wholly determined and irrevocably resolved to follow on the same path as her older sisters.

Thérèse's entrance into the above-mentioned convent was marked by blessings and grace. Thérèse embarked on a foreign visit to Italy, where she attended the House of Loreto and the Eternal City. During the course of Thérèse's visit, on 20 November 1887, amidst a number of pilgrims, Thérèse was in the company of Pope Leo XIII (r.1878-1903), when she requested the Holy Father grant her permission to join the Carmelite Convent. The Pope gave Thérèse his approval and blessing for her solemn request. Thus, at the age of fifteen, Thérèse was granted the requisite permission to enter the Carmelite Convent in Lisieux.

As a Roman Catholic nun, Thérèse dedicated her life to the service of the sick and poor people of France. Thérèse's early years of childhood made her adult life somewhat difficult. Thérèse struggled with doubt, guilt, and depression, however, she worked tirelessly to become the best version of herself. Thérèse's exemplary behaviour was marked by grace, selfless service, humility, kindness, courtesy, and respect for other people.

Thérèse espoused *the Doctrine of the Little Way*, in which she found solace and strength during her troubled childhood and teenage years. *The Little Way* also become the basis for Thérèse's spirituality and devotion to God. In the year 1898, Thérèse's ideas, writings, and thoughts were published posthumously in the work *Histoire d'une âme* (the Story of a Soul). In fact, *the Story of a Soul* made such a strong and favourable impression upon Pope Pius X (r. 1903-1914), that this text is partially credited with the aforesaid Pope signing a decree for the commencement of the formal process of Thérèse's future canonisation as a Saint of the Roman Catholic Church. On 29 July 1894, Thérèse's father, Louis Martin passed away, the gravity of this personal loss tested, but ultimately strengthened Thérèse's faith in God.

Thérèse's final months were marked by a protracted struggle with tuberculosis, however, she found remarkable strength in and through her suffering. Thérèse unconditionally accepted the sovereign will of God, and handled her final days of life with grace and love for all those around her. On 30 September 1897, Thérèse went to be with the Lord. Thérèse was only twenty-four years old at the time of her ascent into the Heavenly Kingdom of God. On 29 April 1923, Thérèse was beatified by Pope Pius XI (r. 1922-1939). Not to mention, on 17 May 1925, Thérèse was canonised also by Pope Pius XI.

Thereafter, on 19 October 1997, Thérèse was appointed 'Doctor of the Church' by Pope John Paul II (r. 1978-2005). Thérèse is one of only four women to hold this honorific title, and she is the youngest woman to be named a 'Doctor of the Church'. Thérèse's annual Feast Day is commemorated on 1 October. Thérèse is the Patron Saint of missions, the Gardens of Vatican City, orphaned children, tuberculosis, missionaries, France, Russia, florists, and gardeners.

Thérèse's life story is one of simplicity, sisterhood, and service. Thérèse did not find any new religious orders or monasteries, nor did she travel to countless far away towns and many foreign cities to make Holy Pilgrimages. Nor did Thérèse make voluminous original contributions to Catholic theology. It was Thérèse's every day and ordinary actions, that she performed while she was a nun at the Carmelite Convent at Lisieux, that strongly resonated with the French people, and the modern world, at large. For example, consider when Thérèse was a nun, she scattered flowers around the Carmelite Convent, as a sign of her true love and sincere affection towards God.

In addition, Thérèse's struggles during her childhood years, the loss of her mother at a young age, and her many intense emotions, all serve to effectively demonstrate, and perhaps remind us, that saints were once all too human. Most importantly, Thérèse's life story illustrates that it is in the ordinary actions of kindness, compassion, love, and forgiveness that a meaningful life is forged and lived. Saint Thérèse is affectionately referred to as 'the Little Flower'. Blessed is She.

Mother Mary Teresa (Saint Teresa of Calcutta) (1910-1997)

Teresa (Anjezë Gonxhe Bojaxhiu) was born on 26 October 1910 in Skopje, North Macedonia (formerly the sovereign territory of the Ottoman Empire). Teresa's father, Nikollë Bojaxhiu was an Albanian businessman, and her mother was Dranafile Bojaxhiu. Teresa's parents were Albanian grocers, and they had five children, however, two of them did not survive infancy. Thus, Teresa grew up with two siblings, one older brother, Lazar Bojaxhiu, and one older sister, Aga Bojaxhiu.

In the year 1919, Teresa's father passed away, and her mother assumed sole responsibility for raising Teresa, and her two siblings. As a young child, Teresa was fascinated by the countless inspiring stories of missionaries and the Great Saints of Old. At the age of twelve, Teresa received her true calling from God. That is to say, Teresa was instructed to devote her life to serving the poor and destitute people of the modern world. For the remainder of her life, Teresa worked tirelessly to make the world a better place. Indeed, Teresa's inspirational story is one of selfless service and devotion to humankind.

In 1928, at the age of eighteen, Teresa joined *the Sisters of Loreto* in Rathfarnham, Ireland for the purposes of education and instruction in the English language. Thereafter, Teresa departed Ireland to join *the Sisters of Loreto* overseas mission based in Calcutta, India. During Teresa's time in India, she became an inspirational missionary, leaving her global imprint on the modern world. In addition, Teresa continued her missionary work far beyond the territory of India. Indeed, Teresa spread the universal message of love, compassion, charity, and community service across the modern world.

In 1929, Teresa arrived in India, determined to make a difference. First and foremost, understanding 'interculturality' was going to be instrumental to Teresa's success as a nun and missionary in India. In this endeavour, Teresa completed her novitiate in the City of Darjeeling in West Bengal. Furthermore, Teresa also learnt the Bengali language, and she taught at a local school in Bengal. Such early experiences helped Teresa to better assimilate with the language, culture, people, and society of her newfound home nation, India.

Teresa served for almost twenty years at the Loreto Convent School in the neighbourhood of Entally located in Calcutta, India. In 1944, Teresa was appointed as the Headmistress of the aforesaid school. During Teresa's time in India, she witnessed many dire circumstances attributed to intercommunal violence, poverty, and war. For example, consider *the Bengal Famine of 1943* (which transpired during the course of *World War II*), and *the 1946 Calcutta Killings* (also known as *Direct Action Day*). In the year 1946, while Teresa was travelling on a train for her annual retreat, she received her second calling from God. This time Teresa's inner calling directed her to continue her charitable work amongst the poorest of the poor, and she did not hesitate to attend to the exalted call of religious duty.

In 1948, Teresa began to undertake missionary work in the infamous slums situated in the Indian City of Calcutta. Teresa was soon to realise that the tremendous toil and bureaucratic burden of missionary work far exceeded the previous demands placed upon her, in particular, when positioned in comparison to the conveniences and comfort of life in a Catholic convent. Nonetheless, Teresa continued her missionary work, undeterred by the many privations that she confronted, and soon enough she attracted a small following of sisters. Teresa had attracted a sufficient number of people to create an informal religious community that served many destitute and impoverished people across the City of Calcutta in India.

Subsequently, within the period of a few years, Teresa received the blessing and consent of the Roman Catholic city-state, the Vatican City during the reign of Pope Pius XII (r. 1939-1958), to begin her own religious order, namely *the Missionaries of Charity* (est. 1950). Following in the footsteps of the congregation's founder, Mother Teresa, the nuns of the *Missionaries of Charity* wear the traditional Indian dress known as a *sari*. This Indian dress is primarily of white cotton fabric material, with a distinct blue coloured borderline across the head scarf.

The purpose of the aforesaid religious organisation is to serve some of the most unfortunate people in India, and across the modern world. *The Missionaries of Charity* provide much needed love, a place of residence, and medical care for destitute people that have been abandoned or rejected. In the year 1965, Pope Paul VI (r. 1963-1978) issued a *Decree of Praise* upon the aforesaid religious institution. Thus, *the Missionaries of Charity* went on to become an International Religious Family, it has numerous active and contemplative branches of Catholic Brothers and Sisters throughout the contemporary world.

Teresa's missionary work in India was truly broad in its scope and endeavour. Among Teresa's countless achievements, in 1952, she established *the Home of the Pure Heart*. This hospice was created for the most vulnerable people of the modern Indian society who require essential medical care, in particular, end-of-life care. Furthermore, Teresa went on to establish another hospice, namely *the City of Peace*, this institution was founded for people with Hansen's disease. In addition, in the year 1955, Teresa founded *the Children's Home of the Immaculate*

Heart for orphans and vulnerable youth. Last but not least, Teresa was also instrumental in the establishment of both *the Missionaries of Charity Brothers* (1963) and *the Missionaries of Charity Sisters* (1976).

Furthermore, Teresa travelled widely during her lifetime, spreading her charitable work through overseas missions, sharing universal teachings of faith, and preaching the Catholic values. Beyond India, Teresa also visited the rural town of Bourke located in New South Wales, Australia where she assisted some of the most socially and economically disadvantaged people in the community, including the Indigenous Australian people. Teresa's other notable foreign visits included Italy, Sri Lanka, Tanzania, the United States of America, and Venezuela.

Throughout Teresa's lifetime, she was the recipient of several accolades as recognition for her charitable work and tireless service to the poor and sick people of India. For example, consider in 1969, Teresa received the Jawaharlal Nehru Award for International Understanding. Not to mention, in the year 1979, Teresa received the prestigious Nobel Peace Prize. Thereafter, in 1980, Teresa was awarded the Republic of India's highest civilian award - *the Bharat Ratna*. Last but not least, on 20 June 1985, Teresa received the Presidential Medal of Freedom by the U.S. President, Ronald Reagan (r. 1981-1989) at a White House ceremony in Washington D.C.

Teresa was a truly global and inspirational leader in her impact and reach. Teresa was born a subject of the Ottoman Empire, she was of Albanian heritage, possessed Indian citizenship, and was a devout member of the Catholic faith. Indisputably, Teresa was truly a representative world citizen and a cosmopolitan individual. Not to mention, Teresa was a spiritual person who went above and beyond the artificial boundaries, social constructs, and traditional contours of language, culture, society, race, gender, sex, ethnicity, nation-state, social status, wealth, history, and politics, to provide assistance to some of the most destitute people in the world.

On 5 September 1997, Teresa went to be with the Lord. Teresa was 87 years old at the time of her passing into the Heavenly Kingdom of God. As a mark of great honour, Teresa received a state funeral by the Indian government, a privilege that is usually reserved for prime ministers and presidents. On 19 October 2003, Teresa was beatified by Pope John Paul II (r. 1978-2005). Shortly thereafter, on 4 September 2016, Teresa was formally canonised by Pope Francis (r. 2013-Present). Saint Teresa's annual Feast Day is commemorated on 5 September. Saint Teresa is a Patron Saint of World Youth Day and Missionaries of Charity. Last but not least, Saint Teresa is a co-Patron Saint of the Roman Catholic Metropolitan Archdiocese of Calcutta. Blessed is She.

CHAPTER THREE

WOMEN IN SCIENCE

'You are no better than anyone else, and no one is better than you.'

Katherine Johnson

Science is a field that is constantly changing and evolving, with new discoveries and technologies redefining the world around us in many consequential ways. In the contemporary world, science impacts nearly every dimension of human life, both in experience and understanding. From the complexity of the laws of astrophysics, to the simplicity of a telephone call, science performs an integral part of modern human life. The natural sciences have revolutionised the modern world, and women have performed an equally important role in the Scientific Revolution.

This chapter examines several women who have made monumental contributions to the field of modern science. This chapter will present accomplished and intellectual women in the fields of astronomy, astrophysics, chemistry, computing science, crystallography, cytogenetics, geophysics, mathematics, meteorology, physics, radiology, and seismology. This chapter introduces the scientific research, ideas, findings, and discoveries of Janet Taylor, Ada Lovelace, Marie Curie, Lise Meitner, Inge Lehmann, Cecilia Payne-Gaposchkin, Barbara McClintock, Dorothy Crowfoot Hodgkin, Katherine Johnson, and Rosalind Franklin.

The notable scientific discoveries and advancements accomplished by the aforesaid women, will inspire men and women to achieve their highest potential. Advancing human knowledge is a shared responsibility that vests in both sexes. Female scientists have equally important ideas, concepts, principles, doctrines, and theories to propose, that will further enlighten human understanding of the physical world, and the known universe.

Janet Taylor (1804-1870)

Janet Taylor (Jane Ann Ionn) was born on 13 May 1804 in Wolsingham, County Durham, England. Janet's father was the Reverend Peter Ionn and her mother was Jane Deighton. Janet came from a family of eight children, and she was the sixth child in her family. From a young age, Janet's father had a significant influence on her life trajectory. The Reverend Peter Ionn was a curate and schoolmaster at the Free Grammar School, where he taught classes in navigation. In addition, Peter allowed his daughter, Janet to attend classes at the school where he taught, including attending his advanced lessons on theoretical navigation and astronomy.

Janet was a child proc gy, and she excelled in mathematics and science, which proved immensely useful to her future career choice as a navigation expert. At the young age of nine, Janet was the recipient of a national scholarship which made possible her first-rate education at the Queen Charlotte's School located at Ampthill, Bedfordshire. Aspiring students usually commenced their studies at the aforesaid school from fourteen years of age. In Janet's case, her remarkable aptitude for mathematics, coupled with the early instruction and learning from her father, made her advanced start possible. Janet had a determined mind, and she wished to embark on a career in nautical science, and therefore, she pursued a formal education in theoretical navigation studies.

In 1830, Janet married a widower by the name of George Taylor, with whom she had eight children, this was in addition to the three stepchildren from George's previous marriage. The institution of marriage, and a large family did not hinder Janet's aspirations and ambitions in her chosen career. In fact, Janet went from success to success in her chosen career. Of great importance, Janet published widely in the field of maritime navigation. Janet was an accomplished writer in her field. Some of Janet's many invaluable works include:

- *Luni-Solar and Horary Tables*
- *Principles of Navigation Simplified: with Luni-Solar and Horary Tables*
- *An Epitome of Navigation and Nautical Astronomy*
- *Planisphere of the Fixed Stars with Book of Directions*
- *Diurnal Register for Barometer, Sympiesometer, Thermometer, and Hygrometer*
- *A Guide Book to Lt Maury's Wind and Current Charts*
- *Handbook to the Local Marine Board Examinations for Officers of the British Mercantile Marine Board*

Janet's aforementioned publications were highly theoretical, they included mathematical charts and lunar tables. Not to mention, Janet's scholarly writing often espoused complex navigational and astronomical principles. Beyond the domain of technical and scientific writing, Janet was also an inventor of maritime equipment. For example, consider Janet was responsible for the invention of the Mariner's Compass. In addition, Janet also developed a personalised Quintant for the Prince of Wales, who subsequently inherited the British throne as His Majesty King Edward VII (r. 1901-1910).

Furthermore, Janet also made noticeable improvements to bronze binnacles, sextants, marine compasses, and chronometers. Last but not least, Janet also developed an instrument known as the 'Sea Artificial Horizon'. Janet's pioneering inventions were displayed at *the Great Exhibition of 1851* and *the 1862 London International Exhibition of Industry and Art*. When considered in the historical context of the first-half of the nineteenth century, Janet's inventions represented sophisticated technological advances in the field of marine navigation.

Janet's contribution to marine navigation went beyond her influential writings and useful inventions. Janet, alongside her husband, founded *the George Taylor Nautical Academy* in 1833. The Nautical Academy primarily served merchant service officers. Janet was one of the first English women to work in the male-dominated field of maritime navigation, and she made significant contributions to the field in her own capacity. Janet was responsible for the provision of sea charts, the training of sailors and mariners, the manufacturing of nautical instruments, and even the servicing of iron ships!

Unfortunately, Janet's husband passed away in the year 1853. The remainder of Janet's life was plagued with financial difficulties and ill health. The many stresses on Janet's health and her personal finances, led her to formally declare bankruptcy in 1866. Regrettably, Janet's state of affairs did not improve in the final years of her life. Unfortunately, Janet passed away in 1870 suffering from bronchitis. Janet's death certificate formally acknowledged her occupation as a 'Teacher of Navigation'. What makes Janet's stellar achievements all the more remarkable is that English women had limited education and employment opportunities in the early nineteenth English society. Not to mention, Janet made her mark in marine navigation, a predominantly male-dominated profession.

Furthermore, Janet's contribution to the field of marine navigation is wide-spanning. Janet published books and created sea charts, she invented navigation equipment, established an academy, trained sailors, serviced ships, and she was also involved in the manufacturing and supply of navigation instruments. Considered in their totality, Janet's admirable achievements were unprecedented for a woman in marine navigation at her time in English history. Janet's story has made it all the more possible for women to integrate into the esteemed profession of marine navigation over the later-half of the nineteenth century and throughout the twentieth century. In fact, Janet Taylor was much more than just a navigation expert, she was an inspirational teacher, prolific writer, polymath, mathematician, original thinker, meteorologist, and peerless inventor of all things 'navigation'.

Ada Lovelace (1815-1852)

Ada Lovelace was born on 10 December 1815 in London, England. Ada's father was one of the greatest English poets of all time, namely George Gordon Byron (Lord Byron). Regrettably, Lord Byron was expecting a baby boy, and he became most disheartened when his wife, Annabella Milbanke (Lady Byron) gave birth to a baby girl. Shortly after the birth of Ada, Lord Byron and Lady Byron separated.

Upon Ada's parents legal separation, Lord Byron requested that Lady Byron retain sole custody of their legitimate child, Ada. At the time, in English Common Law, child custody arrangements almost exclusively favoured the father over the mother of the children. Subsequently, Ada's father relocated to Greece, where he passed away when his daughter was only eight years old. As a child, Ada had no substantive relationship with her father. Ada's mother, Lady Byron, and her grandmother, Judith Milbanke, were the two primary parental figures during Ada's childhood years.

In Ada's childhood years, she was privately tutored. As part of Ada's first-rate education, she received lessons in French and music. During Ada's lifetime, English women were generally not permitted to study at universities in England and Wales. However, as Ada was of an aristocratic and wealthy English family, she was privately educated by, and also able to associate with, some of the best and brightest minds of the nineteenth century English society, including English clergyman and social reformer, William Frend, British physician, William King, Scottish scientist and writer, Mary Somerville, and British mathematician and logician, Augustus De Morgan. Ada also corresponded with several notable intellectual figures, including English mathematician and inventor, Charles Babbage, British scientist, Andrew Crosse, English writer and social critic, Charles Dickens, British scientist and author, Sir David Brewster, English scientist, Michael Faraday, and English scientist and inventor, Sir Charles Wheatstone.

On 5 June 1833, when Ada was seventeen years old, she attended a social gathering, where she met a number of socialites, including the renowned inventor, Charles Babbage. Charles conversed with Ada on his latest invention and personal project, the 'Difference Machine'. Following their aforesaid introductory meeting, Ada's mother took Ada to Charles' place of residence located at 1 Dorset Street, Manchester Square, Marylebone, the City of Westminster in London. Of prime significance herein is Ada's relationship with Charles Babbage. The two intellectuals formed a close academic and intellectual relationship that lasted a lifetime, until the year of Ada's death. Following Ada's inspection of *the Difference Engine*, she began to converse with Charles through the exchange of letters. The two individuals corresponded via letters for almost two decades, from 10 June 1835 until 12 August 1852.

With respect to Ada's personal life, on 8 July 1835, at the age of nineteen, Ada married English nobleman and scientist, William King-Noel, with whom she had three children, namely, Anne Isabella Noel Blunt, Byron King-Noel, and Ralph Gordon King-Noel Milbanke. The conventional reality of a married life, and the birth of three children did not prevent Ada from pursuing her limitless curiosity and infinite imagination into the vast array of possibilities that Charles Babbage's newfound machine could be utilised for.

Over the course of 1842, Ada provided a language translation (from French into English) of the Italian engineer and mathematician, Luigi Federico Menabrea's academic paper on Charles Babbage's latest invention known as *the Analytical Engine*. This scholarly paper was originally published in the French language in the Swiss academic journal known as *The Bibliothèque universelle* in October of 1842. Beyond Ada's language translation efforts of the approximately 8,000-word original paper, she also made her own significant contribution to the recently published paper by annexing a voluminous set of notes which detailed the function and working of *the Analytical Engine*. Ada's 'English' translated version of the paper, including her notes, made the revised scholarly paper circa. 20,000 words in length, it was published in the year 1843.

Ada's second important academic relationship was with the British mathematician and logician, Augustus De Morgan of the London University (now known as the University College of London). Ada and Augustus worked together in the field of mathematics. To the present time there remains some controversy over Ada's original contribution to the field of computer science. Influential scholars, historians, and contemporary writers continue to debate and argue over the true scope of Ada's contribution to the field. For example, consider the perspective of American historian, Bruce Collier who makes the case that Ada's contribution was inconsequential and fundamentally overstated. Whereas, British author and writer, James Essinger, and American author and researcher, Betty Alexandria Toole present the argument that Ada was essentially a 'pioneer' in the field of Computer Science, alongside the world-renowned Charles Babbage.

Unfortunately, Ada passed away at the young age of thirty-six due to the onset of uterine cancer. Ada has been honoured by a number of prominent institutions for her seminal contributions to the field of Computing Science, including *the Association for Women in Computing* (AWC), which inaugurated the Ada Lovelace Award in 1981, and *the British Computer Society* (BCS), which established the Lovelace Medal in 1998. In addition, on 27 July 2013, the U.S. Senator, Ronald Lee Wyden proposed to the United States Senate that 9 October 2018 be designated as 'National Ada Lovelace' Day. Last but not least, in the year 2020, Trinity College Dublin announced that a bust of Ada Lovelace was to be unveiled at its library.

Marie Curie (1867-1934)

Marie Curie was born on 7 November 1867 in the City of Warsaw, Poland. Marie was born to reputable teachers. Marie's father, Władysław Skłodowski was a mathematics and physics teacher. Marie's mother, Bronisława Boguska was employed at a prestigious boarding school for girls in the capital City of Warsaw. Marie was the youngest of five children in her family. Marie had three older sisters, namely, Bronisława Dłuska, Zofia Skłodowska, Helena Skłodowska-Szalay, and one older brother named Józef Skłodowski.

Marie endured a difficult childhood in Poland. Marie's parents had lost the vast majority of their wealth, personal assets, and private property in support of Polish Independence Movements and Nationalist Uprisings, for example, consider the *January Uprising (1863-1865)*. In addition, in the year 1876, Marie's oldest sister, Zofia died of typhus. Furthermore, and shortly thereafter, in the year 1878, Marie's mother died from tuberculosis. Although Marie's mother was a pious Catholic, following Marie's traumatic experience of grief and loss, Marie turned away from her Catholic faith, and she became agnostic.

From 1877 to 1882, Marie's early education was completed at Sikorska Boarding School in Warsaw. Marie excelled academically in her school studies, and she was fluent in five languages, namely English, French, German, Polish, and Russian. Marie was unable to attend university in Poland due to her sex. Thus, Marie decided to study at *the Sorbonne* located in the City of Paris, France, an institution of higher-learning which accepted women at the time. Due to financial limitations, Marie reached an agreement with one of her sisters, Bronisława. The two sisters agreed that Marie would work while she initially remained in Poland, in order to support Bronisława's university studies in medicine at *the Sorbonne* in Paris, France. This arrangement assisted Bronisława to achieve her prime objective of becoming a Medical Doctor. In return, once Bronisława became a Medical Doctor, she agreed to financially support Marie to relocate to Paris and pursue university studies of her own interest.

In 1891, Marie left Warsaw for Paris, she enrolled at *the Sorbonne*, where she studied chemistry, mathematics, and physics. In 1893, Marie was awarded her first degree in physics from the University of Paris. In this achievement alone Marie made history, as she was the first woman to earn a Master's Degree in Physics from the University of Paris. Marie's second degree in mathematics was achieved with the assistance of a University of Paris fellowship in 1894. During Marie's time at *the Sorbonne*, she fell in love with French physicist and Professor in the School of Physics, Pierre Curie. Marie and Pierre got married in 1895, and they had two daughters, namely, Ève and Irène.

Marie and Pierre were more than just a romantic union. The two talented physicists became a force for a life-long intellectual partnership in modern science. Marie was an immensely talented university student and she went on to complete her doctorate studies in science. Marie's doctoral advisor was the world-renowned Franco-Luxembourgish physicist and future recipient of the Nobel Prize in Physics (awarded in 1908), Jonas Ferdinand Gabriel Lippmann (1845-1921). Marie's Ph.D. thesis was entitled *Recherches sur les substances radioactives* (Research on Radioactive Substances). Marie was awarded her Ph.D. award from the University of Paris in 1903. In fact, Marie was the first woman in France to obtain a Doctoral Degree in the year 1903. Most importantly, Marie utilised her first-rate university education and newfound scientific knowledge to make unprecedented progress in the field of modern science.

The ground-breaking research of Marie and Pierre in the natural sciences led to the discovery of two new chemical elements, namely Polonium (Metalloid) and Radium (Alkaline Earth Metal). As a result, Marie and Pierre were jointly awarded the Nobel Prize in Physics (1903) for their combined research on radiation. Marie and Pierre's individual share of the Nobel prize was an equal twenty-five per cent. The remainder fifty per cent share of the Nobel Prize in Physics (1903) was awarded to French engineer and physicist, Antoine Henri Becquerel (1852-1908) for his remarkable discovery of 'Spontaneous Radioactivity'.

On 19 April 1906, Marie's husband, Pierre died due to an accident, however, Marie remained undeterred by this significant tragedy and loss. Marie found the determination and conviction to continue to move forward in the pursuit of her scholarly endeavours. After Pierre's death, Marie was appointed Professor of Physics, and she succeeded Pierre to become the Chair of General Physics in the Faculty of Science at the University of Paris. Once again, Marie made history, this time she was the first female Professor of Physics, and also the first female Chair of the Physics Department at the University of Paris in France.

In the year 1911, Marie was named the recipient of a second Nobel Prize. This time around, Marie was awarded the Nobel Prize in Chemistry (1911) for the discovery of the chemical elements, Radium (Ra) and Polonium (Po), and the isolation of 'Pure Radium'. At the time of writing this book, Marie remains the only female Nobel laureate to have received two of the prestigious Nobel Prizes in two distinct fields.

Marie's life was not without scandal and controversy, and she made headlines for more than her advanced scientific research. During the same year that Marie received the Nobel Prize in Chemistry, her affair with French physicist, Paul Langevin (1872-1946) came into the French public spotlight. Paul was a French physicist, he also happened to be a talented student of Marie's late husband, Pierre Curie. Not to mention, Paul was five years younger than Marie, and he was married at the time of their affair, however, Paul was also estranged from his wife. Their extramarital affair was exploited to discredit Marie's intellectual reputation and scientific achievements. Setting aside the question of immortality, this affair serves to highlight the double standards of the modern society, in which a woman struggles to separate her vocation from her private life, whereas, such a 'personal' and 'professional' distinction is non-existent for a learned man.

Beyond Marie's laboratory and research work at university, she made an outsized humanitarian contribution to the medical treatment and surgery of wounded French soldiers during the course of *World War I (1914-1918)*. Most notably, Marie was appointed Director of the Red Cross Radiology Service. Furthermore, Marie also established France's first Military Radiology Centre. Not to mention, Marie was directly involved in the development of Mobile Radiography Units to assist surgeons and medical doctors to perform emergency war surgery on wounded French soldiers at the frontlines of the battlefield.

In the year 1922, Marie was appointed Fellow of the French Academy of Medicine. Furthermore, the tradition of excellence and scientific achievement continued in the Curie family line. Marie's eldest daughter, French chemist, Irène Joliot-Curie (1897-1956), went on to jointly win the Nobel Prize in Chemistry (1935) with her husband, French physicist, Jean Frédéric Joliot-Curie (1900-1958), for their shared scientific discovery of 'Artificial Radioactivity'.

In the case of Marie, the list of awards, accomplishments, accolades, and achievements are almost endless. In 1922, Marie became a prominent member of *the International Committee on Intellectual Cooperation*, an advisory organisation to *the League of Nations* (est. 1920). Furthermore, in 1930, Marie was elected to serve on *the International Atomic Weights Committee*. Thereafter, in the year 1931, Marie was awarded the Cameron Prize for Therapeutics of the University of Edinburgh by the College of Medicine and Veterinary Medicine. The aforementioned record of achievement represents only a minor selection of Marie's lifetime achievements in science.

Furthermore, Marie has left behind a rich intellectual collection of scientific writings which include, *Radiology in War*, an insightful biography of her late husband titled *Pierre Curie*, a two volume *Treatise on Radioactivity*, and *The Discovery of Radium: Research on Radioactive Substances*. Marie's scholarly work and scientific writings have influenced a generation of scientists, including French physicist, Marguerite Catherine Perey (1909-1975), French chemist, Émile Henriot (1885-1961), and American physicist, William Duane (1872-1935).

On 4 July 1934, Marie died from aplastic anemia in *Sancellemoz* located in *the Commune of Passy* situated in *Haute-Savoie*, France. Marie was 66 years of age at the time of her death. Initially, Marie was interred at *the Sceaux Cemetery*, however, six decades later, in the year 1995, Marie's ashes were re-interred at France's National Museum, *the Panthéon* in Paris. Marie's intellectual legacy and many scientific achievements are truly inspirational for all men and women. Marie's story demonstrates and vividly illustrates the ability of a person to overcome privations, struggles, adverse experiences, unfortunate circumstances, world war, patriarchy, sex discrimination, institutionalised gender inequality, and the personal loss of a spouse. Indisputably, Marie Curie is a towering figure of modern science.

Lise Meitner (1878-1968)

Lise Meitner (Elise Meitner) was born on 7 November 1878 in Vienna, Austria-Hungary. Lise came from a Jewish family. Lise was of middle-class origins, and she came from a family of eight children. Lise's father, Philipp Meitner was a lawyer by profession. Lise's mother, Hedwig Meitner was a talented musician. Lise was a child prodigy, and she most certainly possessed an inquisitive mind. At the age of eight, Lise started diligently keeping records of her studies and research in mathematics and the natural sciences. In addition, Lise also enjoyed playing the piano and reading books.

Due to Lise's sex, she was unable to receive a conventional education in a grammar school located in Vienna during her late teenage years. As a matter of fact, for the overwhelming majority of Austrian teenage girls, school education ceased at the age of fourteen. Not to mention, enrolment at an Austrian university for women remained a distant dream.

In Lise's particular case, she was fortunate enough to have her parents afford her a significant private education in the earlier years of her life, in particular, between the developmental ages of fourteen and twenty-two. Furthermore, upon reaching adulthood, Lise converted to Christianity. Lise was not only concerned with purely scholarly endeavours, spiritualty and faith also performed an integral part in her life.

Beginning in the year 1898, Lise was privately tutored by Austrian physicist, Arthur Szarvassy (1873-1919) for her school leaving certificate. In July of 1901, Lise sat the university entrance exam at *the Akademisches Gymnasium* located in Vienna. Lise passed the university entrance exam with a commendable score, thus, permitting her to pursue tertiary studies in mathematics and physics. Subsequently, in October of 1901, Lise was admitted to the University of Vienna, where she diligently studied physics. In 1906, Lise was awarded her Doctorate Degree from the University of Vienna. Lise's doctoral supervisor was Austrian physicist, Franz Serafin Exner (1849-1926), and her Ph.D. thesis was titled 'Thermal Conductivity in Non-Homogeneous Bodies'. Most notably, Lise was the second woman to receive a Ph.D. in Physics from the University of Vienna, after Austrian physicist, Olga Steindler (1879-1933) in the year 1903.

Once Lise had completed her doctoral studies, she departed Vienna for Berlin. It was in the German City of Berlin that Lise's research and academic career in science began to flourish, albeit not without sex discrimination. Lise started to attend the insightful and inspiring lectures of the world-renowned German physicist, Max Planck (1858-1947) at the Friedrich Wilhelm University (now known as the Humboldt University of Berlin). Furthermore, Max Planck was quite supportive of Lise's research work in the field of physics. Max even personally invited Lise to his place of residence.

Beyond Lise's time learning from Max Planck, Lise also collaborated with the German chemist, Otto Hahn (1879-1968). The two distinguished scientists formed a close working relationship conducting novel research work, theoretical experiments, and several laboratory studies in the field of chemistry. Over the course of 1908 and 1909, Otto and Lise co-authored nine academic papers in the natural sciences. Unfortunately, Lise's father, Philipp Meitner passed away in the year 1910, and financial support was no longer readily available to Lise. At this point, Max Planck demonstrated the initiative to employ Lise as his first female teaching assistant at the Institute for Theoretical Physics (the Friedrich Wilhelm University).

In 1912, Otto and Lise secured research positions at the Kaiser Wilhelm Institute for Chemistry which was established in 1911 (now known as the Free University of Berlin). The onset of *the Great War (1914-1918)* disrupted both the lives and research work of Lise and Otto. During the long war years, Otto worked in the Special War Gas Unit, while Lise worked as an X-ray Nurse Technician. Most noticeably, the aforesaid war temporarily put on hold Lise and Otto's advanced scientific research endeavours; however, the two scientists returned to their work in the final year of *the Great War*.

In the year 1918, Otto and Lise jointly discovered the chemical element, Protactinium (Actinide). However, the end of *the Great War (1914-1918)* was not the end of Lise's difficulties in Berlin. In the 1930's, the rapid rise of Austrian-born German politician, Adolf Hitler (1889-1945), and the NAZI Party in Germany, meant that the domestic politics of Germany became a major issue for Lise, in particular, given her Jewish heritage. In 1938, the annexation of Austria by the NAZI Germany prompted Lise to depart Berlin via the Netherlands for Stockholm. Lise's journey to secure her safety was undertaken with the assistance of the Dutch physicist, Dirk Coster (1889-1950). Upon arriving in Stockholm, Sweden, Lise commenced her research work at the Manne Siegbahn's Institute based in Stockholm.

During this time, Lise also worked with the Danish physicist, Niels Henrik David Bohr (1885-1962).

Despite the political disturbance in Germany and the newfound physical distance, Otto and Lise remained in close contact. Otto and Lise continued to communicate, and the two scientists also secretly met on 13 November 1938 to formulate new scientific experiments in Copenhagen, Denmark. In December of 1938, Otto Hahn in connection with the German chemist, Fritz Strassmann (1902-1980), performed novel experiments in Berlin that bombarded Uranium with neutrons, producing lighter elements.

Subsequently, Otto Hahn wrote to Lise, sharing the experimental observations and preliminary results produced from these experiments. In addition, Otto requested that Lise provide her analysis and appraisal of Fritz and Otto's novel experiments. On 6 January 1939, Otto Hahn and Fritz Strassmann published their novel findings in the scientific journal *Naturwissenschaften* (the Science of Nature). Despite their scientific research and advancements, Otto Hahn and Fritz Strassmann were unable to wholly explain the emergence of Barium, when Uranium was bombarded with neutrons. This crucial knowledge gap, which concerned the phenomenon of Barium, was addressed by Lise Meitner and Austrian-British physicist, Otto Robert Frisch (1904-1979).

On 11 February 1939, Lise Meitner in connection with Otto Frisch published their conclusions and findings with respect to the bombardment of Uranium with neutrons in an academic paper titled *Disintegration of Uranium by Neutrons: A New Type of Nuclear Reaction*. The aforesaid academic paper detailed an explanation and accounted for the intricate process of 'Nuclear Fission' in the prestigious scientific journal *Nature*. However, Otto Hahn publicly refused to provision due credit to Lise Meitner for her invaluable contribution, even after the end of *World War II (1939-1945)*, Hahn did not change his position. Furthermore,

Lise Meitner was not universally acknowledged for her prominent role in the scientific research efforts that she conducted with Otto Hahn. In 1944, the Nobel Prize in Chemistry was awarded solely to Otto Hahn for the discovery of the 'Fission of Heavy Nuclei'. Notwithstanding the aforementioned lack of international recognition, Lise was belatedly awarded the prestigious United States' *Enrico Fermi Award* in 1966.

Regrettably, Lise's story illustrates the profound sexism and racism that she confronted throughout her scientific career, despite being one of the most competent, accomplished, and educated female scientists of the twentieth century. Furthermore, Lise was a gentlelady of intellectual giftedness, high ethical principles, and uncompromising morals, she refused to work on *the Manhattan Project (1942-1945)* in the United States of America, in order to create the destructive atomic bomb, which was ultimately unleashed on the two Japanese cities of Hiroshima and Nagasaki during the final stages of *World War II (1939-1945)*.

On 27 October 1968, Lise passed away in Cambridge, England. Lise was 89 years old at the time of her death. The synthetic chemical element, Atomic Number 109 which was discovered by two German physicists, Peter Armbruster and Gottfried Münzenberg in the year 1982 was named 'Meitnerium' in Lise Meitner's honour. The conventional name of 'Meitnerium' was first proposed in 1992, and then it was recommended by *the International Union of Pure and Applied Chemistry* (IUPAC) in 1994, before being made official in the year 1997. Lise Meitner's epitaph recorded by Austrian-British physicist, Otto Robert Frisch states 'Lise Meitner: a physicist who never lost her humanity'.

Inge Lehmann (1888-1993)

Inge Lehmann was born on 13 May 1888 in Østerbro, Copenhagen, Denmark. Inge's father, Alfred Georg Ludvik Lehmann was a Professor of Psychology. Inge's mother, Ida Sophie Tørsleff was a housewife. Inge was educated at *Fællesskolen*, a private co-educational school. This was a progressive school that promoted equal treatment and opportunities for boys and girls. Not to mention, the private co-educational school was founded by Hanna Adler, a wealthy gentlelady who was the aunt of the world-renowned Danish physicist, Niels Henrik David Bohr (1885-1962).

In the year 1906, Inge achieved a first-rank score for the university entrance exam, permitting her entry into Copenhagen University, Denmark. In 1907, Inge commenced her studies at Copenhagen University. During Inge's time as a student, she studied chemistry, mathematics, and physics. For a short interval of time, between 1910 and 1911, Inge also studied mathematics at Cambridge University in Cambridge, England.

During Inge's time at Newnham College, Cambridge University, she experienced first-hand the dismal reality of sex discrimination in England. Female students were only permitted to attend lectures, they were not allowed to utilise Cambridge University's laboratories or access its libraries. This was a culture shock for Inge in the twentieth century English society, given her liberal and equitable gender experience with education in Denmark. Whilst at Cambridge University, Inge also suffered from poor health and mental exhaustion, therefore, she decided to return to Denmark in 1911. Upon Inge's return to Denmark, she temporarily placed her university studies on hold. Instead, Inge secured employment in the field of actuarial science with an insurance company.

Finally, in the year 1920, Inge was awarded her Degree in Mathematics from the University of Copenhagen. In 1923, Inge accepted a position of employment as an assistant to Professor of Actuarial Science, Johan Frederik Steffensen (1873-1961) in Copenhagen University's Actuarial Department. In 1925, Inge's scientific career ventured into the field of Seismology. Inge commenced working as an assistant to the Head of the Royal Danish Geodetic Institute (RDGI) and Professor of Mathematics, Niels Erik Nørlund (1885-1981). As part of Inge's scientific research, she had the opportunity to travel overseas to a number of seismic stations located in France, Germany, and the Netherlands. In 1928, Inge continued further postgraduate studies in the natural sciences, and she earned a second degree in the field of Geodesy, which was also awarded from the University of Copenhagen.

After Inge completed her second university degree, she conducted scientific research that developed the novel ideas and empirical work of the British Geologist, Richard Dixon Oldham (1858-1936). Furthermore, in the year 1928, Inge secured the position of 'State Geodesist', and she was also appointed as Head of the Seismological Department at the Royal Danish Geodetic Institute (RDGI). Inge held the latter position of employment for twenty-five years, until her retirement in the year 1953.

In 1936, Inge published her scientific research and empirical findings on a three-layered model of the Earth in an academic paper simply known as *P'* in *Publications du Bureau Central Seismologique International*. This important article was Inge's greatest contribution to modern science. Inge's paper titled *P'* suggested a new discontinuity paradigm in the seismic structure of the Earth. This newfound paradigm is now referred to as the 'Lehmann Discontinuity' in the Iinternational cientific Community.

Other seminal publications by Inge include: *On the travel times of P as determined from nuclear explosions* and *Seismology in the Days of Old*.

Inge received numerous awards and accolades for her original contribution to the scientific understanding of the Earth's inner structure. Some of Inge's awards include:

- The Gordon Wood Award
- The *Emil Wiechert* Medal of the German Geophysical Society
- The Gold Medal of the Danish Royal Society of Science and Letters
- The *Tagea Brandt Rejselegat*
- The William Bowie Medal
- The Medal of the Seismological Society of America

Furthermore, in the year 1997, the American Geophysical Union (AGU) established the Inge Lehmann Medal in Inge's honour. On 21 February 1993, Inge passed away in Copenhagen, Denmark. Inge was 104 years old at the time of her death. Inge did not marry, nor did she have any children during her lifetime. Inge donated all her personal belongings to the Danish Academy.

Inge's numerous academic accomplishments demonstrate that a combination of diligence, resolve, perseverance, and passion, can make success possible in one's chosen career or personal endeavour. Inge's meteoric rise was not without its fair share of challenges and opposition, with the greatest hindrance being systematic sex discrimination, however, Inge demonstrated her resolve to stay the course. At all times, Inge continued to work to the best of her ability. Indeed, it was Inge's growth mindset which ultimately ensured that she finished her career at the pinnacle of scientific advances and human knowledge in the newly emergent fields of Geodesy and Seismology.

Cecilia Payne-Gaposchkin (1900-1979)

Cecilia Helena Payne-Gaposchkin was born on 10 May 1900 in Wendover, Buckinghamshire, England. Cecilia's father, Edward John Payne was a barrister-at-law, historian, musician, and scholar. Cecilia's mother, Emma Leonora Helena Pertz was of noble Prussian origin. Unfortunately, Cecilia's father passed away when she was only four years old. Cecilia was one of three children in her family, she had one brother and a sister. Initially, Cecilia attended St. Mary's College in Paddington, London, however, the school curriculum did not emphasise learning in mathematics and the natural sciences. Thus, Inge transferred schools, and in her final years of schooling, she was educated at St. Paul's Girls' School in West London, England.

Following the completion of Cecilia's school education, in 1919, she was awarded a scholarship to attend Newnham College at Cambridge University. Whilst at Cambridge University, Cecilia studied botany, chemistry, and physics. In the year 1923, Cecilia completed her studies at Cambridge University, however, she was denied the official award of a university degree. At the time, Cambridge University did not award degrees to women, not until the year 1948. With limited career options for women in the United Kingdom, and Cecilia not desiring to become a school teacher, she decided to relocate across the North Atlantic Ocean to the United States of America, in order to commence study in advanced astronomy.

Cecilia was successful in obtaining a Pickering Fellowship from Harvard University to study astronomy under the auspices of Director of the Harvard College Observatory, Harlow Shapley (1885-1972). Under the direction and guidance of American scientist, Harlow Shapley, Cecilia completed her Doctoral Thesis on Astronomy. In the year 1925, Cecilia became the first woman to obtain a Ph.D. in the field of Astronomy from Radcliffe College. Unfortunately, Cecilia did not receive her Ph.D. award from Harvard University, as it did not grant Doctoral Degrees to women at the time.

Cecilia's Ph.D. dissertation was titled 'Stellar Atmospheres: A Contribution to the Observational Study of High Temperature in the Reversing Layers of Stars'. Most importantly, Cecilia's Doctoral Thesis made ground-breaking advances in the human understanding of astronomy. Cecilia's Harvard Ph.D. thesis built on the pioneering work of Indian astrophysicist, Meghnad Saha (1893-1956), who proposed *the Theory of Ionisation*. However, American astronomer, Professor Henry Norris Russell (1877-1957), advised Cecilia against concluding that the Sun was overwhelmingly composed of Hydrogen. Henry's advice was on the basis that Cecilia's findings contradicted the status quo of the American Scientific Community at the time, namely, that the Sun and the Earth both possessed similar elemental compositions.

However, several years later, in July of 1929, Professor Henry Norris Russell independently arrived at the conclusion that Cecilia was correct in her initial assessment of Hydrogen being 'much more abundant in the Sun's atmosphere than on the Earth'. Henry published this scientific finding in an academic article titled 'On the Composition of the Sun's Atmosphere' in *the Astrophysical Journal*. While Professor Henry Russell's academic paper did make a minor acknowledgement of the previous novel research findings of Cecilia, he received the majority credit and overwhelming recognition for what was Cecilia's original idea and scientific discovery.

The year 1925 marked the commencement of Cecilia's academic career at Harvard University, albeit it was not without sex discrimination. When Cecilia started her research career, solely on the basis of sex, women were excluded from being appointed as Professors at Harvard University. However, Professor of Astronomy, Harlow Shapley continued to support Cecilia's employment at Harvard University. From 1925 to 1938, Cecilia was employed as a 'Technical Assistant' to Professor Harlow Shapley. In 1926, Cecilia received the honour of being named the youngest scientist in *American Men of Science*. Notwithstanding such a stellar achievement, Cecilia's academic position at Harvard University remained largely unofficial and inconsequential.

In 1934, Cecilia married a Russian gentleman by the name of Sergei Gaposchkin (1898-1984) who was an astrophysicist and astronomer. The married couple had three children. In addition, Cecilia and Sergei's romantic union was intertwined with a productive academic relationship. For Cecilia and Sergei worked together on numerous scientific projects, including research on Variable Stars, the Milky Way, and the Magellanic Clouds. Also in the year 1934, Cecilia was awarded the Annie J. Cannon Prize from *the American Astronomical Society* (AAS) for her many contributions to the field of astronomy. Despite Cecilia's impressive record of scholarly achievement, it was not until the year 1938, that Cecilia was afforded the title 'Astronomer' in overdue recognition for her scientific work as a university lecturer and researcher. Cecilia later requested that her official title be amended to 'Phillips Astronomer'.

Regrettably, and once again on the basis of Cecilia's female sex, her invaluable university courses on astronomy were also not recorded in the Harvard University Catalogue until the year 1945. Not to mention, it was not until 1956 that Cecilia was finally promoted to the distinguished rank of Professor, and provisioned with a salary that was commensurate to her distinguished position of academic employment. In addition, Cecilia was belatedly named Chairperson of the Department of Astronomy. Of great importance, Cecilia became the first woman to be appointed as Chair of the Department of Astronomy at Harvard University.

Cecilia also published several books as a researcher and academic in the field of astrophysics. Cecilia's many notable publications include: *The Stars of High Luminosity*, *Variable Stars*, *Variable Stars and Galactic Structure*, *Introduction to Astronomy*, and *The Galactic Novae*. Not to mention, Cecilia published in excess of 150 academic papers in the field of astronomy, along with several monographs. In 1966, Cecilia officially retired from teaching. Cecilia was subsequently awarded the prestigious title of Emeritus Professor at Harvard University. During Cecilia's retirement years, she remained an active intellectual. Cecilia continued her scientific research activities at the Smithsonian Astrophysical Observatory in Cambridge, Massachusetts, the United States. Furthermore, Cecilia also edited scientific journals and a number of academic publications for the Harvard College Observatory (HCO).

In 1976, Cecilia became the first woman to be awarded the prestigious Henry Norris Russell Prize from *the American Astronomical Society* for her outstanding scientific work in the field of astronomy. As recognition for Cecilia's invaluable contribution to astronomy, she received numerous honorary degrees, including from Colby College, Wilson College, and the Woman's Medical College of Pennsylvania. Arguably, the most unique and exceptional award Cecilia has received is the naming of a planet in her honour. In the year 1977, the Planet 1974 CA was officially named 'Payne-Gaposchkin'. Last but not least, the University of Cambridge, which once denied Cecilia the award of a university degree, due to her sex, now awarded her two degrees, namely, an honorary Master of Arts and a Doctorate in Science.

On 7 December 1979, Cecilia passed away in Cambridge, Massachusetts. Cecilia was 79 years old at the time of her death. Cecilia's remarkable life highlights the protracted struggle of a learned woman to rise to the highest heights in the world of academia. Cecilia's incredible story is an inextinguishable inspiration to all men and women that grit, passion, determination, intelligence, unrelenting resolve, unwavering commitment, diligence, and tenacity, are ultimately the traits that ought to be acknowledged (and rewarded), regardless of one's sex.

Barbara McClintock (1902-1992)

Barbara McClintock (Eleanor McClintock) was born on 16 June 1902 in Hartford, Connecticut, the United States of America. Barbara came from an Anglo-American family of four children, she had two sisters and one brother. Barbara's father was Thomas Henry McClintock, and her mother was Sara Handy McClintock. During the early years of Barbara's life, she demonstrated a highly independent personality. Not to mention, Barbara was a solitary child. For a period of time, Barbara also lived with her aunt and uncle in Brooklyn, New York City, the United States.

Barbara was educated at Erasmus Hall High School in Brooklyn. During Barbara's high school years, she desired to study the natural sciences at university. Despite Barbara's conflict with her mother over attending university, Barbara's father permitted her to continue higher education. Barbara's mother was overly concerned that a university education might make Barbara 'unmarriageable' in the twentieth century American society.

In 1919, Barbara commenced her undergraduate studies in Plant Science (i.e., Botany) at the College of Agriculture, Cornell University in Ithaca, New York. In 1923, Barbara graduated with a Bachelor of Science (BSc) degree. Following Barbara's interest and passion in science, she was inclined to continue her university studies in the field of Genetics. In the furtherance of this endeavour, Barbara corresponded with American Botanist and Geneticist, Claude Burton Hutchison (1885-1980), who encouraged her interest in botany. In addition, Claude also invited Barbara to a graduate-level university course on Genetics taught at Cornell University. As a result, Barbara went on to complete a Master's Degree in Botany at Cornell University, she graduated in the year 1925. Thereafter, Barbara completed her Doctoral studies, also at Cornell University, where she conducted novel research in the fields of Cytology, Genetics, and Zoology. Barbara's Doctoral Dissertation was titled 'A Cytological and Genetical Study of Triploid Maize'.

After completing her Ph.D. thesis in the year 1927, Barbara devoted her post-doctoral research endeavours into the scientific analysis of chromosomes of corn (i.e., Corn Genetics). In 1931, Barbara along with American Botanist and Geneticist, Harriet Baldwin Creighton (1909-2004), published an academic paper titled 'A Correlation of Cytological and Genetic Crossing-over in Zea Mays' in the multi-disciplinary scientific serial known as *the Proceedings of the National Academy of Sciences of the*

United States of America. Barbara's laboratory research served to augment her stellar reputation and newfound influence in the field of science. Over the course of Barbara's academic career, she published several papers and articles in prestigious scientific journals including *the American Journal of Botany*, *Genetics*, and *The American Naturalist*.

Despite Barbara's invaluable research contribution to modern science, her academic career was not all smooth-sailing. Regrettably, Barbara's three-time alumni university, Cornell University, would not employ a female Professor in the early 1930's, however, Barbara secured funding from *the Rockefeller Foundation* in New York, to continue her novel research work on Corn Genetics. Furthermore, in 1936, Barbara found suitable employment at the University of Missouri in Columbia, Missouri.

Slowly and steadily throughout the course of the 1930's, Barbara's profile as an academic, scholar, researcher, and scientist reached newfound heights. For example, consider in 1939, Barbara was elected Vice-President of *the Genetics Society of America* (GSA). Not to mention, in 1944, Barbara was appointed as President of the aforesaid society. Barbara became the first woman to achieve this senior leadership position in the aforesaid scientific society. In addition, also in the year 1944, Barbara became the third woman to be appointed to *the National Academy of Sciences* (NAS).

In 1941, Barbara accepted an opportunity to conduct scientific research at the Cold Spring Harbor Laboratory situated at Long Island in New York City (NYC). The remainder of Barbara's scientific research work was carried out at the aforesaid laboratory. Most importantly, Barbara's greatest contribution to the field of Genetics was her 1948 discovery of 'controlling elements' and novel ideas surrounding 'gene regulation'. In plain English, Barbara's scientific discovery is commonly referred to as 'jumping genes'.

Barbara's pioneering scientific research uncovered that genetic information is not fixed and static. That is to say, genetic information is not constitutive of fixed instructions that are passed on from one generation to the next generation (with the primary - although not sole - factor for genetic variation from parent to offspring being 'dominant' and 'recessive' genes). Rather, Barbara rightly inferred that genes and genetic information are mobile, that is to infer, they can 'move around' the chromosome. For example, genes can 'express' or 'not express' select physical traits (i.e., phenotypes) in corn depending on select controlling elements.

Barbara's original contribution to human knowledge on genetics earnt her many awards and accolades throughout her lifetime, both nationally and internationally. For example, in 1971, Barbara was named the recipient of the National Medal of Science (NMS) which was awarded to her by the United States President, Richard Nixon (r. 1969-1974). Furthermore, in 1983, Barbara was awarded the Nobel Prize for Physiology or Medicine. Most notably, Barbara was the first woman to become a sole recipient of the prestigious Nobel Prize Award in the category of 'Physiology or Medicine'.

On 2 September 1992, Barbara passed away from natural causes at New York's Huntington Hospital in New York, the United States of America. Barbara was 90 years old at the time of her death. Barbara was a genius scientist that challenged the orthodoxy of the prevailing scientific ideas of her time. Not to mention, Barbara defended her novel research in spite of the institutionalised assumptions and the mainstream scientific community's outdated perceptions.

Barbara's evolutionary thinking fundamentally changed the manner in which contemporary scientists perceive an organism's genome. Barbara's advanced perception, that an organism's genome is not stationary, but rather it is subject to alteration was a truly ground-breaking proposition at the time that it was first proposed. Barbara's life-long scientific research and voluminous scholarly publications in the fields of Genetics and Cytology, in addition to her contribution in the newfound field of Cytogenetics, have led to a 'paradigm shift' in modern science.

Dorothy Mary Crowfoot Hodgkin (1910-1994)

Dorothy Mary Crowfoot was born on 12 May 1910 in the City of Cairo, Egypt. Dorothy's father, John Winter Crowfoot worked for the Ministry of Education in Cairo. Dorothy's mother, Grace Mary Crowfoot specialised in archaeological textiles. Dorothy was educated at Sir John Leman Grammar School in Suffolk, England. During the earlier years of Dorothy's school studies, she developed a strong interest in the natural sciences, in particular, the field of chemistry. Dorothy received encouragement and support to pursue her interest in the natural sciences from her mother, father, and two esteemed chemists, namely Charles Harington and A.F. Joseph.

During Dorothy's teenage years, she received personalised and private tuition which enabled her to adequately prepare for and pass the university entrance exam to gain admission into the University of Oxford in Oxford, England. In the year 1928, Dorothy matriculated at Somerville College, Oxford University, where she studied chemistry. In 1932, Dorothy was conferred with a first-class honours degree from the University of

Oxford. Later in the year 1932, Dorothy enrolled into a Ph.D. program at Newnham College, the University of Cambridge in Cambridge, England.

Dorothy's Doctoral Dissertation supervisor was Irish Scientist and Professor, John Desmond Bernal (1901-1971). Dorothy was awarded the Doctor of Philosophy Degree from the University of Cambridge in 1937 for her ground-breaking scientific research in X-ray Crystallography. Dorothy's Cambridge Ph.D. thesis was titled 'X-ray Crystallography and the Chemistry of the Sterols'. Not to mention, Dorothy's 1937 Ph.D. award was an exception to the rule, where female students were generally not conferred degrees at the University of Cambridge until the year 1948.

Furthermore, in 1937, Dorothy married English historian and lecturer, Thomas Lionel Hodgkin (1910-1982) who had a strong interest in African history and politics. Dorothy and her husband had three children during their marriage, a daughter named Elizabeth Hodgkin, and two sons named Toby and Luke Hodgkin. The couple were married for over four decades, until the death of Thomas on 25 March 1982 in the village of Tolo in Greece.

Dorothy's scientific discoveries advanced human understanding of science in profound ways. In 1945, Dorothy and C. H. Carlisle worked together on the molecular structure of Cholesteryl Iodide. Subsequently, the two scientists published their empirical findings in an academic paper titled 'The Crystal Structure of Cholesteryl Iodide' in *the Proceedings of the Royal Society A: Mathematical, Physical, and Engineering Sciences.*

In collaboration with several other scientists, Dorothy and British biochemist, Barbara Wharton Low (1920-2019) were instrumental in identifying the structure of Penicillin in the year 1945. Understanding the atomic structure of Penicillin has had immense consequences for the modern development and use of antibiotics. In the contemporary world, antibiotics are widely used to treat people with infections and diseases that are caused by bacteria. For example, consider the following antibiotics, Amoxicillin, Azithromycin, Cephalexin, Ciprofloxacin, Clindamycin, Doxycycline, Levofloxacin, Metronidazole, Sulfamethoxazole, Trimethoprim, and Vancomycin.

Furthermore, Dorothy conducted scientific research on the molecular structure of Vitamin B_{12}. Dorothy utilised X-ray Crystallography analysis in order to ascertain the entire structure of Vitamin B_{12}. The invaluable results of Dorothy's scientific research, which was completed in connection with other esteemed scientists, namely, Jenny Pickworth, Kenneth N. Trueblood, John G. White, Jennifer Kamper, and Maureen MacKay, was published in an article titled 'Structure of Vitamin B_{12}-: The Crystal Structure of the Hexacarboxylic Acid derived from B_{12} and the Molecular Structure of the Vitamin' in the British scientific journal known as *Nature*. Most notably, Dorothy was awarded the 1964 Nobel Prize in Chemistry for her advanced scientific work which employed X-ray techniques to identify the molecular structures of several biochemical substances.

Last but not least, Dorothy's additional grand contribution to modern science was understanding the atomic structure of the hormone Insulin in 1969. This was thirty-four years after Dorothy had captured her first X-ray image of an insulin crystal. Once again, Dorothy employed X-ray Crystallography in conjunction with advanced computing techniques to identify the complex structure of Insulin. This scientific achievement had immense consequences for the contemporary medical treatment of patients with Type-one and Type-two Diabetes across the modern world.

In terms of Dorothy's political views, she was a committed socialist and an ardent supporter of the Labour Party in the United Kingdom. Intellectually, Dorothy was truly an international collaborator in science, bridging the post-colonial divides between the East and the West. Dorothy also surmounted the rigid twentieth century ideological divide between the Free World and the Communist and Socialist Countries. In fact, from 1975 to 1988, Dorothy was President of *the Pugwash Conferences on Science and World Affairs*. In addition, Dorothy encouraged a number of Chinese scientists from the People's Republic of China (PRC) to participate in scientific meetings and academic conferences at *the International Union of Crystallography* (IUCr). Not to mention, Dorothy often visited China, India, and the Union of Soviet Socialist Republics (USSR). In 1982, Dorothy was awarded *the Lomonosov Medal* by the Soviet Academy of Sciences. Furthermore, Dorothy received the Lenin Peace Prize in 1987 from the Union of Soviet Socialist Republics during the memorable years of the Mikhail Gorbachev government. Dorothy's last international journey was in 1993 to the City of Beijing in China, where she attended the 16th International Congress of Crystallography.

Dorothy was recognised and awarded for her immense contribution to modern science, in particular, to the specialised field of chemistry. In 1947, Dorothy was elected as a Fellow of the Royal Society (FRS). In addition, in the year 1956, Dorothy was a recipient of the Royal Medal. Furthermore, also in 1956, Dorothy became a Foreign Member of the Royal Netherlands Academy of Sciences. Not to mention, in 1958, Dorothy was admitted to the American Academy of Arts and Sciences. Last but not least, in 1965, Dorothy was granted the Order of Merit (OM). On 29 July 1994, Dorothy passed away in Ilmington, Warwickshire, England. Dorothy was 84 years old at the time of her death.

Dorothy's pioneering scientific work on Cholesteryl Iodide, Insulin, Penicillin, and Vitamin B_{12} has positively changed the modern world in which we live. Beyond Dorothy's notable scientific achievements, is the humanity and decency of a learned English gentlelady who was truly cosmopolitan in her world perception. Dorothy worked with people across continents and nations, regardless of colour, sex, gender, ethnicity, wealth, culture, race, social status, creed, political ideology, or religion. Indeed, Dorothy's distinguished awards from Europe, the Soviet Union, Sweden, and the United Kingdom are truly reflective of her international stature as an accomplished scientist.

Katherine Johnson (1918-2020)

Katherine Johnson (Creola Katherine Coleman) was born on 26 August 1918 in White Sulphur Springs, West Virginia, the United States of America. Katherine's father, Joshua McKinley Coleman was a lumberman, janitor, and farmer. Katherine's mother, Joylette Roberta was a teacher. Katherine was the youngest child of four children in her family. Katherine had two older brothers, namely, Charles and Horace, as well as one older sister named Margaret.

From an early age, Katherine was strongly interested in the field of mathematics. In fact, during Katherine's school years she loved solving mathematical equations and performing numerical calculations. The socio-economic realities of inequity in education for the African American children directly impacted Katherine while she was a young student in school. For example, consider that in Greenbrier County, West Virginia, there was no state funded school education beyond eighth grade for the African American children. Thus, Katherine's parents made arrangements for Katherine, when she was only ten years old, to continue her studies at

West Virginia State High School. Katherine completed her schooling when she was fourteen years of age.

At the age of fifteen, Katherine attended West Virginia State College (now known as West Virginia State University), where she studied French and mathematics. During Katherine's time at university, she was educated by some of the best and brightest minds, including African American mathematician, William Schieffelin Claytor (1908-1967), and African American chemist and mathematician, Angie Lena Turner King (1905-2004). Katherine studied in a supportive and encouraging university environment. Not to mention, Katherine was a diligent student of considerable potential, and often her teachers further developed her academic talent and ability.

Following the completion of Katherine's university education, she became a school teacher at Carnegie High School, a school for the African American children in Marion, Virginia. During Katherine's employment at Carnegie High School, she met a chemistry teacher named James Francis Goble. In 1939, Katherine and James got married. Katherine and James had three children together, all of whom were daughters, namely Constance, Joylette, and Katherine.

Following Katherine's marriage, she resigned from her aforesaid teaching position. Katherine decided to study graduate mathematics at West Virginia University in Morgantown, West Virginia. Graduate level university study was now possible for African American students due to the United States Supreme Court ruling in *Missouri ex rel. Gaines v. Canada (1938)*, which was implemented by West Virginia's Governor. However, Katherine withdrew from her graduate study in mathematics at West Virginia University due to her first pregnancy. Most notably, Katherine was one of three African American students, and she was the first African

American female student to study mathematics at the graduate level at West Virginia University.

On 20 December 1956, Katherine's first husband James Goble, passed away due to the onset of brain cancer, which was deemed inoperable. Thus, Katherine was left a widow at the age of thirty-eight. Not to mention, Katherine also had to support her family of three young children. Following the death of Katherine's first husband, three years later, in the year 1959, Katherine re-married to a United States Army Officer, James Arthur Johnson. Katherine and James were married for sixty years, until James's death on 13 March 2019. Katherine had no children during the course of her second marriage.

In the year 1953, Katherine accepted an offer of employment at *the National Advisory Committee for Aeronautics* (NACA). The NACA employed African American people, therefore, ethnicity was not an institutional barrier to employment for Katherine. During the first five years, from 1953 to 1958, Katherine worked in the West Area Computing Unit with several other African American women. In 1958, the NACA was superseded by *the National Aeronautics and Space Administration* (NASA). Thereupon, the NACA's official policies surrounding racial segregation ceased, however, African American employees continued to experience racial discrimination in the NASA's workplace.

With large-scale organisation change at the NASA came newfound opportunities for the African American employees. From 1958 until 1986, Katherine was employed as an Aerospace Technologist at the NASA. During Katherine's remarkable career, she was responsible for authoring or co-authoring some twenty-six research papers and reports. In addition, during Katherine's stellar career, she worked on several important missions, such as:

- The 1961 Mercury-Redstone 3 (Freedom 7) Spaceflight
- The 1969 Apollo 11 Moon Mission
- The 1970 Apollo 13 Moon Mission

On 24 November 2015, Katherine was awarded the Presidential Medal of Freedom, the highest civilian honour in the United States, by the U.S. President, Barack Obama (r. 2009-2017) at the White House. Furthermore, in the year 2016, the NASA named one of its buildings the 'Katherine G. Johnson Computational Research Facility' in acknowledgement of Katherine's invaluable contribution to the organisation. In addition, in 2019, the NASA renamed another facility located in West Virginia in Katherine's honour - the 'Katherine Johnson Independent Verification and Validation Facility'. Furthermore, Katherine was the recipient of several honorary degrees awarded to her. Katherine received a Presidential Honorary Doctorate of Humane Letters by West Virginia University in West Virginia. Not to mention, Katherine was awarded an Honorary Doctorate from the College of William and Mary in Virginia. In addition, Katherine also received an Honorary Doctorate from the University of Johannesburg in South Africa.

On 24 February 2020, Katherine passed away in Newport News, Virginia, the United States of America. Katherine was 101 years old at the time of her death. Katherine's exceptional story of success is an inspiration to all people of the modern world. Katherine overcome sex, gender, colour, and race discrimination in the twentieth century American society. Katherine achieved her full potential.

Rosalind Franklin (1920-1958)

Rosalind Elise Franklin was born on 25 July 1920 in Notting Hill, London, the United Kingdom. Rosalind came from an opulent and noble English family of Jewish origin. Rosalind's father, Ellis Arthur Franklin was an English Merchant Banker. Rosalind's mother was Muriel Frances Waley. Rosalind came from a family of five children. Rosalind had three brothers, namely, Colin, Roland, and David, as well as one younger sister named Jenifer Franklin (now known as Jenifer Glynn).

Rosalind was educated at Saint Paul's Girls' School in West London. Upon the completion of her school studies, at the age of eighteen, Rosalind decided to study the natural sciences, concentrating on chemistry and physics at Newnham College, the University of Cambridge in Cambridge, England. From 1938 to 1941, Rosalind completed her undergraduate studies at Cambridge University. Upon Rosalind's graduation from university, she received a fellowship to perform scientific research at the Physical Chemistry Laboratory also at Cambridge University. Rosalind conducted her scientific research under the supervision and guidance of the world-renowned British chemist, Ronald George Wreyford Norrish (1897-1978). In fact, Ronald Norrish was a future recipient of the 1967 Nobel Prize in Chemistry.

Unfortunately, Rosalind did not have a constructive working relationship with Ronald Norrish, and she decided to resign from her research position at the University of Cambridge after one year. The onset of *World War II (1939-1945)* changed Rosalind's immediate priorities.

Rosalind fulfilled her conscription requirements pursuant to *the National Service Acts* by serving as a London Air Raid Warden. In addition, Rosalind also contributed to the British war effort by working for *the British Coal Utilisation Research Association* (BCURA). It was during Rosalind's time at the BCURA, that she performed advanced scientific research into the chemistry of Carbon and Coal.

The pioneering scientific research that Rosalind performed at *the British Coal Utilisation Research Association* later became the foundational basis for her Doctoral studies. Rosalind's University of Cambridge Ph.D. Dissertation was titled 'The Physical Chemistry of Solid Organic Colloids with Special Reference to Coal'. Rosalind completed her Doctoral Thesis in the year 1945.

The end of *World War II (1939-1945)* represented an opportune time for Rosalind's scientific career. From 1947 to 1950, Rosalind worked as a Researcher under the direction of French engineer, Doctor Jacques Méring (1904-1973), who specialised in X-ray Crystallography at the State Chemical Laboratory located in Paris, France. At the State Chemical Laboratory, Rosalind learned the scientific procedures and proven techniques associated with X-ray Crystallography.

In the year 1951, Rosalind returned to London, the United Kingdom, where she was appointed Research Fellow at the Biophysical Laboratory at King's College. During Rosalind's tenure at the King's College, she continued her advanced scientific research. In particular, Rosalind utilised X-ray diffraction techniques to examine the structure of Deoxyribonucleic Acid (DNA).

The English Physicist and Biophysicist, Sir John Turton Randall (1905-1984), who was also Director of the Biophysical Laboratory, instructed Rosalind to conduct further scientific research on DNA fibres. Randall also assigned graduate student, Raymond George Gosling as

Rosalind's research assistant at King's College. Rosalind and Raymond's scientific work produced a number of famous X-ray diffraction pictures, including the instrumental 'Image 51'. Most importantly, 'Image 51' proved to be the decisive piece of visual evidence to understanding the structural properties of DNA.

Due to differences in personality and communication styles, Rosalind and the British Biophysicist, Maurice Wilkins (1916-2004), were unable to work together at King's College, and both of them ended up working independently of each other. With Maurice Wilkins feeling alienated, and preferring a more collaborative approach to scientific research, he corresponded with his learned friend, the British Molecular Biologist, Francis Crick (1916-2004), who was collaborating with the American Molecular Biologist, James Dewey Watson on the construction of a DNA model at the Cavendish Laboratory at the University of Cambridge.

Unbeknown to Rosalind at the time, Watson and Crick had reviewed some of Rosalind's unpublished research material, including the invaluable 'Image 51' which was produced by Raymond Gosling. Most importantly, Wilkins had revealed 'Image 51' to Watson. With the knowledge of Rosalind's research work, combined with Watson and Crick's own scientific research on DNA, the two constructed their DNA model (i.e., *the Watson-Crick Model of DNA*). In the year 1953, Watson and Crick published their results and research work in the prestigious scientific journal *Nature*. Watson and Crick's scientific paper was titled 'Molecular Structure of Nucleic Acids: A Structure for Deoxyribose Nucleic Acid'. Regrettably, Rosalind's major contribution to the scientific understanding of the DNA structure was largely unacknowledged at the time.

From 1953 until Rosalind's death in 1958, she was employed at the Crystallography Laboratory at Birkbeck College, London. During Rosalind's time at Birkbeck College she worked on Ribonucleic Acid (RNA) and DNA. In addition, Rosalind also studied the molecular structure of the Tobacco Mosaic Virus.

On 16 April 1958, Rosalind passed away due to the onset of ovarian cancer. Rosalind was thirty-seven years old at the time of her death. Despite several months of cancer treatment at the time, Rosalind succumbed to her illness. Crick, Watson, and Wilkins went on to become joint recipients of the 1962 Nobel Prize in Physiology or Medicine, for their shared discovery of the molecular structure of DNA. To this day, there remains considerable controversy on how sexism and racism performed an instrumental role in Rosalind's scientific career. Not to mention, the lack of recognition for Rosalind's original scientific work. In the final analysis, Rosalind's resolve to further the frontiers of scientific knowledge in her unapologetic and panache manner is admirable, Nobel Prize or not.

Chapter Four

WOMEN IN MEDICINE

'Live your life while you have it. Life is a splendid gift. There is nothing small in it. For the greatest things grow by God's Law out of the smallest. But to live your life you must discipline it. You must not fritter it away in 'fair purpose, erring act, inconstant will' but make your thoughts, your acts, all work to the same end and that end, not self but God. That is what we call character.'

Florence Nightingale

The institution of medicine has been predominantly practiced by privileged and learned men in society. Medicine is a noble profession, however, not an equal one. The participation of women in medicine is very much a modern world reality, with the nineteenth-century proving to be the turning point, which witnessed the inclusion of women into this ancient profession. The entry of women into medicine has been (and continues to be) obstructed by several factors, beyond the most notable one of sex, including private wealth, the inequities in common law, gender stereotypes, social norms, educational disparities, and even parental expectations of their daughters to marry and produce children.

This chapter examines several women who have made exceptional contributions to the field of medicine. This chapter will present accomplished and talented women in the fields of anaesthesiology, biological chemistry, cardiology, neurology, nursing, obstetric anaesthesiology, paediatric cardiology, pharmacology, psychiatry, and surgery. This chapter introduces the scientific research and notable accomplishments of Florence Nightingale, Elizabeth Blackwell, Clara Barton, Rebecca Lee Crumpler, Mary Edwards Walker, Mary Putnam Jacobi, Susan La Flesche Picotte, Gerty Theresa Cori, Helen Brooke Taussig, Virginia Apgar, Rita Levi-Montalcini, Gertrude Belle Elion, Rosalyn Sussman Yalow, and Elisabeth Kübler-Ross.

While the twenty-first century demonstrates lettered women working across a wide variety of specialisations in medicine across the modern world, this chapter will highlight, this present-day reality was not always the case. Remarkable (in fact, unprecedented) progress has been accomplished in the former two centuries, however, so much more remains to be attained in bridging the divide when it comes to the distinction of sex in medicine.

Florence Nightingale (1820-1910)

Florence Nightingale was born on 12 May 1820 in Florence, Tuscany, Italy. Florence came from a wealthy and influential English family. Florence's father, William Edward Nightingale was an affluent landlord and university graduate of Trinity College, the University of Cambridge, he also inherited two estates. Florence's mother was Frances Nightingale. Furthermore, Florence was one of two children in her family, she had an older sister, namely, Frances Parthenope.

From a young age, Florence was immersed in a world of learning and education. Florence's father held liberal views, he was openly supportive of women's education, and he even personally educated Florence. Florence was educated in history, literature, mathematics, and philosophy. In addition, Florence was also fluent in several languages including English, French, German, and Italian. Furthermore, Florence was a voracious reader, and she studied philosophy in quite some detail during the earlier years of her life.

At the age of sixteen, Florence experienced a divine calling from God. Florence's personal interpretation of this mystical experience was to serve humanity by alleviating human suffering in the world. To Florence, this spiritual calling meant becoming a nurse, however, her mother and sister were unsupportive of her personal decision regarding a vocation in nursing. While Florence respected her mother and sister's perspectives, Florence was no conformist. Florence did not intend to create a life for herself in accordance with the prevailing conventional expectations of women of her stature in the nineteenth century British society, which was to solely become a housewife and mother.

Florence surmounted her family's initial reservations, surrounding her preferred vocation. As a result, from 1850 to 1851, Florence studied nursing at the Institution of Protestant Deaconesses located at Kaiserswerth in Germany. Thereafter, in the year 1853, Florence was appointed Superintendent of the Institute for the Care of Sick Gentlewomen in London, England. Florence remained in this senior leadership position for just over one year. During Florence's short-lived tenure, she was able to noticeably improve the efficiency and administration of the aforesaid medical institution.

The outbreak of *the Crimean War (1853-1856)* not only changed the course of world history, however, it also forever changed Florence's nursing career trajectory in a profound manner. With the steadfast support and glowing recommendation of the Secretary of State for War for the British government, Sir Sidney Herbert (1810-1861), on 21 October 1854, Florence departed for the Army Base Hospital (i.e., the Barrack Hospital) situated at Scutari located in the great City of Constantinople. As part of a joint nursing team with thirty-eight other women, Florence was sent to provide medical care and attention for the sick and wounded soldiers at war.

During Florence's tenure at the Barrack Hospital (also known as the Scutari Hospital), she had to contend with an under-resourced facility. Most notably, the lack of medical equipment and essential medicines being in short supply, poor sanitisation, lack of good hygiene practices, and the overcrowding of wounded soldiers at the aforesaid hospital. Furthermore, matters were not assisted with an influx of additional wounded soldiers from *the Battle of Balaklava* and *the Battle of Inkerman*. As a result, Florence personally described the deplorable situation that she confronted as the 'Kingdom of Hell'.

Making the best out of the worst possible situation, Florence greatly improved basic standards of medical care and hygiene at the Barrack Hospital. Florence implemented strict hand washing practices, she ensured the injured soldiers were bathed and their clothes were regularly cleaned, she also improved the hospital dressing standards of wounded soldiers, and she advised the nurses to often clean the hospital wards. All of the aforementioned practices assisted in preventing the spread of infectious diseases and reducing the death toll at the Barrack Hospital. In addition to Florence's nursing duties during the day, she also monitored the injured patients at right time. Through Florence's untiring work and selfless actions at the Scutari Hospital, she became known as 'the Lady with the Lamp'. Not to mention, Florence remained at the Barrack Hospital until well after the end of *the Crimean War* on 30 March 1856. Given the prevailing circumstances, Florence assisted to the best of her ability until the closure of the Barrack Hospital. On 7 August 1856, Florence returned to Derbyshire, England.

As a direct result of Florence's invaluable nursing work at the Scutari Hospital, she had established quite a good reputation for herself on her return to England. On 17 September of 1856, Florence had the honour and privilege to meet with Her Majesty Queen Victoria (r. 1837-1901) and Prince Albert at the Queen's summer royal residence located in Balmoral. During this meeting, Florence made her case surrounding the pressing need for substantial reforms in the British Army medical establishment. Thereafter, Florence was instrumental in the creation of *the Royal Commission for the Health of the Army* in 1857. Furthermore, Florence's meticulous records kept from her time as a nurse at the Scutari Hospital greatly assisted the aforesaid Royal Commission's work. For Florence provided the Royal Commission with statistical data on diseases, patient management best practices, good hygiene protocols, and the causes of patient's medical conditions, illnesses, and death.

In addition, Florence's well-known seminal publication *Notes on Nursing: What It Is and What It Is Not* was first published in 1859. In fact, *Notes on Nursing* established the Nursing Profession's best standards for the care and management of sick and wounded patients in London. Furthermore, with the generous financial contributions of *the Nightingale Fund* (est. 1855), in 1860 Florence established *the Nightingale School of Nursing* at Saint Thomas' Hospital in London, England.

In the year 1863, a second Royal Commission was established in which Florence was an instrumental figure. During the course of *The Royal Commission on the Sanitary State of the Army in India*, Florence was actively involved in this Royal Commission's work. In addition, Florence wrote much of the Royal Commission's report, she created the questionnaires for research and assessment, she analysed the results and findings, and she also advocated for the implementation of this Royal Commission's insightful recommendations.

Florence was honoured for her lifelong commitment, dedication, and service to the Nursing Profession. In 1883, Florence was the recipient of the Royal Red Cross (RRC) Medal. Subsequently, in the year 1904, Florence was awarded the title of 'Lady of Grace of the Order of Saint John of Jerusalem'. In addition, in the year 1907, Florence became the first woman to be bestowed with the 'Order of Merit' (OM). Furthermore, Florence's monumental legacy has been honoured with a number of statues across England, including one located at Waterloo Place in St. James, London, and another statue on London Road in Derby, Derbyshire. Last but not least, in the year 2021, a bronze bust of Florence was established at the Gun Hill Park in Aldershot, Hampshire, England.

On 13 August 1910, Florence died peacefully in her sleep at Mayfair in London, England. Florence was 90 years old at the time of her death. In accordance with Florence's wishes, a state funeral and offer of burial at Westminster Abbey in London was declined. Instead, Florence received a memorial service at Saint Paul's Cathedral in London.

Florence was buried at Saint Margaret's Church located at East Wellow, Hampshire. Florence's idealistic philosophy of nursing was constructed into a conventional rea. ty, in large part, due to her unwavering resolve and strong determination to enact lasting change. Florence's immense contribution to the profession of modern nursing cannot be overstated.

Elizabeth Blackwell (1821-1910)

Elizabeth Blackwell was born on 3 February 1821 in Bristol, England. Elizabeth's father, Samuel Blackwell worked as a sugar refiner. Elizabeth's mother was Hannah Lane Blackwell. Hannah came from a Bristol family of proud goldsmiths and fire jewellers. Elizabeth's parents had nine children during their lifetime, of which Elizabeth was the third child. In the year 1832, when Elizabeth was still a child, her family emigrated from England to New York, the United States of America.

Elizabeth's father, Samuel was a positive influence, and a force for good in Elizabeth's childhood years. In many respects, Samuel was a role model father, respected gentleman, and loving husband. In addition, Samuel was a Quaker by faith and an anti-slavery activist (i.e., an abolitionist). Furthermore, Samuel strongly believed in the opportunity for an equal education for his daughters. Not to mention, Samuel treated his wife with dignity, respect, love, and courtesy. Elizabeth's family held and espoused morally righteous, liberal, religious, anti-slavery, and anti-child labour views in their household.

Elizabeth desired to secure admission into medical school, and she made a number of applications to gain formal acceptance as a medical student. Unfortunately, Elizabeth was rejected from twenty-nine medical schools, primarily due to her sex. In the early 1840's, women were considered 'intellectually inferior' and 'unfit' to practice the noble and distinguished profession of Medicine. In the year 1847, Elizabeth was finally accepted into medical school at Geneva Medical College (now known as the Norton College of Medicine) located in Syracuse, New York, the United States.

During Elizabeth's time at medical school, she completed her graduation thesis on Typhus. Elizabeth's medical thesis was titled *The Causes and Treatment of Typhus, or Ship Fever*. Most notably, the empirical findings of Elizabeth's graduation thesis were published in *the Buffalo Medical Journal*. On 23 January 1849, Elizabeth made history, she became the first female student to graduate from a medical school in the United States of America. Not to mention, Elizabeth was ranked first in her medical class upon her historic graduation.

Despite the many barriers to entry for women in the practice of medicine, Elizabeth achieved much success in the male-dominated medical establishment due to her perseverance, tenacity, and determination. Following Elizabeth's graduation from medical school in the United States, in June of 1849, Elizabeth enrolled as a student midwife at the maternity hospital, *La Maternité* located in the City of Paris in France. During Elizabeth's time at *La Maternité*, she gained invaluable clinical experience, and she also learnt important patient interaction skills, which greatly assisted in her professional development and training as a practicing physician.

As Elizabeth learnt first-hand, the practice of Medicine was an inherently hazardous enterprise, and one that contained real risks to both the patient and medical doctor. On 4 November 1849, disaster struck when Elizabeth was treating an infant patient with a medical condition known as ophthalmia neonatorum. During treatment, a portion of the patient's contaminated eye fluid accidently entered Elizabeth's own eyes, and she contracted the infection, which left her temporarily blinded. As a consequence, Elizabeth required surgery, and her left eye was removed and replaced with a glass eye, however, she regained eyesight in her right eye. This most unfortunate event practically diminished Elizabeth's future prospects for becoming a surgeon. As a result, Elizabeth continued to write, lecture, and practice as a Medical Doctor (MD).

In the year 1850, Elizabeth relocated to England, where she worked at the Saint Bartholomew's Hospital in London under the guidance of the renowned English surgeon and pathologist, Doctor Sir James Paget (1814-1899). Elizabeth also attended James Paget's insightful lectures on Medicine. In 1851, Elizabeth returned to New York City, despite being qualified, educated, trained, and experienced, she continued to confront numerous obstacles in securing employment at New York's clinics, dispensaries, and hospitals. In addition, Elizabeth was also unable to successfully lease a private consulting space to independently practice her chosen profession of Medicine.

In light of the noted difficulties, Elizabeth opted to establish a dispensary in 1851 which was located near Tompkins Square, Manhattan, New York City. The purpose of this dispensary was to provision medical care for underprivileged American women. During the next several years of Elizabeth's medical career, she worked tirelessly to alleviate the suffering and sickness of socio-economically disadvantaged New York women. In the year 1857, Elizabeth in connection with her younger sister, Doctor Emily Blackwell (1826-1910), and Doctor Marie Zakrzewska (1829-1902), Marie was a former female medical student of Elizabeth Blackwell, established the New York Infirmary for Indigent Women and Children. Furthermore, in 1858, Elizabeth also travelled to Great Britain, where she became the first woman to have her name listed on the General Medical Council's Medical Register on 1 January 1859.

With the onset of *the American Civil War (1861-1865)*, Elizabeth assisted to train and educate countless nurses. Furthermore, Elizabeth also established the Women's Central Relief Association (WCRA), an organisation which was later incorporated into the United States' Sanitary Commission (USSC).

Unfortunately, Elizabeth was unable to procure many patients during the earlier years of her career as a qualified and competent Doctor in Medical Practice. This unjust reality was due to the presence of systematic bias, widespread injustice, and institutionalised prejudice that Elizabeth encountered being a woman in the Medical Profession. Thus, Elizabeth effectively utilised her time to write and publish on Medicine. Some of Elizabeth's notable works in the field of Medicine include:

- *The Laws of Life, with Special Reference to the Physical Education of Girls*
- *The Religion of Health*
- *Counsel to Parents on the Moral Education of Their Children in Relation to Sex*
- *The Human Element in Sex*
- *Pioneer Work in Opening the Medical Profession to Women*
- *Scientific Method in Biology*
- *Essays in Medical Sociology*

In the year 1871, Elizabeth pioneered major social and public health reforms in Great Britain. In addition, Elizabeth was instrumental in the founding of the National Health Society. Among other things, the National Health Society serves to promote public health awareness campaigns about hygiene and sanitation. In 1874, while Elizabeth was in London, she worked in connection with English physician, teacher, and feminist, Sophia Louisa Jex-Blake (1840-1912). Sophia was an English physician who had studied medicine at the University of Edinburgh, and she was also one of the 'Edinburgh Seven'. Most notably, Elizabeth and Sophia jointly established the London School of Medicine for Women. In 1875, Elizabeth was appointed as Professor of Gynaecology at the London School of Medicine. In 1907, Elizabeth formally retired from her Professorship due to an injury that she had sustained.

On 31 May 1910, Elizabeth passed away from a paralytic stroke at her home in Hastings, East Sussex, England. Elizabeth was 89 years old at the time of her death. While modern history will remember Elizabeth as the first woman to be awarded a Doctor of Medicine (MD) in the United States of America, and thereafter, practice, and widely publish in the field of Medicine, it is timely and prudent to emphasise the noble values that Elizabeth embedded when she practiced Medicine. In many respects, Elizabeth was a role model Medical Doctor, and some of the values that she espoused included equity in access to health care, Christian morality, social justice, compassion, respect, and fair treatment, without regard to one's sex, colour, social class, race, education, wealth, gender, socio-economic status, creed, ethnicity, or religious beliefs.

Clara Barton (1821-1912)

Clara Barton (Clarissa Harlowe Barton) was born on 25 December 1821 in North Oxford, Massachusetts, the United States of America. Clara's father, Captain Stephen Barton was a soldier. Clara's mother was Sarah Stone Barton. Clara came from a family of five children, and she was the youngest child in her family. Clara's four siblings included two brothers, namely, David and Stephen Barton, and two sisters, namely, Sarah and Dorothea Barton.

Clara was educated at Colonel Stones High School, and she also received home tutoring. During Clara's childhood years, she was an introverted and timid child, however, she excelled at reading and spelling. Clara was quite close to her siblings, and she also looked after their well-being. In particular, Clara assisted in gently nursing her older brother, David Barton, when he sustained a traumatic head injury from falling off the roof of a barn.

Clara's first career was as a school teacher. In fact, teaching was one of the only respectable career options available to women during Clara's early adult years. Clara received a formal qualification studying writing and languages from the Clinton Liberal Institute in Kirkland, New York City. In 1852, Clara established a school to provide free education to underprivileged children, namely, Barton's Bordentown School located at Bordentown, New Jersey.

Barton's Bordentown School, the school that Clara founded, became so successful that the influential people in the local town of Bordentown found it necessary to hire a 'male' principal to govern the school. The aforesaid school's board elected a 'male' principal, and Clara was removed from the position of school principal. In fact, Clara was demoted to a position that was considered 'more fitting' of a woman, namely a 'female assistant'. Clara was strongly infuriated, and rather than become a subordinate to a male principle, she resigned in protest of the sex discrimination that she had encountered. To add insult to injury, the newly elected male principal at Barton's Bordentown School was remunerated twice what Clara had received for her remuneration in the same position of principal at the aforesaid school.

In 1855, Clara began her second career as a clerk at the U.S. Patent Office at Washington, D.C. Although Clara was initially employed with 'equal remuneration' as men for the work that she completed (a rarity in the American society in 1855), she continued to confront strong opposition from her male co-workers. Furthermore, Clara also experienced several instances of sex discrimination in her employment at the U.S. Patent Office. Not to mention, the United States' domestic politics and entrenched sexist views continued to thwart Clara's significant latent potential at the U.S. Patent Office. Over the course of her employment, Clara was demoted to the position of a 'copyist', and she also had her remuneration reduced, all because Clara was a woman. Eventually, Clara had her employment terminated in 1858, on the unjust basis of her sex.

In the year 1861, with a change of the United States government and a new political administration, the future for American women looked slightly brighter. Under the auspices of the liberal, progressive, anti-slavery, pro-Union leader, and lawyer, the 16th President of the United States, Abraham Lincoln (r. 1861-1865), Clara returned to the U.S. Patent Office as a 'copyist' in the year 1861. While Clara was employed at the U.S. Patent Office, she strongly advocated for the employment of more American women in the U.S. federal government's agencies and offices.

The outbreak of *the American Civil War (1861-1865)* changed U.S. history forever, it also constituted the opportune time that Clara was to realise her immense potential and destiny as a leader, nurse, and feminist. On 19 April 1861, *the Baltimore Riot* unfolded at Pratt Street in Baltimore, Maryland. The wounded soldiers from the Massachusetts Battalion were transported to Washington, D.C., as Clara was in the vicinity of the railroad station where the injured soldiers were arriving, she immediately began rendering crucial first-aid and nursing the injured soldiers. This experience was to become the start of Clara's instrumental role as a nurse in *the American Civil War*.

Clara was involved in considerably more than simply nursing the sick and wounded Union soldiers, she collected and organised food packages and medical supplies, including bandages, clothing, first-aid equipment, and essential medicines to provide medical care for the injured soldiers. Furthermore, Clara treated soldiers across several prominent battles of *the American Civil War*, including *the First Battle of Bull Run in 1861*, *the Battle of Cedar Mountain in 1862*, *the Second Battle of Bull Run in 1862*, *the Battle of Antietam in 1862*, and *the Battle of Fredericksburg in 1862*. Due to Clara's untiring efforts and selflessness in supporting the just cause of the Union, and the assistance that she rendered to countless injured soldiers of the Union Army, she earned the title 'Angel of the Battlefield'.

In June of 1864, Clara was appointed 'Superintendent of Nurses' for the Army of James. In the year 1865, the U.S. President, Abraham Lincoln granted official permission for Clara to establish the 'Bureau of Records' to assist in the monumental search of the many missing U.S. Army soldiers. In addition, Clara also managed 'the Office of Missing Soldiers' (also known as 'the Office of Correspondence with Friends of the Missing Men of the United States Army') located at Northwest, Washington, D.C. The aforesaid office was instrumental in responding to circa. 63,000 letters of inquiry and identifying in excess of 20,000 missing U.S. soldiers. Regrettably, of the circa. 22,000 missing soldiers, approximately 13,000 were Prisoners of War (POWs), who had died at the Andersonville Prison Camp in Georgia.

In the year 1869, Clara travelled to Europe to rest and recover from her prodigious contribution to *the American Civil War* effort. During Clara's time in Europe, she learnt about the international humanitarian efforts that were being promoted across the European continent. Clara also came across the ideas and work of Swiss humanitarian and social activist, Henry Dunant (1828-1910). Henry was a staunch advocate of international agreements to protect the sick and wounded soldiers in times of war. In addition, Clara also became knowledgeable of *the International Committee of the Red Cross* (ICRC) that was recently established in 1863 and headquartered in Geneva, Switzerland. Clara also learnt about the 'First Geneva Convention for the Amelioration of the Condition of the Wounded in Armies in the Field', which was also held in the City of Geneva, Switzerland in the year 1864.

Being an experienced war-time nurse that Clara was, when *the Franco-Prussian War* broke out in 1870, Clara rendered her invaluable assistance to wounded soldiers. Furthermore, Clara also utilised her invaluable expertise to assist with the functioning of military hospitals, and she organised the logistics of securing medical supplies. For Clara's important humanitarian work in *the Franco-Prussian War*, she was awarded the Golden Cross of Baden and the Prussian Iron Cross.

Upon Clara's return to the United States, she successfully founded *the American Association of the Red Cross* on 21 May 1881. The aforesaid association was later renamed to *the American National Red Cross* in 1893. Clara went on to serve as the 'President' of the *American National Red Cross* for a period of twenty-three years, from its inception until she resigned in 1904. Furthermore, Clara also managed to convince the 21st

U.S. President, Chester Alan Arthur (r. 1881-1885) to execute *the Geneva Convention of 1864*, which the U.S. President Arthur did in 1882. Shortly thereafter, the United States Senate ratified the aforesaid Convention, giving it legal effect in the United States of America.

Clara never ceased to promote the selfless mission of her life, being that of humanitarian assistance. In 1905, Clara founded the National First Aid Society (also known as the National First Aid Association of America) to promote first aid programs and education in the United States of America. Not to mention, Clara served as the 'Honorary President' of the aforesaid society from 1905 for the next five years. Eventually, the National First Aid Society ceased to exist as an independent entity, and its activities and functions were absorbed into *the American Red Cross*.

Beyond Clara's humanitarian work, her profound contribution to the field of Nursing, and the establishment of influential organisations, Clara also published several influential books during her lifetime. Clara's books include *History of the Red Cross*, *The Red Cross in Peace and War*, and *The Story of My Childhood*. Furthermore, the United States Library of Congress (LOC) holds *the Clara Barton Papers*. This historical collection consists of some 62,000 archived items on Clara Barton, including family papers, diaries and journals, general correspondence, letters, books, speeches, scrapbooks, reports, notes, printed matter, lectures, biographical material, telegrams, postcards, miscellaneous items, and memorabilia.

On 12 April 1912, Clara passed away from pneumonia at Glen Echo, Maryland, the United States of America. Clara was 90 years old at the time of her death. Clara's legacy and life is a towering example of a woman rising to the challenge, in the face of adversity, opposition, discrimination, and difficulties. Clara refused to accept the inferior status quo of women in the nineteenth century American society. Not to mention, Clara was a truly aspirational leader for women's rights. Clara lived, worked, and fought for the high moral principles of equality, justice, liberty, respect, loyalty, humanity, and courage. In contemporary times, men and women alike have a lot to learn from Clara's memorable life story.

Rebecca Lee Crumpler (1831-1895)

Rebecca Lee Crumpler (Rebecca Davis) was born on 8 February 1831 in Christiana, Delaware, the United States of America. Rebecca's father was Absolum Davis, and her mother was Matilda Webber. Rebecca was raised by her aunt in Pennsylvania, her aunt cared for the many sick and infirm people within the local community. Rebecca's aunt's humanitarian and social work had a profound influence on Rebecca's development as a child, and her future career choice of Clinical Medicine.

Rebecca was educated at a prestigious private school, namely West Newton English and Classical School in West Newton, Massachusetts. In the year 1852, at the age of twenty-one, Rebecca commenced work as a nurse in Charlestown, Middlesex County, Massachusetts. Rebecca practiced as a nurse for the next eight years. At the time, Rebecca had no formal training as a nurse, and she predominantly assisted qualified Medical Doctors in their clinical duties. Not to mention, in the 1850's, there were very limited opportunities for American women to pursue a medical education or secure employment as a Medical Doctor in the United States.

In understanding the success and remarkable story of Rebecca, it is important to place her achievements in their historical context. In the mid-nineteenth century American society, the real prospects for African American women, such as Rebecca, to secure a place as a medical student in a U.S. medical school were practically zero. This was due to several reasons, including racism, gender roles, unconscious bias, sexism, prejudice, wealth inequalities, slavery, and socio-economic disparities, all of which performed an integral part in denying educational opportunities for the African American people, and African American women more broadly.

Notwithstanding the many complex and often interconnected social, political, economic, and racial challenges that were present during Rebecca's time as a nurse, progress was beginning to be made. Most importantly, educational opportunities for American women to study and enter into the field of Medicine were starting to become a reality. In this respect, *the New England Female Medical College* was founded by Dr. Samuel Gregory and Dr. Israel Tisdale Talbot in 1848. *The New England Female Medical College* was located in Boston, and it was associated with the New England Hospital for Women and Children. The aforesaid college served to advance the visionary and unprecedented cause of women to practice Medicine in the nineteenth century American society. In 1850, *the New England Female Medical College* accepted its first class of twelve female medical students, challenging the long-held institutionalised stereotypes, that American women should be predominantly consigned to the traditionally female roles of a nurse or midwife.

In the year 1860, Rebecca was successful in securing her place as a medical student at *the New England Female Medical College* located at Boston. At the time, Rebecca was the first and the only African American woman to be admitted to the aforesaid medical college. In addition, Rebecca was the recipient of a scholarship courtesy of the Wade Scholarship Fund, which assisted in financing her medical studies. The aforesaid scholarship fund was created by Ohio abolitionist, Benjamin Franklin Wade (1800-1878).

Rebecca's medical studies were briefly interrupted due to the sickness and subsequent death of her first husband, Wyatt Lee, a former slave from Virginia. Wyatt died of tuberculosis on 18 April 1863, however, Rebecca re-enrolled at the aforesaid medical college, and she continued to complete her Medical Degree. On 1 March 1864, Rebecca made history, she became the first African American woman, at the age of thirty-three, to graduate from *the New England Female Medical College*. At Rebecca's historic graduation, she was conferred with the award of 'Doctress of Medicine'.

Following Rebecca's graduation from medical college, she re-married to Arthur Crumpler on 24 May 1865. Rebecca's second husband, Arthur was also a former slave. Arthur had served in the Union Army during *the American Civil War (1861-1865)*. The end of *the American Civil War* provided many newfound opportunities and challenges. The African American people were now emancipated from their former status as slaves, and began to integrate into the modern American society.

While the newfound freedom of the African American people constituted moral progress in the right direction, however, the former slaves had virtually next to nothing in terms of higher education, private wealth, social influence, political power, the right to vote, personal agency in the United States legal system, the privilege of noble birth, honourable standing in the American society, access to well-paid and respectable employment opportunities, nor a high and reliable personal income. In practical effect, the African American people were confined to the occupation of unskilled labourers, and positioned on the lowest level in terms of social stratification in the nineteenth century American society.

The abovementioned newfound reality created significant U.S. public health challenges, in particular, when it came to the issue of 'health inequity' in the American society. For example, African American soldiers who had served in *the American Civil War* and were wounded, they were often unable to access or receive continuity of medical care after the civil war had ended. This injustice was primarily due to the economic, civil, social, and racial disparities that denied equal treatment to the African American people.

Not to mention, the dismal reality of the majority of ordinary African American people, who had only known life as a slave. In this historical context, Rebecca assisted in providing medical treatment to the underprivileged people, including the African American people who were unable to afford her medical services. In 1865, following the conclusion of *the American Civil War*, Rebecca worked tirelessly at the Bureau of Refugees, Freedmen, and Abandoned Lands (commonly known as the Freedmen's Bureau) in Richmond, Virginia, to provide medical treatment for the former African American slaves, who were often denied medical attention by the Anglo American and other European descent physicians.

Following Rebecca's service at the Freedmen's Bureau, she relocated to Boston. Rebecca lived on Joy Street in Beacon Hill; this was a predominantly African American neighbourhood. Rebecca continued to serve the underprivileged African American people of her home town, including those men, women, and families with dependent children, who were unable to remunerate Rebecca for access to such medical services and professional advice. As a result, Rebecca was tasked with providing appropriate medical care to African American patients who were often denied care at state hospitals, unable to afford prescription medication, and were not treated by other learned Medical Doctors, due to factors such as race, ethnicity, colour, socio-economic status, social inequity, illiteracy, unemployment, and abject poverty.

In 1870, Arthur and Rebecca had one child, a daughter whom they named Lizzie Sinclair Crumpler. In the year 1880, Rebecca and her family moved to Hyde Park in Massachusetts. Thereafter, Rebecca ceased practicing as a Medical Doctor, and she devoted her time and efforts to writing and publishing in the field of Medicine. Subsequently, in the year 1883, Rebecca published 'A Book of Medical Discourses' through the publisher Cashman, Keating, and Co., Printers of Boston. Rebecca's technical discourse on Medicine was divided into two parts. The first part of Rebecca's book dealt with infantile bowel complaints, and the second part dealt with the life and growth of beings, motherhood, and the cause, prevention, and cure of distressing complaints of women. At the time, Rebecca's book was an unprecedented publishing accomplishment in the noble field of Medicine, in particular, for an African American female Medical Doctor in the nineteenth century American society this was a historic first.

On 9 March 1895, Rebecca passed away due to fibroid tumours in Hyde Park, Boston, Massachusetts. Rebecca was 64 years old at the time of her death. Rebecca was buried at the Fairview Cemetery in Hyde Park, Boston, Massachusetts. Rebecca's life narrative and distinguished career in Medicine serves as a timeless anecdote that even the most disadvantaged and marginalised people of the modern society can achieve great success in their careers. Not only was Rebecca a woman, but she was a woman of colour, not only was she any woman of colour, she was an African American woman of colour. In addition, Rebecca did not commit to any profession, but the most noble, privileged, and male-dominated profession of her time, namely, that of Medicine.

Most importantly, Rebecca made her ideal vision into a living reality, and she did it during the height of *the American Civil War*. This was a time in the United States' modern history, when race, colour, gender, ethnicity, and sex mattered considerably. Not to mention, the future of slavery in the United States was hanging in the balance, along with the eventual fate of the Union. Rebecca's extraordinary story vividly illustrates that... it *was* possible.

Mary Edwards Walker (1832-1919)

Mary Edwards Walker was born on 26 November 1832 in Oswego, New York City, the United States of America. Mary's father was Alvah Walker, and her mother was Vesta Whitcomb Walker. Mary came from a Christian family of seven children, and she was the youngest child in her family. Mary was educated at Falley Seminary School in Fulton, New York. While Mary came from a devout Christian family, her parents were liberal and progressive in their views. As a child Mary grew up questioning just about everything from gender roles, the traditional role of a woman, dress codes, social norms, and even employment occupations for men and women. Mary's interest in Medicine began at an early age, and she often perused her father's medical books on human anatomy and physiology.

Initially, Mary gained paid employment as a school teacher at Minetto Union School in Minetto, New York. The aforesaid employment opportunity as a school teacher allowed Mary to save sufficient money for her further education at medical school. In the year 1853, Mary enrolled at *Syracuse Medical College* to study Medicine. In 1855, Mary graduated with honours, and she was awarded the 'Doctor of Medicine' Degree from *Syracuse Medical College*. At the time of Mary's graduation, she was the only woman in her medical class to have successfully completed medical school.

Following Mary's graduation from medical school, on 16 November 1855, she married a fellow medical student who also graduated to become a qualified Medical Doctor, Albert Miller. The two opened up a medical practice together in Rome, New York City. The medical practice was ultimately unsuccessful, due to the American people not wanting to visit a female Medical Doctor. Regrettably, such were the widely held gender stereotypes, expectations, roles, and norms in the nineteenth century American society.

In the year 1859, Mary found out about her husband, Albert Miller's infidelity. Albert had been involved in multiple extramarital affairs during the course of their marriage, including an instance where Albert had seduced a female patient that was in his care. Mary wanted a divorce, instead Albert advised Mary to consider finding lovers outside of their marriage. At the time, New York's Divorce Laws made it difficult to secure a divorce without the consent of both the husband and wife. Not to mention, Mary was 'the wife' in their marriage, which made filing for and being granted a divorce that much more difficult in her case, even though Mary had genuine grounds to seek a divorce, namely, her husband's adultery.

After nine years of attempting to lawfully secure a divorce in New York, Mary decided to leave her husband, and her medical career in New York. As a result, Mary relocated to Iowa. It is important to note that even if Mary had been successful in her application for a divorce in New York, there was a five-year waiting period before the divorce became final and settled.

In the year 1860, while Mary was domiciled in Iowa, she attended the Bowen Collegiate Institute in Hopkinton, Delaware County. Regrettably, Mary also confronted institutionalised sex discrimination at the Bowen Collegiate Institute. Most noticeably, Mary was suspended for her refusal to resign from the aforesaid institute's debating society, in which she was the first woman to participate.

The outbreak of *the American Civil War (1861-1865)* was a significant turning point, both in Mary's personal life and her professional career. Initially, Mary volunteered to work as a Surgeon for the Union Army, however, she was rejected because she was a woman. The Union Army offered Mary a position that was presumably more 'fitting' of the stature of her sex, that of a nurse. Initially, Mary declined the offer of employment as a nurse with the Union Army. Given the universal sexist impediments of being a woman in the U.S. Medical Profession, the prospects of Mary securing her preferred posting as a Medical Doctor or Surgeon were so negligible, they were almost zero. Thus, Mary subsequently settled on serving as a nurse at the U.S. Patent Office Hospital located at Washington, D.C.

In 1863, Mary provided medical treatment for the sick and wounded soldiers in Cumberland County, Virginia. In light of Mary's experience and competency, she was appointed as a 'Contract Acting Assistant Surgeon (Civilian)' in the Army of Cumberland by the Union Army General, George Henry Thomas (1816-1870). Despite the belittling titles of 'contract', 'acting', 'assistant', and 'civilian' that were applied to Mary's position of employment, she became the first Surgeon to be employed by the United States Army. Mary was often on the frontlines of *the American Civil War*, and she risked her life to assist injured soldiers on the battlefield. In 1864, Mary was captured and detained as a suspected spy by the Confederate Army. Mary was held as a Prisoner of War (POW) at Castle Thunder in Richmond,

Virginia, for several months, from April to August of 1864. Finally, Mary was released in a prisoner exchange agreement for a Confederate Surgeon with the Union Army.

At the conclusion of the *American Civil War*, Mary received a disability pension for muscular atrophy that she had suffered during her incarceration by the Confederate Army. The receipt of a pension allowed Mary to focus on her other ambitions and endeavours, such as writing, lecturing, promoting women's legal and political rights, advocating for women's voting rights, engagement in the United States' domestic politics, public health care advocacy, and engaging in suffrage movements. Mary also published two books during her lifetime, *Hit: Essays on Women's Rights* in the year 1871, and *Unmasked, or the Science of Immortality* in the year 1878.

In 1865, Mary was awarded the Presidential Medal of Honour, she became the first woman to receive this grand prize. At the time of writing this book, Mary remains the only American woman to have received the esteemed Medal of Honour. Regrettably, the award of this distinguished medal to Mary was rescinded by a U.S. Army Board in 1917, however, Mary's receipt of the medal was later restored during the Jimmy Carter Administration in 1977.

In the year 1871, Mary attempted to register to vote in the United States, however, she was categorically denied on the basis of her sex. Mary campaigned intensely for women's legal right to vote in the United States, including working closely with American feminist, author, and lawyer, Belva Ann Lockwood (1830-1917), on the just cause of Women's Suffrage. Most notably, Belva Ann Lockwood was the first American woman to be admitted to practice law at the United States Supreme Court.

Beyond the campaigning and public advocacy for women's legal right to vote, Mary also directly and actively participated in United States' domestic politics. Mary campaigned for a seat at the United States Senate in 1881, and she also campaigned as a Democratic candidate for the United States Congress in 1890, albeit, Mary was unsuccessful on both occasions. Furthermore, in the year 1912, and again in 1914, Mary testified in front of committees at the United States House of Representatives in relation to the Women's Suffrage Movement.

On 21 February 1919, Mary passed away at her home in Oswego, New York. Mary was 86 years old at the time of her death. Mary was buried at the Rural Cemetery in Oswego, New York. The year following Mary's death, *the Nineteenth Amendment* to the United States Constitution was passed, thereby, provisioning American women with the legal right to vote in the United States of America.

Mary held many titles in her lifetime, including that of military surgeon, medical doctor, military nurse, physician, medical officer for the U.S. Army, writer, abolitionist, lecturer, author, feminist, human rights activist, medal of honour recipient, wife, prisoner of war, war veteran, freedom fighter, war hero, and suffragette. Mary's life explicitly testifies to the indisputable fact that a woman is just as capable as a man. That is to say, a woman can achieve just as much as a man, given the opportunity, resources, education, and civil, political, legal, economic, and social rights. Universal rights, that one should never have to protest for, and must be blindly afforded to all people of the modern world, regardless of one's sex, race, gender, colour, ethnicity, wealth, education, religion, socio-economic status, or any other discriminatory factor.

Mary Putnam Jacobi (1842-1906)

Mary Corinna Putnam Jacobi was born on 31 August 1842 in London, England. Mary came from an influential and wealthy Anglo-American family of eleven children. Mary was the oldest child in her family. Mary's father was American author and publisher, George Palmer Putnam. Mary's mother was Victorine Haven Putnam. In 1848, when Mary was six years old, the Putnam family relocated to New York, the United States of America. In the early years of Mary's life, she was privately educated by her mother. Thereafter, Mary went on to complete her school education at the Twelfth Street School for girls in New York. This was a public and progressive school from which Mary graduated in the year 1859.

Following the completion of Mary's school studies, she decided to embark on a career in Medicine. Although Mary's father, George Palmer Putnam was personally against her decision, he financially supported Mary's tertiary education and university studies. In 1861, Mary matriculated at the New York College of Pharmacy. Mary graduated in 1863, she became the first Anglo-American woman in the history of the United States of America to graduate from a U.S. School of Pharmacy.

Thereafter, Mary pursued further university studies in Medicine, and she obtained a Doctor of Medicine (MD) from the Female Medical College of Pennsylvania (later known as the Woman's Medical College of Pennsylvania) in 1864. Mary's Doctoral Thesis was written in Latin, and it was titled *Theorae aa lienis officium* (Theory on the Function of the Spleen). Following Mary's qualification as a Medical Doctor, she had the opportunity to obtain clinical exposure and practice Medicine at *the New*

England Hospital for Women and Children (est. 1862) in the City of Boston, Massachusetts, the United States.

In 1866, Mary decided to travel to Europe to further her medical studies and clinical experience. While in the City of Paris in France, Mary attended the *École Pratique*, and thereafter, she sought and was granted ministerial permission in 1868 to enrol in the *École de Médecine* at the University of Paris. In the year 1871, Mary graduated with honours from the *École de Médecine*, and she was also awarded a bronze medal for her impressive medical thesis. Most notably, Mary was the second woman to be awarded a Medical Degree from the *École de Médecine*, the University of Paris.

Late in 1871, Mary returned to New York City, where she founded her own private medical practice. In addition, also in the year 1871, Mary began to lecture and conduct scientific research at the Woman's Medical College of the New York Infirmary for Women and Children. Not to mention, from 1873 to 1889, Mary was appointed Professor of *materia medica* and therapeutics at the aforesaid medical college. The Woman's Medical College of the New York Infirmary for Women and Children was established on 12 May 1857. Not to mention, the Woman's Medical College was founded by Doctor Elizabeth Blackwell (1821-1910), and her younger sister, Doctor Emily Blackwell (1826-1910).

Furthermore, in the year 1872, Mary was admitted to the Academy of Medicine by the slightest of majorities, that is to say, a majority of only one vote. Mary was the first Anglo-American woman to be afforded the privilege and honour of membership to the Academy of Medicine. Also in the year 1872, Mary went on to establish the Association for the Advancement of the Medical Education of Women (later known as the Women's Medical Association of New York City). Mary served as the aforesaid association's President from 1874 to 1903. Furthermore, in 1873, Mary married German-born physician, researcher, physicist, and socialist,

Abraham Jacobi (1830-1919). The two physicians had three children together, however, only one of them survived childhood, namely, Marjorie Jacobi McAneny.

During Mary's vocation as Medical Doctor, she wrote several significant essays on Medicine, including, 'The Question of Rest for Women during Menstruation', for which she was awarded the Boylston Prize in 1876 from Harvard University. In addition, Mary also wrote, 'Description of the Early Symptoms of the Meningeal Tumour Compressing the Cerebellum. From Which the Writer Died. Written by Herself'. Mary's countless publications on Medicine are too numerous to detail here, however, some of them include:

- *The Value of Life*
- *Acute Fatty Degeneration of the New-Born*
- *On the Use of the Cold Pack Followed by Massage in the Treatment of Anaemia*
- *The Prophylaxis of Insanity*
- *Essays on Hysteric, Brain-Tumour, and Some Other Cases of Nervous Disease*
- *Physiological Notes on Primary Education and the Study of Language*
- *Studies in Endometritis*
- *The Question of Rest for Women during Menstruation*
- *Common Sense Applied to Woman Suffrage*

On 10 June 1906, Mary died from meningioma in New York City. Mary was 86 years old at the time of her death. In 1993, Mary was inducted into the National Women's Hall of Fame (est. 1969) located at Seneca Falls, New York. Mary never let her sex define who she was, what she was capable of, or what she could achieve in her lifetime. Mary surpassed the societal expectations and institutional barriers that were all too common for American women in the nineteenth century American society.

Mary was among the first of several American women to attend a U.S. medical school, become a practicing physician, join prominent and prestigious medical societies, academies, and associations. Not to mention, Mary also published journal articles, insightful essays, and thought-provoking books on Medicine. In many respects, Mary's unprecedented journey has made it possible for the generations of women who have come after her, and will continue to come, in their aspirational quest to join the noble profession of Medicine.

Susan La Flesche Picotte (1865-1915)

Susan La Flesche Picotte was born on 17 June 1865 on the Omaha Reservation, Eastern Nebraska, the United States of America. Susan was of multi-racial heritage and identity. Susan's father, Joseph La Flesche was Head Chief of the Omaha Tribe of Native Americans. Susan's mother, Mary Gale was the daughter of John Gale, a U.S. Army Surgeon of Anglo-American descent. As a child, Susan learnt to speak her native mother tongue, Omaha-Ponca, and the English language.

Susan's early education was at the Omaha Agency Indian School, and she was later educated at the Elizabeth Institute for Young Ladies in the City of Elizabeth, New Jersey. Thereafter, Susan completed further study and education at the Hampton Normal and Agricultural Institute in Hampton, Virginia. In the year 1886, Susan made the valiant decision to apply for medical school. This decision was strongly motivated by a terrible incident, a preventable tragedy, that Susan had witnessed in her childhood years. Regrettably, Susan witnessed the death of a Native American woman, as an Anglo-American Medical Doctor refused to render medical assistance, presumably, on the basis of her Native American race.

Against all odds, Susan was accepted into the Woman's Medical College of Pennsylvania (est. 1850). Susan's acceptance into medical school was only the overcoming of one impediment, however, funding for medical textbooks, tuition fees, and other ancillary costs associated with study at medical school were far beyond Susan's financial capacity to afford. Susan had limited options at the time, therefore, she wrote to the Connecticut Indian Association, an association that had a strong relationship to the Women's National Indian Association. Susan requested financial assistance for her medical education to become a Physician, in order to support the Native American people. Susan intended to assist the Indian American people by educating them on better hygiene practices, diagnose and treat illnesses, and promote better public health awareness. Susan's ambitions were well aligned with the Connecticut Indian Association's promotion of Victorian values amongst the Indian American people in the United States. Thus, the Connecticut Indian Association readily agreed to sponsor Susan's medical studies.

In 1886, Susan matriculated at the Woman's Medical College of Pennsylvania. Susan studied a range of courses during her time at medical college, including anatomy, general medicine, histology, obstetrics, pharmaceutical science, and physiology. On 14 March 1889, Susan graduated with a Medical Degree from the Woman's Medical College of Pennsylvania. Not to mention, Susan was the first in her class of thirty-six medical students, and therefore, she was rightly bestowed the academic title of Valedictorian.

Following Susan's graduation from medical school, she completed a short internship also in 1889 at the Woman's Hospital in Philadelphia. From 1889 to 1893, Susan worked to benefit the Omaha people situated on the Omaha Reservation. During this time, Susan worked tirelessly as a government Physician at the Omaha Reservation in Nebraska, and she was also actively involved at the Omaha Agency Indian School. During Susan's time as a Medical Doctor, she was responsible for the care of approximately 1,200 patients. Not to mention, Susan often worked twenty hour days. Most importantly, Susan treated both Indigenous and non-Indigenous American patients with equal respect, dignity, and courtesy.

In the year 1894, Susan married a Sioux Indian gentleman, Henry Picotte. Susan and Henry had two children together, both of whom were sons, namely, Caryl and Pierre. Susan was a religious person, and she espoused her Christian beliefs and values amongst the Indian American people. In 1905, Susan was appointed 'Medical Missionary' by the Presbyterian Board of Home Missions. As a result, Susan spread Christian values amongst the Indigenous American people, she read the Holy Bible in the Omaha language, and she also conducted church services for the benefit of countless community members.

Beyond the medical and religious domains, Susan made immense economic, social, and political contributions to the Omaha community. For example, consider that Susan promoted the nineteenth century Temperance Movement amongst the Indian American people. In addition, Susan was a staunch supporter of public health campaigns. In particular, Susan was instrumental in the promotion of hygiene measures to prevent the onset of influenza and tuberculosis amongst the Native American people. Last but not least, Susan also worked with the Office of Indian Affairs (also known as the Bureau of Indian Affairs) to secure land allotments for the Native American people.

On 18 September 1916, Susan passed away from bone cancer in Walthill, Nebraska. Susan was fifty years old at the time of her death. Susan was buried at the Bancroft Cemetery in Bancroft, Nebraska. Susan was the first Native American female Medical Doctor in the United States of America. In addition, Susan was an indispensable bridge between two distinct cultures, peoples, ideas, languages, religions, societies, and environments. Susan's legacy and work serve as an inspiration to all the Indigenous people across the modern world, that social, gender, race, sex, colour, personal income, and private wealth inequities can be surmounted, and a better life is within reach.

In many respects, Susan encouraged 'interculturality' and 'sexual equality' in the United States' Medical Profession by working across distinct races, ethnic groups, Indian tribes, and Indigenous people. When all is said and done, Susan made a profound difference through her tireless work as a Medical Doctor. Most notably, Susan often addressed some of the worst health inequities found across the American Indian population in the modern American society.

Considered in their historical context, Susan's achievements were unprecedented for a woman of Indian American heritage. Susan received opportunities that many people would only have dreamt of in her time. Namely, the ability to receive a quality school education, attend medical college, become a trained and qualified Medical Doctor, dutifully serve her Indigenous community members, fight for natural justice in native land rights for the Indian American people, and contribute to public health campaigns. Susan is an exemplary role model to all members of the modern American society, but also the people situated across the numerous continents and many countries of the modern world, that a single individual can make a noticeable difference in the lives of many people in their local community.

Gerty Theresa Radnitz Cori (1896-1957)

Gerty Theresa Radnitz Cori was born on 15 August 1896 in Prague, then part of the Austro-Hungarian Empire. Gerty came from a Jewish family, and she was one of three children in her family. Gerty's father, Otto Radnitz was a chemist who worked in the sugar refinery industry. Gerty's mother was Martha Neustadt Radnitz. Initially, Gerty was privately schooled at home until the age of ten. In 1906, Gerty was educated at a *Lyceum* for girls, from which she graduated in the year 1912.

Gerty was a precocious child. From a young age, Gerty exhibited strong interests in mathematics, medicine, and the natural sciences. Gerty also desired to complete tertiary study at university, a dream that was not possible for many women during the early twentieth century. In the pursuit of her dream endeavour to become a Medical Doctor, Gerty studied diligently throughout the course of 1913 in preparation for her university entrance exam. During this time, Gerty learned the important principles and foundational knowledge of chemistry, Latin, mathematics, and physics. In 1914, Gerty undertook the university entrance exam at the Tetschen Real Gymnasium, and she passed with a commendable score.

Also in the year 1914, at the age of eighteen, Gerty was accepted into medical school at *the Karl-Ferdinands-Universität*, a German University located in the City of Prague. While Gerty was studying at medical school, she met a fellow medical student, Carl Ferdinand Cori (1896-1984), and the two students exhibited strong chemistry and mutual affection for one another. The onset of *the Great War (1914-1918)* disrupted their medical studies. Consequently, Carl was drafted into the Austrian Army for military service in 1916, whereas Gerty remained in medical school as an assistant. After the conclusion of *the Great War*, Gerty and Carl resumed their studies at medical school.

The year 1920 proved to be quite a significant one in Gerty's personal and professional life. Gerty graduated from medical school receiving her Doctorate in Medicine. In addition, Gerty married Carl Ferdinand Cori in the City of Vienna. Last but not least, also in the year 1920, Gerty and Carl authored and published their first joint research paper on Immune Bodies in Disease. Gerty and Carl were natural partners in science, and they had just set the stage for a lifetime of scientific research and collaboration together.

From 1921 to 1922, Gerty was employed as a postdoctoral researcher at the Karolinen Children's Hospital in Vienna. During this time Gerty researched Paediatric Diseases, and she worked under the auspices of Professor W. Knoepfelmacher. In 1922, Gerty and Carl emigrated to Buffalo, New York, the United States of America. Carl secured a position as a Biochemist at the State Institute for the Study of Malignant Diseases (later known as the Roswell Park Memorial Institute) in Buffalo, New York. In stark comparison, Gerty was only offered an 'Assistant Pathologist' position, even though she possessed the exact same Medical Degree and comparable research experience to Carl, regrettably, sex mattered. Three years on, Gerty was able to secure the position of 'Assistant Biochemist', and Gerty and Carl commenced their joint scientific and medical research.

In 1928, Gerty and Cori became citizens of the United States of America. The two scientists continued to collaborate on a number of experiments, and they published together throughout their remarkable research career. For example, consider that in the year 1929, the two researchers proposed the 'Cori Cycle'. This is a scientific theory which provides a plausible explanation for the utilisation of energy throughout the human body. Gerty and Cori's pioneering work had tremendous consequences for the modern medical treatment of Diabetes. In addition, Gerty and Cori's scientific research contributed to the advancement of human knowledge of how carbohydrates are utilised as an energy source in the human body.

After several productive years at the State Institute for the Study of Malignant Diseases, in 1931, Carl secured a research position within the Department of Pharmacology at the Washington University School of Medicine. Despite, Gerty and Carl's many years of collaborative scientific research, prominent academic publications, and appropriate work experience, Gerty only managed to secure a 'Research Associate' position. Not to mention, Gerty received a meagre one tenth of the remuneration of her husband. In fact, it was over the course of an additional decade for Gerty to become her husband's equal in academic stature, namely, receive a full Professorship at Washington University.

Unfortunately, the presence of sex discrimination was rampant, in fact, it was a constant difficulty that Gerty had to contend with during her many years as an academic in university research laboratories. Only in 1943, was Gerty belatedly appointed to the position of Associate Professor of Research (Biological Chemistry and Pharmacology). Finally, in the year 1947, Gerty was awarded the deserving rank of Professor of Biological Chemistry.

During Gerty and Carl's tenure at Washington University, they discovered the intricate processes that enable the breakdown of Glycogen into Glucose-1-Phosphate. In addition, the two university researchers also described how the intermediate compound (i.e., Glucose 1-Phosphate) is one of the essential steps in the catalytic conversion of Glycogen (the primary carbohydrate stored in the liver) into Glucose. Both Gerty and Carl went on to receive a combined total 50 per cent share of the 1947 Nobel Prize in Physiology or Medicine for their original work. The remainder 50 per cent share of the 1947 Nobel Prize in Physiology or Medicine was awarded to the Argentinian physiologist, Bernardo Alberto Houssay (1887-1971).

Beyond the 1947 Nobel Prize, Gerty has been honoured with numerous awards and accolades for her notable contribution to scientific research. Some of the distinctions awarded to Gerty include:

- The Midwest Award of the American Chemical Society (1946)
- The Squibb Award in Endocrinology (1947)
- The St. Louis Award (1948)
- The Garvan Medal of the American Chemical Society for Women in Chemistry (1948)
- The Sugar Research Prize of the National Academy of Sciences (1950)

In addition, Gerty also received several honorary degrees in recognition for her monumental contribution to Clinical Medicine and Science. Gerty was awarded university degrees from Boston University, Columbia University, Smith College, the University of Rochester, and Yale University. Indeed, Gerty's research and findings have served to enhance the human understanding of how the human body functions, in particular, how the body stores, processes, and utilises energy.

On 26 October 1957, Gerty passed away at her home in Glendale, Missouri, the United States of America. Gerty had experienced a ten-year struggle with myelofibrosis (myelosclerosis). Gerty was 61 years old at the time of her death. Gerty was survived by her only child, her son named Thomas Cori, and her husband, Carl Ferdinand Cori. In 1998, Gerty was inducted into the United States National Women's Hall of Fame. Last but not least, in 2008, the United States Postal Service issued a 41-cent commemorative stamp in Gerty's memory.

Helen Brooke Taussig (1898-1986)

Helen Brooke Taussig was born on 24 May 1898 in Cambridge, Massachusetts, the United States of America. Helen's father, Professor Frank William Taussig, was a Harvard University educated American economist who made original contributions to Trade Theory. Helen's mother, Edith Thomas Guild was educated at Radcliffe College in Cambridge, Massachusetts. Helen came from a family of four children, and she was the youngest child in her family. Helen had two sisters, namely, Catherine Crombie and Mary Guild, and one brother, namely, William Guild.

Helen's childhood years were marked by a number of significant challenges. As a teenager, Helen had a learning disorder known as Dyslexia, which was not well understood during her time as a child. This disorder made reading and comprehension difficult, however, Helen's father, Frank William Taussig actively assisted his daughter with reading and provided encouragement. Frank's involvement in his daughter's education made for a strong father-daughter relationship, and Helen was quite close to her father. Unfortunately, Helen's mother passed away due to tuberculosis when Helen was only eleven years old.

Helen was educated at the Cambridge School for Girls. Helen successfully completed her school studies in the year 1917. Subsequently, Helen matriculated at Radcliffe College, where she studied the natural sciences, concentrating her learning on biology and zoology for the next two years. In the year 1919, Helen transferred her undergraduate studies to the University of California in Berkeley, from where she graduated with a Bachelor's Degree in 1921.

Following Helen's studies at the University of California, she intended to study Medicine at the Harvard Medical School, Harvard University, however, at the time, this renowned graduate medical school did not allow women to matriculate. As a result, Helen matriculated at Boston University in Boston, Massachusetts, where she studied anatomy, bacteriology, and histology. In fact, in the year 1925, when Helen was only a university student, she co-authored her very first medical paper titled 'Rhythmic Contractions in Isolated Strips of Mammalian Ventricle' in the peer-reviewed scientific journal of physiology known as *the American Journal of Physiology*.

Given Helen's ambition, intelligence, and capability, the University of Boston Professor of Anatomy, Alexander Begg, strongly encouraged Helen to apply to the Johns Hopkins University School of Medicine in Baltimore, Maryland. At the time, women were able to study Medicine, and thereafter, graduate with a Medical Degree from the Johns Hopkins University. Helen accepted her Professor's advice, and she transferred her studies across to the Johns Hopkins University, where she completed the remainder of her medical studies. Subsequently, Helen was awarded the Doctor of Medicine (MD) award in 1927 from the Johns Hopkins University.

After graduating from the Johns Hopkins University School of Medicine in 1927, Helen commenced her academic career as a researcher in the specialist field of Cardiology. Initially, Helen served as a 'Fellow' in the Department of Cardiology for one year at the Johns Hopkins Hospital. From 1928 to 1929, Helen completed a two-year internship in the specialist field of Paediatrics. In 1930, Helen was promoted to Head of the Children's Heart Clinic at the Johns Hopkins Hospital Paediatric Unit, also known as the Harriet Lane Home. Helen conducted the overwhelming majority of her medical research and clinical studies at the Children's Heart Clinic, until she retired in the year 1963. Helen never married, and she had no children during her lifetime.

During Helen's distinguished research career as a Cardiologist, she clinically examined babies that presented with Congenital Heart Defects (CHD) (for example, consider Tetralogy of Fallot, or Pulmonary Atresia), and complaints of Rheumatic Fever. During Helen's time at the Children's Heart Clinic, she utilised a medical imaging technique known as 'Fluoroscopy', this is a diagnostic instrument that can identify babies which suffer from a medical condition known as 'Anoxemia' (also known as Blue Baby Syndrome, or alternatively, Infant Methemoglobinemia).

In the year 1941, Helen proposed a novel surgical treatment option to perform surgery on babies with Anoxemia. In this endeavour, Helen collaborated with American surgeon, Alfred Blalock (1899-1964), and American surgical assistant, Vivien Thomas (1910-1985), to refine a surgical procedure to treat the underdeveloped heart of babies. This procedure later came to be known as 'the Blalock-Thomas-Taussig Shunt' (alternatively known as the Blalock-Taussig Operation).

On 9 November 1944, after several years of experimentation and animal testing, the surgical procedure, now known as the Blalock-Taussig Operation, was first performed on a human patient. The first patient was Eileen Saxon, a fifteen-month-old baby girl who was diagnosed with Tetralogy of Fallot. This surgical operation on Eileen proved successful, and thereafter, it was performed again on two other children, one being an eleven-year-old girl, and the other being a nine-year-old boy. Subsequently, the results of Alfred and Helen's research and surgical operations were published in a 1945 article titled 'The Surgical Treatments of Malformations of the Heart in which there is Pulmonary Stenosis or Pulmonary Atresia' within the *Journal of the American Medical Association*.

Beyond the innovative surgical procedure on treating the human heart of infants, in the year 1947, Helen published her seminal research and clinical findings on the human heart in a book known as 'Congenital Malformations of the Heart'. In total, Helen published some 129 scientific papers throughout her research career and into her retirement years. In addition, in 1959 Helen was appointed Professor of Paediatrics at the Johns Hopkins University. Not to mention, in 1965, Helen was elected as President of *the American Heart Association* (AHA).

Helen received numerous prestigious awards, prizes, honours, and accolades for her lifetime of contribution to the noble institution of Medicine. In particular, Helen was widely recognised for her invaluable advancements in the specialist field of Paediatric Cardiology. Some of Helen's awards include:

- The E. Mead Johnson Award (1947)
- The *Chevalier Légion d'Honneur* (1947)

- The Passano Foundation Award (1948)
- An Honorary Medal from the American College of Chest Physicians (1953)
- The Albert Lasker Award for Outstanding Contributions to Medicine (1954)
- The Feltrinelli Prize (1954)
- The Eleanor Roosevelt Achievement Award (1957)
- The Gairdner Foundation Award of Merit (1959)
- The American Heart Association Gold Heart Award (1963)
- The Presidential Medal of Freedom (1965)
- The Carl Ludwig Medal of Honour (1967)
- The Blackwell Award (1970)
- The American Paediatric Society Howland Award (1971)
- The Tokyo Society of Medical Sciences and Faculty of Medicine Plaque (1971)
- The Milton S. Eisenhower Medal for Distinguished Service (1976)
- The Elizabeth Blackwell Medal (1982)

Furthermore, as recognition for Helen's original contribution to the specialist field of Paediatric Cardiology, she was awarded many honorary degrees from respectable and esteemed institutions all over the world. Helen received honorary degrees from the University of Athens, Boston University School of Medicine, Columbia University, Harvard University, the Woman's Medical College of Pennsylvania, Northwestern University, Göttingen University, University of Vienna, University of Massachusetts, the Jefferson Medical College, Duke University, and the Medical College of Wisconsin.

On 20 May 1986, Helen was fatally injured in a tragic motor vehicle accident. Despite earnest attempts to save Helen's life at the Chester

County Hospital in Pennsylvania, she subsequently passed away. Helen was 87 years old at the time of her sudden death. In accordance with Helen's wishes, her body was donated to the Johns Hopkins University.

Virginia Apgar (1909-1974)

Virginia Apgar was born on 7 June 1909 in Westfield, New Jersey, the United States of America. Virginia came from a family of three children, and she was the youngest child in her family. Virginia's father, Charles Emory Apgar was an American business executive. Virginia's mother was Helen May Apgar. Virginia had a childhood passion for playing the violin, and she also loved the natural sciences. As a young child, Virginia had a strong inclination to become a Medical Doctor when she became an adult.

Virginia was educated at Westfield High School and she graduated in the year 1925. After the completion of Virginia's school studies, she matriculated at Mount Holyoke College, where she studied chemistry, physiology, and zoology. In 1929, Virginia graduated with a Degree in Zoology from Mount Holyoke College. In line with her ideal career of becoming a Medical Doctor, Virginia attended the Columbia University Vagelos College of Physicians and Surgeons to study Medicine. Virginia graduated from medical school in the year 1933. Following the completion of medical school, Virginia went on to commence her residency training in Surgery.

Initially, Virginia attended the Presbyterian Hospital in New York City to complete her internship. To Virginia's displeasure, the renowned

American surgeon, Allen Oldfather Whipple (1881-1963) discouraged her ambitions in the field of Surgery. This was not to dishearten Virginia, however, Allen Whipple was genuinely concerned about her future employment prospects in Surgery, given the remote possibility of women establishing successful careers in this speciality at the time. Rather, Allen encouraged Virginia to specialise in the field of Anaesthesiology.

Virginia was in agreement with Allen's practical and well-intended advice. Thus, Virginia completed the first-half of her medical education and training under the guidance of American anaesthesiologist, Ralph Milton Waters (1883-1979) at the University of Wisconsin (now known as the University of Wisconsin-Madison). The second-half of Virginia's medical education and training was completed under the auspices of American anaesthesiologist, Ernest Andrew Rovenstine (1895-1960) at the Bellevue Hospital in New York. In the year 1937, Virginia made history, when she became the first female board-certified Anaesthesiologist in the United States of America.

In 1938, Virginia was appointed Director of the newly established speciality division of Anaesthesiology at the Columbia-Presbyterian Medical Centre (now known as the New York-Presbyterian Hospital) in New York. In 1949, Virginia was appointed Professor at the Columbia University Vagelos College of Physicians and Surgeons. Over the next ten years, Virginia continued her clinical work, medical research, teaching, writing, and scholarly publications at the aforesaid college. In addition, over the next several years, Virginia continued to work with newborn infants, and she developed a scientific model to clinically evaluate a neonate's health condition and vital signs at the time of birth.

In 1952, Virginia presented her clinical model for the evaluation of a newborn baby upon birth, known as the 'Apgar Score', at a meeting of esteemed scientists. Subsequently, in the year 1953, the Apgar

Score System was officially published. The Apgar Score is now utilised worldwide in hospitals to assess the health condition of newborn infants. In 1959, after a decade at the Columbia University Vagelos College of Physicians and Surgeons, Virginia went on sabbatical leave. Thereafter, Virginia undertook graduate studies in the field of Public Health at the Johns Hopkins University, she graduated with a Master of Public Health Degree.

From 1959 until 1967, Virginia held a senior leadership position as Head of the Division of Congenital Malformations at the National Foundation for Infantile Paralysis (est. 1938) (now known as the March of Dimes Foundation). Thereafter, from 1967 to 1972, Virginia was Vice President and Director of Basic Medical Research also at the National Foundation for Infantile Paralysis. In addition, in the year 1972, Virginia, in connection with American author, Joan Beck, co-authored the book *Is My Baby All Right? A Guide to Birth Defects*. Last but not least, from 1973 until 1974, Virginia was the Senior Vice President for Medical Affairs at the National Foundation for Infantile Paralysis.

During Virginia's productive career in Anaesthesiology, which spanned over three and a half decades, she also published widely in her specialist field. In fact, Virginia wrote some sixty articles in prestigious peer-reviewed medical journals. Some of Virginia's sole authored and co-authored papers include:

- Evaluation of the Newborn Infant-Second Report in *the Journal of American Medical Association*
- Further observations on the Newborn Scoring-System in *the American Journal of Diseases of Children*
- The acid-base status of human infants in relation to birth asphyxia and the onset of respiration in *the Journal of Paediatrics*

- The transmission of meperidine across the human placenta in *the American Journal of Obstetrics and Gynaecology*
- Transmission of Drugs Across the Placenta in *Anaesthesia and Analgesia*

In recognition of Virginia's monumental contribution to the specialist field of Anaesthesiology, she was awarded honorary degrees from the Woman's Medical College of Pennsylvania, Mount Holyoke College, and the New Jersey College of Medicine and Dentistry.

On 7 August 1974, Virginia passed away from cirrhosis of the liver at the Columba-Presbyterian Medical Centre. Virginia was 65 years old at the time of her death. Virginia was buried at Fairview Cemetery in Westfield, New Jersey. During Virginia's lifetime, she never married, neither did she have any children. In the year 1995, Virginia was admitted to the United States' National Women's Hall of Fame for her instrumental contribution to modern science.

Rita Levi-Montalcini (1909-2012)

Rita Levi-Montalcini was born on 22 April 1909 in Turin, Italy. Rita came from a cultured and wealthy Italian family of Jewish origins. Rita's father,

Adamo Levi was an electrical engineer and mathematician. Rita's mother, Adele Montalcini was a painter. Rita was one of four children in her family. Not to mention, Rita had an identical twin sister named Paola Levi-Montalcini.

After the completion of Rita's high school studies, against the wishes of her father, Rita decided to become a Medical Doctor and pursue further study at university. Although Rita's father wished for her not to attend university, and rather embrace the traditional role of a wife and thereafter, motherhood, Rita felt that the orthodox and conservative feminine archetype was not well suited to her personality, motivations, ambitions, and interests. Gradually, Rita's father embraced Rita's wishes, and he also supported her university studies in the field of Medicine. As a result, Rita took courses in Greek, Latin, and mathematics to adequately prepare her for entrance into medical school.

In the year 1930, Rita matriculated in the Faculty of Medicine at the University of Turin, Italy. After six years of strenuous and intellectually-demanding study, Rita graduated *summa cum laude* (with the highest distinction) from the University of Turin in 1936. Rita was awarded a Degree in Medicine and Surgery. Rita's speciality in Medicine was a combination of Neurology and Psychiatry.

The rapid rise of Italian journalist, intellectual, and politician, Benito Amilcare Andrea Mussolini (1883-1945), in Italian politics made race and ethnicity critical factors in the Italian state, society, and culture. In 1938, Mussolini published *the Manifesto per la Difesa della Razza* (the Manifesto of Race, also known as the Charter of Race). Mussolini's manifesto marginalised and targeted the many Jewish people living in Italy. In addition, the passage of *Italian Racial Laws* in Fascist Italy made prestigious careers in law, medicine, surgery, academia, philosophy, and theology, extremely difficult for the Jewish people. Not to mention, the onset of *World War II (1939-1945)* disrupted Rita's ambitions and early career in Medicine.

Unfortunately, the long war years and racial discrimination made every day life difficult for Rita in Italy. Not to mention, in the year 1938, Rita lost her position as a Research Assistant in Neurobiology at the Institute of Anatomy, the University of Turin. During the course of *World War II*, Rita established a private laboratory at her home to continue her scientific research. Rita spent her time examining the growth of nerve fibres in chicken embryos. Due to aerial bombardment by the United Kingdom and United States' Air Force, in 1941 Rita left Turin and moved to Piemonte. However, the political and social situation in Italy took a turn for the worst, and in 1943 Rita had to leave Piemonte and evacuate to the Italian City of Florence.

After the cessation of *World War II*, Rita returned to the City of Turin in 1945, where she resumed her academic position at the University of Turin in Italy. In the year 1947, Rita accepted a Research Fellowship to work with German-American Neuro-Embryologist and Professor of Zoology, Viktor Hamburger (1900-2001) at Washington University in St. Louis, Missouri, the United States of America. While at the Washington University, Rita performed several novel experiments during her first semester at the university. Subsequently, Viktor offered Rita a Research Associate position of employment with the Washington University. Thus, Rita went on to stay as a Researcher at the Washington University for the next three decades.

In the 1950's, Rita continued her ground-breaking scientific research at the Washington University with Viktor Hamburger, and she also collaborated with American biochemist, Stanley Cohen (1922-2020). In connection with Stanley and Viktor, Rita's pioneering scientific research identified that a select type of mouse tumour stimulated nerve growth when it was implanted into chick embryos. The specific substance in the tumour that was responsible for the uncontrolled growth of nerve cells was named the Nerve Growth Factor (NGF). Subsequently, the combined research and laboratory work of Rita and Stanley was able to isolate the Nerve Growth Factor, a protein molecule for cell growth and the broader development of the nervous system, from the tumour. During Rita's tenure at the Washington University, she was promoted to Associate Professor in the year 1956, and thereafter, to full Professor in 1958.

Throughout Rita's research career, her many accomplishments, prizes, awards, and achievements were grand, and they were attributable to the far-reaching impact of her pioneering scientific work. In 1962, Rita founded the Institute of Cell Biology in Rome. Thereafter, Rita divided her time between the aforesaid Institute at Rome and the Washington University in St. Louis. In 1986, Rita along with Stanley, were jointly awarded the Nobel Prize in Physiology or Medicine for their discovery of the Nerve Growth Factor. In the year 2001, Italian President, the Honourable Carlo Azeglio Ciampi (r. 1999-2006), appointed Rita as 'Senator for Life' in the Italian Parliament. In addition, in the year 2002, Rita established the European Brain Research Institute (EBRI). Not to mention, Rita also served as the aforesaid Institute's founding President.

Last but not least, Rita was bestowed with several high-profile accolades in acknowledgement of her monumental contribution to Clinical Science and Medicine. Some of Rita's distinguished awards include:

- The Golden Plate Award of the American Academy of Achievement (1970)
- The Louisa Gross Horwitz Prize from Columbia University (1983)
- The Ralph W. Gerald Prize in Neuroscience (1985)
- The National Medal of Science (1987)

- The Leonardo da Vinci Award from the European Academy of Sciences (2009)

Rita was also awarded honorary degrees from the University of Brazil, the Complutense University of Madrid, Harvard University, the University of London, McGill University, Polytechnic University, the University of Uppsala, and the Weitzman Institute of Science. On 30 December 2012, Rita passed away from natural causes in Rome, Italy. Rita was 103 years old at the time of her death. Rita never married during her lifetime, neither did she have children.

Gertrude Belle Elion (1918-1999)

Gertrude Belle Elion was born on 23 January 1918 in New York City, the United States of America. Gertrude's father, Robert Elion was a dentist, and her mother was Bertha Cohen. Gertrude came from a Jewish family of immigrants who had settled in New York for a brighter future and better life.

Gertrude was educated at Walton High School in New York. Gertrude completed her school studies with commendable results at the age of fifteen. The devastating loss of Gertrude's grandfather due to stomach cancer influenced Gertrude's early life development and thought in a profound manner. Of great importance herein is that this unfortunate event gave rise to Gertrude's strong interest in Clinical Science and Medicine. Following the completion of high school, *the Great Depression (1929-1933)* had deteriorated the social, political, and economic environment in the United States of America. In addition, Gertrude's family had lost much of their private wealth in *the Wall Street Crash of 1929.*

Needless to say, the 1930's did not provide the requisite conditions conducive for tertiary education and employment opportunities involving research work in Clinical Science. Not to mention, systematic sex discrimination was also a factor that limited employment opportunities for women. Last but not least, Gertrude also had to compete with unemployed American men for employment during this terribly difficult time. All things considered; Gertrude decided to matriculate at Hunter College in New York to study chemistry. To Gertrude's benefit, she was able to secure enrolment without having to pay any university course fees, this was due to her exceptionally good high school grades. In 1937, Gertrude graduated *summa cum laude* (with the highest distinction) with a Degree in Chemistry from Hunter College in New York.

After Gertrude was awarded her university degree, she worked as a secretary and high school chemistry teacher to financially support herself. Once Gertrude had saved sufficient funds, she returned to pursue further education at New York University (NYU) in New York. At the time, Gertrude was the only female student in her graduate chemistry class at New York University, however, she was not one to be discouraged. As a result, Gertrude strived for excellence in her university studies. In the year 1941, Gertrude obtained her Master of Science Degree in the field of Chemistry from New York University.

The outbreak of *World War II (1939-1945)* proved to be the ideal turn in fortune for Gertrude. *World War II* created additional demand for the employment of chemists in industrial laboratories throughout the United States of America. In addition, *World War II* also created unprecedent demand for women in the American workforce. Gertrude initially secured employment at Johnson & Johnson in New Jersey, however, her tenure here was short-lived. In the year 1944, Gertrude secured work as an 'Assistant' to American pharmacologist, George Herbert Hitchings (1905-1998), at the Burroughs Wellcome Laboratories (now known as GlaxoSmithKline) in Tuckahoe, New York. Most notably, Gertrude's scientific research partnership with George continued over the course of the next four decades.

Whilst Gertrude worked by day at the Burroughs Wellcome Laboratories, she pursued doctoral studies by night at the Brooklyn Polytechnic Institute (now known as the New York University Tandon School of Engineering). However, after several years of this work and study arrangement, Gertrude was more or less informed by the aforesaid institute that she needed to resign from her position of employment, in order to concentrate full-time on the completion of her Doctoral Dissertation. At this critical inflection point in Gertrude's life, she decided to withdraw from her Ph.D. study program, and continue her research career as a chemist. Gertrude never formally completed a Ph.D. during her lifetime; however, she was awarded numerous honorary degrees in recognition of her original contribution to Clinical Science and Medicine.

Gertrude and George developed several drugs to address numerous medical conditions, including cancer, gout, leukemia, and malaria. From 1967 until Gertrude's retirement in the year 1983, she was Head of the Department of Experimental Therapy at the Burroughs Wellcome Laboratories. While Gertrude was at the Burroughs Wellcome

Laboratories, she had the opportunity to work across the specialist fields of Enzymology, Immunology, Pharmacology, and Virology. Following Gertrude's retirement, she continued her relationship with the Burroughs Wellcome Laboratories, where she remained as a Scientist Emeritus.

During the latter half of Gertrude's research career, she was closely affiliated with the world of academia. From 1971 to 1983, Gertrude worked at Duke University in Durham, North Carolina as an Adjunct Professor of Pharmacology and Experimental Medicine. Thereafter, from 1983 to 1999, Gertrude was a Research Professor also at Duke University. During Gertrude's remarkable research career, and her time as an academic, she authored and co-authored more than twenty papers in scientific journals. Some of Gertrude's publications include:

- Historical background of 6-mercaptopurine in *Toxicology and Industrial Health*
- An overview of the role of nucleosides in chemotherapy in *Advances in Enzyme Regulation*
- Mercaptopurine 'bioavailability' in *the New England Journal of Medicine*
- Effects of acyclovir and its metabolites on hypoxanthine-guanine phosphoribosyltransferase in *Biochemical Pharmacology*
- The biochemistry and mechanism of action of acyclovir in *the Journal of Antimicrobial Chemotherapy*
- Mechanism of action and selectivity of acyclovir in *the American Journal of Medicine*
- The disposition of acyclovir in different species in *the Journal of Pharmacology and Experimental Therapeutics*

Gertrude was awarded three honorary degrees for her outstanding scientific achievements and laboratory research in the field of Medicine. The honorary degree awarding institutions included Brown University, George Washington University, and the University of Michigan. In addition, Gertrude received numerous awards, prizes, and accolades for her contribution to Medicine, such as:

- The Francis P. Garvan - John M. Olin Medal (1968)
- The Sloan - Kettering Institute Judd Award (1983)
- The American Chemical Society Distinguished Chemist Award (1985)
- The American Association of Cancer Research Cain Award (1985)
- The Nobel Prize in Physiology or Medicine (1988)
- The American Academy of Achievement's Golden Plate Award (1989)
- The American Cancer Society Medal of Honour (1990)
- The National Medal of Science (1991)
- The Lemelson-MIT Lifetime Achievement Award (1997)

On 21 February 1999, Gertrude passed away from a haemorrhagic stroke in Chapel Hill, North Carolina, the United States of America. Gertrude was 81 years old at the time of her death. Gertrude's life story illustrates her strong resolve, bold determination, optimistic outlook on life, and perseverance in overcoming some substantial challenges of her time (i.e., the Wall Street Crash of 1929, the Great Depression, and World War II), in order to create the conventional reality, and life that Gertrude most desired for herself.

The monumental legacy Gertrude leaves behind in the field of Medicine, has had positive implications and outcomes for humankind all across the modern world. Due to Gertrude's innovative research contribution to the chemical and molecular composition of drugs, treatment options are now readily available for numerous medical conditions, such as: herpes, gout, immune disorders, leukemia, malaria, acquired immunodeficiency syndrome, organ transplants, cancer, meningitis, sepsis, and bacterial infections.

Rosalyn Sussman Yalow (1921-2011)

Rosalyn Sussman Yalow was born on 19 July 1921 in New York City, the United States of America. Rosalyn's father was Simon Sussman, and her mother was Clara Zipper. Rosalyn's parents were working-class immigrants from Europe, and neither of them had completed their high school education. Not to mention, Rosalyn did not come from a privileged or aristocratic family. A lack of financial resources and originating from a low socio-economic class did not discourage Rosalyn's prudent ambitions to achieve a quality education. During Rosalyn's childhood years, she often obtained books on loan from the local public library to study, and thereby, proactively facilitated her early learning and development.

Rosalyn was educated at Walton High School in New York. Rosalyn's early interests during high school were in the natural sciences, most notably, chemistry, physics, and also mathematics. Following Rosalyn's completion of her high school studies, she attended Hunter College (the City University of New York), at the time, an all-female and tuition-free college. At Hunter College, Rosalyn studied physics, in particular, nuclear physics, and she was greatly influenced by two notable Professors of

Physics, namely, Herbert Otis and Duane Roller. In the year 1941, at the age of nineteen, Rosalyn graduated *magna cum laude* (with great distinction) from Hunter College with a Degree in Physics.

Following the completion of university, Rosalyn was firmly decided on a research career in physics. However, this was not without some contention, for Rosalyn's mother desired that her daughter become a school teacher. In the early to mid-twentieth century American society, teaching was an occupation that was more in accordance with the societal norms, custom, and gender expectations of women at that time. However, with the outbreak of *World War II (1939-1945)*, more employment opportunities began to open up for American women, and numerous learned professions became more accepting of the employment of American women in historically and traditionally male-dominated trades and guilds (i.e., law, medicine, clinical science, philosophy, and research positions in universities). No doubt that this tumultuous period of time in world history assisted Rosalyn immensely to advance her scientific research career.

In the year 1941, Rosalyn was offered an assistant teaching position in the Department of Physics at the University of Illinois in Illinois. In addition, Rosalyn went on to complete her Doctoral studies in Physics at the University of Illinois. During Rosalyn's Doctoral studies, she married Aaron Yalow in 1943. Aaron was a fellow graduate physics student at the University of Illinois. Rosalyn graduated in 1945 with her Ph.D. in Nuclear Physics, her Doctoral Thesis was titled 'Doubly ionised K-shell following Radioactive Decay'. Aaron and Rosalyn were married just short of half-a-century, 49 years to be precise, until the death of Rosalyn's spouse. Unfortunately, Aaron Yalow passed away at 72 years of age in the year 1992. Aaron and Rosalyn had two children during their time together, a son named Benjamin, and a daughter named Elanna.

Following the completion of Rosalyn's Doctoral Dissertation, she accepted the position of Assistant Engineer at the Federal Telecommunications Laboratory for a brief period of time. Subsequently, in the year 1946, Rosalyn returned to Hunter College in New York as a physics teacher. In 1947, Rosalyn began a lifelong scientific research partnership with the Bronx Veteran's Administration Hospital. Over the course of the next several years, Rosalyn and the Veteran's Administration Hospital's interests aligned, namely in the field of researching the medical use of radioactive substances. In the year 1950, American physician and scientist, Solomon Aaron Berson (1918-1972), joined Rosalyn's research division at the Bronx Veteran's Administration Hospital. Thus, Rosalyn and Solomon commenced a twenty-two-year research partnership that lasted until Solomon's death from a heart attack in 1972.

From 1950 to 1972, over the course of two productive decades together, Rosalyn and Solomon dedicated their scientific research endeavours on the practical application of radioactive isotopes to more accurately measure blood volume, identify thyroid diseases, examine iodine metabolism, and investigate the distribution of globin. Subsequently, the two scientific researchers also studied the disease known as Diabetes Mellitus.

In addition, during the course of their scientific research, Rosalyn and Solomon developed Radioimmunoassay (RIA). Radioimmunoassay is a radioisotope detection technique which permits the accurate measurement of minor concentrations of biological substances in the human blood. Rosalyn and Solomon's scientific work has made possible the accurate medical diagnosis of hormone-related conditions and endocrine diseases. For example, consider the following conditions and diseases, Acromegaly, Addison's disease, Amenorrhoea, Cushing's syndrome, diabetes, Gastrinomas, Glucagonoma, Graves' disease, Hurthle Cell Thyroid Cancer, hyperthyroidism, hypopituitarism, hypothyroidism, osteoporosis, polycystic ovary syndrome, prolactinoma, Sheehan's syndrome, Thyrotoxicosis, and Turner syndrome. Furthermore, in the year 1959, Rosalyn and Solomon published their scientific research on Radioimmunoassay in a paper titled 'Assay of Plasma Insulin in Human Subjects by Immunological Methods' in the prestigious scientific journal *Nature*.

Not to mention, Rosalyn and Solomon's ground-breaking scientific research uncovered that people with Type II Diabetes are not able to process insulin, not because they lacked the requisite hormone, but rather because their bodies produced an antibody which rejected insulin. Beyond the medical diagnosis and treatment of hormone-related conditions and endocrine diseases, Rosalyn and Solomon's evolutionary technique of Radioimmunoassay has been able to detect extremely small quantities of biologically active substances in the human blood, such as drugs, viruses, non-hormonal proteins, vitamins, hormones, and enzymes.

In the year 1968, Rosalyn successfully secured a Research Professorship in the Department of Medicine at Mount Sinai Hospital in New York. Furthermore, in 1977, Rosalyn was jointly awarded the Nobel Prize in Physiology or Medicine. Rosalyn's share of the Nobel Prize was fifty per cent. Unfortunately, Rosalyn's long-standing research partner, Solomon Berson passed away in 1972, and thus, Solomon did not receive a share of the 1977 Nobel Prize. The Norwegian Nobel Committee does not consider applicants posthumously. Thus, the remainder fifty per cent share of the prize was equally awarded amongst French American neuroscientist, Roger Guillemin and American endocrinologist, Andrew Viktor Schally. That is to say, the two learned gentlemen, namely, Roger and Andrew were each awarded a twenty-five per cent share of the 1977 Nobel Prize in Physiology or Medicine.

During Rosalyn's research career, she widely published articles and papers in a number of prestigious scientific and medical journals. Some of Rosalyn's notable publications include:

- Dynamics of Insulin secretion in early diabetes in humans in *Advances in Metabolic Disorders*
- Human Growth Hormone (HGH) and Adrenocorticotropic hormone (ACTH) secretory responses to stress in *Hormone and Metabolic Research*
- Immunochemical heterogeneity of parathyroid hormone in plasma in *the Journal of Clinical Endocrinology and Metabolism*
- Radioimmunoassays of peptide hormones in plasma in *the New England Journal of Medicine*
- Detection of Australia antigen and antibody by means of Radioimmunoassay techniques in *the Journal of Infectious Diseases*

In recognition of Rosalyn's immense contribution to the field of Medicine, she was awarded many prestigious awards, honours, prizes, and accolades. Some of Rosalyn's awards include:

- The Eli Lilly Award of the American Diabetes Association (1961)
- The Gairdner International Award (1971)
- The American Medical Association Scientific Achievement Award (1975)
- The Albert Lasker Award for Basic Medical Research (1976)
- The National Medal of Science for Biological Sciences (1988)

On 30 May 2011, Rosalyn passed away from undisclosed causes in the Bronx, New York, the United States of America. Rosalyn had suffered recurrent strokes and ill health during the final years of her life. Rosalyn was 89 years old at the time of her death. Rosalyn's exceptional life story is noteworthy for many reasons. Rosalyn was born into a family of working-class immigrants whose parents had not been educated beyond school. In addition, Rosalyn overcame the challenges of poverty and privations in her childhood years. Furthermore, Rosalyn accessed books in public libraries to improve her reading, comprehension, literacy, and knowledge. Most importantly, Rosalyn did not let the mainstream American society of her time define her ambitions and dreams. Not to mention, Rosalyn worked in male-dominated fields in which the very presence of women was far and few between.

Furthermore, Rosalyn demonstrated the natural capacity to work well with other scientists. Rosalyn was determined, unrelenting, and passionate about her career choice. Not to mention, Rosalyn achieved the world-renowned Nobel Prize in her chosen field. Last but not least, Rosalyn's joint scientific research and development of Radioimmunoassay has resulted in immense benefits to human civilisation. Rosalyn's life narrative is almost a perfect example of where we start in our life, what our sex is, or who are parents are, do not necessarily determine where we finish in life, or how high we can strive to achieve. For all these reasons and more, Rosalyn was a truly admirable and inspirational person.

Elisabeth Kübler-Ross (1926-2004)

Elisabeth Kübler-Ross was born on 8 July 1926 in Zürich, Switzerland. Elisabeth's father was Ernst Kübler and her mother was Emma Villiger Kübler. Elisabeth came from a Protestant Christian family of three children. Elisabeth had two sisters, namely, Erika Faust-Kübler and Eva Bacher-Kübler. Unfortunately, Elisabeth's birth and early childhood was not a pleasant or ideal one. Not to mention, Elisabeth was born weighing just under one kilogram (her birthweight was ca. 907 grams).

Notwithstanding the inherent complications of Elisabeth's birth, she received considerable unconditional love and 'kangaroo care' from her mother, Emma Villiger Kübler. Thus, Elisabeth went on to grow from a very small neonate into a healthy baby girl. Unfortunately, overcoming the significant challenges of her birth was not the end of Elisabeth's childhood difficulties. At five years of age, Elisabeth was hospitalised due to pneumonia. During Elisabeth's time at hospital, she witnessed the death of a patient. This traumatic second-hand experience of death had a profound psychological effect on Elisabeth's life.

As a child growing up, Elisabeth intended to become a Medical Doctor, however, her father, Ernst Kübler strongly disagreed with her career ambitions and endeavours. Ernst expected his daughter to become a secretary in his business. At the age of sixteen, Elisabeth left home and started to support herself by seeking suitable employment opportunities. Ultimately, Elisabeth made the decision to pursue her dreams, albeit without the support of her immediate family. In the year 1951, Elisabeth matriculated in medical school at the University of Zürich in Zürich, Switzerland, where she studied Medicine for the next several years. In 1957, Elisabeth graduated from the University of Zürich with a Medical

Degree. Given Elisabeth's childhood experiences in life, she intended to specialise and practice in the field of Psychiatry.

During Elisabeth's time at medical school, she met a Jewish American gentleman and fellow medical student named Emanuel Ross. In the year 1958, Elisabeth and Emanuel got married, and the two immigrated to New York, the United States of America. In 1961, Elisabeth became a naturalised citizen of the United States of America. Elisabeth and Emanuel had two children during their time together, namely, Barbara and Ken Ross. Regrettably, Elisabeth and Emanuel filed for divorce in the year 1978.

In the year 1959, Elisabeth commenced her residency in Psychiatry as a 'Research Fellow' at the Manhattan State Hospital in New York, the United States. Shortly after, in the year 1961, Elisabeth secured work as a 'Resident' at the Montefiore Hospital located in Bronx, New York. Subsequently, from 1962 to 1965, Elisabeth worked as a 'Fellow in Psychiatry' at the Psychopathic Hospital, the University of Colorado School of Medicine. Thereafter, from 1965 to 1970, Elisabeth served as an 'Assistant Professor of Psychiatry' at the Albert Merritt Billings Hospital, the University of Chicago located in Chicago, Illinois.

In addition, Elisabeth also published a book in 1969 titled *On Death and Dying*. Elisabeth's book was based on her clinical experiences and profound conversations with terminally ill patients. In the aforesaid book, Elisabeth proposed a simple five-stage model of grief known as 'the Five Stages of Grief' (i.e., denial, anger, bargaining, depression, and acceptance). Elisabeth's book *On Death and Dying* went on to become an international best-seller, and it has been translated into twenty-six languages.

Throughout the later years of Elisabeth's life, she became a vocal advocate of compassionate care and the provision of adequate medical attention for mentally and terminally ill patients. In the 1970's and the

1980's, Elisabeth was an instrumental figure in the Worldwide Hospice Movement, and she was also an advocate for palliative care. In addition, Elisabeth founded *the Shanti Nilaya* (the Home of Peace) in Escondido, California, and she was also a co-founder of the American Holistic Medical Association. Beyond Elisabeth's notable interest and work in the hospice movement, she also had an interest in the qualitative study of near-death experiences, and she assisted many patients with acquired immunodeficiency syndrome (AIDS).

In 1998, Elisabeth published another book titled *The Wheel of Life: A Memoir of Living and Dying*. This book dealt with the themes of suffering, worldly existence, birth, death, and pain. In fact, during Elisabeth's lifetime, she authored in excess of twenty books on bereavement, illness, terminally ill patients, gr ef, grieving, the psychology of death, and finding meaning in life. Some of Elisabeth's other books include *Questions and Answers on Death and Dying*, *Death: The Final Stage of Growth*, *To Live Until We Say Goodbye*, *Working It Through*, *Living with Death and Dying*, *Remember the Secret*, *On Children and Death*, *AIDS: The Ultimate Challenge*, *On Life After Death*, *Death is of Vital Importance*, *Making the Most of the In-between*, *Longing to Go Back Home*, *Why Are We Here*, and *The Tunnel and the Light*.

Furthermore, Elisabeth received several honorary degrees for her outstanding contr bution to the specialised field of Psychiatry. A number of world-renowned universities and higher education institutions recognised Elisabeth's important advocacy work in relation to the hospice movement and the pro notion of palliative care, including the University of Notre Dame, Smith College, Amherst College, the University of Miami, and the Fairleigh Dickinson University.

On 24 August 2004, Elisabeth passed away from natural cases in a nursing home in Scottsdale, Arizona, the United States of America.

Elisabeth was 78 years old at the time of her death. Elisabeth's advocacy work, academic research, publications, books, lectures, and university teaching have greatly enriched the institution of Psychiatry. In particular, Elisabeth was a strong promoter of compassionate care, and she openly discussed end-of-life care. In many respects, Elisabeth's work has elevated the fundamental importance of empathy, human dignity, compassion, kindness, integrity, tolerance, ethics, and respect in doctor-patient interactions, and good care in the hospital environment, more broadly.

Elisabeth's legacy remains well and truly alive in the early twenty-first century. In the year 2005, Elisabeth's son, Ken Ross, established the Elizabeth Kübler-Ross Foundation in her memory. In 2007, Elisabeth was inducted into the United States National Women's Hall of Fame in Seneca Falls, New York. In addition, the *Time Magazine* named Elisabeth as one the '100 Most Important Thinkers' of the twentieth century.

Indeed, Elisabeth's pivotal message of compassion and empathy are universal in their application to humankind. Not to mention, Elisabeth's writings and publications serve to make the unfamiliar, but unavoidable experience of death, a more approachable one. Death ought to be a phenomenon that people can more willingly and transparently communicate about in the contemporary society. In many respects, Helen broached the human condition and the destined reality of human mortality in a transparent and direct manner. Last but not least, Helen ensured that we are more attuned to not only the wonderful aspects of life and living, but also the more sombre aspects of death and dying.

Chapter Five

Women in Politics

'I was often asked the question, how I functioned with an all-male Cabinet. I must say that I had no problems. They all co-operated and gave me all the support necessary. Well, I appointed my Cabinet of Ministers.'

Sirimavo Bandaranaike

This chapter examines a number of important women who have made lasting contributions in the domain of politics. This chapter will present influential women who have seized the initiative of their time to leave their mark on world history and create their own towering legacy in the tumultuous and chaotic sphere of politics. This chapter introduces women from all over the modern world, including England, India, New Zealand, Russia, Sri Lanka, the United Kingdom, and the United States of America.

This chapter explores the lives, ideas, and achievements of women who were of royalty, and those women who were elected democratically. This chapter investigates women who forged their political career during the height of the British Empire, and women of colour who grasped the newfound social, economic, and political currents of the mid-twentieth century. Furthermore, this chapter examines the *post-World War II* global political environment, in which a new world order was fashioned out of the last vestiges of Western colonialism. That is to say, an international order consisting of an independent third-world bloc of post-colonial nation-states that had recovered their lost political independence, territorial integrity, and inviolable sovereignty. In addition, this chapter will also introduce several influential women who were instrumental in the Women's Suffrage Movement, a just cause that was not won without a bitter struggle for equality at the ballot box.

This chapter investigates the remarkable political accomplishments of Her Majesty Queen Mary I, Her Majesty Queen Elizabeth I, Catherine the Great, Mary Wollstonecraft, Lucretia Mott, Sojourner Truth, Elizabeth Cady Stanton, Lucy Stone, Her Majesty Queen Victoria, Susan Brownell Anthony, Elizabeth Yates, Kate Sheppard, Emmeline Pankhurst, Ida Bell Wells-Barnett, Mary Eliza Church Terrell, Elizabeth McCombs, Lucy Burns, Frances Perkins, Jeannette Rankin, Alice Paul, Sirimavo Bandaranaike, Indira Gandhi, and Margaret Thatcher.

Her Majesty Queen Mary I (1516-1558)

Her Majesty Queen Mary I (Mary Tudor) was born into royalty and privilege on 18 February 1516 in the Palace of Placentia in Greenwich, England. Mary's royal father was His Majesty King Henry VIII (r. 1509-1547).

Mary's mother was Her Majesty Queen Catherine of Aragon. From birth, Mary was baptised as a Catholic by faith, and she was well-educated during her childhood years. Mary learnt to speak many languages beyond English, including French, German, Greek, Italian, Latin, Spanish, and Welsh. Mary was well versed in the aforesaid foreign languages, although she was not fluent in all of them.

Despite the privilege and honour of English royalty, Mary had her fair share of challenges to contend with during her lifetime. During the early years of Mary's life, His Majesty King Henry VIII had attempted to arrange several marriages for her. Firstly, a royal marriage for Mary was proposed with Francis, the cultured son of King of France, His Majesty King Francis I (r. 1515-1547), and secondly, with the Holy Roman Emperor and King of Spain, His Majesty Charles V (r. 1516-1556). Last but not least, the idea of Mary's marriage to His Majesty King of Scotland James V (r. 1513-1542) was also considered, however, all such marriage arrangements were ultimately unsuccessful.

While Mary's early marriage proposals were beyond her control, so was her father's irrevocable decision to divorce her mother. His Majesty King Henry VIII was dismayed by the inability of his wife, Her Majesty Queen Catherine of Aragon, to conceive a legitimate son, which was pivotal to King Henry VIII's royal succession plans for the English throne. Thus, King Henry VIII directly appealed to Pope Clement VII (r. 1523-1534) to grant him a legitimate divorce, however, the Italian Pope categorically refused. As a result, King Henry VIII made his utter displeasure known in no uncertain terms.

Consequently, King Henry VIII concurrently refused to accept the Italian Pope's authority in the jurisdiction of the Kingdom of England. In fact, in 1531, King Henry VIII separated from Catherine of Aragon, and he also declared himself the 'Supreme Head of the Church of England'. Thus,

King Henry VIII began the process of formally distancing the Church of England from the Papacy, the Italian Pope, and the Roman Catholic Church. In addition, in the year 1533, King Henry VIII had his marriage to Queen Catherine of Aragon formally annulled through the patronage of the Archbishop of Canterbury, Thomas Cranmer (1489-1556).

In 1533, Mary was declared an illegitimate child, and she was also dispossessed of her royal title of Princess. These decisions had great political ramifications and social consequences for Mary. Over the next three years, Mary had a strained relationship with her father, and it was only in 1536 that she made sincere attempts via English lawyer and statesperson, Thomas Cromwell (1485-1540) to correspond with His Majesty King Henry VIII, in order to restore their important relationship.

The death of Mary Tudor's father in 1547 changed the dynamics of royal succession to the English throne. A bitter power struggle ensued between Lady Jane Grey (also known as the Nine Days Queen) and Mary Tudor, in which Lady Jane was initially successful in securing succession to the English throne, however, her reign as sovereign was not destined to be, and it only lasted several days. Within a very short period of time, Lady Jane Grey was deposed of as the Queen of England and Ireland on 19 July 1553. Almost immediately thereafter, Mary was proclaimed the Queen of England and Ireland.

On 25 July 1554, Her Majesty Queen Mary I married His Majesty King Phillip II (r. 1556-1598) of the Kingdom of Spain. Their royal marriage did not produce any children, and it was short lived, ending upon Queen Mary's death in the year 1558. Not to mention, the royal marriage was not without domestic controversy in the Kingdom of England. The English royalty and nobility were most concerned about the undeserving influence this royal marriage granted King Phillip II in the internal affairs of the Kingdom of England. Not to mention, the English Peerage had legitimate concerns about a future foreign successor to the English throne. Notwithstanding the presence of such legitimate concerns, the royal marriage did serve a diplomatic purpose, namely to improve relations between the two European Powers, England and Spain.

Her Majesty Queen Mary's greatest influence was in matters of religion. Queen Mary was a devout Roman Catholic, and she was responsible for repivoting England away from Protestantism and towards Catholicism. In doing so, Her Majesty Queen Mary restored the sacrosanct religious authority of the Roman Catholic Church and the Pope. During Queen Mary's reign she persecuted English Protestants, including the Archbishop of Canterbury, Thomas Cranmer (1489-1556), English clergyman, John Rogers (1505-1555), English Protestant Bishop of Worcester, Hugh Latimer (1487-1555), English reformer, John Bradford (1510-1555), and Protestant reformer, John Hooper (1495-1555).

In addition, from 1553 to 1556, hundreds of politically connected, affluent, learned, and aristocratic English Protestants were incarcerated, exiled, burnt at the stake, or executed. This religious tyranny and persecution earnt Her Majesty Queen Mary I the infamous name 'Bloody Mary'. Indeed, hundreds of years later, Queen Mary is still best remembered for restoring the primacy of Roman Catholicism in England.

On 17 November 1558, Her Majesty Queen Mary I passed away from uterine cancer during the course of the Influenza Pandemic. Her Majesty Queen Mary died at the royal residence known as St James' Palace in London, England. Queen Mary was 42 years old at the time of her death. Her Majesty Queen Mary I was buried at Westminster Abbey in London. Queen Mary's half-sister, Elizabeth I was her legitimate successor to the English throne, and she went on to rule the Kingdom of England for the next four decades.

Her Majesty Queen Elizabeth I (1533-1603)

Her Majesty Queen Elizabeth I was born on 7 September 1533 at Greenwich Palace (also known as the Palace of Placentia) in Greenwich, England. Elizabeth was a child of His Majesty King Henry VIII (r. 1509-1547) of England, and her mother was the second wife of King Henry VIII, namely, the Queen of England, Her Majesty Anne Boleyn. When Elizabeth was only two years and eight months old, her mother, Queen Anne Boleyn was beheaded. From childhood, Elizabeth was deemed an illegitimate child, and she was also denied her rightful place in the royal succession of the English monarchy.

Elizabeth was an extremely talented and highly intelligent young girl. Most notably, Elizabeth demonstrated a remarkable love of languages. Not to mention, Elizabeth received a first-rate education, and she also attained the mastery of several languages as a child, including Dutch, English, French, Greek, Italian, Latin, and Spanish. Later on in Elizabeth's life, she was also able to converse in Cornish, Irish, Scottish, and Welsh. Elizabeth was privately tutored by the leading English scholars of her time, including William Grindal and Roger Ascham.

At the age of twenty-five, Elizabeth became the Queen of England, succeeding her half-sister, Her Majesty Queen Mary I, upon her untimely death from uterine cancer. As a matter of fact, shortly before Queen Mary's death in 1558, Queen Mary I had formally recognised Elizabeth as the next legitimate heiress to the English throne. One of the major points of discord and contention between the two gentleladies was that of faith. For Queen Mary I was a devout Roman Catholic, and Queen Elizabeth I was a faithful Protestant. However, Queen Elizabeth I was much more astute diplomatically, and she demonstrated far greater finesse in her handling of the English Protestant and Roman Catholic doctrinal and theological distinctions than Queen Mary I had done during her reign as sovereign.

During the time of Her Majesty Queen Elizabeth's rule, she embraced qualities of both Roman Catholicism and Protestantism in order to preserve the peace and promote religious harmony amongst the English people. Regrettably, due to her sex, Her Majesty Queen Elizabeth was bestowed the title of 'Supreme Governor of the Church of England', as opposed to 'Supreme Head of the Church of England', as the latter title was considered inappropriate for a woman. In addition, the former title was more acceptable to English Protestants who found a woman being a 'Supreme Head' to be intolerable. The title of 'Supreme Governor' also appeased the English Catholics who considered the Pope of the Roman Catholic Church to be the sole 'Supreme Head' of the faith.

Furthermore, Her Majesty Queen Elizabeth I promoted genuine compromise between Roman Catholicism and English Protestantism during her reign as sovereign of England. For example, consider the formal adoption of the *Thirty-Nine Articles of Religion of 1563*. The aforesaid *Articles of Religion* were enacted with the expert theological guidance of the Archbishop of Canterbury, Matthew Parker (1504-1575). *The Thirty-Nine Articles of Religion* served to address some of the major and deep-rooted doctrinal differences between the two major religious denominations in England.

During Her Majesty Queen Elizabeth's reign as sovereign, she received countless marriage proposals, both within the Kingdom of England and from foreign nations, however, she most admired English statesman and the First Earl of Leicester, Robert Dudley (1532-1588). Robert Dudley was a childhood friend of Queen Elizabeth, and he remained a potential suitor for many years. While Robert was married to Amy Dudley, his wife tragically passed away on 8 September 1560 at Cumnor Place in Oxford, England. At the time of Amy's death, she was only twenty-eight years of age, and the cause of her death was a cervical fracture (i.e., a broken neck).

There were unfounded suggestions that Robert was behind the death of Amy, in order to secure his marriage to Queen Elizabeth. Indeed, the very circumstances surrounding Amy's death were mysterious and misfortunate to say the least. Amy was found dead at the bottom of a set of stairs, whether she was forced down, or accidently fell, we will never know for sure. In any event, Her Majesty Queen Elizabeth's closest royal advisors, including English diplomat and politician, Sir Nicholas Throckmorton (1515-1571), discouraged her from marrying Robert Dudley. Notwithstanding the numerous possibilities of a spouse afforded to her, Queen Elizabeth I never married, and she is commonly known as 'the Virgin Queen' of England.

During Queen Elizabeth's forty-five year reign as sovereign of the Kingdom of England, Her Majesty Queen Elizabeth I enacted many prudent and judicious foreign policy determinations that ultimately benefited England, and its people for centuries to come. In the realm of international affairs, Her Majesty Queen Elizabeth I was a grand political master of her time. Her Majesty Queen Elizabeth I accomplished many important objectives and endeavours during her reign, such as:

- Promoting English naval expeditions to the Americas (i.e., the New World)
- The 1588 victory of Her Majesty's Royal English Navy against the Spanish Armada

- The granting of a Royal Charter to the Levant Company in 1592 to promote diplomacy and trade with the Ottoman Empire
- The granting of a Royal Charter to the East India Company on 31 December 1600
- Queen Elizabeth I militarily supported the French Protestant King Henry IV (r. 1589-1610)
- Queen Elizabeth I's defiant and authoritarian resolve to keep Ireland subservient to the British Crown during *the Nine Years' War (1594-1603)*. During the course of this war, the Kingdom of Spain assisted Ireland to rebel against English rule.
- The promotion of trade and diplomatic relations with Russia during the rule of Tsar Ivan the Terrible (r. 1547-1584). Her Majesty Queen Elizabeth I appointed Anthony Jenkins as Special Ambassador to the Court of Ivan the Terrible.

On 24 March 1603, Queen Elizabeth I passed away at Richmond Palace in Surrey, England. Queen Elizabeth was 69 years old at the time of her death. Her Majesty Queen Elizabeth was succeeded by His Majesty King James VI of Scotland, King James I ruled England from 1603 to 1625. Her Majesty Queen Elizabeth I has been considered to be one of the greatest English monarchs of all time. Although Her Majesty Queen Elizabeth I did not marry, nor did she produce an heir to the English throne, her period of rule as sovereign brought remarkable stability, law and order, and peace and justice across the Kingdom of England. Arguably, Queen Elizabeth I's two greatest contributions to the English society and state are religious reformation and foreign policy, respectively. In her own royal right, Her Majesty Queen Elizabeth I was as bold, bright, and brilliant as the best kings of England.

Catherine the Great (1729-1796)

Catherine the Great (also known as Catherine II) was born on 2 May 1729 in Stettin, Pomerania, the Kingdom of Prussia. Catherine was born a princess, and she received a quality education, with learning in French and instruction in Lutheran theology. At the age of ten, Catherine met her future spouse, who later became Emperor Peter III of Russia. Catherine the Great and Russian Emperor Peter III were married from 1745 until 1762.

Catherine the Great's spouse, Tsar Peter III ruled Russia in 1762 for a very brief period of time, that is only six months. During this time Catherine was Queen Consort, and the couple lived in the Winter Palace in Saint Petersburg, Russia. The royal couple had a contentious marriage, and Catherine the Great was constantly suspicious of her husband's motives, desires, and intentions. Tsar Peter III's character, temperament, and personality certainly did not assist their relationship to flourish. Catherine the Great had two children while she was married to Tsar Peter III, namely, a son named Paul, and a daughter named Anna, however, there remains dispute as to Tsar Peter III being the biological father of the two aforesaid children. Furthermore, Catherine's daughter, Anna did not survive childhood.

The chaotic events of July 1762 led to the downfall and demise of Tsar Peter III from the Russian throne. For Catherine the Great plotted against her spouse, with the assistance of her lover, Grigory Orlov who was a military officer. On 9 July 1762, Catherine and Grigory overthrew Tsar Peter

III in a *coup d'état* with the might of some 14,000 Russian soldiers. As a result, Peter III abdicated as Russian emperor. Shortly thereafter, Peter III was murdered by Grigory's brother, Alexei Orlov. Subsequently, Catherine the Great was installed as the Empress of Russia.

On 22 September 1762, Catherine was formally crowned at the Cathedral of the Dormition. Catherine the Great ruled Russia as sovereign for the next three decades. As a result, Catherine personally shaped much of the nation's foreign policy, culture, art, society, economy, and she also restored Russia's status as an Imperial Power to newfound heights. In addition, Catherine the Great was actively involved in the diplomatic settlement of the all-important questions of war and peace across Europe.

During Catherine's rule as the Empress of Russia, the sovereign territory of Russia expanded significantly to incorporate Belarus, Courland, Crimea, Lithuania, and Ukraine. In addition, Russia entered into a formal treaty with Great Britain, known as *the Treaty of Commerce between Great Britain and Russia 1766,* promoting trade and cordial diplomatic relations between the two Great Powers. Furthermore, Catherine the Great agreed to protect Georgia from Persian influence and military power, executing *the Treaty of Georgievsk (1783),* in order to keep Persian might and territorial conquest in check. Not to mention, during Catherine's reign as sovereign, she bravely commenced the Persian Expedition of Catherine the Great in 1796, waging war against Persia.

Catherine the Great also made genuine efforts to salvage and promote peace where possible throughout Europe. For example, consider Russia's role as an international mediator during *the War of the Bavarian Succession (1778-1779).* Furthermore, in 1780, Catherine the Great was instrumental in institutionalising *the League of Armed Neutrality* which promoted the honourable cause of peace between the European Naval

Powers. *The League of Armed Neutrality* advocated for the protection of neutral shipping from unlimited search by the British Royal Navy.

In this respect, Russia secured considerable international support from a number of Western nations in its diplomatic endeavours, including Denmark-Norway, France, Sweden, and the United States of America, which all supported Russia's position on free and open neutral shipping. In the year 1781, Austria, Portugal, and Prussia also joined *the League of Neutrality*, however, Great Britain never became a member of the aforesaid league, as it was engaged in wars with the Netherlands and the Kingdom of Spain.

Catherine the Great's love life was marked by unbridled passion, and it was just as grand and stupendous as her foreign policy adventures. Catherine entertained romantic and erotic affairs with at least twelve gentlemen. Catherine granted her many lovers with material benefits and financial rewards, she bestowed them with serfs, peasants, Russian Rubles, esteemed positions in Court, and generous state pensions. Some of Catherine the Great's well-known lovers included: Russian Prince, Grigory Orlov, Russian aristocrat, Alexander Vasilchikov, Russian military leader and statesperson, Grigory Potemkin, Russian statesperson, Pyotr Zavadovsky, Russian officer, Semyon Zorich, Russian courtier and guard officer, Ivan Rimsky-Korsakov, Provincial Youth, Alexander Lanskoy, Russian Imperial General, Alexander Petrovich Yermolov, Russian noble, Alexander Dmitriev-Mamonov, and Russian Prince, Platon Alexandrovich Zubov.

Beyond the domains of foreign policy and love-making, Catherine the Great made significant contributions to Russian educational reform, financial reform, and public health. Although Catherine was not always successful in her many ambitions, she always had high hopes and embodied great expectations. Last but not least, Catherine the Great had a strong personal interest in the arts and literature. In fact, Catherine left behind an impressive collection and vast array of books, paintings, Western jewellery, drawings, gems, Chinese art, and Egyptian antiquities. Catherine's countless treasured items that make up her vast personal collection are exhibited in the State Hermitage Museum in Saint Petersburg, Russia.

On 17 November 1796, Empress Catherine the Great passed away from a stroke at the Winter Palace in Saint Petersburg. Catherine the Great was 67 years old at the time of her death. Catherine was buried at the Peter and Paul Cathedral located in Saint Petersburg, Russia. Catherine imprinted her towering legacy as sovereign on Russia and the modern world. In particular, Catherine's notable territorial expansion of the sovereign territory of the Russian Empire, made it a peer competitor with the greatest empires and kingdoms of her time, including Great Britain, France, Portugal, and Spain.

Mary Wollstonecraft (1759-1797)

Mary Wollstonecraft was born on 27 April 1759 in Spitalfields, London, England. Mary's father was Edward John Wollstonecraft and her mother was Elizabeth Dixon. Mary came from an Anglo-Irish family of seven children. Mary's father was a farmer by occupation; however, he was also an unsuccessful entrepreneur and investor. In addition, Edward John Wollstonecraft completely squandered the family's private wealth and fortune. Not to mention, Edward often turned to alcohol as a maladaptive remedy of his countless troubles. Furthermore, Mary's father, Edward did not treat his wife with love, respect, and courtesy, and he was often violent towards her. As a further matter, Edward kept his wife in a state of servitude.

In Mary's early life, two relationships positively influenced her intellectual development, namely, British schoolmistress and grammarian, Jane Arden Gardiner (1758-1840), and English illustrator and educator, Frances Blood (1758-1785). In 1780, Mary lost her beloved mother, and the next several years constituted a bitter socio-economic struggle. Mary also supported her younger sister, Elizabeth Wollstonecraft Bishop to leave her abusive husband, Meredith Bishop and arrange a legal separation to end their crestfallen marriage. Regrettably, Mary's sister, Elizabeth was disparaged by the local English populace, given that she was a divorced woman. Unfortunately, such were the sexist and discriminatory social norms and prevailing customs of the eighteenth-century English society. While Elizabeth had secured her prized liberty, she was now resigned to a life of hard labour and abject poverty in England.

Throughout the early 1780's, Mary spent considerable time in the company of her close companion, Frances Blood, until Frances's death in the year 1785. Thereafter, during the years 1786 to 1787, Mary was employed as a governess (i.e., private tutor) to the two privileged daughters of Lord and Lady Kingsborough of Mitchelstown, namely, Margaret and Mary King. During this time Mary decided to embark on a career as an author, writer, and philosopher. Mary's career determination was a combination of her strengths, abilities, and talents, but also the realistic assessment that respectable, yet underprivileged women like herself, had limited opportunities for suitable paid employment in the eighteenth-century English society.

In the year 1788, Mary secured employment as a literary advisor and translator to the English bookseller and publisher, Joseph Johnson (1738-1809). Joseph demonstrated a notable interest in the publication and sale of liberal and radical texts. Not to mention, Mary also learnt the French and German languages, which greatly assisted her work as a translator of foreign texts from prominent European authors into the English language. During Mary's tenure working with Joseph, she translated *Of the Importance of Religious Opinions* written by Genevan banker and statesperson, Jacques Necker (1732-1804), and *Elements of Morality, for the Use of Children* written by German theologian, author, and writer, Christian Gotthilf Salzmann (1744-1811).

Furthermore, also in the year 1788, Mary published two books herself, namely, *Mary: A Fiction* and *Original Stories from Real Life: With Conversations Calculated to Regulate the Affections and Form the Mind to Truth and Goodness*. The two aforesaid publications marked the beginning of Mary's first-rate career as a prolific writer. In addition, Mary's access to Joseph Johnson opened the door to immense opportunities and newfound privileges for her as a writer and author.

Not to mention, Mary had unfettered access to intellectuals, great thinkers, and radical writers, for example, English-born American political activist, philosopher, and political theorist, Thomas Paine (1737-1809), and English philosopher, novelist, and journalist, William Godwin (1756-1836). In addition, Mary's first-rate writings were also influenced by the original ideas and thoughtful writings of English philosopher, John Locke (1632-1704), Welsh philosopher and mathematician, Richard Price (1723-1791), and Anglo-Irish statesperson, economist and philosopher, Edmund Burke (1729-1797). Furthermore, of great importance herein, Joseph Johnson provided a platform for Mary to publish her writings. Some of Mary's influential writings include:

- *A Vindication of the Rights of Men, in a Letter to the Right Honourable Edmund Burke*
- *A Vindication of the Rights of Woman: With Strictures on Political and Moral Subjects*
- *Letters Written during a Short Residence in Sweden, Norway, and Denmark*
- *Maria: or, The Wrongs of Woman* (posthumously published)

Mary experienced an affectionate and passionate love life. Mary was deeply in love with the American author, businessman, and diplomat, Gilbert Imlay (1754-1828), with whom she became pregnant, and bore her first child named Fanny. However, Gilbert's intimacy and interest in Mary was short-lived, and he eventually left her along with their child, Fanny. Mary went on to forge a second relationship. On this occasion, Mary became intimately involved with the English political philosopher, William Godwin. Upon Mary and William's realisation of Mary's pregnancy, the two intellectuals got married, in order that their future child be a legitimate one. Mary and William's daughter was also named Mary.

Although Mary was a writer, intellectual, author, and feminist philosopher, her 1792 work 'A Vindication on the Rights of Woman: With Strictures on Political and Moral Subjects' came to define much of the Women's Suffrage Movement and Feminist Movement across the Anglophone world. Not to mention, Mary's 1792 seminal publication has indirectly influenced the women's worldwide struggle for political, social, economic, civil, and legal rights. In addition, Mary's influential 1792 publication also promoted the ideas of classical republicanism. In fact, following the earlier years of *the French Revolution (1789-1799)*, Mary was a strong advocate that France become a republic.

On 10 September 1797, Mary passed away from septicaemia in Somers Town, London, England. Mary was only 38 years old at the time of her death. Mary was buried at the Old Saint Pancras Churchyard in London. In such a short lifetime, Mary transcended the struggles of her formative years, and made her outsized impression on the just struggle for equal rights of women in the eighteenth-century English society, but also across the modern world, at large. It is not a misleading statement to assert that Mary's 1792 text 'A Vindication on the Rights of Woman: With Strictures on Political and Moral Subjects' proved to be the intellectual stimulus and original impetus for the 19th and 20th century political and legal struggle for women's enfranchisement across the Anglophone world.

Lucretia Mott (1793-1880)

Lucretia Coffin Mott was born on 3 January 1793 in Nantucket, Massachusetts, the United States of America. Lucretia's father was Thomas Coffin, and her mother was Anna Folger. Lucretia came from an Anglo-American family, and she was raised as a Quaker. The formative years of Lucretia's life were spent in Boston. Lucretia was educated at the Nine Partners School which was administered by the Religious Society of Friends in Dutchess County, New York.

Upon Lucretia's completion of her high school studies, she briefly taught at the Nine Partners School. During Lucretia's employment tenure as a school teacher, she directly experienced the noticeable income inequality that was associated with teaching work completed by American women. Often male American school teachers were paid considerably more then their female counterparts, for the same work, solely due to the discriminatory distinction of sex. Being a Quaker woman of faith, Lucretia held strong opinions in relation to the equality of humankind, natural justice, the equality of women, women's civil, legal, and political rights, and the abolition of slavery. These moral ideals ultimately influenced Lucretia's occupation and social associations in the near future.

In the year 1811, Lucretia married Quaker leader, teacher, and anti-slavery activist, James Mott (1788-1868), at Pine Street Meeting in Philadelphia. The married couple had six children during the course of their time together. James was a supportive spouse, and he assisted Lucretia in the achievement of her political, social, and economic objectives, and her ambition to reform the modern American civil society. In the year 1821, Lucretia became a Quaker minister, and her husband, James Mott supported her preaching and ministry activities. Often Lucretia lectured on religious doctrine, social and political reform, human rights, the abolition of slavery, women's rights, universal suffrage, the temperance movement, and the just cause for peace.

Furthermore, Lucretia was also involved in the activities of *the American Anti-Slavery Society* (est. 1833), and so was her husband. In addition, Lucretia was active across several other anti-slavery and women's rights organisations and associations during her lifetime, including *the Anti-Slavery Convention of American Women* (first held in 1837, second held in 1838, and third held in 1839), *the Philadelphia Female Anti-Slavery Society* (est. 1833), *the American Free Produce Association* (est. 1838), and *the Pennsylvania Anti-Slavery Society* (est. 1838).

In the year 1840, Lucretia attended *the World's Anti-Slavery Convention* (also known as the General Anti-Slavery Convention) held in London,

England. During Lucretia's visit to the aforesaid Convention, she met with American women's rights activist, Elizabeth Cady Stanton (1815-1902). As a result, Lucretia and Elizabeth forged a collaborative partnership that endured for several years, the two activists focused on addressing women's rights and the just cause of anti-slavery.

Furthermore, in the year 1848, Lucretia and Elizabeth were instrumental in the organisation of *the Seneca Falls Convention* that was held in Seneca Falls, New York. Although the two activists did not always agree with each other, they set aside their differences for the greater good of the Women's Suffragette Movement, and the abolition of slavery in the United States of America. Furthermore, two years later, Lucretia also published her thoughts and ideas on women's rights in the *Discourse on Woman (1849).*

Lucretia's passionate involvement on social issues went much further. For example, Lucretia became the founding President of *the American Equal Rights Association* (est. 1866). This organisation worked to promote the enlightened message of universal suffrage for all people, regardless of a person's sex, colour, education, income, wealth, private property, socio-economic status, race, ethnicity, social class, gender, creed, or faith. During Lucretia's time as a political activist and social reformer, she collaborated with some of the greatest suffragettes and well-known advocates of women's rights, including Susan Brownell Anthony (1820-1906), Lucy Stone (1818-1893), Abigail Kelley Foster (1811-1887), Angelina Emily Grimké Weld (1805-1879), Elizabeth Cady Stanton (1815-1902), Sarah Moore Grimké (1792-1873), and Mary Ann M'Clintock (1800-1834). In addition, Lucretia was instrumental in the inner workings of *the Free Religious Association* (est. 1867), and she also worked with a number of enlightened religious liberals, including American Unitarian minister and abolitionist, Thomas Wentworth Higginson

(1823-1911), American philosopher, poet, and abolitionist, Ralph Waldo Emerson (1803-1882), and American author and educator, Isaac Mayer Wise (1819-1900).

Lucretia was a life-long pacifist. Not to mention, Lucretia was a member of *the New England Non-Resistance Society* (est. 1838) and *the Universal Peace Union* (est. 1866). In addition, Lucretia was strongly opposed to *the Mexican-American War (1846-1848)*. In fact, Lucretia was categorically against the Doctrine of War, as a means to settle disputes and grievances between sovereign nations. In Lucretia's world view, being bellicose was not a solution to the problems and challenges of the modern world. In the final analysis, Lucretia understood that the 'use of force' was not the ideal principle in solving the many global challenges of the modern world.

On 11 November 1880, Lucretia passed away from pneumonia in Cheltenham, Pennsylvania, the United States of America. Lucretia was 87 years old at the time of her death. Lucretia was buried at the Fair Hill Burial Ground in North Philadelphia. Lucretia's tireless advocacy work and selfless dedication to the noble causes of justice, liberty, enfranchisement, and freedom have been recognised throughout the United States of America. In the year 1921, a sculpture was designed by American sculptor, Adelaide Johnson, which commemorated the three great American suffragette leaders, Elizabeth Cady Stanton, Susan Brownell Anthony, and Lucretia Mott. Furthermore, in 1948, a commemorative postage stamp which featured Lucretia Mott, along with the American women's suffrage leaders, Elizabeth Cady Stanton and Carrie Chapman Catt was issued by the United States Postal Service. Last but not least, in the year 1983, Lucretia was inducted into the United States National Women's Hall of Fame.

Lucretia is an inspirational role model for all the people of the modern world. Lucretia's tireless advocacy work has made significant contributions to the American civil society, making it more equitable for women and people of colour. Lucretia achieved much over the extraordinary course of her lifetime. Indeed, Lucretia has set the 'gold standard' for contemporary activists who desire to initiate meaningful social, political, legal, and economic change in the modern world, to construct a future that is more just, humane, peaceful, and equitable.

Sojourner Truth (1797-1883)

Sojourner Truth (Isabella Baumfree) was born in slavery in the year ca. 1797 in Swartekill, Ulster County, New York, the United States of America. Sojourner's father was James Baumfree, and her mother was Elizabeth Baumfree. Sojourner's childhood was one of servitude, hard labour, physical and sexual assault, bondage, and many other privations. Sojourner's first language was Dutch, and later on, she also learnt the English language.

Sojourner had a short-lived romantic relationship with a slave by the name of Robert, however, Robert's owner, Charles Catton, did not want his slaves to produce children, and therefore, he forbade the intimate relationship between the two aforesaid slaves of different households. When Robert escaped to secretly visit Sojourner, and his master (Charles) found out, Robert was severely beaten. As a result, Sojourner and Robert were unable to meet again. Thereafter, Sojourner married a slave by the name of Thomas, and she had five children. Not all of Sojourner's children were with Thomas, for she had been raped by her master and slave owner, John Dumont. Consequently, Sojourner had previously given birth to her master's biological child.

In 1826, Sojourner escaped enslavement by her master, John Dumont in a desperate bid for her freedom. Sojourner left with her daughter, Sophia, her liberation journey is commonly referred to as the 'Walk of Freedom'. Sojourner and her infant daughter accepted refuge with an abolitionist family, Isaac and Maria Van Wagenen in New Paltz, New York. Furthermore, the Wagenen family assisted Sojourner and her daughter to secure their freedom in New York for USD $20, which her master accepted as settlement payment. During the first three decades of the 1800's, chattel slavery was also gradually being abolished in New York, by active measures of the New York State legislature, for example, consider *An Act for the Gradual Abolition of Slavery of 1799*.

In addition, the Wagenen family also assisted Sojourner to pursue legal proceedings for the sole custody and return of her five-year-old son, Peter, who had been illegally sold into slavery in the state of Alabama by her former owner and master, John Dumont. In 1828, Sojourner successfully mounted her legal challenge in a U.S. court of law, for the return of her son. In summary, Sojourner's legal argument soundly demonstrated that the unlawful sale of her son circumvented *the New York Anti-Slavery Law* which came into force in 1827. Sojourner was successful in court action, and her son was thereafter reunited with her. Sojourner is often known as the first African American woman to have won a court case against an American man of Anglo-Saxon or European origin. Of great significance, Sojourner overcame the formidable barriers of race, colour, gender, poverty, and sex, to secure the deliverance of natural justice in the nineteenth century United States of America.

In 1829, Sojourner moved to New York City, where she worked for Christian Evangelist, Elijah Pierson. Thereafter, in 1832, Sojourner became acquainted with American businessman and religious figure, Robert Matthews. Sojourner worked for Robert as a housemaid at the Matthias Kingdom Communal Colony. Most notably, Sojourner demonstrated her ability to successfully integrate into the modern nineteenth century American society, at a time when race, colour, sex, slavery, and ethnicity were major factors in the aforesaid society.

The year 1843 witnessed Sojourner become a Methodist. Thereafter, Sojourner dedicated her time, wisdom, knowledge, and energy to preaching the just message of women's rights and advocating for the abolition of slavery in the United States of America. The following year, that is 1844, Sojourner joined *the Northampton Association of Education and Industry* in Florence, Massachusetts. Sojourner's membership to the aforesaid Association introduced her to the great American abolitionist leaders of her time, such as David Ruggles (1810-1849), William Lloyd Garrison (1805-1879), and Frederick Douglass (1818-1895). In the year 1850, with the support and assistance of American journalist and social reformer, William Lloyd Garrison, Sojourner managed to publish her remarkable story which was titled *The Narrative of Sojourner Truth: A Northern Slave*. The sale proceeds from Sojourner's book greatly assisted her financially, in particular, to meet the living costs and daily expenses that she encountered.

Furthermore, Sojourner was a gifted orator, and she made several prominent speeches during her lifetime. Arguably, Sojourner's most famous speech was *Ain't I A Woman?* which was presented at the 1851 *Ohio Women's Rights Convention*. In addition, Sojourner spoke or sang at the following significant events:

- *The Northampton Camp Meeting (1844)*
- *The First National Women's Rights Convention (1850)*
- *The Mob Convention (1853)*
- *The American Equal Rights Association (1867)*
- *The Eighth Anniversary of Negro Freedom (1871)*
- *The Second Annual Convention of the American Woman Suffrage Association (1871)*

Despite the many institutional barriers that women, and the people of African American descent confronted, Sojourner actively participated in the current affairs of the American society and state to the best of her ability. By any measure, Sojourner made an outsized positive contribution to her country. For example, consider that Sojourner assisted in the recruitment of African American men in the Union Army during *the American Civil War (1861-1865)*. In addition, Sojourner assisted in the efforts of *the National Freedman's Relief Association* located in Washington, D.C., to integrate African American people into civil society, and improve their living conditions. During Sojourner's tenure at the aforesaid Relief Association, she shared her expertise, knowledge, and life experience to provide counselling to former slaves on how to better integrate as free people into the modern American society. In addition, Sojourner also encouraged the migration and settlement of free African American people to the U.S. states of Kansas and Missouri.

Last but not least, Sojourner's notable efforts to assist the Union in *the American Civil War* earnt her the high privilege of meeting with the United States President, Abraham Lincoln (r. 1861-1865) at the White House in Washington D.C., on 29 October 1864. Following several more years of intense advocacy work and social activism in the cause of women's rights, not to mention, the moral battle for greater civil liberties for the African

American people, in the year 1875, Sojourner retired at her home in Battle Creek, Michigan.

In the later years of Sojourner's life, she progressively became deaf and blind. On 26 November 1883, Sojourner passed away at her place of residence in Battle Creek, Michigan. Sojourner was 86 years old at the time of her death. Sojourner was buried at Battle Creek's Oak Hill Cemetery in Michigan. In the year 2009, Sojourner Truth was honoured with a memorial bust that was sculpted by Canadian sculptor and painter, Artis Lane, it was installed at the United States Capitol in Washington D.C. In recognition of Sojourner's towering legacy, she became the first African American woman to receive such a prestigious honour at the United States Capitol.

Elizabeth Cady Stanton (1815-1902)

Elizabeth Cady Stanton was born on 12 November 1815 in Johnstown, New York, the United States of America. Elizabeth was born into a family of privilege, private wealth, abundant resources (including her family's ownership of several African American slaves), political affiliations, and high socio-economic class. Elizabeth's father was American lawyer, politician, and judge, Daniel Cady. Elizabeth's mother was Margaret Livingston Cady. In addition, Elizabeth came from a family of eleven children.

Elizabeth was educated at the Johnstown Academy, where she studied several subjects, including French, Greek, Latin, religion, the natural sciences, and mathematics, until the age of sixteen. Elizabeth excelled academically, she outperformed many of the boys at the aforesaid Academy. Elizabeth's strongest achievement was her mastery of the Greek language. In the year 1830, Elizabeth graduated from the aforesaid Academy.

Upon the completion of school, Elizabeth desired to attend New York Union College, however, this was not possible at the time, solely due to the discriminatory factor of Elizabeth's sex. Consequently, Elizabeth matriculated at Emma Willard's Troy Female Seminary in Troy, New York. Emma Willard's Troy Female Seminary was an educational institution for women which was founded in 1821 by American women's rights and education activist, Emma Hart Willard (1787-1870). From 1831 to 1832, Elizabeth studied at Emma Willard's Troy Female Seminary.

Elizabeth's father, Daniel Cady had a profound impact on her intellectual development and thought. In fact, it was through her father, that Elizabeth became well acquainted with New York law, and she gained somewhat of an informal education in the United States law. Elizabeth's father was a very influential, wealthy, learned, and respected figure in the New York society, an accomplished gentleman in his own right. Daniel Cady was a member of the Federalist Party, he was elected to the New York State Assembly, and he had also served one term in the United States Congress. Furthermore, Daniel had served as a Justice in the New York Supreme Court, and last but not least, he was an ex officio judge of the New York Court of Appeals.

During Elizabeth's teenage years, she attended her father's law office, where she often immersed herself in legal publications, scholarly articles, and law books. Thus, Elizabeth became quite familiar with the inequalities that the United States law presented for American women, solely on the basis of their sex. As a symbol of passive protest, Elizabeth often cut out the unfair laws that discriminated against American women from her father's expensive law books!

Following the completion of Elizabeth's formal education, she was most interested in the abolitionist movement, women's rights, and the promotion of temperance. Elizabeth's cousin and American abolitionist, Gerrit Smith (1797-1874), introduced her to *the New York State Anti-Slavery Society*. During Elizabeth's abolitionist work, she met her future spouse, American abolitionist and lawyer, Henry Brewster Stanton. On 1 May 1840, Elizabeth, at the age of twenty-four, got married to Henry (then aged thirty-four) in Johnstown, New York. Most notably, Elizabeth outright refused to say the word 'obey' during the exchange of vows at their wedding ceremony. After all, the 'ideal' marriage is established on the moral principle of equal relations between the husband and wife. Elizabeth's family was against her marriage, as her husband was an abolitionist. Nonetheless, Elizabeth's family's diplomatic protests were ignored, and the two social activists got married. Not to mention, Elizabeth and Henry went on to have seven children together.

Beyond Elizabeth's marriage to Henry, 1840 was an important year for her in respect to advocacy work on women's rights. While Elizabeth and Henry were in London, England on their honeymoon, both individuals attended *the World's Anti-Slavery Convention* at Exeter Hall. It was at this important Convention that Elizabeth met American abolitionist and women's rights activist, Lucretia Mott (1793-1880). Of great importance herein, Elizabeth and Lucretia's meeting set into motion an important partnership, one that witnessed them collaborate together on social, legal, civil, and political endeavours across the United States of America.

Through Elizabeth's father's vocation in the United States Legal Profession, Elizabeth came to more adequately understand the intricacies of the United States law, and how it functioned to oppress and alienate women in the modern American society, depriving them of their civil, political, and legal rights, solely on the basis of their sex. In addition, Elizabeth's experience at *the World's Anti-Slavery Convention* in London, acquainted her with the broader social, political, and economic realities of how women were treated in the modern English society. For example, consider that women were not allowed to vote at *the World's Anti-Slavery Convention*, the women in attendance were also seated separately to the men, and women were positioned in an area that was distant to the main proceedings of the aforesaid Convention. Over the course of the next several years, from 1840 to 1848, Elizabeth worked with Lucretia Mott, who was the more experienced activist, and Elizabeth also learnt from Lucretia's life experiences. In addition, Elizabeth also listened to Lucretia publicly speak and preach about the profound importance of women's rights.

Most importantly, Elizabeth Cady Stanton emerged as one of the five primary female architects, along with Lucretia Mott (1793-1880), Martha Coffin Wright (1806-1875), Mary Ann M'Clintock (1800-1884), and Jane Clothier Hunt (1812-1889), in the organisation of *the Seneca Falls Convention* which was held on 19 and 20 July 1848 at the Wesleyan Methodist Chapel, Seneca Falls in New York, the United States of America. This was a historic Convention in its own right, for it was the first Women's Rights Convention organised by women in the United States of America. Many influential American abolitions and women's rights activists attended the aforesaid Convention, including Frederick Douglass, Lucretia Mott, Mary Ann M'Clintock, Susan Brownell Anthony, Amelia Jenks Bloomer, Amy Post, Rhoda Palmer, Thomas M'Clintock, Ansel Bascom, James Mott, Betsy Tewksbury, Martha Coffin Wright, Malvina Seymour, Charlotte Woodward Pierce, and Eunice Newton Foote, among many other influential and learned American people.

Over the course of two short days, the distinguished participants of *the 1848 Seneca Falls Convention*, both gentlemen and gentlewomen, vigorously debated and del berated on the inequities confronting women in the modern American society. At the formal conclusion of the aforesaid Convention, the majority cf people in attendance reached a consensus on several grievances and resolutions. In essence, *the Declaration of Sentiments* demanded the political, social, legal, and economic equality of American women.

Shortly thereafter, on 2 August 1848, *the Rochester Women's Rights Convention* was held in New York, the United States of America. Elizabeth was also in attendance at this notable Convention. The Chairperson of this Convention was an American abolitionist and women's rights activist, Abigail Norton Bush (1810-1898). The fact that *the Rochester Women's Rights Convention* was chaired by an American woman, was a first, and it represented a deviation from the orthodox and long-standing practice of American men presiding as 'the Chairperson' on national conferences and conventions in the United States of America.

In the year 1863, Elizabeth Cady Stanton, in connection with Susan Brownell Anthony, founded *the Women's Loyal National League* to campaign for the abolition of slavery in the United States of America, and also to secure equal legal and voting rights for American women. Elizabeth served as the aforesaid league's President, while Susan was its Secretary. However, the 1860's was consumed with *the American Civil War* and the abolition of slavery in the United States. Consequently, the all-important issue of American women's rights was considerably marginalised.

Throughout the 1860's, the abolition of slavery was one of the major political issues in the United States of America. In fact, the issue of slavery was a major sticking point in *the American Civil War (1861-1865)* between the belligerent parties (i.e., the United States of America and the Confederate States of America). Not to mention, the United States President, Abraham Lincoln (r. 1861-1865) had issued the *Emancipation Proclamation in 1863* formally announcing that the time of slavery was coming to its end. Furthermore, with the Union's decisive victory over the Confederacy in 1865, slavery came to be abolished throughout the United States of America. The final nail in the coffin for American slavery was the 1865 passage of *the Thirteen Amendment* to the United States Constitution.

As the aforementioned narrative demonstrates, during the 1860's, the political discourse and public debate shifted away from the equality for American women (including the Women's Suffragette Movement), and strongly towards the abolition of slavery and the advancement of racial equality. The time had arrived to abolish the immoral institution of slavery of the African American people, and secure the vote for the African American man. As a result, American women became somewhat alienated in the public discourse and domestic politics of the United States of America.

In response, *the American Equal Rights Association* (est. 1866) was formed. The purpose of this Association was to bring the issues of race, civil rights, ethnicity, gender, colour, and sex on an equal footing for all the American people. As a result, the aforesaid Association sought to promote the issue of equality of all the U.S. citizens, regardless of race, colour, ethnicity, gender, or sex, and also advocate for American women's equal right to vote. In practical effect, universal suffrage was the grand aim of *the American Equal Rights Association.*

In the year 1869, Elizabeth Cady Stanton and Susan Brownell Anthony formed another major association, known as *the National Woman Suffrage Association* (NWSA), with the aim of advancing the political and legal cause of women's right to vote in the United States of

America. Unfortunately, division, disagreement, and discord ensued, and several months after its establishment, an alternative association was formed, namely the American Woman Suffrage Association (AWSA) which was headed by American abolitionists and suffragettes, including Julia Ward Howe (1819-1910) and Lucy Stone (1818-1893). The two aforementioned associations (i.e., the AWSA and the NWSA), became rivals and competitors in the identical cause for women's suffrage, with each association adopting a different political and legal strategy. The rivalry of the NWSA and the AWSA is a classic textbook case of the pursuit of the same end, only by different means.

Beyond the presentation of public speeches at associations and passionate debates at conventions, Elizabeth also focused on writing about the social injustices that American women confronted in the modern American society. In connection with Susan Brownell Anthony, Matilda Joslyn Gage, and Ida Husted Harper, Elizabeth co-authored the History of Woman Suffrage, a six-volume book that was published from 1881 to 1922. Elizabeth was primarily involved in the writing of the first three volumes of this seminal text. In addition, Elizabeth was one of many learned women that were involved in co-authoring the Women's Bible (1895). The Women's Bible openly challenges the orthodox, institutionalised, traditional, and conservative religious views on the role, identity, and status of women in the modern American society.

In the 1870's, Elizabeth was employed as a lecturer at the Boston Lyceum Bureau. During Elizabeth's tenure at the Boston Lyceum Bureau, she gave informative lectures on the female and male sex, women's rights, co-education, marriage, divorce, the oppression of women, and critical interpretations of Bible Studies. In many respects, Elizabeth was a polymath. Elizabeth was well learned and deeply knowledgeable of the pivotal issues that were of prime importance to women in the nineteenth century American society.

In the year 1890, Elizabeth Cady Stanton, along with Susan Brownell Anthony, Alice Stone Blackwell, and Lucy Stone were all instrumental figures in the merger of *the National Woman Suffrage Association* and *the American Woman Suffrage Association*. The new institution was known as *the National American Woman Suffrage Association* (NAWSA) and it was established on 18 February 1890. The disappointing conventional reality was that American women remained subject to religious, political, legal, economic, educational, and social inequalities in the United States of America. This dismal reality meant that the 'common ground' for American women's causes, far outweighed the 'initial differences' in opinions and divergent thoughts amongst the leading American suffragettes.

In addition, the passage of *the Fifteenth Amendment* to the United States Constitution, which was passed, and subsequently ratified by the United States Congress on 26 February 1869 and 3 February 1870, respectively, now ensured the vote for the African American man. As a result, *the Fifteenth Amendment* fundamentally changed the political calculation for the two aforesaid women's associations (i.e., the NWSA and the AWSA). The public debate was now no longer about the two critical elements of the abolition of slavery and the African American man's right to suffrage, it was now all about securing American women's rights! The hour of the African American man had come, and now it was the hour of American women that was upon the United States of America. Thus, the establishment of *the National American Woman Suffrage Association* served to unite the many American suffragettes in the furtherance of their common endeavour.

Throughout the 1890's, which were the later years of Elizabeth's life, she remained politically active with the promotion of the Women's Suffrage Movement. Furthermore, in the year 1898, Elizabeth published her memoirs *Eighty Years and More.* Elizabeth's extraordinary life narrative demonstrates that an American woman, who was without the proper and formal legal education, possessed an equally brilliant mind as any American man. In fact, Elizabeth was well able to understand the advanced principles of jurisprudence and abstract concepts of the United States law, which allowed her to make such a positive and effective contribution to the greater American Women's Suffrage Movement.

On 26 October 1902, Elizabeth passed away from heart failure in New York City, the United States of America. Elizabeth was 86 years old at the time of her death. Elizabeth was buried alongside her husband, Henry Brewster Stanton at the Woodlawn Cemetery in the Bronx, New York City. Elizabeth's beloved daughter, Harriot Eaton Stanton Blatch (1856-1940), continued the struggle for women's rights in Great Britain and the United States of America. Short of two decades after Elizabeth's death, the United States Congress passed *the Nineteenth Amendment* to the United States Constitution on 4 June 1919, which was later ratified by the United States Congress on 18 August 1920, granting American women the legal right to vote.

In 1973, Elizabeth Cady Stanton was inducted into the United States National Women's Hall of Fame. Furthermore, in 2020, on the 100th anniversary of the passage of *the Nineteenth Amendment*, the Women's Rights Pioneers Monument designed by American sculptor, Meredith Bergmann was unveiled at Central Park in New York City. This monument portrays Elizabeth Cady Stanton in the company of the two famed American women's rights activists, Susan Brownell Anthony and Sojourner Truth.

Lucy Stone (1818-1893)

Lucy Stone was born on 13 August 1818 in West Brookfield, Massachusetts, the United States of America. Lucy's father was Francis Stone, and her mother was Hannah Matthews. Lucy came from a family of nine children, regrettably, two of her siblings did not survive childhood. Most of Lucy's early life was spent on the family farm located at Coy's Hill in West Brookfield. Unfortunately, Lucy's first experience of the inequality between man and woman, and the existence of sex discrimination was in her own household. The prime example herein being that Lucy's mother was treated poorly by Lucy's father. Not to mention, the household's affairs and finances were strictly managed by her father, Francis Stone, who imposed his unquestionable will in all matters, great and small. As a result, Lucy's mother, Hannah Matthews had no autonomy, agency, or liberty in her marriage or household.

At the age of sixteen, Lucy began to teach in order to earn an income and save money to attend college in the future. Regrettably, Lucy was paid significantly less than her male counterparts for the identical teaching work that she performed. In the year 1839, at the age of twenty-one, Lucy attended Mount Holyoke College in South Hadley, Massachusetts, where she studied for one semester, however, Lucy discontinued her studies. Lucy also briefly studied at the Wesleyan Academy (now known as Wilbraham and Monson Academy) in Wilbraham, Massachusetts, a co-educational institution. In preparation for Lucy's entrance examination into college, she studied at the Quaboag Seminary in Warren, Massachusetts, where she learnt the Greek and Latin language, as well as Greco-Roman Philosophy.

Lucy passed her college entrance examination with a commendable score. Subsequently, in the year 1843, at the age of twenty-five, Lucy matriculated at Oberlin College in Ohio. Oberlin College was one of the first colleges to admit American women (and African American men) to study and graduate with a college degree in the United States of America. During Lucy's memorable time at Oberlin College, she became good friends with Antoinette Louisa Brown (1825-1921), who went on to become an abolitionist and suffragette. In order for Lucy to financially support herself throughout her studies at college, she secured teaching work as a student. Lucy graduated with a college degree on 25 August 1847, she became the first American woman from Massachusetts to graduate with a college degree.

Following the completion of Lucy's formal education, she became involved in public speaking and speech writing. Most notably, Lucy worked tirelessly to advocate for the abolition of slavery in the United States of America, and she also promoted American women's rights in the modern American society. Throughout Lucy's lifetime of advocacy, she was directly or indirectly involved in several eminent social and political institutions, such as:

- *the Massachusetts Anti-Slavery Society*
- *the American Anti-Slavery Society*
- *the Seneca Falls Convention*
- *the Rochester Women's Rights Convention*
- *the New England Anti-Slavery Society*
- *the American Woman Suffrage Association*

- *the Women's Loyal National League*
- *the American Equal Rights Association*
- *the New England Woman Suffrage Association*
- *the National American Woman Suffrage Association*
- *the World's Congress of Representative Women*

Initially, the pursuit of the institution of marriage was not of prime importance to Lucy Stone, however, in the year 1853, American human rights activist and women's rights campaigner, Henry Browne Blackwell commenced courting Lucy. Henry remained adamant and persistent in his courtship endeavours, a delicate process that lasted well over twelve months. Over this period of time, the two parties exchanged views on love, marriage, human nature, individual personality traits, sexuality, sexual intercourse, pregnancy, property rights, children, financial control, autonomy, liberty, and bodily integrity. Clearly, Lucy was not going to leave the fine details of their relationship to chance. For Lucy, marriage was much more than love.

After several rounds of communication and negotiation, Lucy and Henry finally came to a mutually agreeable understanding, a meeting of the minds and hearts. In the end, a valid consensus was reached between Lucy and Henry, in which their marriage was seen as a 'partnership of equals'. On 1 May 1855, Lucy married Henry Browne Blackwell. One of the articles of their marriage agreement was that Lucy kept her surname, she did not take the title Mrs. Blackwell, period. On 14 September 1857, Lucy and Henry had a daughter whom they named Alice Stone Blackwell. In 1859, Lucy was pregnant with her second child, this time she was expecting a baby boy, however, she had a miscarriage on this most unfortunate occasion.

During Lucy's lifetime of untiring work on the Women's Suffrage Movement, she cooperated with many leading suffragettes, including American educator and temperance reformer, Frances Elizabeth Caroline Willard (1839-1898), American women's rights advocate, Abigail Scott Duniway (1834-1915), American women's rights activist, Rachel Foster Avery (1858-1919), American women's rights leader, Carrie Chapman Catt (1859-1947), American publisher and journalist, Josephine St. Pierre Ruffin (1842-1924), American social reformer, Susan Brownell Anthony (1820-1906), and American author and poet, Julia Ward Howe (1819-1910). Lucy's final public appearance was at *the World's Congress of Representative Women* (1893) held in Chicago, the United States of America.

In the year 1893, Lucy was diagnosed with stomach cancer. As a result, Lucy was unable to further participate in important social events, public gatherings, prominent speeches, and organised activities in relation to the Women's Rights Movement. On 18 October 1893, Lucy passed away from stomach cancer in Dorchester, Boston, Massachusetts, the United States. Lucy was 75 years old at the time of her death. In accordance with Lucy's personal wishes, upon Lucy's death, her body was cremated. Lucy's cremation took place at the Forest Hills Cemetery in Boston, Massachusetts.

Lucy's trailblazing legacy, pioneering reform work, and honourable memory were survived by her daughter, Alice Stone Blackwell (1857-1950), who continued the moral struggle for women's rights across the United States of America. Lucy's legacy was honoured across the United States of America in several ways. In 1968, the United States Postal Service issued a U.S. 50 cent commemorative stamp in Lucy's honour. Furthermore, in 1986, Lucy was inducted into the United States National Women's Hall of Fame. Last but not least, in the year 1999, the

Massachusetts State House unveiled a bust of Lucy in recognition of her vast contribution to the modern American society.

Her Majesty Queen Victoria (1819-1901)

Her Majesty Alexandrina Victoria was born on 24 May 1819 at Kensington Palace, London, England. Victoria's father was Duke of Kent and Strathearn, Prince Edward. Victoria's mother was Princess Victoria Mary Louisa of Saxe-Coburg-Saalfeld. Upon Victoria's birth, she was fifth in line to the English throne, however, a royal succession crisis witnessed Victoria become the Queen of England at the young age of eighteen. Regrettably, Victoria's father died when she was only eight months old.

During Victoria's childhood years, she was privately educated at her home. Victoria was tutored by the Right Reverend George Davys (1780-1864), and Baroness Louise Lehzen (1784-1870). Victoria learnt how to play the piano, and she also received private lessons in arithmetic, astronomy, geography, modern history, moral teachings, natural history, and Western philosophy. In addition, Victoria learnt a number of languages beyond English, including French, German, Italian, and Latin.

On 20 June 1837, upon the death of His Majesty King William IV (r. 1830-1837), Alexandrina Victoria was proclaimed the Queen of England. Victoria was only eighteen years old at the time of her coronation, and she was destined to reign as sovereign of England for the next 63 years and 7 months. Victoria's coronation was effectuated on 28 June 1838 at

Westminster Abbey in London, England. Given the young age at which Victoria had become the Queen of England, the earlier years of her reign as sovereign were greatly influenced by the Whig Prime Minister, the Right Honourable Lord Melbourne (r. 1834, 1835-1841). In addition, as Her Majesty Queen Victoria was unmarried upon her coronation as the Queen of the United Kingdom, in accordance with the dictates of custom, she resided with her mother in the earlier years of her rule as sovereign.

On 10 February 1840, Queen Victoria married Prince Albert of Saxe-Coburg and Gotha at the Chapel Royal, Saint James Palace in London, England. Queen Victoria and Prince Albert's marriage was founded on mutual love and affection, however, in line with social conventions of the time, it also served an immediate purpose, Queen Victoria no longer had to reside with her mother! Following the royal couple's marriage, Prince Albert became the more influential advisor in Queen Victoria's life, he effectively replaced the Right Honourable Lord Melbourne. Not to mention, Prince Albert was also a positive force in Queen Victoria's life. Most notably, Prince Albert earnestly attempted to improve Queen Victoria's strained relationship with her mother. In addition, Her Majesty Queen Victoria and Prince Albert had nine children during the course of their marriage. From 1840 to 1857, the royal couple had four boys and five girls.

Following Her Majesty Queen Victoria and Prince Albert's eventful marriage, not all of royal life was smooth sailing. On 10 June 1840, a young unemployed Londoner by the name of Edward Oxford attempted to assassinate Her Majesty Queen Victoria, however, he was unsuccessful. In fact, during Her Majesty Queen Victoria's lifetime, a total of eight assassination attempts were made against her life, none of the assassins were successful in their ignoble cause.

1861 was a year of terrible tragedy and great personal loss for Her Majesty Queen Victoria. On 16 March 1861, Queen Victoria's mother, Princess Victoria Mary Louisa of Saxe-Coburg-Saalfeld passed away at the age of 74. In addition, Queen Victoria's spouse, Prince Albert passed away on 14 December 1861 from typhoid fever. Prince Albert was only 42 years old at the time of his death. Needless to say, Her Majesty Queen Victoria was heart-broken and devastated by the loss of two influential and important figures in her life.

The devastating grief of death, in particular, that of Queen Victoria's spouse of twenty-one years, psychologically impacted the remainder of Queen Victoria's life in several ways. In fact, Her Majesty Queen Victoria entered into a terminal state of mourning, from which, in many respects, she never totally recovered. For example, consider Queen Victoria wore black clothes for the remainder of her life, her outer attire reflected her inner sombre mood. In addition, Queen Victoria became more secluded and isolated in her daily living, she avoided public gatherings and high-profile events. Last but not least, Queen Victoria turned to comfort food and writing to gain solace and personally cope in her immeasurable grief. In fact, Queen Victoria kept a private journal from a very young age until the later years of her life, and she wrote daily. Most notably, Queen Victoria's private diaries constitute some 141 volumes in length!

For the majority of Queen Victoria's remaining years, she spent her time between Windsor Castle in Windsor, England and Balmoral Castle in Aberdeenshire, Scotland. During the 1860's, Her Majesty Queen Victoria had a close friendship with her Scottish personal attendant, John Brown. In many respects, John was the Queen's confidant and favourite personality. Queen Victoria and John conversed often, and Queen Victoria shared many of her private thoughts, intimate feelings, and personal concerns with him.

In matters of foreign affairs, Her Majesty Queen Victoria ruled England during the height of the British Empire. For example, consider that in the Indian subcontinent, after the events of *the Indian Mutiny of 1857*, the civil administration and government of India was transferred from the East India Company to the British Crown. Furthermore, in the year 1877, Her Majesty Queen Victoria was also proclaimed the 'Empress of India'.

In addition, Queen Victoria also worked closely with both the democratically elected governments of Prime Minister Benjamin Disraeli (r. 1868, 1874-1880) and William Ewart Gladstone (r. 1868-1874, 1880-1885, 1886, 1892-1894). Furthermore, there were a number of foreign wars fought during Queen Victoria's reign as sovereign of the United Kingdom. For example, consider *the Anglo-Zulu War 1879* and *the Second Anglo-Afghan War 1878-1880*. Last but not least, Her Majesty Queen Victoria also entertained a close relationship with Abdul Karim (also known as the *Munshi*). Abdul was the Queen's personal attendant; he was a gentleman of Indian origin. In fact, Abdul served Her Majesty Queen Victoria diligently for close to fourteen years, until her death in 1901.

On 22 January 1901, Her Majesty Queen Victoria passed away due to a cerebral haemorrhage. Queen Victoria died at the Osborne House in the Isle of Wight, England. Queen Victoria was 81 years old at the time of her death. Queen Victoria was buried at the Frogmore Royal Mausoleum in Berkshire, England. Her Majesty Queen Victoria's legacy is truly universal in its reach. For example, consider the following record:

- Two of the six Australian states are named in Queen Victoria's honour, namely, Queensland and Victoria.
- Zimbabwe's largest lake is named Victoria Falls.
- The Victoria Cross was issued in 1856 to recognise acts of courage and bravery.

- The Victoria Memorial in India is dedicated to the Empress of India.
- Queen Victoria was a recipient of foreign honours from Brazil, Ethiopia, France, Mexico, Portugal, Prussia, Russia, and Spain.
- Queen Victoria was a recipient of several British honours. In addition, Queen Victoria was the Founder and Sovereign of the Order of the Star of India, the Royal Order of Victoria and Albert, Order of the Crown of India, Order of the Indian Empire, Royal Red Cross (RRC), Distinguished Service Order (DSO), and the Royal Victorian Order (RVO).

Susan Brownell Anthony (1820-1906)

Susan Brownell Anthony was born on 15 February 1820 in Adams, Massachusetts, the United States of America. Susan's father, Daniel Anthony was a farmer, cotton mill owner, Quaker, abolitionist, and temperance advocate. Susan's mother was Lucy Read Anthony. Susan came from a family of seven children, and she was a child prodigy. Not to mention, Susan learnt how to read and write by the early age of three. Furthermore, Susan was raised in accordance with Quaker traditions, morals, doctrines, principles, values, and beliefs. Most importantly, Susan grew up with a strong sense of personal independence, moral righteousness, and the equality and dignity of all people.

In 1826, Susan attended a local district school in New York, however, she received an inacequate education as a result of her sex. Consequently, Susan's father, Daniel Anthony accommodated Susan's educational needs in a home school environment, where he taught Susan himself. In the year 1837, Susan attended a Quaker boarding school in Philadelphia, however, her tenure as a student was abruptly ended due to the outbreak of a United States financial crisis known as *the Panic of 1837*. As a result, Susan's family was unable to continue to financially support Susan's higher education endeavours.

Given the dire socio-economic change in Susan's family fortunes and the onset of extenuating circumstances, Susan began to work as a teacher in order to earn a living. During this time, Susan also assisted her father in repaying his overdue debts. In 1839, Susan began to teach at the Eunice Kenyon's Friends' Seminary in Rochelle, New York. Thereafter, in the year 1846, Susan transferred to the Canajoharie Academy in Rochester, New York, where she was employed as Headmistress of the Female Department. Susan directly experienced the dismal reality of economic inequality during her time as a female teacher. For Susan was paid considerably less than her male counterparts, for the performance of teaching work of equal value.

In the year 1849, Susan ended her career in the Teaching Profession. From thereon, Susan became involved in the pressing issues effecting the modern American society, including the abolition of slavery, the African American man's right to vote, temperance activities, the Women's Suffrage Movement, and the advancement of women's political, legal, civil, and economic rights. In 1852, Susan attended a convention known as *the Sons of Temperance* in Albany, New York, where she learnt first-hand about the damaging impact of alcohol on men and women in the modern American society, however, as a woman, Susan had no agency and influence in the aforesaid Convention. In fact, Susan was not even permitted to speak, instead, she was told by the Chairperson that it was her proper place to sit and listen at *the Sons of Temperance* Convention.

Eventually, Susan, in connection with Elizabeth Cady Stanton (1815-1902), became directly involved in the Women's Suffragette Movement and the Women's Temperance Movement. In 1853, the two American suffragettes jointly founded *the Woman's State Temperance Society*, and Elizabeth became its founding President, whereas Susan went on to become the first Secretary of the aforesaid Society. In addition, also in the year 1853, Susan attended *the World's Temperance Convention* which was held in New York City. Not to mention, the most basic civil right of women to publicly speak at this Convention was itself a most contentious issue.

Beyond Susan's considerable involvement in the Temperance Movement, she was also actively involved in the struggle for securing the employment rights of female teachers in the modern American society. For example, consider that Susan attended a meeting of *the New York State Teachers' Association* in 1853, where she continued to advocate for equal pay for equal work, regardless of sex. In addition, Susan was also a staunch advocate for the admission of African American people into American schools and colleges.

The remainder of Susan's activist work was predominantly focused on the abolition of slavery and the Women's Suffrage Movement. In the year 1852, Susan attended *the National Women's Rights Convention* held in Syracuse, New York. Furthermore, in the year 1856, Susan became involved with the all-important work of *the American Anti-Slavery Society* (est. 1833). Unfortunately, not all of Susan's activist work was admired. For example, consider that throughout Susan's time as a social activist, she encountered strong opposition and resistance from American abolitionists and women's rights supporters, for advocating the right of women to seek a divorce from their husband.

In the year 1863, Susan, in connection with American writer and women's rights activist, Elizabeth Cady Stanton (1815-1902), founded *the Women's Loyal National League*. The aforesaid League advocated for the abolition of slavery in the United States of America. Inevitably, there came a conflicting point in the parallel advocacy of several competing social issues, that were all of great importance in the political discourse of the nineteenth century American society. These social issues included, the African American people's emancipation from slavery, the legal right of the African American man to vote, and the American Women's Suffrage Movement, which demanded that American women also be given the legal right to vote.

The inherent conflict involved prioritising the aforesaid social issues, all of which were important, however, it was clear that within the American Political Establishment, there would soon emerge the will and resolve to address certain issues before other issues. At the time, it strongly appeared that the 'Woman Question' will be deferred, thereby, degrading the status of women in the modern American society. As a consequence, in the year 1866, at the proceedings of *the Eleventh National Women's Rights Convention*, Susan proposed a formal resolution to merge the African American's Rights Movement with the American Women's Suffragette Movement, by establishing *the American Equal Rights Association*. This was a strategic decision proposed by Susan, by uniting the several social issues into one association, the select issues concerning American women were no longer 'competing', but rather 'cooperating' for resources, influence, power, and ultimately, social change in the United States of America.

As the name of *the American Equal Rights Association* suggests, the merger of the African American issues with the American women's rights issues, was meant to 'consolidate' the political debate and enhance the 'equality' narrative of the two equally important movements. The grand objective was to extend civil, political, and legal rights to all the American people, regardless of one's sex, colour, race, income, wealth, education, religion, gender, ethnicity, or any other discriminatory factor. In addition to Susan, other prominent American abolitionists and women's rights activists, who formed an important part of this newfound Association included, Lucy Stone (1818-1893), Lucretia Mott (1793-1880), and Frederick Douglass (1818-1895).

In the year 1868, Susan and her activist colleague, Elizabeth Cady Stanton founded a weekly newspaper, *the Revolution*. This American newspaper reported on the Women's Suffrage Movement, women's rights, the United States' domestic politics, discrimination faced by American women, women's pay inequality, and it also advocated for legal reform in the U.S.' Divorce Laws. The newspaper was financed by American entrepreneur, George Francis Train, and its first print issue was dated 8 January 1868. Unfortunately, over the course of the next two years, *the Revolution* became commercially unviable, and it was sold to American writer and women's rights activist, Laura Curtis Bullard (1831-1912). Ultimately, *the Revolution* ceased print publication in the year 1872.

In the year 1869, divergent views began to emerge in the senior leadership ranks of the leading American women's suffragettes, as a result, deep-rooted fissures also began to emerge on how to proceed forward with the Women's Suffrage Movement. Ultimately, there was a break in the movement, Elizabeth Cady Stanton and Susan Brownell Anthony forged ahead with *the National Woman Suffrage Association* (NWSA), while Julia Ward Howe and Lucy Stone founded a separate organisation known as *the American Woman Suffrage Association* (AWSA). The split in the Women's Suffragette Movement was a classic case of distinctions and disagreements along the basis of sex, gender, race, and political affiliations.

In the early 1870's, the grand strategy to advocate for women's suffrage in the United States of America adopted a 'legal' dimension. Most notably, Susan and other American suffragettes began to register to vote for upcoming elections, and then the suffragettes attempted to cast their vote on election day. For example, consider the United States Presidential Election of 1872 which was held on 5 November 1872. In the aforesaid election, Susan Brownell Anthony was arrested for casting her vote in Rochester, New York.

Now according to Susan, the legal basis for her vote was already provided for in 1868 by *the Fourteenth Amendment* to the United States Constitution of 1787, which explicitly states that ... 'no State shall make or enforce any law which shall abridge the privileges or immunities of citizens of the United States', with the key operative word here being 'citizens', a gender neutral and inclusive term. By definition, the term 'citizen' rightly implied there was no legal basis for American women, who were citizens of the United States, to be denied the vote in the United States of America. Most disappointingly, as the 1873 legal case of *the United States v. Susan B. Anthony* demonstrated, as with many aspects of *the United States Constitutional Law*, it was a nuanced matter of legal interpretation.

Susan's criminal trial was heard in a United States Federal Court, and it was presided over by Justice Ward Hunt (1810-1886). Susan utilised the court proceedings as a public platform to advocate for social change and create greater awareness of the Women's Suffrage Movement across the United States of America. By the act of voting, Susan was found guilty of violating *the Enforcement Act of 1870*. Consequently, Susan was sentenced to pay a fine of USD $100, however, in protest Susan categorically refused to pay the fine, and in fact, she never did!

In 1876, Susan worked with her close friend and suffragette activist, Elizabeth Cady Stanton on authoring an authoritative history of the Women's Suffrage Movement, a multi-volume work which was later published as *the History of Woman Suffrage*. Beyond the national struggle for women's right to vote at home, and the countless hours devoted to writing, Susan was also an active participant in the many international associations and conventions pertaining to the Women's Rights Movement. For example, Susan was involved with *the International Council of Women* (est. 1888), *the World's Congress of Representative Women* (est. 1893), and last but not least, *the International Woman Suffrage Alliance* (est. 1904) which was later renamed as *the International Alliance of Women*.

On 13 March 1906, Susan passed away from heart failure and pneumonia in Rochester, New York, the United States of America. Susan was 86 years old at the time of her death. Susan was buried at Mount Hope Cemetery in Rochester. Susan is one of the most pioneering and influential figures in the modern history of the Women's Suffrage Movement. Susan's towering legacy is honoured in countless ways. For example, consider that in 1950, Susan was inducted into the Hall of Fame for Great Americans. Furthermore, in the year 1973, Susan was inducted into the United States National Women's Hall of Fame.

In 2020, the United States President, Donald Trump (r. 2017-2021), pardoned Susan Brownell Anthony for voting illegally, however, the President of the National Susan Brownell Anthony Museum and House, declined to accept the U.S. President's pardon offer, as it would have served to retroactively legitimise and validate the legal proceedings against Susan.

Elizabeth Yates (1845-1918)

Elizabeth Yates (Elizabeth Oman) was born in the year 1845 in Caithness, Scotland. The historical details surrounding Elizabeth's early life are scant. Elizabeth immigrated to New Zealand with her Scottish family in the year 1853. Elizabeth's father was George Oman, and her mother was Eleanor Lannigan. Furthermore, Elizabeth had a younger sister named Eleanor Oman. Upon Elizabeth's family's immigration into New Zealand, they lived in Onehunga.

On 15 December 1875, Elizabeth married a Master Mariner by the name of Captain Michael Yates at Saint Peter's Church in Onehunga, New Zealand. Elizabeth and Michael had no children during the course of their marriage. In the 1880's and early 1890's, Michael was intimately involved in the domestic politics of New Zealand, first as a local Councillor, and then as a Mayor in the Onehunga Borough Council. For Elizabeth's part, she was an active participant in the Women's Suffrage Movement in New Zealand. In addition, Elizabeth also participated in the sessions of the Auckland Union Parliament.

In the year 1892, Elizabeth's husband's health deteriorated, consequently, he decided to resign from his position as Mayor. As a result, in 1893, Elizabeth accepted the nomination for the public Office of the

Mayor of Onehunga. Following Elizabeth's intense political campaign, she narrowly defeated her opponent, F. W. Court in the election held on 28 November 1893. Elizabeth's election victory was marginal, she secured her position as Mayor by an extremely slim majority of only thirteen votes. That is to say, Elizabeth won the Office of Mayor by 120 votes to 107! In addition, the Office of Mayor also granted Elizabeth the distinguished title of 'Justice of the Peace'.

By winning the 1893 election, Elizabeth made history, and not only in New Zealand, but throughout the modern world. That is to say, Elizabeth became the first woman to be sworn into the Office of the Mayor of Onehunga on 16 January 1894. Elizabeth was sworn into Office before the New Zealand Supreme Court Judge, His Honour Edward Tennyson Conolly (1822-1908). In addition, Elizabeth also became the first Lady Mayor in the British Empire. As a result, New Zealand's Premier, the Right Honourable Richard John Seddon (r. 1893-1906), and Her Majesty Queen Victoria (r. 1837-1901), both congratulated Elizabeth on her momentous political achievement.

Elizabeth's time as Lady Mayor was not without controversy and disagreement. A number of Elizabeth's fellow Councillors and town Clerks resigned in formal protest of her appointment as Mayor. Not to mention, Elizabeth's governance style and direct personality were often criticised, she was considered autocratic, dictatorial, and undiplomatic. Some Council members simply opposed every proposal that Elizabeth submitted, without due consideration to its merits. To make matters more challenging, Elizabeth was not very fond of following the established rules of procedure at Council meetings. Put simply, Elizabeth was not of the New Zealand Political Establishment, and she intended to initiate change, rather than promote the status quo in New Zealand.

Despite Lady Mayor Elizabeth Yates' noteworthy accomplishments during her time in public Office, her tenure as the Mayor of Onehunga was short-lived. In the following election, which was held exactly one year later, on 28 November 1894, Elizabeth was defeated by a considerable margin while she recontested her position as the incumbent Mayor. However, Elizabeth's 1894 election defeat did not result in the end of her political career.

Several years later, Elizabeth was appointed Councillor of the Onehunga Borough Council, a position that she held from September 1899 until April 1901. In the capacity of a Councillor, Elizabeth's track record of achievements included: significant improvements to the local fire brigade, major upgrades to public roads and footpaths, and enhancements to public utilities. In spite of Elizabeth's short-lived tenure in New Zealand politics, she demonstrated herself to be a competent Mayor and effective Councillor. Elizabeth even earnt the admiration and respect of her many critics, including local Councillors and town Clerks, who once thought that she would amount to nothing purposeful or constructive in the world of politics.

The social pressures and high expectations of public life performed a significant role in the deterioration of Elizabeth's physical and mental health. In the later years of Elizabeth's life, she suffered from alcoholism and dementia. Regrettably, the health issues that Elizabeth experienced gradually became worse, and consequently, she required psychiatric intervention. In the year 1909, Elizabeth was committed to the Auckland Mental Hospital in Avondale. Elizabeth remained institutionalised at the aforesaid mental hospital until her death on 6 September 1918. Elizabeth was 73 years old at the time of her death. Elizabeth was buried next to her late husband in the Saint Peter's Anglican Churchyard in Onehunga.

In its historical, social, political, and economic context, Elizabeth's life narrative is most encouraging for any man or woman to make a positive contribution to public life, that is to serve their local community, town, county, state, or country. Elizabeth was a charismatic leader, one that was far ahead of her time, not only in her thoughts, values, beliefs, and actions, but also in her many achievements. In fact, it is entirely reasonable to propose that Elizabeth established new standards for the fair and equitable participation of women in New Zealand politics. Most notably, Elizabeth encouraged New Zealand women to take hold of the moral high ground on civic responsibility. Last but not least, Elizabeth promoted the greater participation of women in the political process of this democratic and liberal nation-state, New Zealand.

Kate Sheppard (1847-1934)

Kate Sheppard (Catherine Wilson Malcolm) was born on 10 March 1847 in Liverpool, England. Kate's father was Andrew Wilson Malcolm, and her mother was Jemima Crawford Souter. Kate was English born; however, she was of Scottish heritage. Kate came from a family of five children, she had an older sister, and three younger siblings.

In the year 1862, Kate's father died at the age of forty-two. Several years later, Kate and the remainder of her family immigrated to New Zealand. On 8 February 1869, Kate accompanied by her mother and siblings, onboard the ship known as *Matoaka*, arrived at Lyttelton Harbour in New Zealand.

Kate integrated into the New Zealand society without too much effort. In fact, Kate's sister, Marie Beath, was already domiciled in the City of Christchurch. On 21 July 1871, at the age of twenty-four, Kate married New Zealand grocer and merchant, Walter Allen Sheppard. Thereafter, on 8 October 1880, Kate ad Walter had a son, whom they named Douglas Sheppard.

Kate was a firm believer in the equality of the sexes, and she whole-heartedly desired to secure the political, legal, civil, and economic rights of women to fully participate in all aspects of the modern New Zealand society. Kate's social work and public service in New Zealand strongly embodied both the spirit and letter of *feminism*. In Kate's earlier years, she was actively involved in the Trinity Congregational Church. Furthermore, in the year 1884, Kate was elected as Secretary of the Trinity Ladies' Association.

In the year 1885, American suffragette, activist, and missionary, Mary Greenleaf Clement Leavitt (1830-1912) from *the Woman's Christian Temperance Union* (WCTU) of the United States of America arrived in New Zealand. Mary worked closely with Kate on the Temperance Movement in New Zealand. Furthermore, also in 1885, Kate became a founding member of the newly established *New Zealand Women's Christian Temperance Union* (NZWCTU). Not to mention, in 1887, Kate was promoted to the influential senior leadership position of National Superintendent of the Franchise and Legislation Department of the NZWCTU.

The pressing issue of Temperance was a complex and multi-faceted one in New Zealand. The social, economic, legal, and political dimensions of Temperance adversely impacted women and young children across the country. From the legal perspective, New Zealand women were not permitted to seek a divorce from their husbands. Not to mention, in the case the husband filed for a divorce from the wife, the custody of children, by legal precedent, was almost always given to the father, not the mother of the children. From the economic perspective, the woman was usually a housewife and mother, thus, she was preoccupied with raising children and domestic duties, consequently, unable to earn her own income. This dismal economic reality made the wife subordinate to her husband. From the social perspective, New Zealand women with their dependent children, often ended up residing in toxic domestic environments, whereby, an alcoholic husband was in a position to physically, emotionally, and financially abuse the wife, and neglect their children's best interests. Last but not least, from the political perspective, New Zealand women did not have the vote, and nor did they have adequate representation in the New Zealand Parliament or government. Therefore, New Zealand women were unable to advocate for the social issues that profoundly affected their lives and children in the modern New Zealand society.

In addition, Kate was also part of *the Canterbury Women's Institute* (est. 1892), which advocated for the equality of New Zealand men and women. The aforesaid Institute had four departments, namely, Science, Health, Economics, and Literature, and it intended to cultivate lettered and learned women in the modern New Zealand society, women who were responsible and autonomous individuals in the modern society. At *the Canterbury Women's Institute*, Kate was in charge of the Economics Department. As part of Kate's important leadership position, she educated New Zealand women on the importance of managing their own finances, budgeting for the household, and securing paid employment in the New Zealand society.

In 1879, men aged twenty-one and above were given the legal right to vote in New Zealand, regardless of property ownership, however, women largely remained excluded from this legal right. Kate began to petition the

New Zealand Parliament on the issue of women's suffrage. Thereafter, a number of suffrage bills were introduced to the New Zealand Parliament in 1888, 1891, and again in 1892, however, on all three occasions the bills did not pass Parliament. Finally, after several years of campaigning and political advocacy, *the Electoral Act 1893* was passed by both houses of the New Zealand Parliament on 19 September 1893. The aforesaid Act of Parliament provisioned women with the newfound legal right to vote in New Zealand.

Within a few months of the passage of the aforesaid Act of the New Zealand Parliament, New Zealand women were able to cast their vote in the 1893 general election. The 1893 election was held on 28 November for the European electorates, and on 20 December for the Māori electorates. Kate's monumental advocacy work was recognised by the New Zealand Premier, Richard John Seddon (1845-1906), and also by the New Zealand Governor, Sir David Boyle Glasgow (1833-1915). In addition, by granting women the right to vote, New Zealand made history, it was the first country in the modern world to secure voting rights for women.

Beyond Kate's numerous and significant involvement in New Zealand's domestic politics and its society, she also travelled to Canada, England, and the United States of America, where she continued her important work as a political activist. Most notably, Kate supported the Women's Suffragette Movement on the international stage. For example, in the year 1894, Kate arrived in England, and thereafter, in 1895, she attended *the World's Woman's Christian Temperance Union* biennial convention which was held in the City of London.

In the year 1895, to further support the cause of the Women's Suffrage Movement, Kate, in connection with *the New Zealand Women's Christian Temperance Union,* founded the New Zealand newspaper known as *White Ribbon*. This newspaper was an instrumental platform to disseminate news and current affairs to the wider public on salient issues that impacted women. For example, consider Kate's influential writings on several topics, including health care, women's dress and clothing, women's education, women's political, civil, economic, and legal rights, divorce laws, and employment relations.

Furthermore, Kate was the editor, publisher, and manager of *White Ribbon* newspaper, which gave her unprecedented autonomy to freely write about women's issues in New Zealand. By any measure, Kate was a talented orator and persuasive writer, and this first-rate expertise translated into her remarkable editorship with the *White Ribbon* newspaper. In fact, prior to the establishment of the *White Ribbon* newspaper, Kate had written a concise pamphlet in 1888 titled *Ten Reasons Why the Women of New Zealand Should Vote*. Kate's 1888 pamphlet proposed convincing arguments for women's suffrage in New Zealand. In addition, in the year 1891, Kate had also edited the women's section in *the Prohibitionist*, a National Temperance magazine.

In 1896, Kate founded *the National Council of Women* in New Zealand, and she became its founding President. Kate held this senior leadership position at the aforesaid Council until the year 1903. Kate's resignation from the *National Council of Women* in 1903 was due to poor health. The aforesaid Council argued for greater rights of women in the institution of marriage, the right of women to manage their finances independently of their husbands, and the right of women to campaign for seats in the New Zealand Parliament. Furthermore, in 1909, Kate was elected as Honorary Vice-President of *the International Council of Women* (est. 1888).

Kate's personal life was not without struggle and despair. Regrettably, in the year 1910, Kate's son, Douglas Sheppard passed away from the onset of pernicious anaemia (also known as Addison's anaemia). Unfortunately, Douglas was only twenty-nine years old at the time of his death. In addition, on 24 July 1915, Kate's first husband, Walter Allen Sheppard died in Bath, England. Walter was 78 years old at the time of his death. Consequently, on 15 August 1925, Kate re-married a dear friend, author, and women's suffrage advocate, William Sidney Lovell-Smith (the gentleman authored the *Outline of the Women's Franchise Movement in New Zealand*). Kate also outlived her second husband, William who passed away on 16 April 1929.

On 13 July 1934, Kate passed away at her home in Riccarton, Christchurch. Kate was 86 years old at the time of her death. Kate was buried at the Addington Cemetery in Christchurch, New Zealand. Kate's monumental life and legacy was one of civic duty and public service. New Zealand is a more liberal and progressive country today, in large part, due to Kate's commendable actions, accomplishments, and achievements. In 1993, the Kate Sheppard Memorial was unveiled to commemorate Kate's invaluable contribution to New Zealand.

Emmeline Pankhurst (1858-1921)

Emmeline Pankhurst (Emmeline Goulden) was born on 15 July 1858 in Manchester, England. Emmeline's father was Robert Goulden, and her mother was Sophia Goulden. Emmeline came from an English family of ten children. Unfortunately, one of Emmeline's siblings passed away at the very young age of two. Both of Emmeline's parents were abolitionists and staunch supporters of women's rights, not to mention, they were also politically active. This dynamic family environment greatly influenced and impressed upon Emmeline's early reasoning, experience, and thought.

Emmeline was an avid reader in her childhood years. Some of the great texts that Emmeline read included the Odyssey by ancient Greek author and poet, Homer, the Pilgrim's Progress by English writer, John Bunyan, and the French Revolution: A History by Scottish historian, mathematician, and philosopher, Thomas Carlyle.

Emmeline's interest in women's suffrage started in her teenage years. Emmeline's mother, Sophia Goulden often perused the Women's Suffrage Journal, and Sophia also attended public meetings and important gatherings in relation to the advocacy of women's rights. On one occasion, at the young age of fourteen, Emmeline attended a public meeting on women's rights with her mother in Manchester, England. At the aforesaid meeting, the editor of the Women's Suffrage Journal, British suffragette, Lydia Ernestine Becker (1827-1890), was one of the prominent speakers in attendance. This women's rights meeting inspired Emmeline to dedicate her life to the just cause of the Women's Suffrage Movement.

Emmeline was educated at the École Normale de Neuilly in Paris, France, where she studied bookkeeping, chemistry, and embroidery, among other school subjects. Upon Emmeline's completion of her school education, she returned to her birth City of Manchester in England. In Manchester, Emmeline met English barrister and socialist, Richard Marsden Pankhurst. The two individuals had quite an age gap between them, with Richard being forty-five years old, whereas Emmeline was only twenty-one years old at the time. Notwithstanding the notable age difference, Emmeline and Richard developed mutual affection for one another, and they subsequently got married on 18 December 1879 at Saint Luke's Church in Weaste, Lancashire, England. Emmeline and Richard had five children in the period of ten years, namely, Christabel Pankhurst,

Sylvia Pankhurst, Francis Henry, Adela Pankhurst, and Henry Francis. The completion of Emmeline's formal education, her entrance into the institution of marriage, and the birth of her children, were only the end of the beginning for Emmeline.

In the year 1889, Emmeline Pankhurst founded *the Women's Franchise League*, its inaugural meeting was convened in Russell Square, London on 25 July 1889. The aforesaid League promoted the women's just cause for suffrage. Some of the League's notable members included English feminist, Josephine Elizabeth Butler (1828-1906), English women's rights activist, Elizabeth Clarke Wolstenholme Elmy (1833-1918), and American writer, Harriot Eaton Stanton Blatch (1856-1940).

During *the Women's Franchise League's* short-lived tenure, it made the case for 'married' women to be given the vote in local elections. Historically, it was considered custom that a married woman need not vote, as her husband 'voted on her behalf'. Furthermore, the aforesaid League promoted women's rights in matters of divorce and property inheritance. However, the League's inability to bring about much-needed political and legal reform in the modern English society was obvious to the prominent suffragettes. Thus, *the Women's Franchise League* was disbanded within a year of its inception, primarily due to disagreements amongst the several suffragettes on utilising 'conservative' in contrast to 'radical' methods to secure the vote for English women.

Regrettably, on 5 July 1898, Emmeline's husband, Richard suddenly passed away from the development of a gastric ulcer. Richard was 64 years old at the time of his death. The profound loss of Emmeline's husband meant a change in immediate responsibilities and priorities for her. Consequently, Emmeline resigned from her unpaid position at the Chorlton Board of Guardians, she relocated her residence to 62 Nelson Street in Manchester, and she secured paid employment as the Registrar of

Births and Deaths in Chorlton. These practical changes assisted Emmeline to earn a living, and also support her young children.

On 10 October 1903, Emmeline and her beloved daughter, Christabel Harriette Pankhurst founded *the Women's Social and Political Union* (WSPU). *The Women's Social and Political Union* employed strong militant means to advocate for radical change in the modern English society. Some of the WSPU's methods of protest included: civil disobedience, direct action, public demonstrations, marches, and the promotion of violence. All of these instruments were utilised by the WSPU to ensure increased public attention of the Women's Suffrage Movement. Emmeline and her fellow suffragettes were often imprisoned for their anti-social and radical methods of protesting; however, the determined and resolved English suffragettes vehemently continued their protests in prison by commencing hunger strikes. Consequently, a number of imprisoned English suffragettes were force-fed by the English prison authorities on numerous occasions. However, the unrelenting and determined suffragettes were eventually released from prison, in order to prevent the real possibility of death in police custody.

There were countless instances of the employment of peaceful protests and direct violence as means to achieve the end of women's suffrage by *the Women's Social and Political Union.* For example, consider that on 21 June 1908, the WSPU organised a large-scale protest at Hyde Park in London. The Hyde Park Public Demonstration was attended by some 500,000 protestors, and it is infamously known as 'Women's Sunday'. The dedicated protestors demanded votes for English women. Not to mention, the aforesaid protest march was attended by English women all across the City of London, however, the British Prime Minister, the Right Honourable Herbert Henry Asquith (r. 1908-1916), and the respected members of the British Parliament responded with total indifference.

Following the absence of any notable concern in the British Parliament, two of the WSPU members and suffragettes, Edith Bessie New (1877-1951) and Mary Leigh (1885-1978), turned to the employment of vandalism. Edith and Mary hurled rocks at the windows of 10 Downing Street, the official residence and office of the British Prime Minister, who at the time was the Right Honourable Herbert Henry Asquith. Alternatively, consider the actions of British-Scottish suffragette, Marion Wallace Dunlop (1864-1942), who inscribed an article of *the Bill of Rights 1688* on a wall of the House of Commons, namely, 'it is the right of the subject to petition the King, and all commitments and prosecutions for such petitioning are illegal'.

Furthermore, from 1909 onwards, the WSPU began to officially sanction the use of hunger strikes by its members. Hunger strikes was an effective political weapon that was employed by countless English suffragettes, including Emmeline Pankhurst, Marion Wallace Dunlop, Georgina Fanny Cheffins, Emily Wilding Davison, Janie Terrero, Helen MacRae, Myra Eleanor Sadd Brown, and Charlotte Blacklock. The greater purpose of the hunger strikes was to intensify the political campaign against the British government to immediately act on the British suffragette's demand for the right to vote.

Not to mention, the very act of hunger strikes was symbolised and glorified by the WSPU. Most notably, the WSPU awarded its members with prized 'Hunger Strike Medals' for their gallantry and defiance, while the WSPU portrayed the British government's inhumane and cruel treatment of the suffragettes as the torture of helpless and innocent English women. No doubt the politicisation of hunger-strikes was advantageous to the aims and objectives of the WSPU, most importantly, to secure greater support by the British people, and also to turn the tide of public opinion in the favour of its just and moral cause.

The unavoidable subject of women's voting rights had become such an important issue of public interest, that it could no longer be denied debate in the British Parliament. As a result, *the Coalition Bill of 1910* was introduced to the House of Commons which proposed a select minority of British women be granted the vote (i.e., wealthy land-owning British women), however, the British Prime Minister, the Right Honourable Herbert Henry Asquith had called for a general election on 18 November 1910, which prevented further discussions and debates over the proposed bill in the British Parliament. The WSPU understood the calling of an election at this pivotal time as a 'betrayal' of the all-important issue of women's rights, and commenced its own retaliatory action. The WSPU organised a protest outside the House of Commons known as 'Black Friday'. This confrontational public demonstration was attended by Emmeline, and some 300 of her fellow suffragettes. Following on from the events of 1910, *the Coalition Bill of 1911, and the Coalition Bill of 1912* were introduced to the British Parliament, however, both of them also failed to secure passage.

Between the years of 1910 to 1914, the WSPU continued, and rather intensified its militant campaigns against the British government. During this time, the WSPU's loyal members engaged in arson-related activities, the use of explosives, private property damage, and planned acts of vandalism to enact meaningful social, legal, economic, civil, and political change across Great Britain. In addition, Emmeline Pankhurst even attempted to personally present a petition to His Majesty King George V (r. 1910-1936) in 1914, however, she was arrested by police outside Buckingham Palace.

The British government intended to continue its heavy-handed response to the imprisoned English suffragettes hunger strikes campaign. Not to mention, the British prison authorities began to force-feed the

English women in prison. During this time, British public opinion was mounting against the British Prime Minister, Herbert Henry Asquith's liberal government's handling of the hunger strike issue. In particular, the inhumane treatment of the English women in prison began to attract public outrage and serious condemnation by the British people.

In a compromise, the British government passed *the Prisoner's (Temporary Discharge for Ill Health) Act 1913* (also informally known as *the Cat and Mouse Act)*. This Act of the British Parliament permitted the release of incarcerated English suffragettes on the grounds of ill health due to hunger strikes, however, upon the release and recovery of the English suffragettes, they were subject to being re-arrested, in order to serve out the remainder of their prison term. This compromise was simply a public relations exercise, and it did not address the substantive demands of the Women's Suffrage Movement. In fact, *the Cat and Mouse Act* only served to prevent the deaths of the English suffragettes in police custody.

The outbreak of *World War I (1914-1918)* changed the dynamics of the protracted fight for women's suffrage across Great Britain. Emmeline was a committed suffragette, however, she was no pacificist. Emmeline whole-heartedly supported the British war effort, and she encouraged British women to participate in domestic industry and employment, while the men went to fight on the frontlines of war across the European Theatre. During this time of war, a partial peace pact was endorsed between the British government and the WSPU, and in exchange for the WSPU's agreement to cease all militant activities during war time, the British government released the WSPU's suffragettes from prison.

In addition, Emmeline travelled abroad during *the Great War* years to promote the large-scale industrial mobilisation of women as part of the war effort. The foreign countries that Emmeline visited included Canada, Russia, and the United States of America. During and following the war effort, over the course of several years, the role of women in the first-world industrialised and modernised Western nations had irreversibly changed. It was now nigh impossible to continue to deny the fundamental and categorical principle of the equality of the sexes, and also deny the practical reality of the demonstrable capacities of the female sex to contribute to the public sphere of the twentieth century British society. After all, the female sex had also made significant sacrifices and equally contributed to the British war effort as part of *the Great War*.

Consequently, the Parliament of the United Kingdom passed *the Representation of the People Act 1918*. This was an Act of Parliament which extended the legal right to vote to British women, who were above the age of thirty years, subject to certain qualifications. Although the aforesaid Act did not provide universal suffrage for British women, it marked a significant step in the women's struggle for political and legal equality in the United Kingdom. In addition, the Parliament of the United Kingdom also passed *the Parliament (Qualification of Women) Act 1918*, which permitted British women, who were twenty-one years of age or older, the legal right to stand for election as a member of Parliament.

The two aforesaid Acts of parliament opened the pathway for women to finally become legally involved in British politics. In fact, Emmeline had already begun to make detailed preparations for women to enter into and influence the British Political Establishment. In 1917, Emmeline and her daughter, Christabel Harriette Pankhurst (1880-1958) founded *the Women's Party of Great Britain*, and Emmeline supported Christabel as a candidate in the upcoming 1918 general election. Unfortunately, Christabel, who represented *the Women's Party of Great Britain* was unsuccessful in her campaign to secure an election victory. Christabel was defeated by the Labour Party's candidate, John Davison, by a very small margin of some 775 votes. Thereafter, *the Women's Party of Great Britain* was dissolved in 1919.

In the year 1926, Emmeline became a member of *the Conservative Party*, however, her direct contribution to British politics was short-lived due to her forthcoming illness and death. The decades-long militant struggle for women's suffrage by Emmeline had led to accumulated bodily damage as a result of the numerous hunger strikes, several violent confrontations with the British police, countless instances of incarceration by the British state, and the use of militancy tactics in public protests and demonstrations. All of these notable factors had begun to take a noticeable toll on Emmeline's health and well-being.

In the year 1928, the English Women's Suffrage Movement had achieved its primary objective. The Parliament of the United Kingdom passed *the Representation of the People (Equal Franchise) Act 1928*. As a result, now all British women over the age of twenty-one, without any reference to property qualifications, had finally achieved the legal right to vote in the sovereign territory of the United Kingdom. The enduring struggle for the just cause of British women's right to vote had finally prevailed. The English suffragettes had finally secured victory, and their hard-fought and newfound legal right to vote in the twentieth century British society was irrevocably affirmed.

On 14 June 1928, Emmeline passed away from jaundice in Hampstead, London. Emmeline was 69 years old at the time of her death. Emmeline was buried at Brompton Cemetery in London. On 14 December 2018, a bronze statue of Emmeline Pankhurst was unveiled at Saint Peter's Square, Manchester in honour of her outstanding legacy and extraordinary contribution to the Women's Suffrage Movement.

Emmeline was more than just a feminist, political activist, and a suffragette, she was a leader of a movement, however, even Emmeline understood the principle that the individual is not larger than the movement. Esteemed historians and public intellectuals will continue to debate the legitimacy of the means and methods that Emmeline implemented in the WSPU's fight for the women's right to vote. However, there is no doubt that as long as the human civilisation endures, the long memory of history will continue to remember Emmeline Pankhurst in the ranks of some of the greatest free thinkers and change makers in world history, along with American activist, Rosa Louise McCauley Parks (1913-2005), English physician, teacher, and feminist, Sophia Louisa Jex-Blake (1840-1912), English physician and suffragette, Elizabeth Garrett Anderson (1836-1917), and British philanthropist, Angela Georgina Burdett-Coutts (1814-1906).

Ida Bell Wells-Barnett (1862-1931)

Ida Bell Wells-Barnett was born on 16 July 1862 in Holly Springs, Mississippi, the United States of America. Both of Ida's parents were slaves. Ida's father, James Madison Wells was a carpenter. Ida's mother, Elizabeth Warrenton was a cook and deeply religious individual. Consequently, by the bonds of birth, Ida was herself born into the institution of slavery. Notwithstanding the injustice of slavery present at Ida's birth, the United States President, Abraham Lincoln's *Emancipation Proclamation 1863* forever changed Ida's destiny.

Following the cessation of *the American Civil War (1861-1865)*, with the decisive victory of the United States of America (the Union) over the Confederate States of America (the Confederacy), *the Emancipation Proclamation* was enforced throughout the rebellious Southern states. Ida's newfound freedom at a very young age, meant a life of opportunity and newfound agency. Ida was educated at Rust College (est. 1866) in Holly Springs, Mississippi. In 1878, both of Ida's parents, and one of her younger siblings died from the outbreak of *the Yellow Fever Epidemic*. The tragic loss of Ida's parents meant that she had to shoulder considerable personal responsibility from an early age. Most importantly, Ida had to provide for her siblings. As a result, Ida secured employment as a teacher at a local school for African American students, and she lived with her parental grandmother, Peggy Wells.

In the year 1883, Ida, along with her two sisters moved to Memphis, Tennessee to live with her aunt, Fanny Butler. During Ida's time in Memphis, she worked in the Shelby County school system. Furthermore, Ida concurrently continued her formal education, she studied at Fisk University in Nashville, Tennessee, and also at Lemoyne-Owen College in Memphis. Despite the many challenges that Ida confronted in the early decades of her life, she possessed the admirable traits to create a productive and whole life, including a strong work ethic, diligent attitude, integrity, ethical conduct, honesty, respect, and courage.

During Ida's time as a teacher, she also took an interest in writing about the current issues that affected the African American people. Most notably, Ida wrote for influential newspapers, including *The Living Way* and *The Free Speech and Headlight*. In 1891, Ida was dismissed from her employment as a teacher by the Memphis Board of Education. Regrettably, Ida's dismissal was due to her criticism of the many inadequacies found in the African American schools in the Memphis region. From Ida's point of view, the schools were poorly funded, the conditions were sub-standard, and the learning institutions provided an inadequate education for the African American students.

Following Ida's prejudiced end to her teaching career, she dedicated herself to highlighting the grave injustices faced by the African American people in the United States of America. Ida's writings covered many aspects of perceived and actual inequality in the modern American society, including unfair criminal trails in the United States' law courts, the systematic and racial practice of lynching of the African American people, targeted violence against African Americans, the widespread incidence of the rape of African American women, and the unjust denial of African American people's constitutional rights and civil liberties.

In 1892, Ida published her findings on the lynching of the African American people in a pamphlet known as *the Southern Horrors: Lynch Law in all its Phases*. According to Ida, the lynching was racially motivated, and it represented widespread terror and violence by the Anglo-American people or Americans of European descent, in order to intimidate the African American people. The unjustified violence and systematic racism against the African American people was to prevent them from making substantial economic progress, and to keep them as second-class citizens in the United States of America. A large percentage of the Anglo-American and European-American people, intended to deny the emancipated African American people their rightful and equal access to political, economic, and legal power in the modern American society. In summary, ethnicity, race, colour, and sex mattered in the nineteenth century United States of America.

There is significant truth and logic in Ida's central premise. In fact, some of the Southern states passed new State Laws, or amended their State Constitution to disenfranchise the African American people. For example, consider that in early 1890's, the U.S. state of Mississippi adopted a 'literacy test' and a 'poll tax' to exclude previously eligible African American people from voting. These new voting requirements disproportionality affected the African American people, as a large number of them were uneducated and formerly slaves. In summary, the Anglo-American and European-American peoples disempowerment of the African American people's political, legal, and economic rights, allowed the white minority population to continue to rule and oppress the black majority population in the Southern states. Furthermore, from the 1870's up until the mid 1960's, disenfranchisement was further supported and reinforced by racial segregation in the modern American society by the existence and function of *the Jim Crow Laws*.

In 1893 and 1894, Ida travelled to Great Britain to promote the Anti-Lynching Campaign on the international stage. During this time, Ida worked closely with British Quaker and social activist, Catherine Impey (1847-1923), and Scottish suffragette, poet, and reformer, Isabella Fyvie Mayo (1843-1914). In addition, Ida also toured England, Scotland, and Wales, where she educated the local population on the horrors of lynching in the modern American society. Ida made convincing and compelling arguments that the African American people were victims of injustice, hate crimes, and racial discrimination. Ida's message resonated with the British people, prompting the initiation of much needed change and an urgent call to action.

As a result of Ida's advocacy work abroad, *the London Anti-Lynching Committee* was founded in 1894. The aforesaid Committee's prominent members included British philanthropist, temperance leader, and women's rights advocate, Isabella Caroline Somerset (1851-1921), British suffragette, pacifist, and feminist, Florence Balgarnie (1856-1928), British lawyer and politician, Sir John Eldon Gorst (1835-1916), British politician, Sir Joseph Whitwell Pease (1828-1903), and Irish nationalist, liberal historian, novelist, and politician, Justin McCarthy (1830-1912), and numerous other respected members of the British Parliament. This was the first Anti-Lynching Organisation in the world, and it most effectively employed British public opinion and criticism to confront American attitudes towards the immorality and injustice of lynching the African American people.

Ida continued her detailed examination of the lynching of African American people across the United States of America. In 1895, Ida published *The Red Record*, a 100-page pamphlet that investigated the immoral practice of lynching in the United States. *The Red Record* made use of empirical evidence, statistics, and fact-based findings to promote widespread awareness of the issue of lynching. This publication also relied upon and made use of reputable sources including newspapers, correspondents, and bureau reports to present a credible argument that lynching was a widespread issue in the modern American society.

On 27 June 1895, Ida married American lawyer, civil rights activist, and journalist, Ferdinand Lee Barnett at the Bethel African Methodist Episcopal Church in Chicago, Illinois, the United States of America. The married couple had four children together, namely, Charles Aked Barnett, Herman Kohlsaat Barnett, Ida Bell Wells Barnett, Jr., and Alfreda Marguerita Barnett. Ida's husband, Ferdinand Lee Barnett was an accomplished gentleman; however, he was also the founder of an American newspaper, *the Chicago Conservator*. *The Chicago Conservator* was the first African American newspaper which was founded in 1878. Ida had begun to write for *the Chicago Conservator* since 1893, from the time when the two journalists (i.e., Ida and Ferdinand) had collaborated on publishing a pamphlet highlighting the under-representation of the African American people at *the World's Columbian Exposition* in Chicago.

After Ida and Ferdinand's marriage in the year 1895, Ida became the editor of *the Chicago Conservator.*

Throughout Ida's lifetime, she continued to make countless contributions towards the struggle for racial equality in the United States of America. Ida was a prominent member of many national institutions and organisations that supported the just cause of equality for the African American people. Most notably, Ida was a member of *the National Equal Rights League*, and she also associated with *the National Association of Coloured Women's Clubs*. Not to mention, Ida was the first Secretary of *the National Afro-American Council*. Last but not least, Ida was also one of the founders of *the National Association for the Advancement of Coloured People*.

During the course of *World War I (1914-1918)* and beyond, Ida continued her work as an investigative journalist and civil rights activist. Ida worked with several influential figures, such as Jamaican political activist, Marcus Mosiah Garvey (1887-1940), American civil rights activist and newspaper editor, William Monroe Trotter (1872-1934), and African American political and social activist, Madam C. J. Walker (1867-1919). Furthermore, in 1917, Ida published investigative reports on *the East Saint Louis Race Riots* in the newspaper, *the Chicago Defender*. In addition, Ida personally examined the atrocities and crimes of *the Elaine Massacre of 1919* which had taken place in Philips County, Arkansas. Thereafter, Ida published an informative account that detailed her findings in relation to *the Elaine Massacre* in a book titled *The Arkansas Race Riot (1920)*.

In the later years of Ida's life, she began to write her autobiography, however, she never finished it before her untimely death. In the year 1970, Ida's autobiography was posthumously published by her daughter, Alfreda Barnett Duster (1904-1983). In fact, Alfreda was responsible for editing the publication. The finished work was titled *Crusade for Justice:*

The Autobiography of Ida B. Wells. In addition, Ida's youngest daughter, Alfreda went on to become a prominent civil rights leader and social worker in the City of Chicago. Not to mention, Alfreda worked tirelessly to support the many underprivileged people across the state of Illinois.

On 25 March 1931, Ida passed away from the onset of uraemia (chronic kidney disease). Ida was 68 years old at the time of her death. Ida was buried at the Oak Woods Cemetery in Chicago, Illinois. Ida's legacy has been honoured in the United Kingdom and the United States of America. In 1990, the United States Postal Service dedicated a U.S. 25 cent commemorative stamp in Ida's memory. Furthermore, in the year 2019, a blue plaque was unveiled in Ida's honour at the Edgbaston Community Centre in Birmingham, England. In addition, in 2020, Ida was posthumously awarded the Pulitzer Prize Special Citation for her detailed reporting on the lynching of the African American people. Last but not least, in 2021, a life-sized bronze statue of Ida B. Wells was unveiled at Downtown Memphis in Tennessee.

Ida's work as an investigative journalist, civil rights activist, women's rights activist, and newspaper editor was instrumental in creating a platform for public debate and urgent action on the political, legal, and economic inequalities that the African American people confronted in the nineteenth and twentieth century American society. By any measure, Ida was a talented and lettered gentlelady of remarkable social intelligence.

Furthermore, Ida's ability to gather information from a variety of credible sources, galvanise influential civil rights activists into action, establish new civil rights institutions, influence British public opinion to place due pressure upon the United States to act on lynching, and publish well-written articles and detailed pamphlets, all assisted to create greater awareness of the serious issues that impacted the African

American people, in a free, but not equal nineteenth and twentieth century American society.

Mary Eliza Church Terrell (1863-1954)

Mary Eliza Church Terrell was born on 23 September 1863 in Memphis, Tennessee, the United States of America. Mary's father was African American entrepreneur, businessperson, landlord, and millionaire, Robert Reed Church Sr. Mary's mother was a hairdresser and beauty salon owner named Louisa Ayres Church. Mary's parents were formerly African American slaves, however, they had both secured their freedom, and thereafter, successfully integrated into the modern American society. Mary's father had amassed the majority of his private fortune during *the 1878 Yellow Fever Epidemic* by taking advantage of the once-in-a-generation real estate opportunities that this epidemic had created in the Memphis Real Estate market.

Mary was born and grew up during a period of great change in the United States of America. Shortly before her birth, the United States President, Abraham Lincoln (r. 1861-1865) had issued *the Emancipation Proclamation* on 1 January 1863. *The Emancipation Proclamation* put an end to the immoral question of the legality of slavery in the United States of America. Furthermore, Mary was born in the midst of *the American Civil War (1861-1865)*, a fight over the soul and survival of the Union, in which the Union prevailed over the rebellious Southern states. On 9 April 1865, the Confederacy surrendered to the Union, marking the end of a bitter and decisive conflict in the history of the United States of America. Thereafter, Mary grew up during *the Reconstruction Era (1865-1877)*. This was a time which provided unprecedented opportunities for the African American people to advance in the modern American society. Last but not least, the outbreak of *the 1878 Yellow Fever Epidemic* in the United States was a challenging time in Mary's home town of Memphis, Tennessee.

Mary was initially educated at Antioch College Model School in Yellow Springs, Ohio. Thereafter, Mary completed the remainder of her school studies at Oberlin Public School in Oberlin, Ohio. After the completion of Mary's school studies in the year 1879, she matriculated in Oberlin College in Oberlin, Ohio. Most importantly, Mary did not undertake the standard two-year curriculum of study that was recommended for gentleladies at Oberlin College, instead, Mary undertook the four-year gentlemen's course of college study.

Thus, beginning in the year 1880, Mary studied the Classics and the Greek language. In 1884, Mary graduated with a Bachelor of Arts (BA) Degree from Oberlin College. Subsequently, Mary continued her college studies at the master's level for an additional four years. During Mary's Master's Degree, she studied Education (also at Oberlin College). In the year 1888, Mary graduated with a Master of Arts (MA) Degree from Oberlin College. During Mary's time at Oberlin College, she was an editor of the student newspaper, *the Oberlin Review*. Furthermore, Mary also made lifelong friendships with Anna Julia Haywood Cooper (1858-1964), and Ida Alexander Gibbs Hunt (1862-1957). Both Anna and Ida went on to become influential American activists in their own right.

In the year 1885, Mary commenced her career as a teacher at Wilberforce University in Wilberforce, Ohio. After two years Mary left Ohio, and in 1887, she accepted a position at the M Street Coloured High School in

Washington, D.C., where she taught Latin. During Mary's time as a teacher at the M Street Coloured High School, she met fellow teacher, Robert Heberton Terrell, who also happened to work in the Foreign Language Department. Mary and Robert established a very personable relationship, and Mary enjoyed assisting and working alongside Robert, whom she subsequently married. Mary also briefly travelled abroad to Europe, including England, France, Germany, Italy, and Switzerland, where she learnt French, German, and Italian.

On 18 October 1891, Mary married African American lawyer and school teacher, Robert Heberton Terrell. Mary's spouse, Robert went on to become a Justice of the Peace in Washington D.C., and also serve as a judge at the Municipal Court of the District of Columbia. The major challenge their marriage confronted was that of childbirth. Mary and Robert had four biological children, however, three of their biological children did not survive childbirth or infancy, the one surviving child was a girl named Phyllis Terrell who was born in 1898. The couple also adopted a niece named Terrell Church in the year 1905.

After Mary's marriage to Robert, she was forced to resign from her teaching position at the M Street Coloured High School. In the nineteenth century American society, once a gentlewoman married a gentleman, it was usually considered the definitive end of the married woman's professional career. Notwithstanding, the prevailing societal customs, norms, and traditions of the time in which Mary was a school teacher, she had much more to contribute to the advancement of the modern American society.

During Mary's time away from teaching, she became more involved as a social and political activist in the United States of America. Most notably, in the year 1892, Mary co-founded of the Coloured Women's League in Washington, D.C., and she worked alongside prominent African American activists, including Helen Appo Cook (1837-1913), Ida Bell Wells-Barnett (1862-1931), Anna Julia Haywood Cooper (1858-1964), Charlotte Louise Bridges Forten Grimké (1837-1914), and Mary Jane Patterson (1840-1894).

In the year 1895, Mary resumed her teaching career in a leadership capacity. Mary was appointed Superintendent at the M Street Coloured High School. Mary became the first African American woman to hold this prestigious leadership position at the aforesaid school. In addition, Mary's activist work raised her professional profile as a competent and able leader. Thus, also in the year 1895, Mary was appointed to the District of Columbia Board of Education. Once again, Mary was the first African American woman to secure such a respectable and esteemed position as an esteemed member of the aforesaid Board.

In the later years of Mary's life, she devoted a considerable amount of her time, energy, resources, knowledge, and expertise towards the African American people's protracted struggle for civil rights. In particular, Mary was an influential figure in the fight for African American women's legal rights. In 1896, Mary was involved in the formation of *the National Association of Coloured Women's Clubs*, and she served as the Association's founding President, from its inception in 1896 until the year 1901. Thereafter, Mary was bestowed the position of Honorary President of the aforesaid Association. Furthermore, in 1910, Mary co-founded *the College Alumna Club* (later known as *the National Association of University Women*) which promoted greater access to school and university education for girls and women, respectively.

Mary also became involved with the trailblazing work of *the National American Woman Suffrage Association* (est. 1890). Mary collaborated with some of the leading figures of the American Women's Suffragette Movement, including Susan Brownell Anthony (1820-1906), Elizabeth Cady Stanton (1815-1902), Frederick Douglass (1818-1895), and Ida Bell

Wells-Barnett (1862-1931). In addition, Mary also corresponded with influential figures, such as American historian, William Edward Burghardt DuBois (1868-1963), American educator and author, Booker Taliaferro Washington (1856-1915), and American social worker, Jane Addams (1860-1935).

Mary effectively utilised *the National American Woman Suffrage Association* as a politica. platform to raise greater public awareness of the injustices and inequalit'es that confronted the African American people, in particular, African American women. From Mary's direct experience and first-hand perspective, the African American woman, had to contend with four counts of discrimination in the modern American society, namely, prejudice on the grounds of sex, gender, colour, and race.

In the year 1892, Mary was elected as the first African American woman of *the Bethel Literary and Historical Society* (est. 1881). Not to mention, Mary was also affiliated with *the International Congress of Women*. In fact, on 13 June 1904, Mary gave a speech in the German language at *the International Congress cf Women's* Conference held in Berlin, Germany. Last but not least, Mary was also a founding member of *the National Association for the Advancement of Coloured People* (est. 1909).

Mary's perseverarce and dedication to the advancement of the just causes of gender and racial equality in the modern American society were truly limitless. In addition to working with prominent institutions, Mary continued her advocacy work, through writing in several reputable newspapers and journals, including *the African Methodist Episcopal Church Review*, *the Indianapolis Freeman*, *the Baltimore Afro-American*, *the Chicago Defender*, *the New York Age*, *the Voice of the Negro*, *Washington Evening Star*, and *the Washington Post*.

Furthermore, in 1940, Mary published *A Coloured Woman in a White World*. This book detailed Mary's personal experiences and notable struggles of being an African American woman in the Anglophone World, a minority constituent in the predominantly Anglo-American society of the United States of America. In the year 1948, Oberlin College in Ohio awarded Mary an Honorary Doctorate of Humane Letters. In addition, Mary also received two additional honorary degrees, one from Howard University in Washington, D.C., and another one from Wilberforce University in Ohio.

On 24 July 1954, Mary passed away from cancer in Anne Arundel General Hospital in Highland Beach, Maryland, the United States of America. Mary was 90 years old at the time of her death. Mary was buried at the Lincoln Memorial Cemetery in Washington, D.C. Mary had a true love of languages, and she was a committed teacher, dedicating herself to the noble cause of women's education. Mary was a truly personable, socially astute, intelligent, and talented gentlelady. In the final analysis, Mary is a role model for the present and future generations of men and women, on how to effectively create change in civil society, along the ideal principles of equality, justice, fairness, universal suffrage, liberty, equity, and peace.

Mary's legacy has and continues to be honoured throughout the United States of America. In 2009, the United States Postal Service issued a U.S. 42 cent commemorative stamp with an image of Mary Church Terrell. In 2018, Oberlin College, Mary's former college in Ohio, named its main library the Mary Church Terrell Main Library. Last but not least, in 2020, Mary was inducted into the United States National Women's Hall of Fame.

Elizabeth McCombs (1873-1935)

Elizabeth Reid McCombs (Elizabeth Reid Henderson) was born on 19 November 1873 in Kaiapoi, North Canterbury, New Zealand. Elizabeth's father was Daniel Henderson, and her mother was Alice Henderson. Elizabeth came from a family of nine children. Unfortunately, Elizabeth's father died when she was only thirteen years old.

Elizabeth was educated at Christchurch West School, and thereafter, at Christchurch Girls' High School. Elizabeth came from a family of politically active and educated women, and this influenced her early ambitions and interests in life. Two of Elizabeth's older sisters, Christina Kirk Henderson (1861-1953), and Stella May Henderson (1871-1962), both of whom were university educated, were directly involved in New Zealand's domestic politics. Furthermore, Christina and Stella also actively participated in the National Council of Women (NCW) to promote the legal equality of women.

Some of Elizabeth's early political involvement was with the New Zealand Women's Christian Temperance Union (NZWCTU), which was organised by the New Zealand social reformer, writer, and women's rights campaigner, Katherine Wilson Sheppard (1848-1934). At the NZWCTU, Elizabeth served as its Dominion Treasurer. Throughout Elizabeth's political career, she espoused socialist political doctrines. Elizabeth was left-wing in her political ideology, and she supported the Labour Movement in New Zealand. In addition, Elizabeth also served as Secretary of the Canterbury Children's Aid Society.

In the year 1903, Elizabeth married New Zealand politician, James McCombs. The married couple had two biological children, namely, Alison and Terence. Furthermore, Elizabeth and James also adopted two children, both of them were orphans. James was deeply involved in New Zealand's domestic politics, and Elizabeth and James' marriage also served to facilitate Elizabeth's access into prominent political circles. In many respects, James McCombs provisioned Elizabeth with newfound agency, resources, influence, relationships, and power in New Zealand's domestic politics. In fact, Elizabeth's husband, James was a prominent figure in *the Social Democratic Party*, before he joined the newly founded second *New Zealand Labour Party*, of which he was the founding President from 1916 to 1917. Thereafter, James served as the Deputy Leader of *the New Zealand Labour Party* from 1919 to 1923. Elizabeth's politically convenient marriage to James, and her early life experience with New Zealand's domestic politics, established Elizabeth for an impressive career of public service.

In the year 1921, Elizabeth was elected as Councillor to the Christchurch City Council, she became the second woman to occupy this noble position. During Elizabeth's tenure in public Office, she successfully convinced the aforesaid Council to establish a childcare centre, and also to construct women's rest rooms at the Cathedral Square in the City of Christchurch. From 1925 to 1934, Elizabeth was involved with the North Canterbury Hospital Board, where she advocated for improved work place conditions and higher remuneration for female nurses. In addition, Elizabeth also held several other influential positions during her distinguished career. Most notably, Elizabeth was the Chairperson of the Electricity Committee, where she demanded more competitive electricity prices for consumers. In addition, Elizabeth was also elected to the Christchurch Tramway Board, and she was a Committee member of the Mayor's Relief of Distress Fund. Furthermore, in the year 1926, Elizabeth was appointed as a Justice of the Peace (JP).

On 2 August 1933, Elizabeth's husband, James McCombs passed away from heart failure. Elizabeth passionately contested and vigorously campaigned for her husband's seat of Lyttelton, as his most able and natural successor. In the 1933 Lyttelton seat by-election, Elizabeth was victorious, and she became New Zealand's first female Member of Parliament (MP). Elizabeth won the Lyttelton seat by-election for *the New Zealand Labour Party* by a comfortable majority, winning 6,344 of the 10,347 votes that were cast.

Although Elizabeth had made political history in New Zealand, her time and opportunity to enact meaningful change was severely limited for two major reasons. First, *the New Zealand Labour Party* was in opposition at the time of Elizabeth's appointment as a Member of Parliament. Second, Elizabeth passed away in the year 1935. During Elizabeth's short tenure in the New Zealand Parliament, she advocated for a range of important issues, including sexual equality, changes to employment law, and greater rights for women in New Zealand's Marriage Laws. In addition, Elizabeth promoted discussion on a range of women's issues, such as equal pay for women, equal unemployment benefits for women, the recruitment of women into the New Zealand Police Force, and increasing the legal age of consensual marriage in New Zealand.

On 7 June 1935, Elizabeth passed away from asthma in Christchurch, New Zealand. Elizabeth was 61 years old at the time of her death. In 1935, Elizabeth was awarded the King George V Silver Jubilee Medal for her outstanding contribution to New Zealand politics, society, and the advancement of women's causes. Upon Elizabeth's death, her son, Sir Terence Henderson McCombs (1905-1982), succeeded to her parliamentary seat. Elizabeth's ground-breaking involvement in New Zealand politics set the stage for the entrance of the many New Zealand female politicians who have come after her in the late 1930's and 1940's, including Catherine Campbell Stewart (1881-1957), Hilda Ross (1883-1959), Mary Manson Dreaver (1887-1961), Mabel Bowden Howard

(1894-1972), Mary Victoria Cracroft Grigg (1897-1971), and Iriaka Matiu Rātana (1905-1981).

Lucy Burns (1879-1966)

Lucy Burns was born on 28 July 1879 in Brooklyn, New York, the United States of America. Lucy's came from an Irish-American family with Catholic beliefs and values. Furthermore, Lucy had seven siblings in her family. Lucy's father, Edward Burns was a banker, and her mother was Ann Burns. Lucy's father held liberal and progressive views. Most importantly, Lucy's father espoused equal opportunities for women, and he supported and financed his daughter's educational aspirations.

From 1890 to 1899, Lucy attended a preparatory school, namely, the Brooklyn Female Academy (later known as the Packer Collegiate Institute) in Brooklyn, New York. Thereafter, in the year 1899, Lucy matriculated at Vassar College in Poughkeepsie, New York, where she studied economics, and several languages, including English, French, German, Greek, and Latin. In the year 1902, Lucy completed her undergraduate studies at Vassar College. Subsequently, Lucy continued her higher education, she attended a private Ivy League university, namely, Yale University in New Haven, Connecticut during the years 1902 and 1903, where she completed her graduate studies in linguistics.

After studying at Yale University, Lucy briefly taught at the Erasmus Hall School in Brooklyn. Lucy did not find teaching to be her forte, and therefore, she decided to return to university to complete further graduate studies. In 1906, Lucy enrolled at the University of Berlin in Germany, where she studied linguistics for the next two years. In 1908, Lucy attended the University of Bonn also in Germany, continuing to study in her chosen field of linguistics until the year 1909. Thereafter, also commencing in the year 1909, Lucy enrolled in a Doctorate program of study at the University of Oxford in England; however, she did not complete her Ph.D. studies in linguistics and the English language, as she pursued the just cause of the Women's Suffrage Movement.

Lucy set aside her Doctor of Philosophy aspirations at the University of Oxford, and she joined forces with the well-known English suffragettes and political activists, namely Emmeline Pankhurst (1858-1928), and Christabel Harriette Pankhurst (1880-1958). Most notably, Lucy became a member of the *Women's Social and Political Union* (WSPU). From 1910 to 1912, Lucy was primarily responsible for the WSPU's civil disobedience operations in Edinburgh, Scotland. As a social activist and political protestor, Lucy was arrested by police on numerous occasions for disorderly conduct. Not to mention, Lucy also participated in hunger strikes while she was imprisoned, to create greater public awareness of the women's suffrage cause in the modern British society. Most notably, Lucy's loyal dedication and unbreakable commitment to the Women's Suffrage Movement, earnt her the Hunger Strike Medal awarded by the WSPU.

While Lucy was engaged in political activism with the WSPU, she met American suffragist, feminist, and women's rights activist, Alice Stokes Paul (1885-1977) in the City of London. The two suffragettes exchanged views on the women's rights campaign in the United States of America, and their perceived lack of progress in the United States' Women's Suffrage Movement under the leadership of American suffragette, physician, and Methodist minister, Anna Howard Shaw (1847-1919).

In the year 1912, Lucy and Alice returned to the United States to commence a more radical and liberal program to promote the Women's Suffrage Movement. Both Lucy and Alice joined *the National American Woman Suffrage Association* (NAWSA), and they were appointed as leaders in its Congressional Committee. Lucy and Alice's earlier involvement and previous experience with *the Women's Social and Political Union* (WSPU) in London, England, substantially influenced their unique leadership approach to political activism in the United States of America.

As senior leaders of *the National American Woman Suffrage Association*, Lucy Burns and Alice Paul promoted the employment of more militant tactics and radical methods to achieve the desired objective of women's suffrage in the United States of America. Furthermore, the two American suffragettes were instrumental in the organisation of *the Woman Suffrage Procession of 1913*. Not to mention, Lucy and Alice also called for holding the major United States' political parties in the United States Congress responsible for the lack of progress on the right to vote for American women, however, other influential leaders of the NAWSA did not readily agree with Lucy and Alice's bold proposals.

Differences in the American suffragette's leadership styles, personalities, agendas, and tactics on *the National American Woman Suffrage Association* Congressional Committee led Lucy and Alice to form a separate body within the NAWSA. Thus, Lucy and Alice founded *the Congressional Union of the National American Woman Suffrage Association*. In 1913, the NAWSA distanced itself from the Congressional Union's political activities. In addition, the use of the NAWSA's name was permanently removed from the Congressional Union's official title, and thereafter, it was simply known as 'the Congressional Union'. In 1914, after several months of unsuccessful negotiations, the NAWSA and the Congressional Union officially separated.

The disagreement and split between the NAWSA and the Congressional Union was not just a public relations crisis, it had immense political ramifications for the future trajectory of the American Women's Suffrage Movement in the United States of America. For example, consider that the Congressional Union supported *the Susan B. Anthony Amendment* (also known as *the Bristow-Mondell Resolution*) which advocated for a federal amendment to the United States Constitution for securing American women's legal right to vote. On the other hand, the NAWSA advocated for *the Shafroth-Palmer Woman Suffrage Amendment. The Shafroth-Palmer* amendment advocated for making the women's suffrage demand a state's legal right issue. Without a doubt, the proposed latter amendment made the ideal objective of securing women's suffrage across the United States of America a much more tedious and strenuous endeavour.

In the year 1916, American suffragette, Alice Paul proposed a bold new plan, the creation of a woman's political party in the United States of America. Alice's newfound idea held much logic. Simply put, promote advocacy on the issue of women's suffrage from within the United States Political Establishment. Lucy was a strong supporter of Alice's newfound idea for a political party, and *the National Woman's Party* (NWP) was founded in 1916. Rather than pursue the high and grand ideal that *the Congressional Union's* counterpart - the NAWSA - was committed to, that is, lobby and campaign *the Democratic Party* for political reform on women's legal right to suffrage, *the Congressional Union* adopted a more direct and radical approach to intervention in the United States' domestic politics.

Lucy was personally involved in all the major aspects of the newfound *National Woman's Party*. In fact, Lucy held many positions of important responsibility within the aforesaid party, including chief organiser, newspaper editor, architect of campaigns and protests, suffrage educator, and teacher. The NWP organised highly visible political protests in the

United States of America. For example, consider that in 1917 *the Silent Sentinels* (also known as *the Sentinels of Liberty*) was a group of American suffragettes who picketed outside the White House in Washington D.C. Specifically, *the Silent Sentinels* picketed outside the Executive Office of the President of the United States, which at the time was held by the U.S. President, Thomas Woodrow Wilson (r. 1913-1921).

In 1917, Lucy was arrested and imprisoned at the Occoquan Workhouse (also known as the Lorton Reformatory) in Lorton, Virginia for her organisation and involvement in picketing outside the White House. Despite Lucy's arrest and detention, she remained defiant in the noble cause for women's legal right to vote. Lucy also began a hunger strike as a tactic to protest while she was imprisoned. Beginning in the year 1917, Lucy was arrested a total of six times during her social and political activism in the United States of America. Not to mention, Lucy was also subject to many injustices during her time in prison, including force feeding, severe injuries, denial of medical attention, threats of physical harm by the prison guards, and solitary confinement.

With the military campaigns and battles of *World War I (1914-1918)* officially coming to a close, and international peace and stability secured for the present moment, the U.S. political debate returned to the pressing domestic question of women's suffrage. The U.S. President, Woodrow Wilson came to the inevitable realisation that the Women's Suffrage Movement was gaining popular public support with the American people. To add to the urgency of the women's suffrage issue, the highly publicised arrests and state incarceration of the American suffragettes was not helping the matter. The women's suffrage issue needed a political and legal resolution, and sooner rather than later.

In the year 1918, a constitutional amendment to grant American women the vote passed the United States House of Representatives, however, it narrowly failed in the United States Senate. On 30 September 1918, the U.S. President, Woodrow Wilson gave a historic speech before the U.S. Congress, in which he pledged his unconditional support for the right of American women to vote. Given the failure of the *Nineteenth Amendment* (also known as *the Anthony Amendment*) in 1918, the U.S. President, Woodrow Wilson requested that the United States Congress convene a 'Special Session' to reconsider the vote for American women in 1919.

Finally, after decades of struggle, strife, and suffering, the American suffragettes had secured their hard-fought victory! On 21 May 1919, the U.S. House of Representatives passed *the Anthony Amendment*, with 304 votes in favour to 89 against. Thereafter, on 4 June 1919, the U.S. Senate also passed *the Anthony Amendment*, with 66 votes in favour to 30 against. Over the course of the following year, individual U.S. states also ratified *the Anthony Amendment.* Of great importance, Tennessee became the 36th U.S. state to ratify *the Nineteenth Amendment* on 18 August 1920. Once the state of Tennessee had ratified *the Nineteenth Amendment*, the criteria of securing three-fourths of the individual U.S. states ratification of an amendment to the United States' Constitution had been secured. Thereafter, on 26 August 1920, the U.S. Secretary of State, Bainbridge Colby (1869-1950), officially certified *the Nineteenth Amendment* to the United States' Constitution. The long quest for American women's suffrage had now come to its successful conclusion.

Following this profound victory for the American Women's Suffragette Campaign, Lucy faded away into the countless pages and endless chapters of the United States' history. Lucy had made her outsized and heroic contribution to the just cause of women's right to vote, and therefore, she retired from the life of social and political activism. Thereafter, Lucy dedicated the remainder of her lifetime to spiritual and religious endeavours. Lucy returned to her Catholic faith, and she worked with the Catholic Church.

On 22 December 1966, Lucy passed away in Brooklyn, New York, the United States of America. Lucy was 87 years old at the time of her death. Lucy's monumental legacy is honoured through the United States. In 2020, Lucy was posthumously named an honouree of the National Women's History Alliance. Also in the year 2020, the Lucy Burns Museum in Lorton, Virginia was opened to the American public. The aforesaid museum is located on the historic site of the Occoquan Workhouse, where Lucy was imprisoned for her unrelenting and society-changing political activism.

In the final analysis, Lucy Burns was a free-thinker, intellectual, suffragette, movement leader, and women's rights activist. The historic passage of the Nineteenth Amendment to the United States' Constitution was in large part due to Lucy's untiring efforts and unbreakable commitment to the just cause of the American Women's Suffrage Movement.

Lucy is an inspiration to all the people of the modern world; her life narrative demonstrates that widespread change in the modern society can be enacted through meaningful action. While some of the other prominent American suffragettes may have disagreed with Lucy's methods, there is little doubt that her employment of militant tactics and direct action placed considerable pressure on the U.S. government to enact meaningful change. Lucy made her grand contribution towards the achievement of equal voting rights and greater political participation for American women in the modern American society.

Frances Perkins (1880-1965)

Frances Perkins (Fannie Coralie Perkins) was born on 10 April 1880 in Boston, Massachusetts, the United States of America. Frances' father was Frederick William Perkins, and her mother was Susan Ella Perkins. Frances also had a younger sister named Ethel Perkins Harrington. As a young child, Frances was curious. In fact, Frances often concerned herself with pressing social and economic issues that effected ordinary members of the modern American society. For example, when Frances was a little girl on one occasion, she asked her parents the question, why some American people were poor?

Frances came from a conservative American family, and her parents often dissuaded her from making such socio-economic inquiries. Instead, Frances' parents advised her that 'alcoholism' or 'laziness' were some of the major factors behind select American people's lack of progress or dire poverty in the modern American society. Notwithstanding Frances' parent's limited perspectives, Frances' well-intended concerns with important social and economic issues were a precursor of her life's all-important work in advocating for employee rights, involvement in social work, and important amendments to the United States' Industrial and Labour Laws. Not to mention, Frances' active participation in the United States government, the United States' domestic politics, and public policy initiatives

Frances was educated at the Worcester Classical High School in Worcester, Massachusetts. Following Frances' successful completion of high school, she matriculated at Mount Holyoke College, a college for women. During Frances' time at Mount Holyoke, she studied the natural sciences, in particular, chemistry and physics. In the year 1902, Frances graduated from Mount Holyoke with a Bachelor's Degree in Physics. Upon graduating from college, Frances went into the workforce. The majority of Frances' early life employment consisted of social work and teaching positions.

In the year 1907, Frances relocated to Philadelphia, and she commenced graduate studies in economics at the Wharton School of the University of Pennsylvania. Thereafter, Frances received a scholarship, which made possible her transfer to Columbia University in New York, where she studied sociology. In 1910, Frances graduated from Columbia University with a Master's Degree in Economics and Sociology. Frances' Master's Thesis was titled 'A Study of Malnutrition in 107 Children from Public School 51'.

In addition, also in the year 1910, Frances secured a leadership appointment as Head of the New York Office of *the National Consumers League* (est. 1899). Frances also understood the moral imperative to protect and advance employee work rights across New York. To this end, Frances was a strong advocate for improved workplace conditions for employees. For example, Frances supported maximum weekly hours of work for employees. Furthermore, Frances was supportive of minimum rates of remuneration for New York City's destitute people. For a brief period of time, Frances also taught at the Adelphi University in Garden City, New York.

The 25th of March 1911 proved to be an infamous date that brought Frances into her destiny. It was on this unfortunate day that a catastrophic fire broke out at the Triangle Shirtwaist Factory in Manhattan, New York City. The Triangle Shirtwaist Factory was a clothing sweatshop that employed mostly poor, young, unlettered, and immigrant women. Unfortunately, the factory doors were kept locked on the eleventh floor of the building, in order to prevent the factory workers from taking regular breaks. Regrettably, this most alarming occupational and health safety breach obstructed the workers escape route. To make matters worse, the Fire Brigade rescue ladders were unable to reach the eleventh floor of the building, in order to save the many trapped and helpless occupants. As a consequence, a total of 146 lives were tragically lost in the Triangle Shirtwaist Factory Fire.

Following this tragic incident at the Triangle Shirtwaist Factory, Frances resigned from her position at *the National Consumers League*. Frances knew that she had to make a difference and address the several employee work place rights issues that contributed to the Triangle Shirtwaist Factory Fire. Thus, Frances became the Executive Secretary for the Committee on Safety of the City of New York. During Frances' tenure on the aforesaid Committee, she was instrumental in the passage of the so-called '54-hour bill' which regulated employment law in New York City.

In the year 1913, Frances married Paul Caldwell Wilson, a gentleman who was employed at the New York City's Mayor's Office. The two had a child in 1915, however, their first child died. Subsequently, Frances and Paul had a daughter named Susanna Wilson, she was born on 30 December 1916. Frances' marriage and child did not hinder her professional career. In fact, Frances went on to make further contributions in the United States' domestic politics, and she also served at the highest levels of the United States' government.

In the year 1933, the U.S. President, Franklin Delano Roosevelt (r. 1933-1945) requested that Frances join his Presidential Cabinet. Frances agreed, and she proposed a number of labour programs and reforms, that she intended to advocate for during President Roosevelt's tenure. As a result, the U.S. President, Franklin Roosevelt nominated Frances as the U.S. Secretary of Labour; Frances went on to serve in this capacity for twelve years, from 1933 to 1945. In addition, Frances was the first

American woman to be appointed to a high-ranking cabinet position in the United States federal government. Frances was a true and committed socialist, and her policies reflected her commitment to the most poor, vulnerable, and marginalised people of the modern American society. In addition, Frances was instrumental in the enactment of President Franklin Delano Roosevelt's *New Deal* and the *Social Security Act of 1935*.

The death of the U.S. President Roosevelt in 1945, drew to a close Frances' successful tenure as the U.S. Secretary of Labour. Thereafter, Frances was asked by Roosevelt's successor, the U.S. President, Harry Truman (r. 1945-1953) to serve as Commissioner on the United States Civil Service Commission, which Frances did from 1945 until 1952. Furthermore, Frances wrote a memoir detailing her many experiences working with the Roosevelt administration, it was titled *The Roosevelt I Knew*. Upon the conclusion of Frances' distinguished career in public service and the U.S. federal government, she lectured at the New York State School of Industrial and Labour Relations at Cornell University. In addition, Frances was a Guest Lecturer at the Institute of Labour and Industrial Relations at the University of Illinois.

On 14 May 1965, Frances passed away at Midtown Hospital in New York, she had suffered a debilitating stroke. Frances was 85 years old at the time of her death. Frances was buried at the Glidden Cemetery in Maine, the United States of America. By any measure, Frances was a trailblazer in the United States twentieth century politics. Most importantly, Frances managed to achieve considerable success in many areas of the U.S civil society vis-à-vis political advocacy and legal reform in the United States Labour and Employment Laws.

As a result of Frances' untiring efforts and commitment to industrial relations and the regulation of labour, the United States has many stringent federal laws surrounding social security, federal minimum wage, the regulation of child labour, and unemployment insurance. Frances made history for many reasons, however, more importantly than making history, she utilised her present to make a decisive impact and shape the future of the U.S. civil society in a productive and constructive manner.

Jeannette Rankin (1880-1973)

Jeannette Pickering Rankin was born on 11 June 1880 at Grant Creek Ranch in Missoula County, Montana, the United States of America. Jeannette's father was John Rankin, a Scottish-Canadian immigrant and a mill owner. Jeannette's mother was Olive Pickering, a school teacher. Jeannette came from an American family of seven children, six sisters, and one brother. Unfortunately, one of Jeannette's sisters did not survive childhood. Jeannette was the oldest child in her family.

As a child, Jeannette was a diligent and talented individual. Not to mention, Jeannette often assisted with multiple household duties and chores, such as cleaning, farm work, sewing, and even carpentry. Jeannette completed her high school studies in Missoula in the year 1898. Following high school, Jeannette attended the Montana State University (now known as the University of Montana) to study biology. In 1902, Jeannette graduated from the Montana State University with a Bachelor of Science Degree. Unfortunately, in the year 1904, Jeannette's father, John Rankin passed away. Consequently, Jeannette assumed primary responsibility for the upbringing of her several younger siblings.

After the completion of Jeannette's Bachelor's Degree, she moved to New York City, where she studied, from 1908 until 1909 at the New York School of Philanthropy (now known as the Columbia University School of Social Work). After two years in New York City, Jeannette moved to Spokane, Washington where she temporarily performed social work. In addition, Jeannette also attended the University of Washington in Seattle. During Jeannette's time in Washington, she became involved in the United States' domestic politics, in particular, the American Women's Suffrage Movement.

After American women were afforded the right to vote in Washington state in 1910, Jeannette moved back to New York state in order to assist *the New York State Woman Suffrage Party*. In addition, Jeannette was also affiliated with *the National American Woman Suffrage Association* (NAWSA). Furthermore, Jeannette travelled to Washington, D.C. to intensely lobby the United States Congress on women's political, economic, civil, and legal rights. This was only the end of the beginning for Jeanette's political involvement in the United States of America.

In the year 1911, Jeannette was actively involved in the battle for women's right to vote in her home state of Montana. Not to mention, Jeannette had also become the President of *the Montana Women's Suffrage Association* (MWSA). In February 1911, Jeannette spoke at the Montana State Legislature in support of granting women the right to vote in Montana. After years of struggle and political advocacy, finally in the year 1914, women in Montana were granted the right to vote in State elections.

In 1916, Jeannette made history in the United States of America, she became the first woman to be elected to the U.S. House of Representatives. Jeannette utilised her newfound political agency in the U.S. House of Representatives to espouse her pacifist agenda and progressive political views. In addition, Jeannette also supported the American Women's Suffrage Movement, and she was an advocate for social welfare policies. Furthermore, Jeannette was against the United States involvement in *World War I (1914-1918)*. In fact, when it came to the decisive issue of the United States *1917 Declaration of War on Germany*, Jeannette casted her vote against war.

In the year 1939, Jeannette launched her second political campaign for a seat in the U.S. Congress on an anti-war agenda and the ideal promotion of *American Isolationism* in foreign affairs. In 1940, Jeannette was elected to the U.S. House of Representatives, she defeated her political opponent American attorney and lawyer, Jerry Joseph O'Connell (1909-1956) in the general election. Despite diplomatic endeavours, the many chaotic events of *World War II (1939-1945)* inevitably resulted in the United States of America and the Empire of Japan engaging in direct military conflict.

The state of direct armed conflict between the two Great Powers (i.e., Japan and the United States), was the result of the infamous Japanese surprise military attack on Pearl Harbour on 7 December 1941. Immediately thereafter, the United States voted on a *Declaration of War on the Empire of Japan* on 8 December 1941. Jeannette was the only elected member of Congress to vote against the aforesaid Declaration. The aforesaid War Resolution passed the U.S. House of Representatives with 388 Yea votes and one Nay vote, with the sole dissenting vote being that of Jeannette. Several days later, on a similar Declaration of War against Germany and Italy, Jeannette abstained from voting. While Jeannette was true to her high ideals and moral principles, her anti-war rhetoric and pacificist approach to foreign policy in the midst of *World War II (1939-1945),* ultimately ended her political career.

Following Jeannette's outsized contribution to the United States' domestic politics, she travelled multiple times to India. During Jeannette's visits to India, she became well acquainted with the doctrines and teachings of Indian independence leader, Mahatma Gandhi (1869-1948). Even in the later years of Jeannette's life, she remained active in her support for the Anti-War Movement in the United States of America. For example, Jeannette protested against the United States' involvement in *the Vietnam War (1955-1975)* by organising the Jeannette Rankin Brigade. The aforesaid Brigade was a coalition of some 5,000 committed American women that engaged in an anti-war march in Washington, D.C. in 1968. This large association of women marched from Washington Union Station to the U.S. Capitol Building. Upon their arrival, the women presented a peace petition to the Speaker of the United States House of Representatives, John William McCormack (1891-1980).

On 18 May 1973, Jeannette passed away in Carmel, California, the United States of America. Jeannette was 92 years old at the time of her death. Jeannette's legacy is remembered and honoured throughout the United States of America. In 1985, a bronze statue of Jeannette was erected by American artist, Terry Mimnaugh, it is placed at the National Statuary Hall Collection, the U.S. Capitol Building in Washington, D.C. Furthermore, in the year 1993, Jeannette was inducted into the U.S. National Women's Hall of Fame. In the final analysis, Jeannette was a true hero of peace, liberty, women's rights, equality, and justice.

Alice Paul (1885-1977)

Alice Stokes Paul was born on 11 January 1885 in Mount Laurel Township, New Jersey, the United States of America. Alice's father, William Mickle Paul I was the President of the Burlington County Trust Company, and he was an affluent businessperson. Alice's mother was American suffragette, Tacie Parry Paul. Alice came from a wealthy and privileged Quaker family. Furthermore, Alice had a younger sister, Helen Paul, and two younger brothers, William Mickle Paul II and Parry Haines Paul.

Alice's introduction to the Women's Suffrage Movement came from her mother, Tacie, who was a member of *the National American Woman Suffrage Association* (NAWSA). In addition, Tacie often attended the aforesaid Association's meetings, where contemporary issues that concerned American women were debated and discussed. With Alice being born into a Quaker family, she was raised in an environment that embraced equality of the sexes, equal education for girls, and the espousal of liberal values in the modern American society.

Alice was educated at Moorestown Friends School in Burlington County, New Jersey. Moorestown Friends was a private co-educational Quaker day school that was founded in 1785. From both the religious and social perspective of Quaker life, the aforesaid school embraced the noble principle of gender equality. This doctrine of equality between the sexes, both in the family home and at school, impressed upon Alice's values, thoughts, and beliefs, thus, shaping her attitudes and expectations of the role of women in the modern American society from a very young age. Upon the completion of Alice's school studies, in 1901, she matriculated at the Swarthmore College (est. 1864) in Swarthmore, Pennsylvania. While at college, Alice studied the natural sciences. In the year 1905, Alice graduated from Swarthmore College with a Bachelor's Degree in Biology.

After the completion of college, Alice performed social work for a short period of time in New York City, however, she soon became convinced that social work will not lead to change in the modern American society, at least not at the pace that Alice envisioned and desired. Thus, Alice decided to leave social work as a profession. Subsequently, Alice re-commenced her studies at the University of Pennsylvania in Philadelphia, Pennsylvania. This time Alice studied sociology, political science, and economics. In the year 1907, Alice graduated from the University of Pennsylvania with a Master of Arts (MA) Degree.

Also in the year 1907, Alice travelled to London, England, where she was inspired by the persuasive speeches and activist work of leading British suffragette, Christabel Harriette Pankhurst (1880-1958). As a result, Alice soon became involved with the activities of *the Women's Social and Political Union* (WSPU). During Alice's time in the City of London, she forged a close bond with American suffragette and women's rights activist, Lucy Burns (1879-1966). Most notably, Alice and Lucy later worked very closely together on the American Women's Suffrage Movement in the United States of America.

During Alice's time in England, she participated in several of the WSPU sponsored protests that led to her arrest by police, and her subsequent incarceration by the State. While Alice was affiliated with the WSPU, she also learnt the militant tactics and effective instruments of protest (i.e., organised marches, picketing, public demonstrations, the disruption of public speeches by political leaders, promotion of civil unrest, arson, violence, and vandalism). As a result, Alice became well acquainted with the employment of civil disobedience tactics while she was subjected to a number of State-sanctioned penalties and imprisonment. For example, consider Alice's use of hunger strikes in prison, and the non-payment of State-sanctioned fines. Alice's first-hand experience with the Women's Suffrage Movement in England, ultimately shaped her grand strategy and operational tactics for the American struggle for women's rights.

In the year 1910, Alice returned to the United States of America, and she joined *the National American Woman Suffrage Association* (NAWSA). Alice worked with the NAWSA to promote the political rights of American women and advance the American Suffragette Movement. Concurrently, Alice continued her university studies at the University of Pennsylvania, where she undertook a Doctorate Degree in the Arts and Social Sciences. Alice was awarded her Ph.D. in 1912, her Doctoral Thesis was titled 'The Legal Position of Women in Pennsylvania'. Thereafter, in the year 1913, Alice organised *the Woman Suffrage Procession* in Washington D.C. This notable public demonstration was meant to send a political signal to the incoming U.S. President, Woodrow Wilson (r. 1913-1921), that women's suffrage was an important bipartisan issue that most urgently needed to be addressed by the U.S. politicians and the United States' Congress.

Over the coming years, Alice's radical and militant approach to the American Suffrage Movement diverged from the more conservative and traditional approach to protest that was embodied by the NAWSA's senior leadership. Consequently, Alice, in connection with American suffragette, Lucy Burns (1879-1966), attempted to reconcile and accommodate the noticeable differences between themselves and the NAWSA. Most notably, Alice and Lucy created *the Congressional Union of the National American Woman Suffrage Association,* however, the NAWSA began to distance itself from the militant activities, and the use of more radical methods that were employed by Alice and Lucy. Ultimately, Alice Paul and Lucy Burns split completely from the NAWSA, and they went their separate ways with *the Congressional Union.*

One of the major irreconcilable differences between *the Congressional Union* and the NAWSA, was that the former promoted the original idea of a constitutional amendment, which was first proposed by Susan Brownell Anthony (1820-1906) and Elizabeth Cady Stanton (1815-1902). That is to say, a federal amendment to the United States' Constitution, in order to secure voting rights for American women (i.e., *the Susan B. Anthony Amendment*). Whereas, the latter promoted the objective of securing American Women's Suffrage on a State-by-State basis (i.e., *the Shafroth-Palmer Woman Suffrage Amendment*).

In 1916, Alice founded *the National Woman's Party* (NWP) in an attempt to more directly and forcefully intervene in the United States' Political Establishment. Alice worked closely with American suffragette, Lucy Burns (1879-1966) in the NWP's more radical and militant promotion of the American Women's Suffragette Movement. The NWP was involved in the organisation of several major protests, public demonstrations, and organised marches, including a 1917 picketing campaign at the White House in Washington D.C. This group of protesting American women were popularly known as *the Silent Sentinels* (also known as *the Sentinels of Liberty*). The United States' public interest and the American people's popular support for the Women's Suffragette Movement began to wax and wane throughout the long course of *World War I (1914-1918)*, however, Alice Paul remained persistent and steadfast in her endeavour to secure the legal right to vote for American women.

On several occasions, Alice was arrested and incarcerated at the Occoquan Workhouse (also known as the Lorton Reformatory) in Lorton, Virginia. On 20 October 1917, Alice was arrested, and following her arrest, she received a seven-month prison sentence for her involvement in public demonstrations and protests. This heavy-handed and State-sanctioned punishment was a categorical breach of Alice's legal rights pursuant to *the*

First Amendment of the United States' Constitution (est. 1787). In effect, Alice and her fellow suffragettes were 'political prisoners' in the United States of America.

During Alice's imprisonment at the Occoquan Workhouse, she was subject to harsh conditions and inhumane treatment. Most notably, Alice was stripped naked, and she had her hands chained above her head to the prison cell bars. In addition, Alice was also repeatedly beaten, force-fed, and assaulted by the prison guards. Alice went on a hunger strike to protest against her, and her fellow suffragettes, most unjust incarceration by the United States government. Notwithstanding the gravity of Alice's ill-treatment and the prison brutality that she endured; she had an unbreakable spirit. As a consequence, Alice continued to proceed forward with her just cause, entirely undeterred by the many struggles and countless privations that she confronted. Indeed, Alice was on the noble quest for the American woman's right to vote, and the enactment of meaningful change in the American society was the only plausible end in sight.

Growing United States public outrage and the turn of domestic public opinion, eventually prompted the American suffragettes release from the Occoquan Workhouse. Widespread U.S. media coverage and domestic press reporting also assisted in bringing the issue of the American suffragettes mistreatment to light. Some of the notable print publications that reported on the American Suffragette Movement included *the New York Times*, *the Washington Post*, and *the Boston Journal*. Not to mention, *the National Woman's Party's* in-house newsletter, *the Suffragist* also ensured greater proliferation of information on the American Women's Movement, in order to better educate the U.S. public about the women's protracted struggle for equality, liberty, and justice, and thus, and turn the tide of the U.S. public opinion.

The decisive issue of the Women's Suffrage Movement finally came to a vote in the United States of America. The U.S. President, Woodrow Wilson (r. 1913-1921) also began to publicly promote the moral cause of women's right to vote, which brought much needed influence to bear upon the Democratic and Republican political parties. After a failed attempt in 1918 to pass *the Nineteenth Amendment* in both the U.S. House of Representatives and the U.S. Senate, the issue was reconsidered in 1919. On the second occasion, both the U.S. House of Representatives and the U.S. Senate passed *the Nineteenth Amendment*. Shortly thereafter, in the year 1920, when Tennessee became the 36th U.S. state to ratify *the Nineteenth Amendment*, the aforesaid Amendment was officially incorporated into the United States Constitution, subject to the U.S. Secretary of State's procedural certification of the aforesaid Amendment. After a protracted fight, American women had now secured the legal right to vote in the United States of America.

After securing the passage of *the Nineteenth Amendment* in 1920, Alice knew that this political victory was only the start of the Women's Rights Campaign in the United States of America. Much more needed to be achieved in order for women to have a true sense of equality, autonomy, liberty, and justice in the modern American society. Thus, Alice in connection with American feminist, lawyer, and socialist, Crystal Catherine Eastman (1881-1928), sought to secure further constitutional amendments for women's equality. In effect, Alice and Crystal intended to make sex-based discrimination illegal in the modern American society.

In the year 1922, Alice attained her Law Degree from the Washington College of Law at the American University. During a time in the United States' history when the majority of American women did not receive an equal, or comparable, education to that of American men, Alice was an extremely well-educated woman. Most importantly, Alice earnestly put into practice the vast legal knowledge that she had attained, in order to enact profound and meaningful changes to the fabric of the modern American society.

Furthermore, in 1923, Alice and Crystal jointly drafted *the Equal Rights Amendment* (also known as *the Lucretia Mott Amendment*). Subsequently, Alice and Crystal presented the aforesaid Amendment to the United States Congress. It was not until the year 1972, that Congress passed *the Equal Rights Amendment*, however, it was then within the legal jurisdiction of the individual States to ratify this Amendment, for it to embody the force of law. Regrettably, it was not until the year 2020, that Virginia became the 38th State to ratify the aforesaid Amendment. While the key legal criterion of thirty-eight States (being the three-fourths of the fifty States requirement) needed to ratify the amendment to the U.S. Constitution was finally secured, the 1982 deadline for *the Equal Rights Amendment* to be ratified had lapsed a long time ago. As at 1 January 2020, the procedural and technical barriers continue to be addressed by the United States Congress, in order to rescind the 1982 ratification deadline, and thereby, permit *the Equal Rights Amendment* to be successfully ratified.

Beyond advocating for the women's cause in the United States of America, Alice also made monumental contributions to the international campaign for women's political, civil, economic, and legal rights. Most notably, Alice worked with *the United Nations* (est. 1945), and its affiliated commissions, such as *the United Nations Commission on Human Rights* (est. 1946). Not to mention, Alice was responsible for enshrining women's equality in *the United Nations Charter (1945)* and *the Universal Declaration of Human Rights (1948)*. These are important documents that form part of the contemporary body of International Law.

On 9 July 1977, Alice passed away in Moorestown, New Jersey, the United States of America. Alice was 92 years old at the time of her death. Alice was buried at Westfield Friends Burial Ground in Cinnaminson, New Jersey. In 1979, Alice was honoured for her lifetime contribution towards the American Women's Suffragette Movement by being posthumously inducted into the United States National Women's Hall of Fame. Furthermore, in 1995, the United States Postal Service issued a U.S. 78 cent commemorative stamp in Alice's memory. Last but not least, in the year 2012, the United States Mint issued a USD $10 gold coin, honouring Alice Paul, and the greater American Women's Suffrage Movement.

Sirimavo Bandaranaike (1916-2000)

Sirimavo Ratwatte Dias Bandaranaike was born on 17 April 1916 in Ratnapura, British Ceylon (present day Sri Lanka). Sirimavo was born into a wealthy and prominent Sinhalese family. Sirimavo's father was Barnes Ratwatte, a well-known politician. Sirimavo's mother was Rosalind Hilda Mahawalatenne Kumarihamy, a Ayurvedic physician. Sirimavo came from a family of six children, and she was the oldest child in her family. Sirimavo was educated at Ferguson High School in Ratnapura, followed by Saint Bridget's Convent in Colombo.

Following the completion of high school, Sirimavo became involved in social work. In fact, Sirimavo was part of many local initiatives involving the distribution of medicine, food, water, clothing, and the provision of other forms of material aid to the destitute Sri Lankan people.

Furthermore, Sirimavo also worked as a Treasurer at *the Social Service League*. This early life experience working in Sri Lankan communities and directly with the Sri Lankan people proved instrumental in Sirimavo's distinguished public career as a politician.

On 2 October 1940, Sirimavo married Oxford educated lawyer and British Ceylon politician, Solomon West Ridgeway Dias (S.W.R.D.) Bandaranaike (1899-1959) at the Mahawelatenne Walawwa. The married couple had three children together, two daughters and a son. Following Sirimavo's marriage to S.W.R.D. Bandaranaike, in the early 1940's, Sirimavo continued to generously contribute her time and effort to important social causes in British Ceylon. For example, consider Sirimavo joined *the Lanka Mahila Samiti* (i.e., the Lankan Women's Association). During Sirimavo's time at the aforesaid Association, she was involved in agricultural projects, disaster relief operations, girl's school education programs, family planning initiatives, advocacy for women's political rights, and the empowerment of uneducated, destitute, and rural Sri Lankan women. Sirimavo's social work was truly broad in its scope. In fact, Sirimavo was also associated with *the All-Ceylon Buddhist Women's Association*, *the Ceylon National Association for the Prevention of Tuberculosis*, and *the Nurses Welfare Association*.

Sirimavo's husband, S.W.R.D. Bandaranaike was active in the domestic politics of British Ceylon, he was a prominent member of *the United National Party* (UNP). However, on the astute judgement of Sirimavo, S.W.R.D. Bandaranaike was encouraged to resign from the UNP and establish *the Sri Lanka Freedom Party*. In the 1952 parliamentary elections, Sirimavo's spouse, S.W.R.D. Bandaranaike, was elected to the Parliament of Ceylon, and he became the Leader of the Opposition. Not to mention, in the 1956 general elections, the Right Honourable S.W.R.D. Bandaranaike secured the high public Office of the Prime Minister of the British

Dominion of Ceylon, however, his tenure as the Prime Minister was short-lived. Unfortunately, S.W.R.D. Bandaranaike was the victim of a planned assassination plot on 25 September 1959. S.W.R.D. Bandaranaike died the following day at the Colombo General Hospital due to his fatal wounds.

The death of Sirimavo's husband forever changed the dynamics of British Ceylon's politics and the nation's future trajectory. Not to mention, the infamous death of S.W.R.D. Bandaranaike was to become a destiny-shaping moment for Sirimavo in the very near future. Furthermore, the political fallout of S.W.R.D. Bandaranaike's death was a total catastrophe for the Sri Lankan government. A caretaker government was immediately established, it was headed by the Right Honourable Wijeyananda Dahanayake (1902-1997). Subsequently, general elections were held in March 1960, and *the United National Party* was victorious. As a result, Dudley Shelton Senanayake (1911-1973) became the Prime Minister, however, after several months in power, his political capital, old alliances, and key relationships all fragmented. As a consequence, new elections were held in July 1960, and *the Sri Lanka Freedom Party* won on this occasion. Sirimavo was elected as the 'Party President' of *the Sri Lanka Freedom Party* earlier in 1960, and she went on to become the Prime Minister of British Ceylon.

On 21 July 1960, Sirimavo Bandaranaike was sworn in as the first female Prime Minister in the modern world. Not only had Sirimavo made history in her own capacity, but so had this small island nation of British Ceylon. Sirimavo's appointment as Prime Minister continued to shape Ceylon's society, diplomacy, institutions, culture, politics, religion, language, foreign policy, and education for the next four decades. Indeed, Sirimavo was a dominant force in the twentieth century Asian politics, alongside some of the great leaders of the Asia Pacific, including Mao

Zedong of China, Jawaharlal Nehru of India, Ahmed Sukarno of Indonesia, and Lee Kuan Yew of Singapore.

Sirimavo's first term as the Prime Minister of British Ceylon was from 1960 until 1965. During Sirimavo's first term in public Office some of her notable accomplishments included: the nationalisation of important sectors of the economy, changing the official language to Sinhala, promoting amicable relations with China, India, and the Soviet Union, condemning South Africa's Apartheid Policy, and resolving the issue of the repatriation of stateless Tamils with India. In fact, *the Sirimavo-Shastri Pact of 1964* was a milestone diplomatic achievement that made tangible progress towards the resolution of stateless people of Indian origin domiciled in Sri Lanka. Notwithstanding Sirimavo's many notable accomplishments, she was defeated in the 1965 general elections. Thus, from 1965 to 1970, Sirimavo went on to serve as the Leader of the Opposition Party.

In 1970, Sirimavo was re-elected to a second term in public Office. Sirimavo continued her nationalist, socialist, pro-Buddhist, and pro-Sinhalese political agenda. Sirimavo's second term as Prime Minister lasted until 1977. During this time in public Office, Sirimavo navigated the politics of securing independence and sovereignty of British Ceylon from the United Kingdom. In 1948, Ceylon had been elevated to the status of 'Dominion' within the British Commonwealth. On 22 May 1972, Ceylon become the Democratic Socialist Republic of Sri Lanka, achieving its complete independence. As a result, Her Majesty Queen Elizabeth II of the United Kingdom was no longer the Head of State (i.e., sovereign) of Sri Lanka.

This monumental and seismic political event, was accompanied by many changes in Sri Lankan politics. Some of these changes included, the drafting of a new Constitution, the abolishment of the Senate, and the creation of the National State Assembly. In addition, Sinhala was the only official language of the Sri Lankan state, and Buddhism was promoted to the supreme religion of Sri Lanka. Furthermore, Sirimavo also pursued collectivisation of land by promoting land distribution and farming cooperatives. Sirimavo's ultra-nationalist government policies alienated minority groups, including, but not limited to Sri Lankan Anglicans, Catholics, Muslims, and Tamils.

In addition, Sirimavo continued to make good on Sri Lanka's bilateral relationship with the Republic of India. Following Sirimavo's aforesaid 1964 Pact with the Indian Prime Minister, the Right Honourable Lal Bahadur Shastri (r. 1964-1966), Sirimavo concluded a second Pact with the Indian Prime Minister, the Right Honourable Indira Gandhi (r. 1966-1977, 1980-1984) on 28 June 1974, known as *the Sirimavo-Gandhi Pact of 1974-*. This second Pact more fully resolved the outstanding question of the legality of Indian people residing in Sri Lanka. As settlement of this issue, a number of the Indian people in Sri Lanka were repatriated to India, while a number of Indian people were granted Sri Lankan citizenship.

Following Sirimavo's defeat at the 1977 general elections, Sirimavo remained as Party Leader of *the Sri Lanka Freedom Party* from 1977 to 1988. During this period, Sirimavo confronted several challenges to her reputation, character, and integrity. For example, consider in the year 1980, Sirimavo was subject to a Special Presidential Commission, this was to investigate legitimate concerns surrounding the abuse of power. At the 1989 general election, Sirimavo's performance merited her sufficient political capital to be appointed as the Leader of the Opposition, a post that she held until 1994.

For Sirimavo, family and political life were inseparable. Two of Sirimavo's children had risen to become important figures in *the Sri Lanka Freedom Party*, namely, her son, Anura P.S.D. Bandaranaike, and her daughter, Chandrika Bandaranaike Kumaratunga. Anura held right-wing political views, whereas, Chandrika was part of the socialist left-wing movement. As for Sirimavo, she preferred the Party's leadership be transferred to her daughter, Chandrika, as the two politicians had similar socialist views on government policy. Consequently, Sirimavo's son, Anura defected to *the United National Front Party*.

From 1994 to 2000, Sirimavo served her third and final term as the Prime Minister of Sri Lanka. Sirimavo's daughter, Chandrika Bandaranaike Kumaratunga was elected as the President of Sri Lanka in 1994, and Chandrika appointed her mother, Sirimavo as the Prime Minister in the same year. While mother and daughter agreed on the government policy front, they had their differences in leadership style, personality, and approach to political governance and political administration of the Sri Lankan state. In addition, over the course of the late 1990's, Chandrika came to prefer that a younger person with new ideas occupy the noble position of Prime Minister.

The political fallout between mother and daughter was diplomatically managed. Sirimavo ultimately resigned on 10 August 2000, she cited 'poor health' as her primary reason for leaving Sri Lankan politics. On 10 October 2000, Sirimavo passed away from the onset of a heart attack. Sirimavo was 84 years old at the time of her death. Sirimavo was buried next to her husband at Horagolla in Atthanagalla, Sri Lanka.

In the final analysis, Sirimavo was a bold and powerful force in the twentieth century Sri Lankan and world politics. Sirimavo's socialist and nationalist policies made her a popular politician with the majority of the Sri Lankan people. Not to mention, Sirimavo successfully navigated British Ceylon into full independence and inviolable sovereignty, and she also supported many admirable social causes along the way. Most notably, Sirimavo is admired for her courage, confidence, and conviction, she well understood the essential needs of her people in the poor Third World that is part of the Global South. At the time, British Ceylon was a backward nation that was emerging out of British colonialism. Not to mention, Sri Lanka is a small island country that is surrounded by Great Powers in the Asian region (i.e., China, and India). In this historical context, Sirimavo was well able to navigate the many nuances of international diplomacy, and she demonstrated great finesse as a national leader in the twentieth century world politics.

Despite Sirimavo's grand political accomplishments as a statesperson, where she clearly struggled was in the convergence of the distinct Sri Lankan people and the creation of strong harmony across the different ethnicities, faiths, backgrounds, religions, and races across Sri Lanka. Sirimavo had much difficulty in creating a truly 'intercultural' Sri Lanka. Sirimavo struggled to create a 'united' Sri Lanka out of the many different people. Consequently, this inequitable treatment and blatant discrimination, ultimately caused much bitter resentment and hostility amongst the Tamil population of Sri Lanka. Not to mention, economic inequality and racial discrimination were partially responsible for provoking the Tamil people into a civil war for statehood and independence. Indeed, history records the Tamil people's protracted struggle for identity and homeland known as *the Sri Lankan Civil War (1983-2009)*.

Indira Gandhi (1917-1984)

Indira Priyadarshini Gandhi was born on 19 November 1917 in Allahabad, the United Provinces of Agra and Oudh, British India. Indira's father was the renowned Indian anti-colonial nationalist leader, Jawaharlal Nehru (1889-1964), who later became the first Prime Minister of an independent and sovereign Republic of India, from 1947 to 1964. Indira's mother was Kamala Nehru.

During Indira's childhood years, she was educated at several schools, including the Modern School in New Delhi, Saint Cecilia and Saint Mary Christian Convent Schools, and the International School of Geneva. Thereafter, Indira studied at the *Vishwa Bharati* (now known as *Visva-Bharati* University) in Shantiniketan. Subsequently, Indira transferred her university studies to Somerville College at the University of Oxford in Oxford, England. At the University of Oxford, Indira studied history, however, she never completed her studies.

During Indira's time in Great Britain, she met her future spouse, Feroze Gandhi, who was also from Allahabad, India. At the time, Feroze was studying at the London School of Economics. On 26 March 1942, Indira and Feroze got married. The married couple had two sons, namely, Rajiv Gandhi and Sanjay Gandhi. Married life and young children did not inhibit Indira's involvement in India's domestic politics, which was facilitated by her father and the first Prime Minister of India, the Right Honourable Jawaharlal Nehru (r. 1947-1964).

As alluded to previously, Indira's association with Indian politics began in the early 1950's. When Indira's father, Jawaharlal Nehru became the first Prime Minister of an independent India, Indira became involved in the world of politics. In fact, Indira frequently served as Nehru's unofficial personal assistant, and she also accompanied the Indian Prime Minister Nehru on his official foreign trips. In 1955, Indira became a member of the Congress Working Committee (CWC). Furthermore, in the year 1959, Indira was elected as the President of the Indian National Congress (INC) (also known as the Congress Party).

Following the death of Indira's father, and the Indian Prime Minister, the Right Honourable Jawaharlal Nehru, Indira was appointed to *the Rajya Sabha* (the Upper Chamber of the Indian Parliament). Not to mention, Indira also served in Prime Minister Lal Bahadur Shastri's Cabinet as the Minister of Information and Broadcasting. On 11 January 1966, Indian Prime Minister Shastri (r. 1964-1966) passed away suddenly due to a cardiac arrest while he was overseas. Consequently, Gulzarilal Nanda became the acting Indian Prime Minister for thirteen days, following which Indira was sworn in as the Prime Minister of India on 24 January 1966. Indira was the third Prime Minister of an independent India, and its first female Prime Minister.

Indira served as the Prime Minister of India from 1966 until 1977, and thereafter, from 1980 until 1984. During the first half of Indira Gandhi's rule, she adopted popular socialist policies. This made sense, given India's relative economic poverty, agricultural backwardness, and illiterate and destitute population that needed to be provisioned with food, water, education, clothing, electricity, housing, medicine, and employment. Not to mention, at the time, independent India lacked mature domestic industries to support more liberal policies. The industrialisation and modernisation of India was very much in its early stages. As a result, Indira Gandhi moved to nationalise several of India's largest banking institutions, and she also abolished *the Privy Purse*, which had provisioned exorbitant payments by the Government of India to the Princely States of India.

During the 1970's, Indira promoted her political campaign on the popular cause of *Garibi Hatao* (Eradicate Poverty). This was an admirable socialist cause that strongly resonated with the countless common and poor people of an independent and democratic India. Furthermore, India's decisive victory in *the Indo-Pakistan War of 1971*, and the dissolution of East Pakistan, led to the creation of an independent and sovereign Bangladesh. This political reality served to create most favourable geopolitical conditions for Indira's strong popularity, and secure her mandate for re-election to public Office. In fact, India's military victory over Pakistan in 1971, earnt Indira Gandhi India's highest civilian honour, *the Bharat Ratna*, which was awarded to her in the year 1971.

In the earlier years of Indira's first term as Prime Minister, Indira's approach to politics and ideology was to continue in the footsteps of her learned father, the former Indian Prime Minister, the Right Honourable Jawaharlal Nehru. Indira espoused much of Nehru's political vision for a socialist, democratic, and economically independent India. From an economic perspective, Indira continued the organisation of *Five-Year Plans* to develop India's domestic industries and the national economy on a socialist basis. On the foreign policy front, Indira forged closer relations with the Union of Soviet Socialist Republics. During Indira's time in public Office, *the Indo-Soviet Treaty of Peace, Friendship, and Cooperation of 1971* was executed. The aforesaid Treaty served to strengthen the economic, military, cultural, and diplomatic relations between India and the Soviet Union.

In addition, Indira promoted *the Non-Aligned Movement* (NAM) in the twentieth century international politics. This novel political movement was designed to promote the neutrality of the NAM's member nation-states from the two Cold War Superpowers, the United States of America and the Union of Soviet Socialist Republics. Indira was also an influential statesperson at the Commonwealth Heads of Government Meeting (CHOGM). For example, Indira utilised this international political forum to condemn the South African Apartheid Regime, and she also called for economic sanctions and international boycotts by member states of the CHOGM against South Africa. Furthermore, Indira also advanced India's national security interests. For example, consider during the Right Honourable Indira Gandhi's Prime Ministership, India did not execute *the Treaty on the Non-Proliferation of Nuclear Weapons 1968-*. Furthermore, Indira Gandhi tacitly endorsed India's strategic pursuit of a Nuclear Weapons Program to acquire nuclear weapons for defensive purposes. In fact, during Indira's first term in public Office, India detonated nuclear weapons underground on 18 May 1974. India's 1974 nuclear test was known as *Operation Smiling Buddha*.

Indian politics was not all smooth sailing for Indira Gandhi. On 12 June 1975, Justice Jagmohanlal Sinha of the Allahabad High Court declared Indira's 1971 election to *the Lok Sabha* (the Lower Chamber of the Indian Parliament) void on the basis of 'electoral malpractice'. Consequently, Indira was deprived of her seat in the Indian Parliament, and she was also disqualified from public Office for a period of six years. Indira appealed the judgement of the Allahabad High Court to the Indian Supreme Court, however, Indira did not receive the outcome that she had hoped for, or rather intended. Instead of presenting her resignation to the fifth President of India, Fakhruddin Ali Ahmed (r. 1974-1977), Indira responded with political tact and unchecked ferocity against her opponents.

Indira requested the President of India, Fakhruddin Ali Ahmed to impose a State of Emergency in the Republic India, due to 'disorder' and 'lawlessness' arising from the Allahabad High Court's legal judgement. On 25 June 1975, the State of Emergency came into effect across the sovereign territory of the Republic of India. Thereafter, President Ahmed issued ordinances that permitted Prime Minister Indira Gandhi to rule by decree. During the period of emergency rule, Indira silenced opposition parties, censored the Indian media, outspoken politicians in the Indian Parliament were arrested and incarcerated, Indian court judges were suspended or transferred in the Indian judicial system, and democratic debate in the Indian Parliament was altogether discarded. The State of Emergency continued in India for just short of two years, and ultimately the 1977 general election witnessed the removal of Indira Gandhi from power.

The period from 1977 to 1980 represented the 'opposition years' for Indira Gandhi. During this time, Indira was also briefly imprisoned by her political opponents. Indira's political opponents claimed that she had planned on killing opposition leaders, whom Indira had jailed, when she had imposed a State of Emergency in India. More likely than not, Indira's imprisonment was simply tit-for-tat politics, an act of retribution by Indian politicians.

Indira returned to power in 1980, for her second and final term in public Office. During this time, Indira became embroiled in the politics of the northern Indian State of Punjab, where the Sikh people demanded greater autonomy in accordance with *the Anandpur Sahib Resolution of 1973*. Orthodox Sikh religious leader, Jarnail Singh Bhindranwale (1947-1984), and a group of his loyal followers turned to militancy, in the promotion of their political cause for greater autonomy from the Indian State. Ultimately, Bhindranwale and his loyal followers took armed residence in *the Golden Temple* in the Holy City of Amritsar. Consequently, *the Golden Temple* became a flashpoint for a special military operation that was executed by the Indian Armed Forces, known as *Operation BlueStar 1984*.

Following *Operation BlueStar*, two of Indira's Sikh body guards, Beant Singh and Satwant Singh assassinated Indira Gandhi on 31 October 1984, in revenge for the aforesaid special military operation on *the Golden Temple*. Indira did not survive the assassination attempt. Indira died at the age of 66 at the All-India Institute of Medical Sciences in New Delhi, India.

Margaret Thatcher (1925-2013)

Margaret Hilda Thatcher (Margaret Hilda Roberts) was born on 13 October 1925 in Grantham, Lincolnshire, England. Margaret's father was English politician, entrepreneur, and Methodist preacher, Alfred Roberts. Margaret's mother was Beatrice Ethel Stephenson. Margaret was initially educated at Huntingtower Road Primary School, however, upon the receipt of a scholarship, she was able to complete her school studies at the Kesteven and Grantham Girls' School.

In the year 1943, with the receipt of a bursary and scholarship, Margaret matriculated at Somerville College, the University of Oxford, where she studied chemistry. During Margaret's time at the University of Oxford, she completed her fourth-year dissertation on X-ray crystallography and antibiotic cocktail gramicidin. Margaret studied under the supervision of renowned British chemist and Nobel Prize recipient, Dorothy Mary Crowfoot Hodgkin (1910-1994). In addition, Margaret was active in the University's associations and its many learned societies that were beyond the scientific realm. For example, consider that in 1946, Margaret was President of the University of Oxford Conservative Association. In the year 1947, Margaret graduated from the University of Oxford with a second-class Degree in Chemistry.

During the years 1947 to 1951, Margaret worked as an Industrial and Research Chemist. First, Margaret was employed at the British Xylonite Plastics in Colchester, Essex. Subsequently, Margaret secured employment as a Food Research Chemist at the J. Lyons and Company in Hammersmith, London. In the 1950 and 1951 United Kingdom general elections, Margaret campaigned as a Conservative candidate for the Labour seat of Dartford. Margaret was unsuccessful on both these occasions; however, she demonstrated her capacity as an effective orator. Not to mention, Margaret attracted widespread media attention across the United Kingdom, as she was a formidable and fierce female political candidate.

On 13 December 1951, Margaret married English businessman, Sir Denis Thatcher (1915-2003) at Wesley's Chapel on City Road in London. Their marriage was not 'love at first sight', rather Margaret found Denis to be a genuine and considerate person. Furthermore, Margaret and Denis' marriage also served Margaret's educational and political ends, namely, Denis was a wealthy and privileged Englishman. That is to say, Denis had the financial means to support Margaret's law studies and ambitious career in British politics. In the year 1953, the married couple had twins, namely, Carol and Mark.

With the financial support of her spouse, Sir Denis Thatcher, Margaret managed to study Common Law, she specialised in the field of taxation. In the year 1953, Margaret successfully passed the Bar exam. Thereafter, Margaret was admitted as a Barrister. It was not until 1959, that Margaret's career in British politics gained some serious traction. For in the 1959 United Kingdom general election, Margaret won the Conservative Seat of Finchley in London, and thus, she was elected as a Member of Parliament (MP) to the House of Commons. Margaret's election victory in 1959 was only the start of her steady and gradual rise to the highest position of public Office in British politics, namely, that of Prime Minister.

Throughout the 1960's and 1970's, Margaret held several prominent positions that served to broaden her breadth and depth of experience in British politics, including the Parliamentary Under Secretary in the Ministry of Pensions and National Insurance (1961-1964), the Chief Opposition Spokesperson on Education (1969-1970), and the Secretary of State for Education and Science (1970-1974). In addition, Margaret was responsible for supporting unpopular, and sometimes controversial legislation in the British Parliament. For example, consider the 1971 removal of the free School Milk Program, that previously provided milk to British school children over the age of seven. This British government public relations crisis earnt Margaret the infamous nickname, 'Thatcher, the Milk Snatcher'.

The leader of *the Conservative Party* and British Prime Minister, the Right Honourable Sir Edward Heath (r. 1970-1974), was challenged for *the Conservative Party* Leadership by Margaret Thatcher. Following Prime Minister Edward Heath's lacklustre performance in the February and October 1974 United Kingdom general elections. There was now open division amongst *the Conservative Party* members regarding the party leadership. As a result, Margaret was successful in defeating Prime Minister Edward Heath for the leadership of *the Conservative Party*. Thereafter, the Right Honourable Edward Heath resigned from his position as the Prime Minister of the United Kingdom. Consequently, *the Conservative Party* leadership matter was decisively settled. On 11 February 1975, Margaret became the Conservative Party Leader, with William Stephen Ian Whitelaw (1918-1999), serving as her Deputy Leader.

The next four years, from 1975 to 1979, witnessed Margaret navigate the opposition in British politics. On 4 May 1979, Margaret made history, she was appointed the first female Prime Minister of the United Kingdom. During the next eleven years of Prime Minister Margaret Thatcher's rule, Great Britain underwent transformative change in its society, national economy, institutions, international trade, foreign affairs, industrial relations and labour laws, immigration policy, trade unions, international diplomacy, and special relationship with the European Committee (EC). Not to mention, throughout Margaret's tenure in public office, she was an unapologetic advocate of English liberalism, *laissez-faire* economics, privatisation, liberalisation, nationalism, conservatism, and moral absolutism. In a single word Prime Minister Margaret Thatcher's political ideology is best described as 'Thatcherism'.

During Margaret's eleven years in public Office, she was responsible for numerous social and economic reforms that irreversibly changed the modern British society in a profound manner. Margaret's economic policy was strongly influenced by the influential ideas of American economist, Milton Friedman (1912-2006), and British economist, Sir Alan Arthur Walters (1926-2009). In fact, during the 1980's, Margaret Thatcher pursued bold and ambitious reforms to the British economy along the lines of monetarism and neoliberalism. For example, consider *the Housing Act of 1980* which promoted private home ownership amongst the British working class. The aforesaid Act of the British Parliament facilitated the ability of council tenants to acquire council homes at steeply discounted prices, in order to encourage private home ownership across Great Britain.

Furthermore, in the 1980's, Margaret Thatcher's government was also dealing with the economic fallout of a recession. During this time, the headline economic indicators of inflation and unemployment were both considerably high. Margaret responded by increasing interest rates to restrict the money supply, and thereby, reduce inflation. In addition, Margaret also adjusted the levers of British Tax Policy to deal with the recession, most notably, by reducing personal income taxes. In the 1970's, the highest rate of income tax rate was 83 per cent. Thatcher reduced the highest income tax rate to 60 per cent. The economic rationale for lower effective tax rates was to stimulate aggregate demand and consumer spending in the British economy. In order to compensate for the loss of income tax revenue to the United Kingdom, Margaret Thatcher increased indirect taxes, such as the British Value Added Tax (VAT), which was increased from eight per cent to fifteen per cent.

Margaret also enacted unpopular national spending cuts to public education and housing programs, in order to reduce government expenditure, and thereby, balance the government budget. In addition, Margaret promoted the privatisation of numerous British State-owned Enterprises across several industries, such as British Aerospace (partially privatised in 1981, then the remainder in 1985), British Telecom (1984), Jaguar (1984), British Telecommunications (1984), British Gas (1986), Rolls-Royce Limited (1987), British Airways (1987), British Petroleum (privatisation completed in 1987), British Airports Authority (1987), and British Steel (privatised over a period of time, from 1987 to 1988). The privatisation of British Rail (1994) and British Coal (1997) was wholly effectuated by Margaret Thatcher's successor, the Conservative Prime Minister, the Right Honourable Sir John Major (r. 1990-1997). In addition to the privatisation of British state-owned enterprises, the Margaret Thatcher Conservative Government also deregulated the British Financial Services Industry, this process is commonly referred to as *the Big Bang of 1986*.

Throughout the 1980's, unemployment and inflation remained problematic and contentious socio-economic issues for Margaret Thatcher's government. In fact, in 1979, the United Kingdom unemployment rate stood at ca. twelve per cent, and in 1989, it was only reduced to ca. seven per cent. As a result, Margaret confronted the unemployment issue by curtailing the power of the British Trade Unions. Most notably, Margaret utilised the instrument of statute law (i.e., legislation) to restrict the British Trade Union Movement. For example, consider the British government's implementation of *the Employment Act of 1980*, and *the Employment Act of 1982*. Notwithstanding Prime Minister Margaret Thatcher s practical initiatives to reduce the national unemployment rate, it remained stubbornly high throughout her long tenure in public Office.

In so far as the economic issue of inflation was concerned, Margaret found far greater success in addressing this economic challenge. Margaret accomplished success by the combined adjustments to government taxes, interest rates, exerting control over the money supply, and reducing public spending across the United Kingdom. As a result, the headline inflation figure decreased from its 1980 peak of ca. 18 per cent, to a modest ca. 4.60 per cent in the year 1983.

Despite Margaret's rising unpopularity with the British people, her political fortunes remained favourable. This political reality was in part due to *the Falklands War (1982)*, which was fought between Argentina and the United Kingdom. This war was waged to decide the key political question of sovereignty of the British Overseas Territories of the Falkland Islands, South Georgia, and the South Sandwich Islands. *The Falklands War* was a tactical gambit that ultimately prevailed for Prime Minister Margaret Thatcher. A decisive British military victory over Argentina was achieved, in a short, sharp, and symbolic war. Of great importance herein, this war turned around Margaret's dire public Office fortunes, and it secured her a political victory in the 1983 United Kingdom general election, with a strong mandate to rule.

Beyond the aforesaid war, Prime Minister Margaret Thatcher also reached international agreements concerning questions of peace.

Throughout the 1980's, Margaret Thatcher worked with the Republic of Ireland to construct a more tenable and durable peace across the Irish Sea in respect to the 'troubles and disturbances' in Northern Ireland. The two High Contracting Parties reached an amicable understanding known as *the Anglo-Irish Agreement of 1985*. This Agreement gave the Republic of Ireland an 'advisory role' in the governance of Northern Ireland. Regrettably, some of Margaret Thatcher's foreign policy was marked by outdated vestiges of British imperialism, in particular, on the matter of South Africa. Notwithstanding Margaret Thatcher's perception of Great Britain in the modern world, she ultimately had to accept the reality of a changing World Order in the late twentieth century. A World Order which witnessed a diminished role for Great Britain in foreign affairs, in particular, on the two pivotal matters of Hong Kong and South Africa.

With respect to the question of South Africa, Prime Minister Margaret Thatcher was against the imposition of economic sanctions against the South African Apartheid Regime, however, she remained in favour of peace negotiations. Against mounting world opinion, Prime Minister Margaret Thatcher preserved British trade with South Africa, and in vain she hoped that the South African government will abandon the tyranny of its racist Apartheid Regime. Regretfully, one cannot entirely negate the plausible conclusion that racial prejudice had performed a role in Margaret's flawed political calculations. Indeed, there was the presence of much wishful thinking here, even for a towering politician of Margaret Thatcher's formidable stature. Perhaps, on this point, the British Prime Minister Harold Macmillan (r. 1957-1963), in his 1960 'Winds of Change' speech given in Cape Town, South Africa, was better acquainted with the inevitable reality of the demise of the British Empire, and its colonies across the continent of Africa. Unfortunately, Margaret Thatcher's flawed judgement found herse.⁼ on the wrong side of modern history when it came to South Africa.

During Margaret Thatcher's time in public Office, the important question of Hong Kong's sovereignty also had to be dealt with. In 1982, when Hong Kong was still subject to British extraterritorial jurisdiction, Prime Minister Margaret Thatcher met with Chinese leader, Deng Xiaoping (1904-1997) in China to discuss the transfer of sovereignty of British Hong Kong to the People's Republic of China. In vain, Margaret Thatcher pressed China for assurances on a continued British presence in Hong Kong, however, Great Britain's colonial years were numbered in Hong Kong. Formal negotiations took place between the High Contracting Parties, namely, the People's Republic of China and the United Kingdom, which ultimately led to a diplomatic agreement known as *the Sino-British Joint Declaration of 1984*. In the end, the United Kingdom agreed to peacefully return sovereignty over the territory of Hong Kong to China on 1 July 1997.

On foreign affairs matters closer to home, Prime Minister Margaret Thatcher established a very cordial relationship with the U.S. President, Ronald Reagan (r. 1981-1989). The two major political leaders of the Free World agreed on their approach to diplomatic relations with the Union of Soviet Socialist Republics in World Politics. Margaret Thatcher considered the Soviet Union an 'Enemy' of the Free World that was bent on 'World Domination'. This strong political commentary of the Soviet Union earnt Margaret the title 'Iron Lady', the title remained with her throughout her political career. The two Free World leaders, Reagan and Thatcher also implemented similar domestic economic policies on deregulation, liberalisation, lower taxes, free trade, privatisation, and free-market enterprise in their respective countries.

Although Margaret Thatcher was very confident in her political views, she had a catastrophic fallout with British Foreign Secretary, Sir Richard

Edward Geoffrey Howe (1926-2015), when it came to Great Britain's 'Special Relationship' with Europe. Consequently, Foreign Secretary Howe resigned from his prominent position in November of 1990, and he gave an impressive resignation speech to the House of Commons. Howe's infamous speech ultimately perpetuated the alienation and demise of Margaret Thatcher's regime from within her own political party. As a result, Prime Minister Margaret Thatcher was to exit the Prime Minister's Office before the end of 1990. Subsequently, Margaret Thatcher also retired from the House of Commons in 1992.

Margaret Thatcher's monumental contribution to British politics was well acknowledged during her lifetime. Most notably, in 1992, Margaret was appointed a 'Life Peeress' in the House of Lords. Furthermore, in the year 1995, Margaret was appointed Lady Companion of the Order of the Garter. In addition, Margaret's memoirs are published across two volumes, namely, *The Downing Street Years (1993)*, and *The Path to Power (1995)*.

On 8 April 2013, Margaret passed away after the onset of a stroke in London, England. Margaret was 87 years old at the time of her death. Margaret was afforded a State funeral with full military honours, and she was also provided a church service that was held at Saint Paul's Cathedral. As a gesture of courtesy and respect, Her Majesty Queen Elizabeth II and the Duke of Edinburgh were both in attendance at Margaret Thatcher's funeral service.

Margaret Thatcher's monumental legacy will continue to be debated by eminent historians and noteworthy politicians alike for decades to come. Regardless of how modern history is perceived or written, there exists no doubt that the 'Iron Lady', Prime Minister Margaret Thatcher has left her mark on British foreign policy, people, society, politics, institutions, diplomacy, culture, and industrial relations, among the many other facets of the United Kingdom. While Margaret Thatcher was a political leader not without controversy and unpopular government policies, Margaret Thatcher rightly deserves her distinguished place at the top of the British Political Establishment, amongst some of the greatest British Prime Ministers of the twentieth century, including David Lloyd George (r. 1916-1922), Winston Leonard Spencer Churchill (r. 1940-1945, 1951-1955), and Clement Richard Attlee (r. 1945-1951).

Chapter Six

WOMEN IN LAW

'I would like to be remembered as someone who used whatever talent she had to do her work to the very best of her ability.'

Ruth Bader Ginsburg

This chapter examines several women who have made unprecedented progress in the distinguished and prestigious field of Law. From a historical perspective, learned practitioners of the Legal Profession, regardless they be solicitors, conveyancers, attorneys at law, barristers, legal counsellors, advocates, law clerks, Crown prosecutors, paralegals, judges, magistrates, justices, legal scholars, deans of law schools, or chief justices, have predominantly, and one might argue exclusively, been men. Indeed, throughout the Ages, men have used Law as an instrument to oppress and define women, by restricting women's political and legal rights, civil liberties, economic opportunities in the labour market, and equal participation in society. Indeed, for much of the human civilisation's pre-modern history, the very autonomy, agency, and authority of women was closely correlated to their father, brother, or husband.

The institution of Law, along with the function of prevailing customs, beliefs, traditions, culture, religion, language, government, and other socio-economic-political factors (i.e., private property ownership, marriage and divorce laws, maternity leave laws, abortion laws, surrogacy laws, sterilisation laws, and other birth control measures), have been utilised, in different degrees throughout human history, in order to oppress the unconditional liberty, constitutional rights, natural rights, and natural justice that ought to be blindly afforded to each and every human, without any distinction, concern, or regard to sex, gender, race, colour, religion, wealth, education, social class, ethnicity, disability, age, or creed.

This chapter will explore the life narratives, the personal struggles, the institutional barriers, and the remarkable achievements of the following women, who have made their impression in the practice of Law across the major Anglophone countries, namely, Belva Ann Lockwood, Arabella Mansfield, Eliza Burton Conley, Clara Brett Martin, Ivy Williams, Grata Flos Matilda Greig, Helena Florence Normanton, Florence Ellinwood Allen, Madge Easton Anderson, and Joan Ruth Bader Ginsburg.

Belva Ann Lockwood (1830-1917)

Belva Ann Bennett Lockwood was born on 24 October 1830 in Royalton, Niagara County, New York, the United States of America. Belva's father was a farmer named Lewis Johnson Bennett, and her mother was Hannah Green Bennett. Belva did not come from a privileged, elite, or affluent family, and her early life was a struggle. Belva had four siblings. Furthermore, from the age of five, Belva only received a very basic education. In fact, Belva attended a one-room country school that was located ca. three kilometres away from her home, until she was fourteen years old. Not to mention, Belva walked to and from country schools in order to attend the Summer and Winter sessions, so that she was able to receive a decent education.

After the completion of Belva's rudimentary school education, she was able to attend a private school. Belva attended the Royalton Academy at Royalton Centre for twelve months. At the Academy, Belva studied English, and she received a preparatory education for her admission into college. Unfortunately, Belva's father, Lewis, was not supportive of his daughter's educational aspirations and lofty ambitions. As a result, Belva's father did not financially support Belva's ambitious higher education endeavours. Consequently, with Belva being unable to support her higher education, she stopped attending the Royalton Academy. Thereafter, Belva began to teach school students in her teenage years in order to provide for herself. As a female school teacher, Belva earnt half the remuneration paid to the male school teachers.

On 8 November 1848, at the young age of eighteen, Belva married a local farmer and sawmill operator, Uriah Harrison McNall. The newly married couple moved to the McNall Sawmill and Farm which was located on Mill Road, south of Gasport. On 31 July 1849, Belva and Uriah had a daughter, they named her Lura McNall. Unfortunately, tragedy struck thereafter, Belva's husband was injured operating the sawmill. Two years later, on 11 May 1853, Belva's husband passed away from complications associated with his injuries.

Thus, Belva was left a widow, with sole parental responsibility for raising their young daughter. After much serious thought, Belva decided that she needed a much better education if she was to financially support herself, and also to provide for her young daughter. Following the death of Belva's husband, in the year 1853, Belva briefly studied at the Gasport Academy, before she enrolled at the Genesee Wesleyan Seminary in 1854, where she commenced serious preparatory studies for her entrance into college.

Despite the obstacles of gender, sex, motherhood, and widowhood, Belva managed to secure admission at Genesee College (now known as Syracuse University) in Lima, New York. While at college, Belva studied a range of subjects, including chemistry, English, history, languages, mathematics, and philosophy. On 27 June 1857, Belva graduated with a Bachelor of Science Degree conferred with honours from Genesee College.

Upon Belva's graduation from college, she recommenced her teaching career in New York. From 1857 to 1861, Belva held the position of Preceptress at the Lockport Union School in Lockport, New York. At Lockport Union School, Belva taught the traditional classes in botany, logic, mathematics, and rhetoric. Most notably, Belva was not the orthodox and conservative school teacher. Much to the amazement and astonishment of Belva's colleagues, and the school children's parents, Belva also incorporated public speaking, nature walks, ice skating, and gymnastics into the school curriculum. These additional activities immensely benefited the morale of the school students in Belva's classes. Following Belva's resignation from Lockport Union School, from 1861 to 1863, Belva also briefly taught at the Gainesville Female Seminary in Gainesville, New York. Thereafter, from 1863 to 1865, Belva went on to teach at the Owego Female Seminary in New York.

During *the American Civil War (1861-1865)*, Belva fulfilled her patriotic duty to country by serving as President of the Lockport Ladies Aid. Following the cessation of *the American Civil War*, in the year 1866, Belva relocated from New York to Washington D.C., where she opened a school in the memory of her late first husband, Uriah Harrison McNall, the school was known as McNall's Ladies Seminary. The aforesaid school was a successful venture, and it later went on to admit male students. At the time, McNall's Ladies Seminary was one of the first co-educational private learning institutions in Washington D.C.

On 11 March 1868, Belva re-married Baptist minister and retired dentist, the Reverend Ezekiel Lockwood. At the time of Belva and Ezekiel's marriage, Belva was thirty-eight years old, and Ezekiel was sixty-five years old. In the year 1869, the couple went on to have a daughter named Jessie Belva, however, most regrettably, the newborn baby did not live to see her third birthday. Belva's second husband, Ezekiel supported and encouraged Belva's legal career aspirations. As a result, Ezekiel assumed control over the administration and governance of McNall's Ladies Seminary. This arrangement permitted Belva to concentrate on the pursuit of a legal education, and thereafter, a distinguished career in Law.

In the year 1869, Belva made a number of formal applications for her admission into one of the many United States' prestigious law schools. However, most unfortunately, on the discriminatory basis of sex, Belva was rejected entry into several prominent U.S. law schools, including the Columbian College (now known as the George Washington University), Georgetown University, and Howard University. Finally, in the year 1871, Belva secured an offer of admission to the National University Law School. While at National University Law, Belva studied the U.S. Law, and she satisfied all of her course requirements in 1873. In spite of Belva's fulfilment of her law course requirements, she was not awarded a Diploma, because she was a female university student.

On 3 September 1873, in unavoidable frustration, Belva wrote to the United States President, Ulysses Simpson Grant (r. 1869-1877), who was also the President *ex officio* of the National University Law School. Belva expressed her dismay, disgust, and displeasure with the prevailing institutional injustice of sexism. While Belva did not directly receive a written response from the U.S. President, Ulysses Simpson Grant, she was rightly awarded her Diploma in Law.

Following the receipt of Belva's Diploma, on 24 September 1873, Belva was duly admitted to the District of Columbia Bar to practice Law. Belva utilised her newfound legal knowledge to advance women's legal, civil, economic, and political rights in the United States of America. In addition, Belva also assisted the many disadvantaged and vulnerable members of the District of Columbia Community, including the Native American people, and the many underprivileged members of the modern American society, who were otherwise unable to afford the professional services of legal counsel.

As one of the few female lawyers in the nineteenth century American society, Belva personally confronted numerous accounts of sex discrimination and verbal harassment in the U.S. Legal Profession. In effect, in the nineteenth century America, the U.S. courtroom was considered to be a 'man's place', and if American women were present, it was customary that they remained seated and silent. For example, consider that in the 1820's, American women were not permitted to speak in the Supreme Court of the United States (est. 1789).

Nevertheless, Belva protested, and she continued to vigorously contest such institutionalised sexist views during her tenure as a qualified and practicing American Lawyer. In fact, in 1873, a Maryland judge ruled that Belva was not entitled to practice Law in the U.S. state of Maryland. Also consider that in the year 1875, Belva was denied the right to legally represent clients at the United States Court of Claims. This injustice was due to Belva's sex. Not to mention, the illogical, irrational, and absurd assertion was advanced, namely, that Belva was a married woman, and therefore, her possible 'incompetency' as a lawyer would cause her husband reputational harm and financial damages. Furthermore, in the year 1876, Belva's application for admission to the United States Supreme Court Bar was rejected. This formal rejection was despite Belva having met the required three-year practicing tenure of a lawyer. Disappointingly, Belva was still denied her rightful place, solely on the discriminatory grounds of her sex.

In a constructive and productive manner, Belva took legal matters into her own hands. Belva decided to enact fundamental legal change. Belva intended to address some of the underlying systematic prejudices and institutionalised barriers that female lawyers confronted in their rightful quest to practice Law in the United States of America. In the year 1876, Belva drafted a statute, which became known as *HR1077*, for the consideration of the United States Congress to permit qualified women to practice Law in the highest court of the United States of America. The historic achievement of this noble endeavour permitted female lawyers to gain the requisite admission to practice Law from the U.S. Supreme Court Bar.

On 25 April 1877, Belva's second husband, the Reverend Ezekiel Lockwood passed away at the family residence in Washington, D.C. Ezekiel was 74 years old at the time of his death. Belva was undeterred by the grief and loss of her beloved spouse. Belva understood the immense gravity of the tall endeavour that stood before her. Belva steadily and confidently pressed forward to continue the just struggle for women's political, economic, civil, and legal rights in the United States of America. In 1878 and 1879, Belva continued to tirelessly lobby the United States Congress to pass legislation permitting qualified female lawyers to be duly admitted to the United States Supreme Court Bar. The bill under consideration was titled 'An act to relieve certain legal disabilities of women' (also known as *HR1077* and *the Lockwood Bill*). *The Lockwood Bill* was duly considered, and subsequently, it was passed by both the U.S. House of Representatives and the U.S. Senate in 1879.

On 3 March 1879, Belva made history. Belva became the first woman to be admitted to the practice Law before the United States Supreme Court in Washington, D.C. This was a monumental achievement, not just for Belva personally, but also for the greater cause of women to be able to practice Law in the highest Court of the United States of America. Shortly thereafter, on 6 March 1879, Belva became the first woman to be admitted to practice Law before the United States Court of Claims. Due to the persuasive political advocacy and unprecedented achievements of Belva, it now became possible for other qualified American female lawyers to practice Law more widely across the United States of America. Indeed, Belva, by example, had established the historic precedent for greater female participation in the United States' Legal Profession with her admirable conduct.

In the year 1880, Belva became the first female lawyer to argue a legal case in the United States Supreme Court. The matter before the Supreme Court was *Kaiser v. Stickney, 102 U.S. 176 (1880)*. Although Belva lost the aforesaid legal case on behalf of her client, Caroline Kaiser, she had made history by becoming the first female lawyer to represent and speak on behalf of a client at the U.S. Supreme Court. In addition, the very presence of Belva as a qualified female lawyer in the U.S. Supreme Court finally began to challenge some of the long-held stereotypes about the competency and ability of American women to practice Law.

It is also essential to highlight that Belva worked for justice for all types of people in the United States, not just the cause of American women. Throughout Belva's remarkable legal career, she promoted justice for the African American people, the Native American people, and the many disadvantaged members of the Washington, D.C. Community. In fact, in 1880, Belva sponsored the historic admission of African American lawyer, Samuel R. Lowery (ca. 1832-1900), to be duly admitted to the United States Supreme Court Bar, and this application was successfully granted by the honourable justices of the aforesaid institution.

In the year 1884, Belva accepted the presidential nomination of *the National Equal Rights Party*, and she campaigned for the Office of the United States President. Although Belva did not secure an election victory, her confidence was unshakeable, and she campaigned for the U.S. presidency again in the year 1888. Belva Lockwood was the second American woman to campaign for the Office of the U.S. President, after American women's rights activist, Victoria Claflin Woodhull (1838-1927), of *the Equal Rights Party* in 1871. At the commencement of 2022, the United States President is a high position of public Office that still remains to be successfully secured by an American woman.

In the year 1906, Belva again appeared before the U.S. Supreme Court, this time in the matter of *United States v. Cherokee Nation, 202 U.S. 101 (1906)*. Belva was legal counsel for the Cherokee Nation. Belva convincingly argued that the U.S. government ought to pay the balance and interest for the transfer of native land from the Cherokee Nation to the U.S. federal government. On this occasion, Belva won her legal case! The judgement of the U.S. Supreme Court ordered the U.S. government to pay USD five million as settlement of the aforesaid legal case. At the time, this Supreme Court judgement represented one of the largest native land settlement payments, to be paid by the U.S. federal government to a Native American nation.

On 19 May 1917, Belva passed away at the age of 86. Belva was buried at the Congressional Cemetery in Washington, D.C. During and after Belva's lifetime, countless national honours have been bestowed upon Belva for her immense contribution to the United States' Legal Profession. For example, in 1908, Syracuse University awarded Belva an Honorary Doctorate in Law. Furthermore, in 1983, Belva was inducted into the United States National Women's Hall of Fame in Seneca Falls, New York. Last but not least, in 1986, the United States Postal Service issued a U.S. 17 cent postage stamp in Belva's memory.

Not only did Belva practice the noble and privileged profession of Law in the United States of America, she also set a fine example, and a very high standard for her peers to emulate, men and women alike. Belva upheld the cherished principles of justice, equity, fairness, equality, integrity, honesty, and courtesy in her life, work, and conduct. In addition, Belva's numerous life struggles and countless accomplishments demonstrate that age, private wealth, income, privilege, sex, education, and gender, are all surmountable factors that do not necessarily limit one's ability to achieve greatness, in order to become all that one was destined to be.

Arabella Mansfield (1846-1911)

Arabella Mansfield (Belle Aurelia Babb) was born on 23 May 1846 in Benton Township, Des Moines County, Iowa, the United States of America. Arabella's father was American farmer and miner, Miles Babb. Arabella's mother was Mary Moyer Babb. Furthermore, Arabella had one sibling; an older brother named Washington Irving Babb. On 10 April 1850, while

Arabella was still a young child, her father left Iowa, in order to take advantage of *the California Gold Rush (1848-1855)*. In 1852, Arabella's father was appointed Superintendent of the Bay State Mining Company, however, his life was tragically lost in a mining accident that same year in El Dorado County, California.

Before Arabella's father, Miles Babb had departed for California, he had executed a will that detailed financial provisions for his children's school education. Following Miles Babb's death, Arabella's mother, Mary moved with the two children to Mount Pleasant in Henry County, Iowa, where there were better educational opportunities for both Arabella and Washington. Arabella studied at the co-educational school known as Howe's Academy, before she moved to Mount Pleasant High School. In the year 1862, Arabella graduated from the latter school.

In the latter half of 1862, Arabella matriculated at Iowa Wesleyan University in Mount Pleasant. In 1866, Arabella graduated from Iowa Wesleyan University as valedictorian (i.e., first place in her graduating class). Following the completion of Arabella's university studies, she commenced her career in teaching. Arabella secured employment at Des Moines Conference Seminary (later known as Simpson College) in Indianola, Iowa, where she taught classes in English, history, and political science. After one year at Des Moines Conference Seminary, Arabella left Indianola and returned to Mount Pleasant, where she married Iowa Wesleyan University graduate and Professor of Natural History, John Melvin Mansfield on 23 June 1868. The married couple did not have any children.

During Arabella's time in Mount Pleasant, Arabella studied the United States Law at the Offices of H. and R. Ambler, a legal practice where her older brother Washington Irving was also studying the United States Law for the Iowa Bar Exam. Arabella profusely read Law books in order to advance her knowledge of legal concepts, ideas, theories, principles, and doctrines. Arabella's husband, who was also studying for the Iowa Law Bar Exam, encouraged Arabella's tall ambitions in the field of Law.

In 1869, Arabella sat the Iowa Law Bar Exam, and she passed the exam with a commendable score. At this time in Iowa state history, the Iowa Code implicitly restricted applicants on the basis of gender, race, colour, and sex. That is to say, the archetypal applicant who sat the Iowa Law Bar Exam was an Anglo-American or European descent American man above the age of twenty-one. Thus, American women and people of colour, in particular, the African American people, were not a part of the traditional cohort of the United States' law school applicants.

Despite passing the Iowa Law Bar Exam, Arabella was initially denied the right to be admitted to practice Law in the State of Iowa. Arabella took the matter to Court, and she successfully challenged Iowa State Law. On 15 June 1869, Arabella was duly admitted by the examining Committee to practice Law in Iowa. Arabella's legal victory was in part due to District Court Judge, the Honourable Francis Springer's more favourable interpretation of the Iowa Code. In effect, Judge Francis Springer advanced a more balanced reading of the Iowa State Statute when it came to American women's right to practice Law.

Despite being educated and admitted to practice Law in the State of Iowa, Arabella turned her attention to a different trajectory, for she subsequently determined not to practice as a lawyer. In 1870, Arabella received her second degree, a Master of Arts (MA) from Iowa Wesleyan University. In addition, Arabella also secured a Bachelor of Laws (LLB) Degree in the year 1872 from Iowa Wesleyan University. Parallel to Arabella's keen interest in further university study, Arabella continued to teach as a Professor of English Literature at Iowa Wesleyan University until the year 1876.

Arabella's interests went beyond law and teaching. In fact, Arabella was strongly involved in the American Women's Suffrage Movement. Arabella desired to create a more equitable and fair standing for American women in the modern United States society. In the pursuit of this noble endeavour, Arabella became a member of the Executive Committee of the *National Woman Suffrage Association* (NWSA). In addition, Arabella also worked closely with the great American suffragette, Susan Brownell Anthony (1820-1906). In June of 1870, Arabella assumed the role of Chair and Secretary of the first *Iowa Women's Rights Convention* held in Mount Pleasant, Iowa. Shortly thereafter, in August 1870, Arabella was elected President of *the Henry County Woman Suffrage Association* (HCWSA).

In 1879, Arabella joined the Indiana Asbury University (now known as DePauw University) in Greencastle, Indiana, where she lectured in the history of music and aesthetics. Thereafter, Arabella served as the Dean of the School of Art in 1893, and also the Dean of the School of Music in 1894. Throughout Arabella's time as a University Lecturer, Professor, and as Dean, Arabella continued her resolute commitment to American women's acceptance into the United States' Legal Profession. For example, consider that in 1893, Arabella became an active member of *the National League of Women Lawyers* (NLWL) Subsequently, in the year 1911, Arabella officially retired from her university teaching commitments and senior leadership positions.

On 1 August 1911, Arabella passed away in Aurora, Illinois, the United States of America. Arabella was 65 years old at the time of her death. Arabella was buried at the Forest Home Cemetery in Mount Pleasant, Iowa. In the year 1920, that is nine years after Arabella's death, *the Nineteenth Amendment* to the United States Constitution was passed, securing American women the legal right to vote.

Arabella's legacy was honoured during her lifetime and beyond. In 1980, Arabella was inducted into the Iowa Women's Hall of Fame. Not to mention, in the year 2002, the Iowa Organisation of Women Attorneys (IOWA) established the Arabella Mansfield Award to acknowledge outstanding achievements by American female lawyers in the State of Iowa. Last but not least, in 2008, a bronze statue of Arabella Mansfield designed by American sculptor, Benjamin Victor was unveiled at the Iowa Wesleyan University Campus in recognition of Arabella's exceptional work as a lawyer, and her many other notable achievements.

Eliza Burton Conley (1869-1946)

Eliza Burton Conley was born in the year 1869 in Kansas City, Kansas, the United States of America. Eliza's father was American farmer, Andrew Syrenus Conley of Scots-Irish heritage and English ancestry. Eliza's mother was Elizabeth Burton Zane, a multiracial member of the Wyandotte Tribe from the Wyandot Nation. Eliza had three older siblings in her family, all of whom were sisters.

Eliza was educated at Park College (now known as Park University) in Parkville, Missouri. Thereafter, Eliza pursued further studies at the Kansas City School of Law. Eliza graduated from law school in the year 1902. Eliza became the first native American woman to be admitted to the Missouri and Kansas Bar Associations in 1902 and 1910, respectively. From the year 1906 until Eliza's death in 1946, her life struggle was dedicated to the protection and preservation of the Huron Indian Cemetery in Kansas. The Huron Indian Cemetery held special importance to Eliza's ancestry, history, people, language, cultural identity, heritage, and sense of belonging to the Indian American people. Among other factors, the Huron Indian Cemetery contained the remains of Eliza's Wyandotte ancestors, grandmother (Hannah Zane), mother (Elizabeth Burton Zane), and sister (Sarah Conley).

In the year 1906, the United States Congress passed legislation that approved the sale of the sacred native land upon which the Huron Indian Cemetery in Kansas was situated. The Huron Indian Cemetery was a prime piece of real estate that was surrounded by significant property developments, including the Carnegie Library, the Brund Hotel, and the Scottish Rite Masonic Temple. In response, Eliza petitioned the United States District Court. In 1907, Eliza filed a permanent injunction at the aforesaid Court, to prevent the United States Secretary of the Interior, James Rudolph Garfield (1865-1950), from authorising the sale of the aforesaid Cemetery. Unfortunately, the United States Circuit Court for the District of Kansas rejected the grounds of Eliza's legal argument.

Eliza was not one to accept the lower Court's validity on this deeply personal matter of connection to land, ancestry, and country. Thus, Eliza took her legal case to the Supreme Court of the United States. At the U.S. Supreme Court, Eliza argued *propria persona* (in her own person), in an attempt to secure the Supreme Court's recognition of the legal ownership of the Huron Indian Cemetery. While the matter was proceeding through the routine legal procedures and mechanisms, Eliza and her two sisters, Helena and Ida, took matters into their own hands. The Conley Sisters fortified the Huron Indian Cemetery, in order to protect the Indian Cemetery from trespassers and the U.S. Federal Troops.

The three Conley Sisters protected the burial place of their native ancestors by erecting a shack on the Huron Indian Cemetery which came to be known as 'Fort Conley'. Not to mention, the Conley Sisters also displayed a warning sign to alert potential trespassers not to enter the site, and they also placed locks on the front gate of the Huron Indian Cemetery. In addition, Eliza, Ida, and Helena, all took turns to fervently guard the Huron Indian Cemetery with their lives, both at day and at night. Furthermore, the Conley Sisters were armed with a shot gun to confront any trespassers onto the Huron Indian Cemetery.

On 14 January 1910, Eliza had her day in the Supreme Court of the United States. Eliza, representing herself and the Wyandotte people, effectively argued the case that the 1855 Federal Treaty between the United States government and the Wyandotte Nation prevented the U.S. government from disposing of the native land. In addition, Eliza asserted that the living descendants, namely, herself and her two sisters, Helena and Ida, now possessed the inherited legal right to the exclusive use of the native land, upon which the Huron Indian Cemetery was erected, for the Conley Sisters had inherited this legal right from their Wyandotte ancestors (who had executed the aforesaid Treaty with the U.S. government). Eliza was the first native American woman from Kansas to argue a legal case in her own capacity before the Supreme Court of the United States. On the other hand, the U.S. government contested that both Eliza and her two sisters were now U.S. citizens, and the Huron Indian Cemetery in question was not part of the agreed 'land allotments' in Kansas that belonged to the Wyandotte people.

Notwithstanding the soundness, quality, and merit of Eliza's legal argument, on 31 January 1910, the U.S. Supreme Court Justice, Oliver Wendell Holmes (1841-1935) made a determination in favour of the U.S. government, and he decided not to overturn the decision of the lower

U.S. Court. As a result, the Supreme Court officially approved the U.S. government's actions to sell the sacred land on which the Huron Indian Cemetery was positioned. Undeterred by the closure of this legal avenue by the highest Court in the United States, the three Conley Sisters held an unwavering belief in their just cause and conviction to protect the Huron Indian Cemetery with their lives.

In the year 1913, influential Kansas State Senator, Charles Curtis (1860-1936), drafted and introduced a bill before the U.S. Congress with the express purpose of prohibiting sale of the sacred land upon which the Huron Indian Cemetery was erected. Senator Curtis' sponsored bill was passed by the U.S. Congress, and it repealed certain sections of *the Indian Appropriation Act of 1906*. Senator Curtis' bill also made a recommendation to have the Huron Indian Cemetery designated as a 'National Monument' of great cultural and historical significance. As a result, in 1916, the U.S. Congress set aside funds for the maintenance and preservation of the Huron Indian Cemetery.

In spite of the positive legislative developments to protect the Huron Indian Cemetery, the Conley Sisters kept a close watch and vigilant guard upon their cherished Cemetery in Kansas City, Kansas. In June of 1937, Eliza haphazardly chased away trespassers on the Huron Indian Cemetery with a broomstick. Subsequently, Eliza was charged by the local police authorities with the offence of public disturbance. Thereafter, Eliza appeared before a judge at a U.S. Court of Law. Eliza's conduct was criminalised by the State, and she was offered the choice of a USD $10 fine, or a ten day jail sentence for a breach of the peace. Eliza selected the latter penalty, and she proudly served her brief prison sentence in protest at the injustice levied against her Indigenous American people and their sacred native lands.

For the remaining years of their lifespan, the three Conley Sisters continued the preservation of their ancestor's Cemetery. On 28 May 1946, Eliza passed away due to a tragic incident. Eliza was the victim of a robbery in which she was physically assaulted, causing her serious bodily injuries. Eliza was buried alongside the Wyandotte people at the Huron Indian Cemetery. Eliza's life was dedicated to the preservation of her Wyandotte ancestor's legacy, and their rightful place in the Kansas City's history.

In 1971, the Huron Indian Cemetery was listed on the U.S. National Register of Historic Places. Last but not least, in the year 2016, more than a century after Eliza had first fought in the United States' Courts for the legal ownership of the Kansas City land upon which the Huron Indian Cemetery was situated, the aforesaid Cemetery was designated as a National Historic Landmark. This newfound status irreversibly ended the future possibility of any private development on the sacred land that is occupied by the Huron Indian Cemetery. Rest in Peace the Conley Sisters.

Clara Brett Martin (1874-1923)

Clara Brett Martin was born on 25 January 1874 in Toronto, Ontario, Canada. Clara's father was Abraham Martin, and her mother was Elizabeth Martin. Clara came from an Irish family of farmers. Clara was the youngest child in her family, and she had eleven siblings. In addition, the Martin family members were faithful adherents of the Anglican faith.

In the year 1888, Clara enrolled at Trinity College in Toronto, Canada, where she studied a Bachelor of Arts (BA) Degree, majoring in mathematics. By any measure, Clara was a gifted and talented student. Furthermore, Clara's early college studies inculcated within her the foundations for advanced university study in the later years of her life. On 27 June 1890, Clara graduated from Trinity college, she was awarded a Bachelor of Arts (BA) Degree with honours. Thereafter, Clara turned her attention to the institution of Common Law.

In 1891, Clara submitted a petition to the Law Society of Upper Canada to join as a student member of the Society. The aforesaid Law Society rejected Clara's petition on the grounds of her sex. While the Law Society of Upper Canada's statute incorporated the word 'person' to practice Law in the Dominion of Canada, the Special Committee chaired by Canadian jurist, Samuel Hume Blake (1835-1914), which was tasked with reviewing Clara's petition, narrowly interpreted the meaning of 'person'. That is to say, the Special Committee inferred that the Law Society's statute only allowed 'men' to study and practice Law in the Dominion of Canada. Notwithstanding the regrettable response from the Law Society, Clara's endeavour to become a member of the Canadian Legal Profession did not end here.

Clara sought legislative remedies in order to overcome the injustice, or rather prejudice, that withheld her student membership to become involved in the Canadian Legal Profession. In 1892, the Member of Provincial Parliament (MPP) for Essex South, the Honourable William Douglas Balfour (1851-1896), introduced a bill to the Provincial Parliament that would permit women to practice Law in the Dominion of Canada. Not to mention, Clara also received support from influential women in her endeavour to promote equality between the sexes in the Canadian Legal Profession, including Canadian physician, Doctor Emily Howarde

Stowe (1831-1903), and British author and philanthropist, Ishbel Maria Hamilton-Gordon (also known as Lady Aberdeen) (1857-1939). MPP Balfour's bill received strong support from Canadian lawyer, politician, and *Ontario Liberal Party* Leader, Sir Oliver Mowat (1820-1903), who at the time was Ontario's Premier and Attorney-General.

However, the bill permitting women membership to the Canadian Legal Profession was not passed without the usual disagreement of Canadian domestic politics. The leader of the Opposition Party, Sir William Ralph Meredith (1840-1923), criticised the draft bill, arguing that it was an affront to the Canadian society and its values. Ultimately, with some compromise in the bill, bipartisan support was secured and the legislation under consideration was passed by the Parliament of Canada on 13 April 1892. The final wording of the 1892 Statute empowered the Law Society of Upper Canada with 'discretionary power' to admit Canadian women, up to the standing of a solicitor, in the Canadian Legal Profession.

Despite the existence of a positive affirmation for women enshrined in the Canadian legislation, Clara's protracted struggle with the Law Society of Upper Canada was not over yet. The affluent and privileged members of the Canadian society, who were mostly, if not all, learned men of Anglo-Saxon or European descent of the Law Society of Upper Canada, reconvened several weeks later to discuss the 'implications' of the new legislation on the Canadian Legal Profession. Once again, on 21 June 1892, the honourable members of the aforesaid Society voted to deny Clara's application, on the basis that it was not suitable, or rather it was impracticable, to devise a set of rules to permit women into the Law Society, and the Canadian Legal Profession. To Clara's benefit, on 9 December 1892, Ontario's Premier and Attorney-General, Sir Oliver Mowat, effectively argued the case for Clara's admission into the Law Society and the Legal Profession on her behalf. The decisive matter came to a vote in the Law Society of Upper Canada, and it was a deadlock. Finally, the Chair of the Law Society, the Honourable Sir Aemilius Irving (1823-1913) intervened. Most notably, Sir Aemilius Irving broke the deadlock by voting in favour of Clara's admission.

In June 1893, Clara commenced articling with Toronto based law firm, Mulock, Miller, Crowther, and Montgomery. Regrettably, Clara was treated so badly (on the basis of sex), that she changed law practices, and began to work at the law firm known as Blake, Lash, and Cassels (now known as Blake, Cassels, and Graydon LLP). Clara also studied Common Law at university in considerable detail. Not to mention, Clara obtained a Bachelor of Civil Law (BCL) from Trinity University in 1897. Thereafter, Clara was awarded a Bachelor of Laws (LLB) from the University of Toronto in 1899.

While Clara was now permitted to practice as a solicitor, subject to the 'discretion' of the Law Society of Upper Canada, she aimed much higher and was determined to become a barrister. Thus, Clara sought the requisite admission from the Law Society of Upper Canada to practice as a solicitor and as a barrister. This loftier endeavour of becoming a barrister required the joint lobbying and campaigning efforts of Lady Aberdeen, the International Council of Women (ICW), and the National Council of Women of Canada (NCWC). Of great significance herein, it was the praiseworthy work of the Member of Provincial Parliament (MPP) for Brant North, the Honourable William Bruce Wood (1848-1928), who had introduced a bill to the Parliament of Canada to admit female barristers in the Canadian Legal Profession, that made Clara's ideal vision of becoming a barrister into a plausible and newfound conventional reality.

Once again, the Law Society of Upper Canada utilised the same conventional methods to stall Clara's advance into the Canadian Legal Profession as a barrister, as it had previously done to stop her becoming a solicitor. First, the aforesaid Law Society utilised its 'discretion' to prevent permitting Clara to practice as a barrister, then it referred the matter to a 'Special Committee' for review and adjudication, however, all the Law Society managed to accomplish was a delay of the inevitable decision. Finally, the Law Society permitted Clara to practice as a barrister, on the basis of her ability and competency, without regard to her sex. It was in the year 1897, at the age of twenty-three, that Clara made history. For Clara became the first woman to be admitted as a solicitor and as a barrister not only in the Dominion of Canada, but also the first woman in the British Empire!

Clara made progress remarkably quickly in her legal career. Clara commenced practicing as a lawyer with the Toronto based firm Shilton, Wallbridge, and Company, and she was promoted up the corporate ladder to become a Firm Partner in the year 1901. Thereafter, Clara resigned from Shilton, Wallbridge, and Company, to establish her own legal practice. Clara specialised in the areas of family law, real estate, wills, and probate law.

Beyond the domain of Common Law, Clara was also an active member of the Toronto Collegiate Institute Board from 1896 to 1899, and the Public School Board from 1901 to 1910. Clara utilised her profound legal knowledge, esteemed reputable position in the modern Canadian society, diverse legal career experience, and strong personal influence to promote the legal, economic, political, civil, cultural, and social rights of Canadian women across the Dominion of Canada.

On 30 October 1923, Clara passed away from the onset of a heart attack. Clara was 49 years old at the time of her death. Clara was buried at the Saint James Cemetery in Toronto, Ontario, Canada. Clara's unprecedented accomplishments in the field of Common Law, have made it possible for countless women, who have come after her to study and practice Law in Canada, without the prejudice of blatant sex discrimination, which once barred women for practicing Law in Canada. Clara's battle for equality with the Law Society of Upper Canada challengec the status quo, the outdated assumptions, and the institutionalised ideology, that it was not a woman's place to practice as a lawyer in the modern Canadian society.

Ivy Williams (1877-1966)

Ivy Williams was born on 7 September 1877 in Newton Abbot, Devon, England. Ivy came from an English family. Ivy's father was a respected solicitor by the name of George St Swithin Williams. Ivy's mother was Emma Ewers. Ivy had one older brother named Winter Williams, who went on to become a barrister. Ivy was educated privately, and she studied many languages, including French, German, Greek, Italian, Latin, and Russian. Furthermore, Ivy also travelled briefly to Europe, before she committed herself to the pursuit of Common Law studies in England. Ivy never married, and she did not have any children.

With Ivy's father being a solicitor, and her brother being a barrister, the English Legal Profession was part and parcel of the Williams family tradition. Ivy herself desired to become a lawyer, however, the inequalities and disparities of sex could not be more distinguished in a privileged profession such as Law, and the journey ahead of Ivy was not a convenient one. In the year 1895, Ivy attended the prestigious University of Oxford, where she studied Jurisprudence at the Society of Oxford Home Students (now known as St Anne's College). In 1900, Ivy completed her university degree, fulfilling the inherent requirements of a Bachelor of Arts (BA), she majored in the field of Jurisprudence. Notwithstanding Ivy's satisfactory academic performance, she was unjustly denied an award at the time due to her sex. Regrettably, Oxford University's regulations did not permit women to be granted a university degree in the year 1900, it was not until 1920 that such discriminatory regulations were belatedly amended. As a result, Ivy was retrospectively granted her Degree from the University of Oxford.

Thereafter, Ivy attended the University of London, where she studied a Bachelor of Laws (LLB). In the year 1901, Ivy graduated with her Bachelor of Laws from the University of London. Subsequently, Ivy went on to complete a Doctor of Laws (LLD), also at the University of London in 1903. Despite having undertaken a rigorous education in English Common Law, and being appropriately qualified to practice Law, Ivy was unable to seek admission into the English Legal Profession, due to her sex. It was not until the passage of *the Sex Disqualification (Removal) Act of 1919*, an Act of the Parliament of the United Kingdom, that it become a real possibility for English women to practice Law as barristers in the jurisdiction of England and Wales.

Following the passage of the aforementioned legislation, which no longer disallowed English women from becoming barristers, on 26 January 1920, with the support of British politician, Sir John Allsebrook Simon (1873-1954), Ivy was admitted to the Honourable Society of the Inner Temple (the Inner Temple) as a student member. Most notably, Ivy Williams was the second female student member to join the Inner Temple, after British barrister, writer, and activist, Helena Florence Normanton (1882-1957) in the year 1919. The Inner Temple is one of the Four Inns of

Court, along with Lincoln's Inn, Gray's Inn, and Middle Temple, all of which formally call law students to the Bar of England and Wales.

Thereafter, Ivy completed her Bar exams with a commendable score of 475. Ivy was awarded a Certificate of Honour for her admirable achievement. On 10 May 1922, Ivy was formally called to the Bar of England and Wales, a most historic moment for an English woman of her time. Despite such an unprecedented accomplishment in the field of English Common Law, Ivy ultimately decided not to pursue the distinguished career of a barrister in England. Instead, for the great part of Ivy's working age life, she pursued a respectable career as a Lecturer of Common Law at university.

From 1920 to 1945, Ivy taught as a University Lecturer in the field of Law at the Society of Oxford Home Students, the University of Oxford. Ivy's remarkable teaching career was only enhanced by her eloquent writing and detailed research in the field of Law. Not to mention, Ivy authored two influential texts, which are still widely acknowledged by legal experts and cited by university academics to this day, namely, *the Sources of Law in the Swiss Civil Code* in 1923, and *the Swiss Civil Code: English Version, with Notes and Vocabulary* in 1925.

In fact, Ivy's earlier work *the Sources of Law in the Swiss Civil Code* written in 1923, earnt her the prestigious Doctor of Civil Law (DCL) from the University of Oxford. In addition, Ivy had the honour and privilege of becoming the first English woman to be awarded the DCL award from the University of Oxford. Ivy's authoritative academic work and expertise knowledge in the field of Law, ensured her appointment in 1930 as a Technical Delegate representing Great Britain to *the Conference for the Codification of International Law* held in the Hague, the Netherlands.

In addition, Ivy also worked in the administration of Public Law in the United Kingdom. Specifically, Ivy was involved in the application of the

United Kingdom's Immigration Law, that is to say, the interpretation of *the Aliens Restriction (Amendment) Act of 1919*. Most notably, in the year 1932, Ivy was appointed as a member of *the Aliens Deportation Advisory Committee*. This Committee was tasked with reviewing deportation orders issued by the United Kingdom Home Office for aliens and foreigners residing in the United Kingdom. The aforesaid Committee was formally dissolved by the British government in 1939. In the year 1956, Ivy was appointed as an Honorary Fellow at St Anne's College in recognition of her monumental contribution to the field of Law.

On 18 February 1966, Ivy passed away in her home located at 12 King Edward Street, Oxford, England. Ivy was 88 years old at the time of her death. More recently, Ivy's pioneering legacy in the field of Common Law has been honoured. In 2020, English barrister, Karlia Lykourgou of Doughty Street Chambers established a law clothing company, known as Ivy and Normanton. This company specialises in courtroom appropriate attire that is specifically designed for female lawyers. Last but not least, also in the year 2020, a plaque honouring Ivy Williams was affixed to her aforementioned home address.

Grata Flos Matilda Greig (1880-1958)

Grata Flos Matilda Greig was born on 7 November 1880 in Broughty Ferry, Scotland. Grata's father was a textile merchant named Robert Lindsay Greig. Grata's mother was Jane Greig. Grata had seven siblings, three brothers, namely, James Arthur, Ernest Howard, and Hector Maximus, as well as four sisters, namely, Jane Stocks, Janet Lindsay, Stella Fida, and Clara Puella. Grata's father believed in the principle of equal opportunity in higher education for both boys and girls, and this important belief immensely benefited Grata's ambitions and endeavours. In 1889, Grata and her family immigrated to Melbourne, Victoria, the Commonwealth of Australia.

Grata grew up in the City of Melbourne. From 1894 to 1896, Grata attended the Presbyter an Ladies' College (PLC) in Burwood. While Grata was still at school she decided upon a career in legal practice. In 1897, Grata matriculated at the University of Melbourne to study an Arts and Law Degree. Grata was the first female student to study at the University of Melbourne's Faculty of Law. In the year 1900, Grata received her Bachelor of Arts (BA) Degree. Thereafter, Grata continued her university studies in Common Law at the University of Melbourne. Subsequently, Grata obtained her Bachelor of Laws (LLB) on 28 March 1903. Grata became the first woman in the state of Victoria to graduate with a Law Degree. In addition, Grata was the second woman to be awarded a Law Degree in Australia, after Australian lawyer, Ada Emily Evans (1872-1947) from the University of Sydney in the State of New South Wales. Ada Emily Evans had studied at the Sydney Law School, and she graduated with a Bachelor of Laws (LLB) Degree on 26 November 1902.

At the time, by established legal practice, custom, and convention Australian women were not entitled to practice the noble profession of Law in the Commonwealth State of Victoria. To alter this sexist status quo in Victoria, in the year 1903, the Parliament of Victoria passed *the Women's Disabilities Removal Act of 1903* (also known as *the Flos Greig Enabling Act*). Thereafter, by the virtue of legislation, the State law explicitly permitted Australian women to practice Law in the Commonwealth State of Victoria.

Grata completed her articles of clerkship at the Melbourne-based law firm, Frank Cornwall (now known as Cornwalls). Most importantly, on 1 August 1905, Grata was admitted to the Victorian Bar. With this grand accomplishment, Grata made modern history, she became the first Australian woman to be formally admitted into the Legal Profession of an Australian State. In addition, Grata also joined the Law Institute of Victoria, and again, she was the first Australian woman to do so.

Grata was a pragmatic woman, and she opted to practice as a solicitor, rather than pursue the more rigorous career path of a barrister-at-law. While not lacking the requisite motivation or intelligence, Grata accurately perceived the widespread injustices, sex discrimination, prejudice, and institutional bias that women confronted in the Australian Legal Profession at the commencement of the twentieth century. Thus, from the outset, Grata strategically determined to make her contribution in the field of Law, where she would make her greatest impact.

Notwithstanding the numerous barriers that Australian women faced in the Australian Legal Profession at the time, Grata made quite a remarkable contribution in her capacity as a lawyer. Not to mention, Grata was an influential spokesperson on legal matters in the Victorian community. For example, in 1905, Grata presented an informative speech at the annual National Congress of Women of Victoria, her speech addressed legal matters that involved children and women. Furthermore, Grata worked closely with the Women's Christian Temperance Union (WCTU), where she promoted positive social behaviours in the Victorian community.

In addition, Grata also drafted significant amendments to the Child's Court Act of 1906. The aforesaid State legislation ultimately resulted in the formation of the Children's Court of Victoria, a statutory Court which was established in the year 1906. On the broader social, economic, and political dimensions, the Victorian state, institutions, and society were all beginning to fundamentally change. That is to say, a more equal and fitting role for women was being enacted in the aforesaid Commonwealth State. For example, consider that in 1908, Victorian women were afforded the right to vote in State elections.

Grata continued to proceed from strength-to-strength in her steadfast determination to advance women's involvement in the Australian Legal Profession. For example, in the year 1910, Grata was a founding member of the Catalysts' Society (now known as the Melbourne Lyceum Club). The Melbourne Lyceum Club now provides university educated women with professional networking opportunities in fields diverse as: the arts, education, journalism, literature, the learned professions, and science. In addition, Grata was elected the first President of the Women's Law Society of Victoria, which was established in the year 1914.

Beyond Grata's outsized contribution to the Australian Legal Profession, she was also a keen traveller. In fact, Grata was well traversed across the many countries situated in the Asia Pacific region, including Bali, Burma, China, Java, Malaysia, Siam (now known as Thailand), and Singapore. In the later years of Grata's legal career, she was employed at a law firm known as Cornwall Stodart. Thereafter, Grata practiced at a law firm in Wangaratta headed by Paul McSwiney.

In the year 1942, Grata decided to formally retire from legal practice. Retirement did not cease Grata's proactive involvement in the social, legal, economic, and political affairs of Victoria. Not to mention, Grata was also involved in initiating meaningful change at the federal level, across the Commonwealth of Australia. Furthermore, Grata continued to campaign for greater opportunities for Australian women to receive a university education. Last but not least, Grata also supported the Australian political party known as *the Douglas Credit Party*.

On 31 December 1958, Grata passed away in Moorabbin, Victoria, Australia. Grata was 78 years old at the time of her death. In the year 2015, an Australian not-for-profit public interest advocacy organisation, *the Grata Fund* was established in Grata's memory. *The Grata Fund* assists Australian people and communities with equitable access to the Australian Law Courts, and its lawyers provide expertise in legal counsel in their noble quest for justice.

Helena Florence Normanton (1882-1957)

Helena Florence Normanton was born on 14 December 1882 in East London, England. Helena's father was William Alexander Normanton, and her mother was Jane Amelia. Unfortunately, Helena's parents separated when she was only four years old. As a result, Helena's mother was the sole care provider to Helena and her younger sister, Ethel. In addition, in the year 1886, Helena's father died when Helena was still a very young girl.

Commencing in the year 1900, Helena was initially educated at York Place Secondary School (later known as Margaret Hardy School for Girls) in Brighton. Thereafter, from 1903 to 1905, Helena attended Edge College in Liverpool, where she studied teaching. Helena was an ambitious young gentlelady, and she whole-heartedly continued the pursuit of her higher education. Most notably, Helena went on to study the French language, along with French history and literature at Dijon University in Dijon, France. In 1907, Helena graduated from Dijon University with a Diploma. Furthermore, Helena also studied history at the University of London. In 1912, Helena was awarded a Bachelor of Arts (BA) Degree, she majored in history, with first class honours from the University of London.

From 1913 to 1915, Helena taught history classes at the Glasgow High School for Girls, and she was employed as a Lecturer at the University of Glasgow in Glasgow, Scotland. Subsequently, Helena was appointed as a Lecturer in the History Department at the University of London. While Helena was lecturing at university, she remained interested in a legal career. Unfortunately, Helena's February 1918 application to *the Honourable Society of the Middle Temple* (the Middle Temple) had been rejected, almost certainly due to her sex. As a result, Helena petitioned the House of Lords in relation to the sex discrimination that she confronted when attempting to join the English Legal Profession. In this respect, Helena received the support of Permanent Secretary to the Lord Chancellor, the Right Honourable Claud Schuster (1869-1956), however, upon appeal to the Middle Temple, her application was again refused in January of 1919.

Despite a disappointing start to 1919, Helena remained persistent in her endeavours to join the English Legal Profession. In fact, the year 1919 constituted a major turning point in Helena's professional life and career aspirations to become a practicing lawyer. Most importantly, *the Sex Disqualification (Removal) Act of 1919* was passed by the Parliament of the United Kingdom. Notwithstanding Helena's previous rejections, when *the Sex Disqualification (Removal) Act of 1919* received royal assent on 23 December 1919, Helena immediately reapplied to join the Middle

Temple as a law student on 24 December 1919. This time round Helena's application was successful.

On 26 October 1921, Helena married an accountant by the name of Gavin Bowman Watson Clark. The married couple did not have any children. Not to mention, Helena made the decision to keep her maiden name, she decided not to adopt her husband's surname for professional reasons. In fact, in the year 1924, Helena became the first married British woman to have a British Passport issued in her maiden name by the United Kingdom.

Despite the legal inequities, economic disparities, and social challenges that British women confronted in their desire to become esteemed members of the English Legal Profession, Helena experienced an illustrious and accomplished career as a lawyer. On 17 November 1922, Helena became the second woman, after British lawyer and university lecturer, Doctor Ivy Williams (1877-1966), to be called to the Bar of England and Wales. In addition, in the year 1922, Helena was the first female counsel in a legal case before the High Court of Justice in London (formerly known as Her Majesty's High Court of Justice in England). Furthermore, in the year 1924, Helena became the first female barrister to be briefed at the Old Bailey (also known as the Central Criminal Court of England and Wales). Not to mention, in 1926, Helena was also the first female barrister to attend the North London Sessions. Last but not least, in the year 1949, Helena, along with British barrister, Rose Heilbron (1914-2005), shared the joint honour to become the first two English women to be appointed as King's Counsel (KC) at the English Bar.

Aside from Helena's dedication and commitment to the institution of Common Law, during her lifetime, Helena also dedicated her time to writing and publishing on matters of social, economic, political, legal, cultural, historical, and global importance. Some of Helena's influential writings include: *Sex Differentiation in Salary, India in England, the Trial of Norman Thorne, the Trial of Alfred Arthur Rouse, Everyday Law for Women, the Trial of Mrs. Duncan*, and *What's in a Woman's Name*. The archives of Helena Normanton are held by the Women's Library located at the London School of Economics and Political Science in the United Kingdom.

On 14 October 1957, Helena passed away in a Sydenham nursing home in London, England. Helena was 74 years old at the time of her death. Upon Helena's death, her body was cremated, and her ashes were subsequently buried next to her husband at the Ovingdean Churchyard in Brighton, England, the United Kingdom. Helena continues to be remembered in the English Legal Profession, and her epoch-making legacy is respectfully honoured. In the year 2019, the 218 Strand Chambers was renamed Normanton Chambers after Helena Normanton. Last but not least, in the year 2021, a blue plaque was unveiled at 22 Mecklenburgh Square in Bloomsbury, London, commemorating Helena's admirable and historic contribution to the English Legal Profession.

Florence Ellinwood Allen (1884-1966)

Florence Ellinwood Allen was born on 23 March 1884 in Salt Lake City, Utah, the United States of America. Florence's father was a Professor and Linguist named Clarence Emir Allen. Florence's mother was Corinne Marie Allen. Florence came from a family of seven children, consisting of five girls and two boys, however, one of her sisters did not survive beyond infancy.

Florence was raised in Cleveland, Ohio, and during her childhood she was taught Greek and Latin. Florence was educated at the New Lyme Institute in Ashtabula, Ohio. Most notably, Florence excelled in music and poetry. Upon completion of Florence's school studies, she matriculated at the Western Reserve University (now known as the Case Western Reserve University) in Cleveland, Ohio, where she studied music. In 1904, Florence graduated from the Western Reserve University with a Bachelor of Arts (BA) Degree.

After the completion of Florence's university degree, she travelled to the City of Berlin, Germany. While in Berlin, Florence completed further studies in music for the next two years. Initially, Florence had planned to become a Concert Pianist, however, a nerve injury prevented her from the complete realisation of this personal endeavour. In the year 1906, Florence returned to Ohio, the United States, and she secured employment as a music critic for an Ohio newspaper, *the Plain Dealer*. Florence worked at *the Plain Dealer* newspaper for the next three years, until the year 1909. During Florence's three years at the aforesaid newspaper, she began to intricately examine the structure and function of the modern American society, including its ideas, associations, learned professions, and prominent institutions, matters well beyond her primary domain of music. It was during this time, that Florence realised her newfound interest in law and politics.

As a result, Florence returned to the Western Reserve University to pursue a Master of Arts (MA) Degree, she majored in political science. In the year 1908, Florence graduated with a MA Degree from the Western Reserve University. Florence demonstrated an unwavering interest for university study in the field of Law, however, soon enough, she encountered several difficulties and challenges. Of greatest concern, was the lack of opportunities and acceptance of American women to pursue a legal education in the United States of America. Notwithstanding such institutional barriers and systematic sex inequality in the early twentieth century American society, Florence possessed the tenacity, resolve, and diligence to navigate the unjust inequities that she inevitably confronted.

At the time, the Western Reserve University's Law School did not admit female law students. Thus, Florence enrolled at the University of Chicago Law School, where she studied Law for one year. Subsequently, Florence transferred her law studies to the New York University School of Law. In order to financially support herself during law school, Florence worked as a legal researcher at *the New York League for the Protection of Immigrants*. In 1913, Florence graduated with a Bachelor of Laws (LLB) with honours from the New York University School of Law. Following Florence's graduation from law school, she returned to Ohio and secured admission to the Ohio Bar in the year 1914.

As Florence soon realised, having a Law Degree from a prestigious U.S. law school, and being a certified practicing lawyer by the state of Ohio, did not prove entirely sufficient in her righteous quest to practice Law in the United States of America. Initially, Florence established a legal practice in Ohio, however, she struggled to attract clients, and was earning a meagre USD $25 per month. At this stage Florence only had sufficient financial capital for a work desk, two chairs, and a loaned typewriter. What Florence required most was professional experience and a sterling reputation. Thus, Florence started to work for *the Legal Aid Society of Cleveland*, during this time Florence also became involved in the American Women's Suffrage Movement. In addition, Florence was involved in the activities of *the Cleveland Women's City Club* (CWCC), *the Young Men's Christian Association* (YMCA), and *the Cleveland Business Women's Club* (CBWC).

In the year 1919, Florence was appointed Assistant Prosecutor for Cuyahoga County in Ohio. Florence became the first American woman to hold such an influential position in the state of Ohio. From 1919 onwards, Florence's legal career went from strength to strength. In 1920, Florence was elected as a judge to the Court of Common Pleas in Cuyahoga County. Most notably, during Florence's time as a judge on the Bench of the Court of Common Pleas, Florence adjudicated hundreds of legal cases. Thereafter, in 1922, Florence was appointed to the Ohio Supreme Court, she became the first American woman to achieve this esteemed honour in the Ohio society. To a great extent, and beyond the capacity of Florence's brilliant legal mind, what made her tremendous success possible was the ratification of *the Nineteenth Amendment* in 1920 by the United States Congress. *The Nineteenth Amendment* not only guaranteed American women the legal right to vote, but it also elevated the social, political, civil, and economic standing of women in the modern American society, to unprecedented new heights.

In the year 1928, Florence was elected to a second six-year term as a judge on the Ohio Supreme Court. Florence was an ardent supporter of *the Democratic Party*, however, she kept party politics out of the judiciary. Florence's impartiality in the adjudication of the law, very much assisted her in augmenting her reputation as an independent, objective, and fair-minded judge. Indeed, Florence did not let the politics of the day impede the public administration of justice. Furthermore, the appointment of the U.S. President, Franklin D. Roosevelt in 1933 only assisted Florence to accomplish an impressive record of service in the United States' Legal Profession.

On 6 March 1934, the U.S. President, Franklin D. Roosevelt (r. 1933-1945), nominated Florence to serve on the United States Court of Appeals for the Sixth Circuit. Florence's presidential nomination was later confirmed by the United States Senate on 15 March 1934. As a result, Florence, who was formally commissioned on 21 March 1934, became the second American woman to serve in the United States Federal Judiciary, after American jurist and judge, Genevieve Rose Cline (1877-1959), who served as an Article I judge on the United States Customs Court. Notwithstanding being the second American woman to serve in the U.S. Federal Judiciary, Florence was the first American woman to serve as an Article III federal judge in the United States of America.

Florence served on the United States Court of Appeals for the Sixth Circuit for some twenty-five years. In 1958, Florence assumed Chief Judgeship of the aforesaid Court, after Chief Judge, Charles Casper Simons (1876-1964), relinquished the position of Chief Judge on 17 September 1958. Herein Florence secured another first of an American woman, namely, she became the first woman in the United States of America to be appointed Chief Judge on a United States Federal Court. On 5 February 1959, Florence officially relinquished her position as Chief Judge, and she retired from the United States Federal Bench. Despite Florence's profound intellectual capacity and sound understanding of the United States Legal System and Law, Florence was never appointed to the Supreme Court of the United States.

Throughout Florence's lifetime, she was committed to the just cause of women's rights, and she was a dedicated pacifist. Florence was against war and the use of force to resolve international disputes. As a result, Florence opposed the use of atomic weapons employed against Imperial Japan during the course of *World War II (1939-1945)*. Not to mention, Florence idealised the restoration of the 'morality' of sovereign nation-states as the underlying principle for a safe and secure World Order. According to Florence, the contemporary World Order ought to be underwritten by the tenets of peace, justice, liberty, and equality. Florence never married, and she had no children of her own.

In addition to Florence's commendable career as an American lawyer and United States judge, she also published several books. Some of Florence's writings include: *This Constitution of Ours*, *The Treaty as an Instrument of Legislation*, *Patris*, and *To Do Justly*. Not to mention, Florence also published articles in *the Women Lawyer's Journal*. Florence's invaluable writings reflect her immense breadth and depth of experience across the United States Legal Profession.

On 12 September 1966, Florence passed away from a cerebrovascular accident in Waite Hill, Ohio, the United States of America. Florence was 82 years old at the time of her death. Florence was buried at Waite Hill Village Cemetery in Ohio. In many respects, it was Florence's remarkable achievements and protracted struggles, that made it possible for Justice Sandra Day O'Connor to be appointed as the first American female Justice to the Supreme Court of the United States by the U.S. President, Ronald Reagan (r. 1981-1989) in the year 1981, an honourable position which Justice O'Connor held until 2006.

In 2005, Florence was inducted to the United States National Women's Hall of Fame. In addition, Florence is also a member of the Ohio Women's Hall of Fame. Florence was a distinguished American jurist, and she was awarded the prestigious Albert Gallatin Medal by New York University. Last but not least, Florence was also bestowed numerous honorary degrees from universities and colleges for her outsized contribution to the United States Legal Profession, including degrees from the Ohio State University, the University of Utah, and the University of North Carolina Greensboro.

Madge Easton Anderson (1896-1982)

Madge Easton Anderson was born on 24 April 1896 in Glasgow, Scotland. Madge's father was a surgical instrument maker named Robert Easton. Madge's mother was Anne Catherine Chisholm. Madge was the youngest of three children in her family. Madge had two older sisters, namely, Ellen and Muriel. Initially, Madge was educated at Melville Street Primary School in Scotland. In 1904, Madge changed schools, and she was enrolled as a foundation pupil at Hutcheson's Girls Grammar School in Glasgow, where she completed her school studies in the year 1913.

Madge matriculated at the University of Glasgow, where she studied a Master of Arts (MA) Degree. Madge's university subjects included four languages, namely, English, French, Greek, and Latin, in conjunction with studies in moral philosophy and zoology. On 26 June 1916, Madge graduated with her Master of Arts (MA) Degree from the University of Glasgow. Following the completion of Madge's first university degree, she entered the workforce. As a result, Madge gained first-hand experience in the Scottish Legal Profession.

In the year 1917, Madge secured employment as an apprentice law agent, courtesy of John Alexander Spens at the Glasgow law firm named Maclay, Murray, and Spens (now known as Dentons). After much careful deliberation over the course of 1917, Madge decided to concentrate on and specialise in her chosen career path in the field of Law. Madge went on to complete her Bachelor of Laws (LLB) Degree also from the University of Glasgow, she graduated on 8 November 1919. Whilst Madge was a law student at the University of Glasgow's School of Law, she studied the Law of Scotland, Public International Law, Civil Law, and Constitutional Law and History.

In the year 1917, when Madge was still employed as an apprentice, she applied for registration as a 'law agent' with the Scottish Law Agents Society (now superseded by the Law Society of Scotland) pursuant to *the Law Agents Act of 1873*, however, Madge's application was rejected, in majority part, due to her sex. Madge appealed the outcome to the Court of Session (i.e., the Supreme Civil Court of Scotland). Madge's petition was received by the Inner House (First Division), and it was subject to a formal hearing in December of 1920. Ultimately, it was the sound judgement of Scottish lawyer, John Wilson, Lord Ashmore KC (1857-1932), at the aforesaid Court which resolved that Madge was rightly entitled to have her petition granted. Thus, the aforesaid Law Court upheld Madge's appeal, and the Court's decision was formally registered in January of 1921.

In addition to Madge's successful appeal hearing in a Scottish Court of Law, on a broader legal-political spectrum positive changes were coming into force across the sovereign territory of the United Kingdom. Most notably, the Parliament of the United Kingdom had recently passed *the Sex Disqualification (Removal) Act of 1919*. Consequently, the possibility of practicing Law in Scotland now became a much more plausible reality for Madge. Once again, Madge followed established procedure and protocol, and she applied to register as a 'law agent' with the Scottish Law Agents Society. On this occasion, Madge's application was accepted. As a result, Madge was now entitled to practice as a solicitor in Scotland.

In the year 1922, Madge was employed by a Glasgow law firm known as John Steuart and Gillies. Madge worked at the aforesaid firm for several years, and she gained the requisite experience and competency to establish her own legal practice. In 1931, Madge, in connection with English solicitor, Edith Annie Jones Berthen (1877-1951), and British barrister, Beatrice Honour Davy (1885-1966), came together as Partners to establish their own law practice. This was a historic first in the United Kingdom, namely, a legal practice that was entirely managed and organised by female lawyers.

In 1937, Madge passed her English Law Society exam, and thereby, she fulfilled the inherent requirements to practice as a solicitor in England. As a result, Madge became the first woman to be certified to practice as a solicitor in both England and Scotland. In the year 1951, Madge officially retired from practicing Law, and she relocated to Perth, Scotland. On 9 August 1982, Madge passed away at the Royal Infirmary in Perth, Scotland. Madge was 86 years old at the time of her death. Madge has been honoured with a blue plaque affixed to the Stair Building at the University of Glasgow's School of Law.

Among many things, Madge was a catalyst for profound social, political, and legal change in England and Scotland. The notable (and often unprecedented) accomplishments of Madge have made it possible for the following generations of English and Scottish women to enter the learned profession of Law, as solicitors, law clerks, Crown prosecutors, barristers, judges, university lectures, academics, deans, and scholars.

The unshakeable confidence and unquestionable belief of Madge, made it possible for her to reach towering new heights in the Scottish Legal Profession. Indeed, Madge's remarkable story has empowered countless women to pursue their dreams and aspirations to practice Law. Madge's struggle and accomplishments have made the distant dream of a career in Law into a living reality for many notable women, including Noreen Burrows, Sheila McLean, Lady Cosgrove, and Lady Clark.

Joan Ruth Bader Ginsburg (1933-2020)

Joan Ruth Bader Ginsburg was born on 15 March 1933 at Beth Moses Hospital, New York City, the United States of America. Joan's father was Nathan Bader, and her mother was Celia Amster Bader. Joan came from a Jewish family of immigrant parents, and she had an older sister named Marilyn. Unfortunately, Marilyn passed away at the age of six due to meningitis.

In the early years of Joan's life, she was educated at James Madison High School in Brooklyn, New York City. After Joan finished her high school studies, she matriculated at Cornell University in Ithaca, New York. In the furtherance of Joan's endeavour to attend university, she received a scholarship award for her undergraduate studies. Whilst at Cornell University, Joan studied a Bachelor of Arts (BA) Degree. On 23 June 1954, Joan graduated from Cornell University. Not to mention, Joan was the highest-ranking female student in her graduating class at Cornell University.

During Joan's time as a student at Cornell University, she met her future husband, Martin David Ginsburg, who was also studying a Bachelor of Arts (BA) Degree. The two individuals married a month after Joan's completed her undergraduate degree. Thereafter, Joan and Martin moved to Oklahoma, where Martin was stationed as a Reserve Officer in United States Army Reserve at Fort Sill. Concurrently, Joan secured local employment at the Social Security Administration Office in Lawton, Oklahoma. In the year 1955, Joan was demoted from her position of employment, after her pregnancy with her first baby girl, Jane Carol Ginsburg. Jane was born on 21 July 1955.

In the year 1956, Joan matriculated at Harvard Law School in Cambridge, Massachusetts, where she studied United States' Law for the next two years. During Joan's brief tenure at Harvard Law School, she was also editor of the Harvard Law Review. After Joan's husband, Martin graduated from Harvard Law School in 1958, he managed to secure employment at Weil, Gotshal, and Manges LLP in New York City. Thus, in the same year, Joan requested a formal transfer from the Harvard Law School Dean, Erwin Nathaniel Griswold (1904-1994), to complete her third year of study at Columbia Law School in New York City, New York, however, Dean Griswold denied her transfer request.

Consequently, Joan left Harvard Law School, and she enrolled at the Columbia Law School in 1958, where she studied and graduated with a Law Degree in the year 1959. Joan's academic performance was commendable, and she was tied first place in the graduating Law Class of 1959. During Joan's tenure as a student at the Columbia Law School, she served as an editor of the Columbia Law Review, and she also contributed to this prestigious U.S. law journal as an author.

At the time, finding suitable employment for a qualified female law graduate in New York was a most challenging endeavour. Not to mention, in Joan's particular case, she was of Jewish heritage, and a mother with a dependent child. This reality only served to make matters more difficult in Joan's case. Unfortunately, Joan experienced these unfair challenges associated with sex discrimination and prejudice first-hand. As a result, Joan was unsuccessful in the first twelve firms that interviewed her for a position of employment relating to legal work. For example, consider that the United States Supreme Court Justice, Felix Frankfurter (1882-1965), denied Joan a clerkship because she was a woman and a mother, this was despite Joan receiving a glowing recommendation from American lawyer, Albert Martin Sacks (1920-1991). It was the unwavering support of Columbia Professor of Law, Gerald Gunther (1927-2002), that made it possible for Joan to secure employment in New York. Professor Gunther persuaded Judge Edmund Louis Palmieri (1907-1989) of the United States District Court for the Southern District of New York to employ Joan as a qualified Law Clerk. Thus, from 1959 until 1961, Joan served as a Law Clerk at the aforesaid Court in the jurisdiction of New York.

Following Joan's clerkship with the United States District Court for the Southern District of New York, in 1963, Joan pivoted her law career towards research, publishing, writing, and academia. Joan worked at the Columbia Law School, first as a Research Associate, and then as an Associate Director. Also in the year 1963, Joan was appointed Professor at Rutgers Law School in Newark, New Jersey. As a female Law Professor, Joan was remunerated less than the male Law Professors at Rutgers University. Joan remained at Rutgers Law School for the better part of a decade, where she taught United States Civil Procedure. Not to mention, Joan also earnt tenure at the aforesaid institution in 1969. Joan resigned from her academic position at Rutgers University in 1972. Whilst Joan was employed at Rutgers Law school, she had her second child with Martin, a son named James Steven Ginsburg. James was born on 8 September 1965.

Furthermore, in the year 1965, Joan co-authored a book titled *Civil Procedure in Sweden* with Swedish jurist and judge, Anders Bruzelius (1911-2006). The endeavour of writing the aforesaid book included travelling to Sweden, where Joan conducted primary research in Swedish Law at the Lund University. During Joan's time in Sweden, she encountered a more equitable modern society, a place where relations between men and women were more positive. For example, consider that at the time there were many more female students studying Law at Lund University, than had been the case in the United States universities in which Joan had completed her U.S. Law studies. In addition, Swedish female lawyers were more prevalent in the Swedish Legal Profession, including in more prominent positions, such as a judge. Joan's insightful experiences and newfound observations in the modern Swedish society made a strong impression on her. Not to mention, Joan's time in Sweden, markedly influenced her thinking upon her return to the United States of America.

During the 1970's, Joan became an active participant in women's rights issues throughout the United States of America. In 1970, Joan was one of the founders of the Women's Rights Law Reports, a law journal that reported on women's rights. Thereafter, in the year 1972, Joan was a co-founder of the Women's Rights Project at the American Civil Liberties Union (ACLU). Furthermore, from 1972 to 1980, Joan taught as a Professor at the Columbia Law School, where she authored books on sex discrimination against women. Not to mention, Joan was also briefly employed as a Research Fellow from 1977 to 1978, at the Centre for Advanced Study in the Behavioural Sciences at Stanford University in Stanford, California.

After several years in the world of academia and universities, the year 1980 marked a turning point for Joan in her legal career. On 14 April 1980, Joan was nominated by the Democratic U.S. President, Jimmy Earl Carter (r. 1977-1981) to the United States Court of Appeals for the District of Columbia Circuit in Washington D.C. Joan's nomination was subsequently confirmed by the United States Senate on 18 June 1980. As a result, Joan went on to serve as an appellate judge for the next thirteen years, until her opportune time arrived for her deserving nomination to the Supreme Court of the United States.

On 14 June 1993, the Democratic U.S. President, Bill Clinton (r. 1993-2001), announced his nomination of Joan for the noble position of Associate Justice to the Supreme Court of the United States. Subsequently, Joan's nomination was formally confirmed by the United States Senate on 3 August 1993. Joan received her commission on 5 August 1993, and she took her judicial oath (that is to say, she was formally sworn in) on 10 August 1993. Most notably, Joan became the 107th Supreme Court Justice, and the second American woman in the history of the United States Supreme Court, after Sandra Day O'Connor's historic first appointment to the aforesaid Court on 25 September 1981.

From 1993 until 2020, Joan served on the highest Court in the United States of America. During Joan's long tenure at the Supreme Court, she authored detailed and thoughtful legal opinions on a wide variety of significant legal cases. Some of the landmark legal cases that Joan adjudicated at the Supreme Court of the United States include:

- *United States v. Virginia* (1996)
- *Olmstead v. L.C.,* (1999)
- *Bush v. Gore* (2000)
- *Ledbetter v. Goodyear Tyre & Rubber Co., Inc.* (2007)
- *Shelby County v. Holder* (2013)
- *Burwell v. Hobby Lobby Stores, Inc.* (2014)
- *Obergefell v. Hodges* (2015)
- *Whole Woman's Health v. Hellerstedt* (2016)

On 18 September 2020, Joan passed away in Washington D.C., after her protracted battle with cancer. Joan was 87 years old at the time of her death. Both throughout Joan's lifetime and after her death, she was and continues to be honoured by the American people and its esteemed institutions. For example, consider in the year 2002, Joan was inducted into the United States National Women's Hall of Fame. Not to mention, in the year 2015, Joan was named *Time Magazine's* 100 Most Influential People.

Furthermore, Joan was awarded countless honorary degrees from universities and colleges both in the United States of America, and from foreign countries, including Amherst College, Brown University, DePaul University, Harvard University, Hebrew Union College-Jewish Institute of Religion, Lund University, Princeton University, Vermont Law School, and Yale University. In addition, Joan was also the recipient of several prestigious medals and awards, such as the Golden Plate Award (1995), the Liberty Medal (2020), and the World Peace and Liberty Award (2020).

Chapter Seven

WOMEN IN SPORT

'What does it take to be a champion? Desire, dedication, determination, concentration, and the will to win.'

Patricia Jane Berg

This chapter examines a number of women who have made significant contributions to the institution of sport. The chapter will examine the notable achievements of female athletes across a broad range of sports, including athletics, baseball, basketball, figure skating, golf, gymnastics, high jump, swimming, tennis, and track and field. In addition, this chapter reviews the grand accomplishments of women at the Olympic Games in modern history, and it also considers women who have competed in professional sports from a number of nations across the world, such as Australia, Canada, Czechoslovakia, the Netherlands, New Zealand, Norway, Romania, the United Kingdom, and the United States of America.

Throughout much of human history, women never received equal opportunities to compete in sporting tournaments and championships throughout the world. Historically, the distinction of the female sex was a defining characteristic of a woman's capacity for participation in sport, however, progress has and continues to be made, albeit slowly and steadily. This chapter will explore some of the remarkable sporting achievements of Florence Madeline Syers, Sarah Frances Durack, Fanny Rosenfeld, Gertrude Caroline Ederle, Mildred Ella Didrikson Zaharias, Sonja Henie, Patricia Jane Berg, Francina Elsje Blankers-Koen, Alice Coachman Davis, Sophie Kurys, Althea Neale Gibson, Yvette Winifred Williams, Iolanda Balaş, Wilma Glodean Rudolph, Věra Čáslavská, Patricia Susan Summitt, and Florence Delorez Griffith Joyner.

Florence Madeline Syers (1881-1917)

Florence Madeline Cave Syers was born on 16 September 1881 in Kensington, London, England, the United Kingdom. Florence's father was a property developer and builder by the name of Edward Jarvis Cave. Florence's mother was Elizabeth Ann. Florence came from an English family of fifteen children. From quite a young age, Florence exhibited a passion for sport. In fact, as a child, Florence participated in equestrian, figure skating, and swimming. Florence's favourite sport was figure skating. Most notably, Florence joined the Prince's Skating Rink in Knightsbridge, London, where she diligently practiced her skating technique.

Through Florence's participation in the world-renowned sport of figure skating, she met her future husband and professional coach, British figure skater, Edgar Morris Wood Syers (1863-1946). Edgar carefully critiqued Florence's skating style. In addition, Edgar also encouraged Florence to discontinue the orthodox and conservative 'English' style of figure skating which exhibited limited body movement, and in its place, adopt the contemporary 'International' style of figure skating. Most notably, the latter style of figure skating demonstrated a greater range of movement of the human body.

By any measure, Florence was a dedicated and naturally talented athlete. Florence started participating in a number of tournaments and championships, demonstrating her exceptional ability and skill as a figure skater. For example, in the year 1899, Florence was a member of the team that won the Challenge Shield Championship. Thereafter, in 1900, Florence and her coach, Edgar got married. Throughout Florence and Edgar's lifetime, the two admirable sportspersons competed together and against one another in the international sport of figure skating. In the same year as their marriage, that is 1900, Florence and Edgar secured a respectable second place in an International Pairs Figure Skating Event that was held in the City of Berlin, Germany.

In the year 1902, Florence participated in the World Championships held in the City of London. While there were no explicit rules excluding women from this sporting competition, however, by the dictates of custom, only male participants were involved in the aforesaid Championship. Nonetheless, Florence went on to compete at the World Championships. As a result, Florence finished a commendable second place to Swedish figure skater, Karl Emil Ulrich Salchow (1877-1949). Furthermore, in the year 1903, Florence went on to secure another victory at the British Singles Championship, where she defeated the British figure skater,

Horatio Tertuliano Torromé (1861-1920). In addition, Florence successfully defended her first-place title, against her husband, Edgar Syers in the 1904 British Singles Championship.

Florence's impressive accomplishments, thus far, raised her professional sporting profile on the world stage. Not to mention, Florence's notable success also had tremendous implications for the greater participation of women in World Figure Skating Events and Competitions. Consequently, in 1906, the International Skating Union (ISU) established a Skating Competition for female figure skaters, which came to be known as the Ladies World Championships (LWC). Florence went on to claim victory at the Ladies World Championships in 1906, and again in the year 1907.

In the year 1908, Florence competed at the Olympic Games which were held in London, the United Kingdom. Most notably, Florence went on to secure a gold medal for her host nation in the Women's Single Figure Skating Event. In addition, Florence also won a bronze medal in a Joint Figure Skating Event with her husband and coach, Edgar Morris Wood Syers as her skating partner. Thereafter, also in the year 1908, Florence and Edgar jointly authored their first book titled *The Book of Winter Sports*. Regrettably, the incidence of deteriorating personal health led to Florence's official retirement as an elite athlete. Florence was no longer able to compete in professional sports on the world stage. In 1913, Florence co-authored her second book with her husband, *The Art of Skating: International Style*.

On 9 September 1917, Florence passed away due to heart failure as a result of endocarditis. Regrettably, Florence was only thirty-five years old at the time of her death, which occurred in Weybridge, Surrey, England. In the year 1981, Florence's sporting legacy and her many accomplishments were belatedly honoured by the Figure Skating World, when she was posthumously elected to the World Figure Skating Hall of Fame.

In the early twenty-first century, figure skating is one of the most popular sports in the Winter Olympic Games, and it is contested by male and female elite athletes alike. Much of figure skating's success with the increased participation of women can be directly attributed to Florence. Indeed, Florence demonstrated to the world what a female figure skater can accomplish on the Olympic Ice Rink. Florence had to literally 'break ice' to enter the male-dominated world of figure skating during her lifetime. As a result of what Florence accomplished, many talented women achieved sporting success during Florence's time, and countless women continue to participate as elite athletes in this sport, including American figure skater, Beatrix Suzetta Loughran (1900-1975), American figure skater, Theresa Weld Blanchard (1893-1978), Austrian figure skater, Herma Szabo (1902-1986), and Norwegian figure skater, Sonja Henie (1912-1969).

Sarah Frances Durack (1889-1956)

Sarah Frances Durack was born on 27 October 1889 in Sydney, New South Wales, the Commonwealth of Australia. Sarah's father was Thomas Durack, and her mother was Mary Mason. Sarah came from an

Irish-Australian family. Furthermore, Sarah was the third daughter, and the sixth child of Thomas and Mary.

In Sarah's earlier years, she learned how to swim at Sydney's Coogee Beach and Wylie's Baths. During Sarah's swimming training, she practiced several popular swimming styles, including that of Breaststroke, Freestyle, the Trudgen Stroke, and the Australian Crawl. In 1906, while Sarah was still at high school, she participated in and won her first State Championship Title for Breaststroke. Throughout Sarah's younger years as an amateur swimmer, she forged a strong bond and competitive friendship with fellow Australian swimmer, Wilhelmina Wylie (1891-1984).

As a talented and competitive swimmer, Sarah was a member of the New South Wales Ladies Swimming Association (NSWLSA), however, the aforesaid Association, in accordance with the conventions of the time, was initially against the participation of female swimmers in the Olympic Games. In fact, Sarah was originally refused permission to compete at the 1912 Olympic Games in Stockholm, Sweden. Most notably, the aforesaid Olympic Games were to be the first to permit female swimmers to equally participate in the Olympics' International Swimming Competitions.

Notwithstanding the traditions and customs of the early twentieth century, Sarah's swimming performance was highly impressive to overlook. In fact, prior to the 1912 Olympic Games, Sarah was setting new World Records in the 100 and 200-yards Freestyle Swimming Events. Not to mention, the Australian public was also becoming increasingly supportive of Sarah's inclusion in the Australian Olympic Team. The Australian people desired to witness Sarah compete at the upcoming Olympic Games in Sweden. Thus, the NSWLSA reconsidered its long-standing position, and it permitted Sarah to travel to Sweden in order to participate in the 1912 Olympic Games. Most disappointingly, Sarah had to cover her own expenditure in connection with the 1912 Olympic Games. In addition,

Sarah also had to arrange to cover the ancillary costs associated with an obligatory chaperone.

Sarah's participation in the 1912 Olympic Games were a remarkable success. Most notably, Sarah secured a gold medal for her brilliant performance in the 100-metre Freestyle. Sarah became the first Australian female swimmer to win a gold medal for Australia at the 1912 Olympic Games. Fellow Australian swimmer, Wilhelmina Wylie secured a respectable second place in the same swimming event. As a result, Wilhelmina was awarded a silver medal for her brilliant performance. From 1912 until 1918, Sarah held twelve World Records to her name in the sport of swimming.

Furthermore, Sarah also travelled to Europe and the United States of America to compete as a professional swimmer, however, she did not encounter considerable success. This dismal reality was more or less due to the internal politics of Australian swimming associations and sporting bodies when it came to sponsoring and financing Australian female swimmers to compete abroad. Regrettably, when it came to permitting female Australian swimmers to compete in international swimming events and competitions, the inability to cover the female athletes sporting expenses, as well as the non-payment of their professional coach, and their direct manager's costs, by swimming sporting bodies, made Australian female swimmers elite sporting endeavours 'commercially unviable'. Most notably, male Australian professional swimmers did not confront such financial difficulties and economic challenges at the time.

Regardless of the lack of sponsorship and financial challenges that confronted Australian women in the sport of swimming, Sarah was unable to compete in the 1920 Olympic Games held in Antwerp, Belgium. Sarah's absence from the 1920 Olympic's was due to complications in her health. Unfortunately, Sarah was diagnosed with appendicitis.

Subsequently, Sarah underwent an emergency appendectomy. Following Sarah's successful surgery, she also suffered from episodes of typhoid fever and pneumonia. In the year 1921, Sarah officially retired from professional swimming, however, her passion, commitment, and support for the sport of swimming remained throughout her lifetime.

On 22 January 1921, Sarah married horse-trainer, Bernard Martin Gately at the St Mary's Cathedral in Sydney, New South Wales. In the year 1945, Sarah was made a life member of the New South Wales Ladies' Amateur Swimming Association. This important recognition was for Sarah's unrivalled contribution to the sport of swimming, in particular, due to her continued efforts aimed at the promotion of women in swimming. Furthermore, during Sarah's later years, she dedicated her time, energy, and resources towards coaching younger children to become competitive and professional swimmers.

On 20 March 1956, Sarah passed away from cancer at her home in Stanmore, Sydney, New South Wales. Sarah was 66 years old at the time of her death. Sarah was buried in the Catholic Section at Waverley Cemetery in Sydney. In the year 1967, Sarah was posthumously inducted as an Honour Swimmer in the International Swimming Hall of Fame located at Florida, the United States of America. Last but not least, Sarah's Olympic gold medal was presented by her brother, Frank Clement Durack, to the Commonwealth Government. As a result, Sarah's prized gold medal is now preserved in the historic collection of valuable items at the National Library of Australia in Canberra, the Australian Capital Territory.

Fanny Rosenfeld (1904-1969)

Fanny Rosenfeld was born on 28 December 1904 in Ekaterinoslav, the Russian Empire. Fanny's father was Max Rosenfeld, and her mother was Sarah Rosenfeld. Fanny came from a Jewish family. In addition, Fanny had four siblings, three of whom were sisters, namely, Gertrude, Mary, and Ethel, and she also had one older brother named Maurice. In the year 1905, while Fanny was still an infant, her family immigrated to Barrie, Ontario, the Dominion of Canada.

Fanny was initially educated at Central School, however, in her later school years she attended the Barrie Collegiate Institute. From an early age, Fanny demonstrated a strong passion for sports and athletics, which greatly influenced her personal endeavours and ambitions. In the year 1922, the Rosenfeld family relocated to the City of Toronto, and Fanny enrolled in the Harbord Collegiate Institute. Fanny graduated from the Harbord Collegiate Institute in 1923. After the completion of Fanny's studies, she secured employment as a Stenographer at the Patterson Chocolate Factory in Toronto. To Fanny's great benefit, her newfound employer supported the involvement of women in sports and recreational activities.

As a result, during Fanny's time in Toronto, she became involved in athletics. Among Fanny's numerous sporting commitments, she participated in basketball, hockey, softball, and tennis. Not to mention, Fanny was also involved in a number of local sporting clubs, associations, and teams, including the Patterson Hockey Team, the Hind and Dauche Softball Team, the Young Women's Christian Association (YWCA) Hockey Team, the Young Women's Hebrew Association (YWHA) Hockey and

Basketball Teams, the Toronto Sunnyside Women's League, and the Toronto Ladies Athletic Club.

Fanny demonstrated remarkable talent as an athlete, in particular, as a runner. As a result, Fanny went on to leave her mark in the sport of track and field in Canada, and on the world stage. In the year 1923, in one of Fanny's first important races, she defeated the first-rate Canadian sprinter, Rosa Grosse in a 100-yard race. Fanny's unexpectedly brilliant performance as a novice athlete resulted in her partnering with Canadian track and field coach, Walter Knox. Thereafter, Walter was responsible for Fanny's professional training, coaching, and development. Whilst Fanny was under the supervision of Walter Knox, she trained with some of Canada's best track and field athletes, such as Grace Conacher, Rosa Grosse, and Myrtle Alice Cook.

On 8 September 1923, Fanny was a participant at the Annual Athletic Day, which was held at the Canadian National Exhibition Track Championships in Toronto, where she once again defeated Rosa Grosse. Not to mention, Fanny also claimed victory in a race against the American track and field athlete world record holder, Helen Filkey. During the Annual Athletic Day there was also a four-team relay contest between Canada and the United States of America. The United States was represented by the Chicago Flyers, and Canada was represented by Grace Conacher, Rosa Grosse, Fanny Rosenfeld, and Myrtle Alice Cook. Canada defeated the United States in this team relay event. It is noteworthy to mention, that while the Chicago Flyers were the more experienced team and utilised the latest athletic clothing and sports footwear, Fanny simply raced in her Hind and Dauche Softball Jersey, her father's socks, and her brother's swimming shorts! Fanny was simply too good. Indeed, Fanny was one of the most gifted track and field athletes of her time.

Fanny continued her most impressive track and field winning streak. In the year 1924, Fanny was awarded the prestigious title of the Toronto Ladies Grass Court Tennis Championship. Thereafter, in the year 1925, at the Ontario Ladies Track and Field Championships, Fanny participated in discus throw, javelin, long jump, low hurdles races, and shot put. Fanny's biggest moment in the international spotlight came at the 1928 Olympic Games which were held in Amsterdam, the Netherlands. At the 1928 Olympics, Fanny was one of the team members in the 'Matchless Six' (i.e., the six female track and field athletes which included Fanny Rosenfeld, Florence Jane Bell, Ethel Catherwood, Myrtle Alice Cook, Ethel May Smith, and Jean Thompson).

As a result, Fanny's athletic performance at the 1928 Olympics was both remarkable and memorable. Fanny won two Olympic medals, she secured a gold medal in the Women's 4 x 100-metre Relay Event, and a silver medal in the Women's 100-metre Sprint. Not to mention, Fanny also secured fifth place in the Women's 800-metre Race, where she let her team member, the Canadian runner, Jean Thompson finish the race in fourth place. Fanny embodied and demonstrated the selfless traits and genuine qualities of the Olympic Games spirit.

In the year 1929, a noticeable deterioration in Fanny's health resulted in her temporary withdrawal from professional sports. Most notably, Fanny suffered from arthritis, and consequently, she was bed-ridden for approximately eight months. Fanny's rest and recovery was a slow and painful process. In fact, Fanny employed the aid of crutches to walk for quite some time, close to one year, in order to assist her to regain strength and mobility. Unfortunately, Fanny's return to professional sport was short-lived. In 1931, Fanny was a team member of two professional sports, namely, the Ontario Softball and Hockey Championship Teams. In the year

1932, Fanny was named the best Women's Hockey Player in the Canadian Province of Ontario.

A further deterioration in Fanny's arthritis condition eventually led to her formal retirement from competitive sport, and it also resulted in the end of her stellar athletic career. Notwithstanding Fanny's departure from track and field competition, she adapted to the changing circumstances. In the year 1932, Fanny began to work as a Sports Journalist with *the Montreal Daily Herald*. Thereafter, in 1936, Fanny was employed at the Sports Department of *the Globe and Mail*, where she wrote columns for the Canadian newspaper based in Toronto. During Fanny's time at *the Globe and Mail*, she started a column which was initially known as 'Femmes Sports Reel', however, later on it came to be popularly known as 'Sports Reel'.

The 'Sports Reel' was a noteworthy sports column which reported on both men's and women's sporting achievements across Canada and the modern world. In addition, Fanny utilised her sport's column as a platform to advocate for the greater involvement of Canadian women in sporting events. Not to mention, Fanny also publicly addressed unfounded stereotypes portrayed about female athletes in the modern world, such as women's involvement in competitive sports made women 'unfeminine'.

Furthermore, Fanny was also an active participant in the coaching and administration of Canadian sports. For example, Fanny was Coach of the Canadian Women's Track and Field Team at the 1934 British Commonwealth Games in London, the United Kingdom. In addition, Fanny was also instrumental in the founding of the Provincial Women's Softball Union of Québec. Not to mention, Fanny went on to serve as the founding President of the Provincial Women's Softball Union. Last but not least, Fanny was employed as Manager of a Toronto-based Softball Team known as the Lakeside Langleys.

On 13 November 1969, Fanny passed away in Toronto, Ontario, Canada. Fanny was 65 years old at the time of her death. Fanny never married during her lifetime, nor did she have any children. Fanny was buried at the Lambton Mills Cemetery in Toronto. In the final analysis, Fanny was more than just a famous sports icon. Fanny was a talented writer, a journalist, a professional coach, and an advocate for the greater representation of women in international sporting events. Fanny's unprecedented track record of sporting achievements and accomplishments will continue to inspire men and women to achieve their highest potential.

Last but not least, throughout Fanny's lifetime and posthumously, she was the recipient of numerous awards and honours in recognition of her profound contribution to the sport of Track and Field. In addition, Fanny was also passionately committed to the widespread promotion of women's participation in elite sporting events and tournaments. Some of Fanny's notable accolades include being named Canada's Female Athlete of the Half-Century (1950), Fanny's induction into Canada's Sports Hall of Fame (1955), and also Fanny's induction into the International Jewish Sports Hall of Fame in Israel (1981). Furthermore, in the year 1996, the Canada Post Corporation issued a commemorative stamp in Fanny's memory. Not to mention, also in 1996, Fanny was inducted into the Ontario Sports Hall of Fame.

Gertrude Caroline Ederle (1905-2003)

Gertrude Caroline Ederle was born on 23 October 1905 in Manhattan, New York City, the United States of America. Gertrude's father was Henry Ederle, and her mother was Gertrude Anna Haberstroh. Gertrude came from a German family that had immigrated to the United States of America. Furthermore, Gertrude had five siblings. Gertrude's father, Henry Ederle, had a major influence on Gertrude while she was a child, not to mention, he also introduced her to the sport of swimming.

In Gertrude's youth, she frequently swam in Highlands, New Jersey, where the family spent the summer time on vacation. Gertrude's passion and enthusiasm for swimming led to her joining the Women's Swimming Association (WSA) (est. 1917) in New York. Gertrude often practiced her swimming style and technique at the aforesaid Association's Manhattan indoor pool. From thirteen years of age, Gertrude was professionally trained and extensively coached by American freestyle swimmer, Louis de Breda Handley (1874-1956). Gertrude's swimming training commitments and the associated travel requirements became a priority over her formal education. As a result, Gertrude never graduated from high school, and she solely focused on her training and development as a professional athlete in swimming.

Unfortunately, Gertrude was too young to compete in the 1920 Olympic Games held in Antwerp, Belgium. Thus, Gertrude's immediate priority remained on local and regional swimming competitions. Gertrude secured early accomplishments in her swimming career, with her first great success coming at the age of sixteen. On 1 August 1922, Gertrude secured first place in the circa. 5.6-kilometre Joseph P. Day

Cup Race held across New York Bay, where she defeated great rival swimmers, such as American swimmer, Helen Wainwright (1906-1965), and British champion swimmer, Hilda Marjorie James (1904-1982). Gertrude's swimming performance was remarkable. In fact, from 1921 to 1925, Gertrude held twenty-nine United States National and World Swimming Records to her name!

In the 1924 Olympic Games held in the City of Paris, France, Gertrude was an official member of the United States of America Olympics' Competition Team. Specifically, Gertrude was part of the United States Swimming Team that won gold in the Women's 4 x 100-metre Freestyle Relay Event. Furthermore, Gertrude also secured two bronze medals, one each in the Women's 100 and 400-metre Freestyle Events. In the year 1925, Gertrude pivoted her attention towards open-water endurance swimming. Gertrude performed the circa. thirty-four kilometre swim from Battery Park, Manhattan Island to Sandy Hook, New Jersey. Most notably, Gertrude completed this marathon swim in a World Record-breaking time of seven hours, eleven minutes, and thirty seconds.

On 18 August 1925, Gertrude also made her first unsuccessful attempt at swimming across the English Channel. After completing the majority of the swim, Gertrude was removed from the water at the direction of her coach, English Channel swimmer, Jabez Wolffe (1876-1943). Unfortunately, Jabez instructed English Channel swimmer, Ishak Helmy to recover Gertrude from the water, at this point she was disqualified. Regrettably, Gertrude was only circa. 9.65 kilometres from the English coastline!

Following Gertrude's unsought removal from the waters of the English Channel, bitter resentment and hostility ensued between Gertrude and her swimming coach, Jabez Wolffe. While it is true that Gertrude had not requested any assistance, however, she was positioned horizontally in the water, lying face down for several minutes. In this context, Jabez made the critical decision to intervene on Gertrude's behalf. Gertrude later claimed that she was resting, possibly for the purposes of conserving much needed energy to gather momentum to prepare herself for the finish line to the shore.

Furthermore, there was some speculation that personal bias had performed a role in Jabez's pivotal decision to remove Gertrude from the waters of the English Channel. This assertion is not without some credibility, for Jabez had himself unsuccessfully attempted to swim across the English Channel in excess of twenty times! Not to mention, Jabez had previously stated that women might not be capable of swimming across the English Channel. Last but not least, one cannot wholly negate the contingent possibility, that Jabez himself did not want to be outperformed by a woman. Either way, the end result was that Gertrude and Jabez's relationship was formally terminated.

Gertrude's major, and perhaps most daring, endurance swimming endeavour was the English Channel. The English Channel is a body of water that stretches some fifty-six kilometres, and it separates the United Kingdom and France. After a failed first attempt, Gertrude trained under the guidance of Olympic bronze medal winner, swimmer, and coach, Thomas William Burgess (1872-1950). Most notably, Thomas had successfully completed the endurance swim across the English Channel.

On 6 August 1926, Gertrude made her second attempt to swim across the English Channel. On this occasion, Gertrude made history at twenty-one years of age. Gertrude successfully completed the swim across the English Channel in a World Record-breaking circa. fourteen hours, thirty-nine minutes, and twenty-four seconds. Gertrude dared to believe it was possible, and she achieved success in style. Most notably, Gertrude became the first woman to successfully swim across the English Channel.

Gertrude's completion of the swim across the English Channel was a fine accomplishment in its own right, however, Gertrude also broke the male swim time record, which was then held by Argentine marathon swimmer, Enrique Tirabocchi (1887-1948). Enrique had previously completed the swim across the English Channel in circa. sixteen hours and thirty-three minutes. Gertrude's achievements earnt her the epithet 'Queen of the Waves'. Gertrude's 1926 record swim time across the English Channel was eventually superseded by American swimmer, Florence May Chadwick (1918-1995) on 8 August 1950. Florence completed the swim across the English Channel in circa. fourteen hours and twenty minutes.

Gertrude's monumental swimming achievement resulted in her instant sporting fame. Gertrude's success also questioned the modern world's outdated stereotypes of the female sex. Not to mention, Gertrude's monumental accomplishment directly challenged the old assumptions underwriting the conventional notions of gender roles. Without a doubt, Gertrude had categorically proven to the modern world, that a woman was capable of as much as a man in the sport of swimming. Throughout Gertrude's lifetime, she utilised her newfound fame in a beneficial and prudent manner. Gertrude also featured in the 1927 Hollywood movie, *Swim Girl, Swim* directed by American film director, Clarence Badger. In the year 1933, Gertrude sustained serious bodily injuries, including to her spine. Regrettably, Gertrude was left partially immobilised for the next several years. In 1939, Gertrude made a guest appearance at Billy Rose's Aquacade at the New York World's Fair.

During Gertrude's childhood years she had a hearing problem. This hearing problem progressively worsened as Gertrude got older. In particular, after Gertrude's successful swim across the English Channel in 1926, her hearing ability significantly deteriorated. By the 1940's, Gertrude was practically permanently hearing-impaired in both her ears. In the later years of Gertrude's life, she instructed and coached hearing-impaired school children in swimming lessons at the Lexington School for the Deaf in New York City. Last but not least, Gertrude spent her final years in a nursing home known as the Christian Health Care Centre located in Wyckoff, New Jersey.

On 30 November 2003, Gertrude passed away from natural causes in Wyckoff, New Jersey, the United States of America. Gertrude was 98 years old at the time of her death. Gertrude never married, and she did not have any children. Gertrude was buried at the Woodlawn Cemetery in the Bronx, New York City. Gertrude's grand achievements continue to be remembered by the modern world. In 1965, Gertrude was inducted as an Honour Swimmer into the International Swimming Hall of Fame in Florida, the United States. Last but not least, in 2003, Gertrude was admitted to the United States' National Women's Hall of Fame.

Mildred Ella Didrikson Zaharias (1911-1956)

Mildred Ella Didrikson Zaharias was born on 26 June 1911 in Port Arthur, Texas, the United States of America. Mildred's father was a merchant mariner and ship's carpenter named Ole Didrikson. Mildred's mother was Hannah Marie Didrikson, she worked as a laundress (otherwise known as a washerwoman). Mildred's parents had immigrated to the United States of America from the Kingdom of Norway. Furthermore, Mildred had six siblings, and she was the sixth child of the seven children in her family.

Initially, Mildred attended David Crockett Junior High School. Thereafter, Mildred went to Beaumont High School, however, she was not overly inclined towards the demands of a school education and formal study. Not to mention, Mildred had to repeat eighth grade. Eventually Mildred decided to withdraw from school, and thus, she never graduated from high school. Rather than the intellectual world of academic research and the formalities of study, Mildred's personal interest and strong passion for sports became the centre of her life. In fact, when Mildred was a child, a teenager, and then into her early adult years, she was consumed with participating in a number of sports, including athletics, baseball, basketball, cycling, diving, golf, swimming, tennis, track and field, and volleyball.

From 1929 to 1932, Mildred was employed by the Employer's Casualty Insurance Company (ECIC) in Dallas, Texas. While Mildred was at the ECIC, she was part of the Company Basketball Team, known as the Golden Cyclones. The Golden Cyclones were an all-female Basketball Team that was an integral part of the Amateur Athletic Union (AAU). During this time, Mildred was also a participant in the Women's All-America Basketball Team. Not to mention, in the year 1932, Mildred competed in the Women's Amateur Athletic Association, where she won six individual sporting events!

Mildred had her sights set on grander accomplishments in the world of sport. As a result, Mildred went on to represent the United States in the 1932 Olympic Games held in the City of Los Angeles, California, the United States of America. Based on Mildred's stunning performance, she had qualified for at least five Olympic Sporting Events. Disappointingly, the 1932 Olympic Games rules for female competitors meant that Mildred was only able to compete in three Olympic Sporting Events. Thus, Mildred decided to compete in the high jump, javelin throw, and the 80-metre hurdles. Notwithstanding the unjust procedural rules imposed upon female athletes at the time, Mildred's sporting performance and prowess, as an elite athlete at the 1932 Olympic Games, was simply astonishing.

On 31 July 1932, Mildred won a gold medal in the Women's Javelin Throw, where she outperformed two German track and field athletes, namely, Ellen Braumüller (1910-1991), and Tilly Fleischer (1911-2005). This spectacular Olympics performance was followed by another gold medal win for Mildred. On 3 August 1932, in the Women's 80-metre Hurdles Event, Mildred secured a gold medal victory, by the smallest of margins, over American hurdler, Evelyne Ruth Hall (1909-1993). Last but not least, on 7 August 1932, Mildred secured a silver medal victory in the High Jump Event, after missing out on the gold medal, which was not awarded without some controversy. Initially, Mildred was tied for first place in the High Jump Event at 1.65 metres, with American high jump athlete, Jean Shiley Newhouse (1911-1998). Both female contestants, that is Mildred and Jean, subsequently failed to clear the high jump bar at 1.67 metres. On the 1.65 metres high jump bar, which was a World Record achievement by both athletes, the judges ruled that Mildred had utilised an improper technique to clear the bar, namely, Mildred had jumped (or dived) head first over the bar, which was not permitted at the time. Therefore, Jean Shiley Newhouse was awarded the gold medal at 1.65 metres. Consequently, Mildred secured the second place with a silver medal.

In sum, not only did Mildred secure three Olympic medals at the 1932 Olympic Games, however, she also established new World Records. In the Women's Javelin Throw, Mildred secured a World Record javelin throwing distance of 43.69 metres. Furthermore, in the Women's 80-metre Hurdles, Mildred finished the event in a World Record time of 11.7 seconds. Although Mildred's high jump technique was disqualified, she did manage to clear the high jump bar at an impressive 1.65 metres, which was the World Record at the time (albeit, the World Record and gold medal were awarded to Mildred's competitor, Jean Shiley Newhouse). Beyond Mildred's towering sporting accomplishments in athletics, and track and field at the 1932 Olympics, she subsequently pivoted her ambitions towards the prestigious sport of golf.

In the year 1933, Mildred pursued the elitist sport of golf as an amateur player. Within the period of the first few years Mildred participated across a number of Golf Tournaments, and she secured notable victories. In the year 1935, Mildred secured victory in the Texas Women's Amateur Tournament. At the time, golf was long considered 'a gentleman's sport', and Mildred had to inevitably confront the stereotypes, generalisations, and prejudices of being a female competitive golfer. No doubt, Mildred's incredible sporting abilities and former prize-winning achievements assisted her to confront her many critics in the golfing establishment.

At one point during Mildred's golfing career, she lost her 'Amateur' status. The United States Golf Association (USGA) considered Mildred to be a professional player, due to her advertising endorsements and other commercial earnings from her widespread involvement in sport. Not to mention, Mildred was an Olympic athlete with two gold medals and one silver medal. Mildred was not one to reject a sporting challenge, and she gladly accepted the next level in the professional game of golf. Thereafter, Mildred competed with some of the best and most talented athletes in the sport.

Now that Mildred had to compete with the elite athletes in top Golfing Tournaments, she went on to participate in professional golf at some of the most prestigious and world-renowned Championships. Mildred participated in the 1938 Los Angeles Open, where she also met American professional wrestler, George Zaharias. On 23 December 1938, George and

Mildred got married. The couple did not have any children during their marriage. A turn of events in 1942, witnessed Mildred regain her 'Amateur' status in golf. Subsequently, Mildred continued to professionally compete in a number of Golf Tournaments.

From 1943 to 1947, Mildred won a remarkable seventeen Amateur Tournaments. Not to mention, Mildred was the first American female golfer to win the prestigious British Women's Amateur Golf Championship. In the year 1950, Mildred and American golfer, Patricia Jane Berg (1918-2006), jointly founded the Ladies Professional Golf Association (LPGA). In the year 1953, Mildred was diagnosed with cancer, and consequently, she underwent a surgical procedure known as a colostomy. Several months after Mildred's successful surgery, she returned to the game of golf. Most notably, in the year 1954, Mildred went on to win her third United States Women's Open Championship!

On 27 September 1956, Mildred passed away from colon cancer at John Sealy Hospital in Galveston, Texas, the United States of America. Mildred was only forty-five years old at the time of her death. Mildred was buried at the Forest Lawn Cemetery in Beaumont, Texas. Both during Mildred's lifetime and after, she continues to be remembered for her incredible sporting achievements. For example, in 1951, Mildred was inducted into the Ladies Professional Golf Association (LPGA) Hall of Fame. Not to mention, in the year 1957, Mildred was posthumously awarded the Bob Jones Award by the United States Golf Association (USGA).

In addition, the Babe Didrikson Zaharias Museum in Beaumont, Texas is dedicated to Mildred's memory, and her many grand sporting achievements. Furthermore, in the year 1976, Mildred was inducted into the United States' National Women's Hall of Fame. Thereafter, in 1981, the United States Postal Service issued an U.S. 18 cent commemorative stamp to acknowledge Mildred's sporting prowess. Last but not least, on 7 January 2021, Mildred was posthumously awarded the Presidential Medal of Freedom by the United States President, Donald John Trump (r. 2017-2021).

Mildred's professional sporting career was illustrious and ground-breaking. Tragically Mildred's life ended prematurely by the onset of cancer, however, she lived to realise her full potential, across athletics, baseball, basketball, golf, and track and field. Mildred's commendable accomplishments have made it possible for the subsequent generations of female athletes to more readily compete in a wide variety of professional sports, and the Olympics too.

Sonja Henie (1912-1969)

Sonja Henie was born on 8 April 1912 in Oslo, Norway. Sonja's father was a wealthy Norwegian furrier named Wilhelm Henie. Sonja's mother was Selma Lochmann-Nielsen. Sonja had one older brother named Leif Henie. Sonja's father had a significant impact on her early childhood years and life trajectory. Most notably, Sonja's father, Wilhelm was also a former World Cycling Champion, and he strongly encouraged Sonja to participate in sporting activities from a very young age.

Sonja demonstrated a keen interest in a number of sports, including equestrian, figure skating, skiing, swimming, and tennis. Ultimately, Sonja decided to seriously pursue figure skating, and in doing so she did not formally finish her school studies. Sonja was coached by Russian ballerina,

Tamara Platonovna Karsavina (1885-1978), an internationally renowned teacher of ballet. At the age of ten, Sonja won her first great Figure Skating Competition, the Senior Norwegian Championships. For Sonja, this Championship Victory signalled the beginning of her remarkable professional sporting career as a world-renowned figure skater.

Sonja went on to participate as an elite athlete in her first Olympic Games at the very young age of eleven. In fact, Sonja was a competitor in the 1924 Winter Olympics held in Chamonix, France. Although Sonja finished last (i.e., eighth place) in the Figure Skating Event, her debut experience of being a contestant on the world stage, amongst the top performing athletes, proved an invaluable experience to her future professional development and sporting success.

Beginning in the year 1927, at the age of fourteen, until the year 1936, Sonja went on to consecutively win a total of ten World Figure Skating Championships! In addition, the future Figure Skating Contests at the Olympic Games witnessed some of the very best skating performances of Sonja. Not to mention, Sonja won three Olympic gold medals in Figure Skating, one medal each at the 1928 St. Moritz Olympic Winter Games, the 1932 Lake Placid Olympic Winter Games, and the 1936 Garmisch-Partenkirchen Olympic Winter Games.

Furthermore, from 1931 to 1936, Sonja went on to become a six-time champion of the European Figure Skating Championships. At the time of writing this book, Sonja is considered one of the world's best female figure skaters of all time, only to be rivalled by Russian female figure skater, Irina Eduardovna Slutskaya, and German female figure skater, Katarina Witt. Following Sonja's remarkable successes in the professional sport of figure skating, she went on to become a first-rate actor in the world of entertainment.

Most notably, beyond Sonja's admirable sporting accomplishments, she ventured into the United States' film production industry. With the assistance of her father, Wilhelm Henie, and Hollywood Studio Chief, Darryl Francis Zanuck, Sonja entered into a contractual agreement with Twentieth Century Fox Studios, Inc. As a result, Sonja appeared in several American films during the course of her stellar acting career, including *Seven Days for Elizabeth*, *One in a Million*, *Happy Landing*, *Second Fiddle*, *Thin Ice*, *Everything Happens at Night*, *It's a Pleasure*, *Sun Valley Serenade*, *The Countess of Monte Cristo*, *Ali Baba Goes to Town*, *Hello London*, *My Lucky Star*, *Iceland*, and *Wintertime.* Consequently, Sonja was one of the most influential and highest paid U.S. actresses of her time.

During the course of Sonja's lifetime, she married three times. Sonja's first marriage was in 1940, to the Owner and President of the New York Yankees, Daniel Reid Topping, which lasted until 1946. Thereafter, Sonja was married to an Executive at the Industrial Tape Company in New Brunswick, New Jersey, Winthrop Gardiner Jr. from 1949 until 1956. Sonja's third and final marriage was to Norwegian Shipping Magnate and Art Collector, Niels Onstad from 1956 until the year 1969.

In the 1960's, Sonja was diagnosed with an acute medical condition known as chronic lymphocytic leukaemia. Unfortunately, on 12 October 1969, the aforesaid disease claimed Sonja's life. Sonja was 57 years old at the time of her death. Sonja was buried in close proximity to the Henie Onstad Art Centre in Viken County, Norway. By any measure, Sonja lived a full life, and her countless sporting and acting achievements will inspire people for many generations to come.

Sonja, the three-time Olympic Gold medallist and popular U.S. film icon has been recognised for her outstanding sporting and acting achievements. In 1976, Sonja was inducted into the World Figure Skating Hall of Fame in Colorado Springs, Colorado, the United States of America.

Furthermore, in the year 1982, Sonja was admitted into the International Women's Sports Hall of Fame located in East Meadow, New York. In addition, the Norwegian low-cost airline known as Norwegian Air Shuttle painted the image of Sonja onto its Boeing aeroplanes. Last but not least, in 2012, the Norwegian Postal Service (*the Posten Norge*) issued two commemorative postage stamps in the memory of Sonja Henie.

Sonja's life story is an endless source of inspiration for many aspiring actors, singers, dancers, and figure skaters. In addition, beyond Sonja's areas of expertise and monumental achievements, her life narrative illustrates the epitome of the human condition, that is, to become all that one is destined to be. Most notably, Sonja achieved her remarkable successes in the turmoil of *World War I (1914-1918)* and *World War II (1939-1945)*. Not to mention, Sonja also succeeded in her endeavours during the early phase of the onset of *the Cold War (1947-1991)*. In many respects, Sonja demonstrated a strong 'internal locus of control' in creating her envisioned reality. In the final analysis, Sonja's many notable accomplishments are a testimony to her admirable resilience, unquestionable passion, and towering record of success.

Patricia Jane Berg (1918-2006)

Patricia Jane Berg was born on 13 February 1918 in Minneapolis, Minnesota, the United States of America. Patricia's father was professional U.S. baseball player, Herman Berg. Patricia's mother was Teresa Berg.

From a young age, Patricia demonstrated a natural aptitude for sports, and she displayed a remarkable athletic ability, in particular, in football and golf. Most notably, from eleven to thirteen years of age, Patricia concentrated the majority of her time, energy, and effort on football. Not to mention, Patricia was a Quarterback for the Fiftieth Street Tigers, and she played alongside future great American football player, Charles Burnham Wilkinson.

Patricia attended Washburn High School in Minneapolis; however, she was not the most studious and academic person. Instead, Patricia concentrated the majority of her time and energy on the grand professional sport of golf. From the age of fourteen, Patricia demonstrated a remarkable dedication and passion for golf. As a result, Patricia's father, Herman Berg was her first coach, all while Patricia was still a young student at high school. In 1939, Patricia matriculated at the University of Minnesota. Alongside Patricia's university studies, she continued to participate in the sport of golf. In fact, while Patricia was at university, she was coached and trained by the State Golf Championship Winner, Lester Bolstad. In fact, Lester remained Patricia's golf coach and professional sports mentor over the course of the next four decades.

During Patricia's several years as an amateur golfer, she won many Golfing Tournaments, including the Minneapolis City Championship, the Minnesota State Championship, the Western Derby, the Western Amateur, the National Amateur, the Helen Lee Doherty Championship, and the Trans-Mississippi Championship. Furthermore, in the year 1940, Patricia became a professional golfer. Not to mention, Patricia secured a decent sponsorship from the Wilson Sporting Goods Company in Chicago, Illinois. Thereafter, in the year 1941, Patricia won the Western Open as a professional golfer, an accomplishment that she later repeated on six separate occasions, in 1943, 1948, 1951, 1955, 1957, and 1958. In addition,

Patricia also went on to win the All-American Open on five separate occasions, in 1943, 1945, 1953, 1955, and 1957.

With the outbreak of *World War II (1939-1945)*, Patricia served with the United States Marine Corps (USMC) as a Lieutenant, and she was also a Recruitment Officer for the USMC. From 1942 to 1945, during Patricia's tenure with the U.S. military, she determinedly continued to play golf. Most notably, Patricia did not lose her enthusiasm, keen interest, or athletic ability to perform on the golf course. In 1946, Patricia transitioned from military life to civilian life, and she also went on to win the United States Women's Open Championship.

In the year 1950, Patricia and American athlete, Mildred Ella Didrikson Zaharias (1911-1956), jointly founded the Ladies Professional Golf Association (LPGA). In addition, Patricia served as the founding President of the aforesaid Association. Most notably, Patricia's winning streak as a professional golfer continued. Patricia went on to secure victories in the World Championships, the American Women's Open, the Titleholders Championship, the Richmond California Open, and the Oklahoma Civitan Open. Throughout Patricia's lifetime, she also authored and co-authored books on golf, including *Golf for Women: Illustrated*, and *Inside Golf for Women*. As a result of Patricia's many sporting achievements, in the year 1958, Patricia became the first American woman to be inducted into the Minnesota Sports Hall of Fame.

Patricia overcame the rigid and institutionalised barriers of sex and gender, to achieve a dream career in golf during her lifetime. In all, Patricia won in excess of 80 Amateur and Professional Golf Tournaments! Not to mention, Patricia secured a record fifteen Major Golf Title Victories to her name. Without a doubt, Patricia is one of the greatest all-time female members of both the Ladies Professional Golf Association Hall of Fame and the World Golf Hall of Fame. Furthermore, in the year 1980, Patricia was admitted into the International Women's Sports Hall of Fame in East Meadow, New York, the United States.

On 10 September 2006, Patricia passed away from Alzheimer's disease at Fort Myers, Florida, the United States of America. Patricia was 88 years old at the time of her death. By any measure, Patricia was a talented athlete and dexterous golfer. Patricia's numerous achievements and notable accomplishments in the sport of golf earnt her a considerable number of accolades and honours, including the Bob Jones Sportsmanship Award (the highest honour bestowed by the United States Golf Association), the Old Tom Morris Award (the most prestigious award by the Golf Course Superintendents Association of America), and the Ben Hogan Award (issued by the Golf Writers Association).

Patricia's many prized achievements in the historically male-dominated sport of golf are truly unprecedented. Patricia has shown to the United States of America, and the modern world, at large, that women are just as capable, competent, and competitive, as the best male golfers on the golf course. In many ways, Patricia institutionalised her formidable legacy, not only as a professional golfer, but also as a writer, author, and founder of reputable golf institutions for women. In the final analysis, Patricia was a transformational leader for women's participation in professional golf.

Indeed, Patricia's remarkable journey and sporting success has made it possible for many of the great female professional golfers that came during her lifetime, and the countless female professional golfers that will continue to come after her, including Mary Kathryn Wright (1935-2020), Mae Louise Suggs (1923-2015), Elizabeth May Jameson (1919-2009), Marilynn Louise Smith (1929-2019), Beverly Hanson (1924-2014), and Carol Mann (1941-2018).

Francina Elsje Blankers-Koen (1918-2004)

Francina Elsje Blankers-Koen was born on 26 April 1918 in Lage Vuursche, Utrecht, the Netherlands. Francina's father was a Dutch government official by the name of Arnoldus Koen. Francina's mother was Helena Koen. Francina was the only daughter in her family, she had five siblings, all of whom were her brothers. In the earlier years of Francina's life, she was involved in a number of sports, including fencing, gymnastics, ice skating, running, swimming, and tennis. Furthermore, in Francina's teenage years, she was a member of the Amsterdam Dames' Athletic Club, where she trained indoors as a runner in the Club's gymnasium hallway. Francina was a dedicated athlete, and she demonstrated the admirable attribute of perseverance from a young age. For example, consider that Francina rode her bicycle approximately twenty-nine kilometres from her home to the gymnasium in order train at the aforesaid athletic Club.

Francina ultimately decided to concentrate her sporting abilities on track and field. In the year 1935, at the age of seventeen, Francina won a Dutch National Championship in the 800-metre Race. In addition to Francina's victory, she also set a new National Record. Francina's stellar performance earnt her a place in the Dutch Olympic Team, where she met her future husband and track and field coach, Johan Blankers. Johan encouraged and supported Francina to compete in the 1936 Summer Olympics held in the City of Berlin in Germany.

At eighteen years of age, Francina attended the 1936 Summer Olympics. At the Olympic Games, Francina competed in the Women's 4 x 100 metre Relay Event, and the Women's High Jump Event. In the High Jump Event, Francina secured fifth place for her athletic performance. The combined effort of the Dutch Track and Field Team in the Women's 4 x 100 metre Relay Event also merited a fifth-place finish. Arguably, Francina's most memorable moment at the 1936 Olympic Games was her encounter with African American track and field athlete, James Cleveland Owens (1913-1980). Francina also received Owens' autograph at the 1936 Olympic Games, which was her most valuable and prized possession. Notably, James Owens first-rate sporting performance secured him four Olympic gold medals in track and field events at the 1936 Olympic Games held in Berlin.

In the year 1938, Francina competed in a 100-yard sprint in Amsterdam, the Netherlands, which she managed to finish in a World-Record equalling 11.00 seconds. In addition, at the 1938 European Athletics Championships held in Vienna, Francina secured two bronze medals for her commendable performance in the Women's 100-metre Sprint and the Women's 200-metre Sprint. Most disappointingly, the onset of *World War II (1939-1945)* disrupted the schedule of the next Olympic Games which were to be held in July of 1940 in Helsinki, Finland. Notwithstanding the turbulent geopolitics of the mid-twentieth century Europe, Francina continued to participate in several athletic competitions and sporting events outside of the prestigious Olympic Games. Furthermore, in 1940, Francina married her trusted track and field coach, Johan Blankers. In addition, in the year 1942, Francina and Johan had their first child, a boy named Jan Junior.

During the course of 1942 and 1943, Francina continued to participate in three major Track and Field Sporting Competitions. Not to mention, Francina's brilliant sporting performance earnt her three World Record titles. Namely, the 80-metre Hurdles which Francina completed in 11.00 seconds, the High Jump Event in which Francina cleared the bar at 1.71 metres, and the Long Jump Event in which Francina secured a respectable distance of 6.25 metres. In 1945, Francina and her spouse, Johan had their second child, a girl named Fanneke. Following the conclusion of *World War II*, the next major sporting event was the 1946 European Championships held in Oslo, Norway. At the 1946 European Championships, Francina won first place in the Women's 80-metre Hurdles and also in the Women's 4 x 100 metre Relay Event.

Thereafter, the 1948 Olympic Games were held in the City of London, the United Kingdom. The 1948 Games represented an overwhelming sporting success for Francina. Most notably, Francina won four Olympic gold medals across the Women's 100-metre Sprint, the Women's 200-metre Sprint, the Women's 80-metre Hurdles, and the Women's 4 x 100-metre Relay Event. Interestingly, Francina's sporting prowess earnt her the comical epithets 'the flying housewife' and 'the flying Dutchmam' by the International Sports Press.

Upon Francina's return to the Netherlands, Her Majesty Queen Juliana (r. 1948-1980) endorsed Francina with a Knight of the Order of Orange-Nassau. Despite the negative opinions and criticism that Francina faced leading up to the 1948 Olympic Games, that is being thirty years old, a wife, and a mother of two children, Francina went on to win four gold medals! Needless to say, Francina's first-rate sporting performance at the 1948 Olympic Games unequivocally silenced her many judgemental, ignorant, and ill-informed critics.

Four years later, at the age of thirty-four, Francina competed in the 1952 Summer Olympics held in Helsinki, Finland. Francina participated in the Women's 100-metre Sprint, the Women's 200-metre Sprint, and the Women's 80-metre Hurdles. Unfortunately, Francina did not win any medals during the 1952 Olympic Games. The 1952 Olympic Games represented Francina's last major international sporting event. In the year 1955, Francina formally announced her retirement from Track and Field Sporting Competitions and Events.

Following Francina's retirement, she remained an active member in track and field sports. For example, Francina became the Captain of the Dutch Female Track and Field Team. Not to mention, Francina was bestowed with many honours and accolades for her incredible sporting achievements, including the Dutch Athlete of the Year in 1937, 1940, and 1943, the 1948 Associated Press Female Athlete of the Year, and the 1999 title of 'Female Athlete of the Century' awarded by the International Association of Athletics Federation (IAAF). Last but not least, in the year 2012, Francina was inducted into the IAAF Hall of Fame. Most notably, Francina was one of the first twelve Hall of Fame members of the IAAF Hall of Fame.

In the final years of Francina's life she suffered from Alzheimer's disease, and her hearing was also considerably impaired. On 25 January 2004, Francina passed away in Hoofddorp, the Netherlands. Francina was 85 years old at the time of her death. Francina was buried at the Algemene Begraafplaats Wilgenhof in Hoofddorp. There are two statues that memorialise the extraordinary life and exceptional legacy of Francina. One commemorative statue of Francina was established in 1954, and it is situated at Rotterdam, the Netherlands. A second statue of Francina was erected in 2007, and it is located at Hengelo, the Netherlands.

Beyond the glorious Olympic medals, the newfound World Records, and the countless competition victories, Francina's greatest contribution was that she successfully challenged and dismantled the conventional stereotypes that defined what a woman was capable of accomplishing in sport. In particular, Francina directly confronted the totally unjustified social stigma surrounding a female elite athlete who was married and had children. Francina proved to the modern world, that being a wife, mother, and middle-aged athlete, were no barriers to world-class sporting success! Indeed, Francina is one of the greatest female track and field athletes of all time.

Alice Coachman Davis (1923-2014)

Alice Marie Coachman Davis was born on 9 November 1923 in Albany, Georgia, the United States of America. Alice's father was Fred Coachman, and her mother was Evelyn Coachman. Alice came from an African American family of ten children, and she was the fifth child of Fred and Evelyn. Alice had no privilege, upper social class status, private wealth, access to world-class resources, funding, or adequate training equipment and facilities. Not to mention, the fact that Alice was a girl of colour born in Georgia, the United States of America. During this time, racial segregation and the unjust enforcement of *Jim Crow Laws* dominated the Southern States. As a result, the commencement to Alice's life was less than ideal. In many respects, Alice's inspirational story is one of limitless ambition, raw talent, natural aptitude, perseverance, innovative thinking, tireless dedication, and above all, the noble pursuit of excellence.

Alice was initially educated at Monroe Street Elementary School in Walton County, Georgia. During Alice's school years, she received strong encouragement to pursue track and field sporting activities, most notably, from her fifth-grade school teacher, Cora Bailey, and also from her supportive aunt, Carrie Spry. Thereafter, in the year 1938, Alice attended Madison High School, where she joined the Madison School Track Team to develop her ability and skill as an amateur athlete. Alice was trained by American track and field coach, Harry E. Lash, who quickly realised Alice's remarkable natural talent for high jump. Alice's sporting achievements at Madison High School ensured her merited selection for a scholarship commencing in 1939 to join the Tuskegee Preparatory School in Tuskegee, Alabama. Alice diligently furthered her training and development as an athlete while she studied at the Tuskegee Preparatory School.

Due to the racial segregation policies in place across the Southern states, Alice predominantly trained with the African American school boys. Furthermore, Alice often ran barefoot on dirt roads to practice her running style and technique. Not to mention, Alice utilised materials and equipment sourced from home to create hurdles to practice her jumping technique. In addition, as an amateur athlete, Alice also used rope and sticks to create a make-shift high jump cross bar to continue her personal training. Although Alice was from an underprivileged African American family in the Southern State of Georgia, her dedication and ambition more than supplemented the noticeable material disadvantages that she confronted in her athletic training regime for high jump.

In 1943, Alice further pursued higher education. Alice matriculated at the Tuskegee Institute College (now known as Tuskegee University) in Tuskegee, Alabama. While Alice was a student at the Tuskegee Institute College, she studied dressmaking. To complement Alice's college studies, she also participated in sports, including basketball, high jump, and sprinting. In 1946, Alice graduated from the Tuskegee Institute College with a Degree in Dressmaking.

In the year 1947, Alice decided to pursue a second college degree, this time she enrolled at Albany State College (now known as Albany State University) in Albany, Georgia. Alice studied a Bachelor of Science (BSc) Degree, and she majored in Home Economics. Upon the completion of Alice's university studies at Albany State College, she entered the workforce as a Teacher and Track and Field Instructor.

With the outbreak of *World War II (1939-1945)*, the 1940 Olympic Games (awarded to Japan) and the 1944 Olympic Games (awarded to the United Kingdom) were both cancelled. This most unfortunate turn of world events denied Alice two international opportunities to compete at the Olympic Games during her prime years. The following Olympic Games were not held until 1948 in the City of London, the United Kingdom, commonly referred to as the 'Austerity Games'.

Consequently, from 1939 until 1948, Alice competed in domestic Track and Field Competitions. Alice was a matchless competitor in the Amateur Athletic Union (AAU). In fact, Alice went on to win ten National Championships across the 50-metre Sprint, the 100-metre Sprint, the High Jump, and the 4 x 100-metre Relay Team Event. In addition, Alice also won three Conference Championships during her tenure with the Tuskegee Women's Basketball Team. Last but not least, during the ten years form 1939 until 1948, Alice won the American National Title in High Jump every single year. As a result, Alice secured ten U.S. National Championship Titles to her name!

Finally, Alice's crucial moment on the world stage arrived at the 1948 Olympic Games held in London. On 7 August 1948, at the Olympic High Jump Final Event, in front of approximately 83,000 spectators, Alice made sporting history. Alice cleared the high jump bar at 1.68 metres on her first attempt. Alice's nearest competitor, British high jump athlete, Dorothy Jennifer Beatrice Tyler (1920-2014), secured the second place, and she was awarded the silver medal. However, Alice representing the United States of America was the clear victor. Thus, Alice became the first African American woman to win a gold medal in the Women's High Jump Event at the 1948 Olympic Games. Not to mention, Alice had the high honour of having her Olympic gold medal awarded to her by His Majesty King George VI (r. 1936-1952) of the United Kingdom.

In addition to Alice's spectacular victory at the 1948 Olympic Games, her 1.68-metre high jump performance set both the Women's Olympic High Jump Record and the Women's American High Jump Record. Not to mention, Alice was the only American female athlete to win a gold medal at the 1948 Olympic Games held in London. Alice, most deservedly, received a hero's welcome on her return home to the United States of America. For example, consider that after Alice's 1948 Olympic gold medal victory, she had the high privilege of meeting with the U.S. President, Harry S. Truman (r. 1945-1953) at the United States White House in Washington, D.C.

Furthermore, Alice's home town of Albany in Georgia celebrated her monumental Olympic victory by announcing 'Alice Coachman Day'. In Alice's honour, a motorcade stretching across some 282 kilometres was organised to celebrate Alice's historic Olympic accomplishment. Not to mention, Alice Coachman Day was attended by the Anglo–American and African American people. Disappointingly, the customary practice of racial segregation served to divide the different ethnic groups of the American population that were clustered across the above-mentioned grand procession.

Notwithstanding the aforementioned positive reception, there were some disappointing elements in Alice's Olympic medal victory celebration in the United States of America. For one, Albany Mayor, James W. Smith refused to shake the hand of Olympic gold medal champion, Alice Coachman. Furthermore, Mayor James W. Smith also did not appear to acknowledge Alice's presence, nor provide her with an opportunity to speak at the segregated celebration event. Regrettably, such was the second-rate treatment of the African American people at the time in the mid-twentieth century United States of America.

In addition, the prominent local newspaper, *the Albany Herald* did not provide a front-page news story of the remarkable accomplishment of Alice Coachman, who was an Olympic athlete from Albany. No doubt, the prejudices of race, ethnicity, private wealth, sex, gender, and colour, all performed an integral part in Alice's bittersweet reception to celebrate her prized Olympic Gold Medal achievement in her very own home city. Having achieved what Alice had set out to accomplish, she formally retired after the 1948 Olympic Games. Alice was only twenty-five years old at the time of her retirement from professional sport. Thereafter, Alice married Doctor N. F. Davis. The married couple had two children, a daughter named Evelyn, and a son named Richmond. Alice's first marriage ended in divorce. Subsequently, Alice re-married a gentleman by the name of Frank Davis.

The bitter memories of Alice's unfriendly reception in Albany were soon swept away into the endless pages of the United States' modern sporting history. For the near future promoted and acknowledged Alice's sporting accomplishments in a more positive light. For example, in the year 1952, Coca-Cola signed a lucrative endorsement deal with Alice to be a spokesperson for its products. Alice was the first African American woman to sign such an endorsement deal with a major U.S. company that demonstrated a strong international brand and corporate reputation. Furthermore, in 1975, Alice was inducted into the U.S. National Track and Field Hall of Fame. In the year 1994, Alice founded the Alice Coachman Track and Field Foundation, a not-for-profit foundation established to assist junior athletes, and also to provide support for former Olympic athletes. Last but not least, in 2004, Alice was inducted into the United States Olympic Hall of Fame.

On 14 July 2014, Alice passed away in Albany, Georgia, the United States of America. Alice was 90 years old at the time of her death. The many struggles and sporting successes of Alice set a remarkable precedent for African American female athletes to come after her, across many prestigious sports, including basketball, golf, gymnastics, rugby, swimming, tennis, track and field, and water polo. Alice's accomplishments had shown to the United States of America, and indeed to the modern world, that even without the most sophisticated training equipment, without the best running shoes, with the notable racial injustices and socio-economic inequities present within the modern American society, and without the most experienced track and field coach, in the end... *it was possible*.

Sophie Kurys (1925-2013)

Sophie Mary Kurys was born on 14 May 1925 in Flint, Michigan, the United States of America. Sophie was of mixed ancestry. Sophie's father, Antony Kurys was of Ukrainian origin. Sophie's mother, Antonina Kurys was of Polish origin. Sophie had four siblings, two sisters named Mary Terry and Ann Gensel, and two brothers named Morris and John. Sophie was educated at the All-Saints Catholic School, Emerson Junior High School, and Flint Northern High School. During Sophie's childhood, she displayed a remarkable aptitude and talent as an amateur athlete. Furthermore, as a child, Sophie participated in a number of sports, including baseball, basketball, bowling, softball, swimming, tennis, track and field, and volleyball.

In the year 1939, Sophie participated in the Flint's Mott Decathlon, and she won the City Championship by achieving 4,693 points out of the maximum possible 5,000 points. Remarkably, Sophie was only fourteen years old at the time of her outstanding sporting success. Unfortunately, Sophie withdrew from high school in eleventh grade, this was in part due to the devastating economic impact of *the Great Depression (1929-1939)*. As a result, Sophie entered the workforce in order to financially support her immediate family. Sophie's employment included work as a clerk, administration officer, dry cleaner, and house cleaner.

The onset of *World War II (1939-1945)* dramatically changed the social dynamics of the twentieth century United States society. With American men fighting in the front lines of war in distant theatres and foreign lands across the Asia-Pacific and Europe, the role of American women was elevated domestically, that is to say, within the United States. As a result,

American women were now at the forefront of the United States society, not only in terms of employment, but also advertisement, education, marketing, sport, and teaching. Indeed, *World War II* provided newfound economic opportunities for Sophie, which immensely benefited her sporting career in the United States of America. Not to mention, for a brief period of time, in the year 1942, Sophie played for the CIO Auto's Fast-Pitch Softball Team.

In the year 1943, the All-American Girls Professional Baseball League (AAGPBL) was established in Chicago, Illinois. The AAGPBL was founded by Major League Baseball Executive, Philip Knight Wrigley, to recruit talented American girls to participate in baseball. Due to the protracted nature and severity of *World War II*, the shortage of American male baseball players was telling. As a direct consequence, an alternative baseball league for American female players had to be created to provide sports and entertainment, but also to serve as a much-needed morale booster to the war-tired and weary American people. Furthermore, the advent of television had not become a mainstream household entertainment medium just yet. Thus, live sports were an integral part of the American society's leisure and enjoyment.

Sophie's sporting story with the AAGPBL is truly one of rags-to-riches. From 1943 to 1951, in Sophie's nine-year sporting career with the Baseball League, she was one of the top performing baseball players. In fact, in 1946, Sophie was named the AAGPBL 'Player of the Year'. Sophie earnt the nickname 'the Flirt Flash' for her remarkable speed and agility in the game of baseball. Indeed, Sophie's batting record statistics speak for themselves. For example, Sophie was the greatest AAGPBL Record Holder for career stolen bases, with a total of 1,114. In addition, from 1946 until 1949, Sophie made the AAGPBL All-Star Team. Sophie was a truly remarkable sportsperson who made a name for herself playing baseball and softball.

From 1952 to 1955, Sophie also played softball with the National Girls Baseball League in Chicago, Illinois. Commencing in 1952, Sophie initially played for the Battle Creek Belles, however, she secured a lucrative contract with the Chicago's Admiral Music Maids, where she played for three seasons. The year 1955 was Sophie's final season of fast-pitch softball. Sophie's sporting success was a result of two primary factors. One, Sophie was a naturally talented sportsperson. Two, Sophie knew how to put on a captivating show in American sport. In fact, both the Girl's Baseball and Softball Competition's audience base increased in large part due to Sophie's first-rate performance on the field.

After Sophie made her original mark in the world of American sports, she turned her attention to a more professional career in leadership, management, and business. In the year 1956, Sophie dedicated her time to work for an American manufacturer of automotive and aeroplane components, known as Apex Machine Products, Inc. situated in Racine, Wisconsin. Sophie succeeded in this reputable organisation, as the Secretary-Treasurer and Vice-President of this American company.

In the year 1972, Sophie retired from her influential leadership positions held at Apex Machine Products, Inc. Thereafter, Sophie relocated to Scottsdale in Arizona. In the year 1986, Sophie was inducted into the Greater Flint Area Sports Hall of Fame in Michigan. Following a successful career in baseball and softball, in her later years, Sophie turned to playing recreational golf. In addition, Sophie also spent her leisure time with immediate family, and she attended baseball games, this time, as a spectator of the sport!

On 17 February 2013, Sophie passed away from surgical complications in Scottsdale, Arizona, the United States of America. Sophie was 87 years old at the time of her death. Sophie was buried at the St. Francis Catholic Cemetery in Phoenix, Arizona. In the same year as her death, Sophie was inducted into the National Women's Baseball Hall of Fame in Cooperstown, New York, the United States of America.

Althea Neale Gibson (1927-2003)

Althea Neale Gibson was born on 25 August 1927 in Clarendon County, South Carolina, the United States of America. Althea's father was Daniel Gibson, and her mother was Annie Bell Gibson. Althea's parents were sharecroppers, and they both worked on a cotton farm in the town of Silver in Clarendon County. The onset of *the Great Depression (1929-1939)* meant that the Southern farmers suffered economically. This dismal socio-economic reality took a significant toll on the Gibson family's ability to earn a decent living.

In the year 1930, the Gibson family relocated to Harlem in Upper Manhattan, New York City, in search of a better life. During this time, *the Great Northward Migration (1910-1970)* was taking place. As a result, some six million African American people were migrating from the impoverished rural Southern States, to more prosperous states across the United States of America, in search of new economic opportunities. After Althea's family moved to Harlem, her family grew to include three sisters and a brother.

During the memorable years of Althea's youth, she participated in a variety of sports at the New York Police Athletic League (NYPAL). The NYPAL is a safe play zone designated for children to participate in organised sports in New York. Among the several sports on offer, Althea excelled in paddle tennis. In 1939, Althea became the New York City's Women's Paddle Tennis Champion, she was only twelve years old at the time of this notable achievement. Althea had her fair share of challenges growing up in the twentieth century American society, factors such as sex, colour, gender, socio-economic status, ethnicity, social class, poverty, and race all functioned to make sporting success all the more difficult, but not impossible for her. To Althea's benefit, where there was disadvantage, there was also opportunity. That is to say, generous and thoughtful members of the Cosmopolitan Tennis Club in Harlem paid for Althea's Junior Club Membership. The Cosmopolitan Tennis Club's members also covered the cost of Althea's practice tennis lessons at the Club.

Notwithstanding the aforesaid difficulties, Althea's natural aptitude, drive, ability, and talent for tennis was widely demonstrated in her amateur tennis matches. In 1941, at the age of fourteen, Althea won her first tennis tournament, namely the American Tennis Association (ATA) New York State Championship. The ATA is a sports institution founded in 1916 aimed at specifically promoting the sport of tennis amongst the African American people. Thereafter, Althea went from strength to strength in her tennis performance. In 1944 and 1945, Althea was the winner of the ATA National Championship, and she was also declared the National Junior Champion. From 1947 to 1956, Althea went on to consecutively win the ATA Women's Tennis National Singles Title, every single year.

Over the course of Althea's time playing tennis with the ATA, her track record of achievement gained the favourable attention of American physician, Robert Walter Johnson (1899-1971). Robert Johnson was the founder of the ATA Junior Development Program, and he assisted Althea to secure access to the United States Lawn Tennis Association (now known as the United States Tennis Association), in order to further Althea's tennis training, coaching, and professional development. In addition, American physician and civil rights activist, Hubert Arthur Eaton (1916-1991), also assisted Althea to matriculate at Williston Industrial High School in Wilmington, North Carolina. Following the completion of high school, Althea secured an athletic scholarship to attend Florida Agricultural and Mechanical University (FAMU) in Tallahassee, Florida. Althea graduated from FAMU with a Bachelor's Degree in 1953.

At the time, ethnicity and race were major factors, not exclusive to the popular sport of tennis, but visible across all facets of the modern American society, however, prominent American female tennis players, such as Alice Marble (1913-1990), and Sarah Hammond Palfrey (1912-1996), were publicly calling for Althea's inclusion in the Lawn Tennis Association's Championships, and the United States Women's Tennis Competitions. In fact, Alice Marble had written about Althea in the July 1950 issue of the prestigious *American Lawn Tennis* magazine, and Sarah Hammond Palfrey had done the same in a 1956 issue of the *Sports Illustrated* magazine. This much-needed publicity helped Althea to gain attention amongst the prestigious sport of tennis across the United States of America.

In the year 1955, the United States Department of State (DOS) invited Althea on a 'Goodwill Tour' across Asia to play exhibition tennis matches across several nations, including Burma, Ceylon, India, Pakistan, and Thailand. Accompanying Althea on the 1955 U.S. DOS sponsored Tennis

Tour of Asia were great tennis players, including Robert Perry, Hamilton Farrar Richardson, and Karol Fageros. The brief Asia Tour assisted Althea to develop her confidence, and also to raise her international profile as a capable and talented American tennis player. In 1956, Althea went on to compete in and win the French Championship Women's Singles Event, she became the first African American woman to do so.

1957 represented an even bigger year for Althea in the World of Tennis. In fact, 1957 was Althea's best year, thus far. Althea won several prestigious Tennis Championships, such as the 1957 Wimbledon Ladies' Singles Championship, where she was personally awarded the Venus Rosewater Trophy by Her Majesty Queen Elizabeth II of the United Kingdom. In addition, Althea also won the 1957 United States' Nationals Women's Singles Championship, and on this special occasion, she was awarded the Women's Championship Trophy by the United States Vice-President, Richard Nixon.

Following on from Althea's earlier victories, she had mixed success in the 1957 Australian Open. Althea was the Finalist (i.e., Runner-up) in the Women's Singles Championship. Unfortunately, Althea was defeated by the American tennis player, Shirley Fry Irvin. Thereafter, Althea won the Australian Women's Doubles Competition, her double's tennis partner was also Shirley Fry Irvin. Furthermore, Althea was also a participant in the 1957 United States Wightman Cup Team, which defeated Great Britain in Women's Tennis. Most notably, Althea was the first African American woman to represent the United States of America in this Transatlantic Women's Tennis Contest, which was held from 1923 until 1989. Althea's memorable and remarkable sporting achievements on the tennis court, secured her the top spot of World Number One female tennis player in 1957.

Althea continued to receive favourable press coverage for her many sporting achievements. This was a positive outcome for her public relations image as an accomplished American tennis super star. Althea's successive tennis victories at the French Open, the Wimbledon Championships, the United States National Championships (also known as the United States Open), and the Australian Open, received the attention of prominent American sports writer and journalist, Allison Danzig (1898-1987). In response, Allison penned a short piece of writing on Althea Gibson's legendary performance in *the New York Times* newspaper. In addition, in 1957, and again in 1958, Althea was named the Female Athlete of the Year by *the Associated Press*. Last but not least, Althea secured victory in both the 1958 Wimbledon Ladies' Singles Championship, and the 1958 United States Open Women's Singles Championship.

Beyond the magnificent highlights and sporting achievements in tennis, Althea also played golf in her later years. In 1964, at the age of thirty-seven, Althea became the first African American woman to join the Ladies Professional Golf Association (LPGA) Tour. Althea continued to play professional golf over the next the decade and a half, until she retired in 1978.

Furthermore, beyond the world of sport, Althea published two books during her lifetime, both being her memoirs. The first book was *I Always Wanted to Be Somebody*, published with the assistance of Ed Fitzgerald. The second book was *So Much to Live For*, published with the assistance of Richard Curtis. In addition, Althea also made an appearance in the film *The Horse Soldiers*, which was directed by American film director and naval officer, John Ford.

On 28 September 2003, Althea passed away from respiratory failure at a hospital in East Orange, New Jersey. Althea was 76 years old at the time of her death. Althea's legacy, as a truly inspirational athlete, has been recognised and acknowledged with several prominent awards and honours, both during her lifetime and beyond. For example, consider Althea's 1971 induction into the International Tennis Hall of Fame in Newport, Rhode Island. Not to mention, Althea's 1980 induction into the International Women's Sports Hall of Fame in East Meadow, New York. Furthermore, in the year 2002, Althea was inducted into the National Women's Hall of Fame in Seneca Falls, New York. Last but not the least of Althea's countless honours, a granite statue designed by American sculptor, Eric Goulder, honouring Althea was unveiled in 2019 at the USTA Billie Jean King National Tennis Centre in Flushing Meadows, Queens, New York City, New York, the United States of America.

Yvette Winifred Williams (1929-2019)

Yvette Winifred Williams was born on 25 April 1929 in Dunedin, New Zealand. Yvette's father was Thomas Williams, and her mother was Winifred Fanny Elizabeth Williams. In addition, Yvette also had one younger brother named Roy Williams. Roy was born in the year 1934. Yvette was educated at Otago Girls High School in Otago, New Zealand. During Yvette's high school years, she displayed a strong interest in athletics and sports, such as basketball and netball. In fact, Yvette was part of the Otago Girls High School Netball Team, and she also played basketball for the local Otago Team.

After the completion of high school, Yvette was employed at the Pharmaceutical Office of the Health Department, and thereafter, she also worked as a bookkeeper. Notwithstanding Yvette's work commitments, her true passion and unquestionable drive was in the field of sports. In 1947, Yvette joined the Otago Ladies Athletics Club, where she became socially involved with other female track and field athletes. Also in the year 1947, Yvette won her first National Title at the New Zealand Championships in Shot Put. Yvette's winning streak continued across several sports, including, securing National Titles in Long Jump (1948), Javelin Throw (1950), Discus Throw (1951), and the Women's 80-metre Hurdles (1954).

In order for Yvette to further her sporting potential, she began to intently train under the stewardship of New Zealand athletics coach, James Charles Bellwood (1912-1994). Disappointingly, Yvette was excluded from the New Zealand Olympics Team in the 1948 Olympic Games held in London, the United Kingdom. Notwithstanding this national sporting controversy, Yvette went on to represent New Zealand in the 1950 British Empire Games held in Auckland, New Zealand. At the 1950 British Games, Yvette secured a gold medal for her remarkable performance in the Women's Long Jump, in which she cleared a jump length of 5.91 metres. In addition, Yvette also won a silver medal in the Women's Javelin Throw Event, where she achieved a respectable throw distance of 37.97 metres. Most notably, Yvette's Long Jump performance superseded the New Zealand, the British Empire Games, and the British Empire Women's Long Jump Records!

Yvette's recent sporting prowess ensured her merited selection in the New Zealand Olympic Team in the 1952 Olympic Games held in Helsinki, Finland. At the 1952 Olympics, Yvette outperformed her 1950 British Empire Games sporting performance. Not only did Yvette win a gold medal in the Women's Long Jump, she also established a new Long Jump Olympic Games Record of 6.24 metres! Yvette made sporting history by becoming the first New Zealand female athlete to win a gold medal at the Olympics. At the 1952 Olympic Games Yvette also competed in the Women's Shot Put and the Women's Discus Throw, where she finished in sixth and tenth place, respectively.

On 20 February 1954, Yvette surpassed the existing World Record in the Women's Long Jump, with her unprecedent jump length of 6.28 metres in Gisborne, New Zealand. Yvette's last major sporting triumph was at the 1954 British Empire and Commonwealth Games held in Vancouver, British Columbia, Canada. At the 1954 Games, Yvette won gold medals in the Women's Long Jump, the Women's Discus Throw, and the Women's Shot Put Competitions, however, Yvette finished in sixth place in the Women's 80-metre Hurdles. Most notably, Yvette's stellar performance at the 1954 British Empire Games secured New Zealand three out of its seven gold medals.

The year 1954 proved a pivotal one in respect to Yvette's personal life. On 11 December 1954, Yvette married New Zealand sportsperson, Charles Armistice Corlett (1921-2015). Charles was a member of the New Zealand Men's National Basketball Team. The married couple had four children, three of whom achieved remarkable success in sports, namely, Neville Corlett, he became involved in basketball, Peter Corlett, he became involved in rugby union, and Karen Corlett, she became involved in rhythmic gymnastics. Yvette finally decided to retire from competitive sports, and thus, she did not compete at the 1956 Olympic Games held in

Melbourne, Australia. Yvette dedicated the later years of her life to quality time with her spouse, family life, and raising her four children. In addition, Yvette worked as a Physical Education teacher in Auckland, while she also coached Special Olympians with intellectual disabilities.

On 13 April 2019, Yvette passed away in Auckland, New Zealand. Yvette was 89 years old at the time of her death. Yvette's sporting legacy is remembered and celebrated, both during her lifetime and beyond. In the years 1950 and 1952, Yvette was named the New Zealand Sportsperson of the Year. In addition, in the year 1953, Yvette was made a Member of the Order of the British Empire (MBE). Not to mention, in 1990, Yvette was also inducted into the New Zealand Sports Hall of Fame. In the year 2000, Yvette was voted the Otago Sportsperson of the Century. Furthermore, in 2011, Yvette was appointed a Companion of the New Zealand Order of Merit (CNZM).

Thereafter, in the year 2013, the New Zealand Olympic Committee, in connection with the Glenn Family Foundation, established the Yvette Williams Scholarship. The Yvette Williams Scholarship provides invaluable support with the coaching and development requirements of talented amateur athletes in New Zealand. Last but not the least in Yvette's endless list of accolades, in 2019, Yvette was promoted to Dame Companion of the New Zealand Order of the Merit (DNZM).

Iolanda Balaş (1936-2016)

Iolanda Balaş was born on 12 December 1936 in Timişoara, Romania. Iolanda's Hungarian father was a locksmith named Frigyes Balaş. Iolanda's Romanian mother was a homemaker named Etel Bozó. During the course of *World War II (1939-1945)*, Iolanda's father, Frigyes, fought in the Hungarian Armed Forces. Furthermore, Iolanda was educated at the Roman Catholic High School for Girls in Timişoara. Not to mention, to Iolanda's long-term benefit and personal development, her high school actively encouraged the participation of girls in sporting activities.

It was the watchful eye of Romania's Pentathlon Champion and long jump athlete, Luiza Ernst-Lupşa, who first noticed the athletic potential and hidden talent of Iolanda, when Iolanda was only nine and a half years old. Initially, Iolanda joined the local Electrica Club in Timişoara, where she participated in High Jump Competitions. During Iolanda's time at the Electrica Club, she also met her first coach, Romanian high jump athlete, Ion Söter. Subsequently, Iolanda married her coach and high jump athlete, Ion. In the year 1951, while Iolanda was still a member of the Electrica Club, she won her first National Title in High Jump.

In the year 1953, Iolanda joined the CSA Steaua in Bucharest, where she continued her athletic training and development. Thereafter, at the 1954 European Athletics Championships held in Bern, Switzerland, the seventeen-year-old Iolanda went on to finish in second place. Iolanda managed to achieve a high jump bar clearance of 1.65 metres, which earnt her a well-deserved silver medal.

Iolanda continued to improve her high jump performance, style, and technique. Despite some disappointments, the receipt of greater sporting rewards was only a matter of time. On 14 July 1956, at the age of nineteen, Iolanda set a new World Record in the Women's High Jump, she cleared the high jump bar at a record 1.75 metres in Bucharest, Romania. Iolanda's next major competition was the 1956 Olympic Games held in Melbourne, Australia. Despite Iolanda being the favourite Romanian female athlete, who appeared most promising to secure gold in the Women's High Jump Event, Iolanda was outperformed by the U.S. female athlete, Mildred Louise McDaniel (1933-2004). Mildred not only won the gold medal, but the American also superseded Iolanda's High Jump Record of 1.75 metres, with a jump height of 1.76 metres.

The notable absence of Iolanda's coach, Ion Söter, who himself was also an active sports athlete at the time, significantly impacted Iolanda's 1956 Olympic Games performance. Indeed, Ion's absence was a considerable factor that undermined Iolanda's preparation leading up to the Olympic Games. Unfortunately, Iolanda finished in fifth place in the Women's High Jump Event at the 1956 Melbourne Olympics, however, this sporting performance was the last major upset for Iolanda. Thereafter, Iolanda regained her momentum, and she accomplished much more in the years ahead.

In 1958, Iolanda competed at the Sixth European Athletics Championships held in Stockholm, Sweden. At the Sixth European Athletics Championships, Iolanda secured first place, and she won a gold medal for her deserving performance in the Women's High Jump Event. Most notably, Iolanda cleared the high jump bar at a phenomenal height of 1.77 metres. Iolanda's next major European Sports Event was the 1959 Summer Universiade held in Turin, Italy. This time round, Iolanda managed an astonishing high jump height of 1.80 metres. Once again, Iolanda secured first place in the aforesaid Competition. The following major International Sporting Contest for Iolanda was the 1960 Olympic Games held in Rome, Italy. Not to mention, Iolanda's 1960 Olympics performance was one of her best performances to date in the Women's

High Jump. At the age of twenty-three, Iolanda won the gold medal in the Women's High Jump Event, with an Olympic Record-breaking high jump height of 1.85 metres.

Following her 1960 Olympic Games performance, Iolanda continued to proceed from strength-to-strength. Iolanda's all-time Personal Best for the sport of high jump was an impressive height of 1.91 metres, which she managed to achieve in 1961. This was a World Record in the Women's High Jump that Iolanda held for the next ten years. Iolanda's 1.91 metre World Record was superseded by Austrian high jump athlete, Ilona Maria Gusenbauer in the year 1971. Last but not least, in the 1964 Olympic Games held in Tokyo, Japan, Iolanda secured first place, and she won her second Olympic gold medal in the Women's High Jump Event. Most notably, this time Iolanda won gold with a Record-breaking high jump bar clearance of 1.90 metres!

In 1967, Iolanda retired from Professional Competition in Track and Field, due to an Achilles tendon injury. Unfortunately, Iolanda's forced retirement all but ended her possibility of achieving a dream third Olympic gold medal at the upcoming 1968 Olympic Games held in Mexico City, Mexico. Following Iolanda's retirement, she married her coach, Ion Söter. Subsequently, the married couple had a son named Doru Balaş Söter. Iolanda's personal injury did not prevent her from contributing to the sport that she truly loved, and she assisted in nurturing the next generation of talented athletes.

Furthermore, Iolanda worked as a Physical Education Teacher in Bucharest. In addition, from 1988 until 2005, Iolanda served as the President of the Romanian Athletics Federation (RAF). Not to mention, Iolanda was also the President of the Romanian Track and Field Foundation. Moreover, from 1998 until 2002, Iolanda was the Vice-President of the Romanian Olympic Committee (ROC). Last but not least, in the year 2012, Iolanda was inducted into the International Association of Athletics Federation's Hall of Fame for her remarkable sporting achievements.

On 11 March 2016, Iolanda passed away from gastric complications at the Elias Hospital in Bucharest, Romania. Iolanda was 79 years old at the time of her death. Iolanda was buried at Ghencea Cemetery in Bucharest. During Iolanda's lifetime and beyond, she was awarded a number of prized medals and accolades which recognised her distinct contribution to athletics and Romania. Some of Iolanda's honours include, the Emeritus Master of Sport, the Order of Sports Merit, the Romanian Steaua Order, the Golden Column, and the National Order of Steaua Romaniei (in the Rank of Officer).

Wilma Glodean Rudolph (1940-1994)

Wilma Glodean Rudolph was born on 23 June 1940 in Saint Bethlehem, Tennessee, the United States of America. Wilma's father was a railway porter named Ed Rudolph. Wilma's mother was a housemaid named Blanche Rudolph. Beyond the notable social, economic, legal, and political inequalities of being an African American girl born in the racially segregated Southern States, Wilma had significant personal challenges in her infancy and childhood years. Wilma had to endure a premature birth, followed by several medical conditions, including parotitis, pneumonia, poliomyelitis, rubeola, scarlatina, and varicella. In addition, Wilma was unable to walk, without the assistance of a leg brace and orthopedic shoes, until she was twelve years old.

During Wilma's youth, she received ongoing treatment for her medical conditions at Meharry Medical College in Nashville, Tennessee. In the year 1947, Wilma attended Cobb Elementary School in Clarksville, Tennessee. Thereafter, Wilma was educated at Burt High School for African American school children, this school was also situated in Clarksville. During Wilma's high school years, she became involved in basketball and track and field related sports. Most notably, Wilma played on the High School Girls' Basketball Team, and her first coach was Clinton Gray. Most importantly, Wilma's gifted sporting abilities and natural talent were recognised by Women's Track and Field Coach, Ed Temple. As a result, Ed invited Wilma to participate in the High School Girl's Track and Field Program held at Tennessee State University in Nashville.

Wilma trained with unrelenting commitment and perseverance under the tutelage of Ed Temple. Wilma's track and field training regime was rigorous, requiring her to practice five days a week, and run a distance of circa. thirty-two kilometres each day. Notwithstanding Wilma's unrelenting training regime and strenuous personal effort, she shortly witnessed the remarkable results of her training. Wilma participated in competition at the Amateur Athletic Union (AAU) Junior Division Championship held in Philadelphia, Pennsylvania. Wilma won nine races, including the 75-metre Sprint, the 100-metre Sprint, and the 400-metre Relay Event at the aforementioned Championship Event.

Wilma's intense involvement in track and field was to the detriment of her high school studies, however, the time and effort she invested into her training and development, did produce tangible results. At the age of sixteen, Wilma was selected as the youngest team member to be part of the United States Olympic Women's Track and Field Team to compete at the 1956 Olympic Games held in Melbourne, Australia. Wilma competed in the Women's 200-metre Race and the Women's 4 x 100-metre Relay Event; she secured a bronze medal in the latter Track and Field Event. Wilma's three relay race team members at the 1956 Olympics were, Isabelle Daniels, Mae Faggs, and Margaret Matthews.

Following the 1956 Olympic Games, Wilma had an intimate relationship with her high school boyfriend, Robert Eldridge. Subsequently, Wilma became pregnant in the year 1957. To Wilma's ultimate benefit, her family generously assisted with raising the new-born baby girl named Yolanda. This family arrangement allowed Wilma to complete her high school studies, and it also permitted her to concentrate on her track and field sporting commitments. In 1958, Wilma graduated from high school, and thereafter, she was awarded an athletic scholarship to study at the Tennessee State University, where she pursued a Bachelor of Education (BEd) Degree. Once again, Wilma's studies were interrupted by her sporting commitments, and the next Global Sporting Event was the 1960 Olympic Games held in Rome, Italy.

To Wilma's advantage, Ed Temple was nominated as the Coach of the 1960 U.S. Women's Olympic Team. Wilma's long-standing track and field working relationship with Ed, from her former school days, greatly assisted her upcoming Olympic Games preparation and training regimen. Wilma's athletic performance in Rome was astonishing. Wilma won three gold medals, one each across the Women's 100-metre Sprint, the Women's 200-metre Sprint, and the Women's 4 x 100-metre Relay Event. Winning three gold medals at the 1960 Olympic Games was an extraordinary achievement for Wilma, and it was the highlight of her remarkable sporting career!

Following Wilma's track and field performance, she became an international sports star. Wilma gained publicity and fame across Italy, France, the United Kingdom, the United States, and many other foreign countries. In particular, greater recognition of Wilma's ground-breaking sporting accomplishments and profound talent followed at home, that is to say, in the United States of America. In 1961, Wilma was awarded the Associated Press 'Female Athlete of the Year' Award. In addition, also in the year 1961, Wilma won the Amateur Athletic Union (AAU) Sullivan Award. The year 1961 also witnessed Wilma marry fellow track and field athlete, William Ward, however, their marriage only lasted seventeen months.

In 1962, Wilma retired from Track and Field Competition. Despite being in exceptional form, Wilma made the decision not to compete in the 1964 Olympic Games held in Tokyo, Japan. Having won three gold medals at the 1960 Olympics, Wilma wanted to retire on an all-time high record of achievement. Wilma had accomplished sporting success at the highest of heights, there was nothing greater left for her to 'master' in track and field. From Wilma's perspective, she had rivalled the stunning performance of the all-time great, the African American track and field athlete, Jesse Owens (1913-1980), at the 1936 Olympic Games held in the City of Berlin, Germany. Jesse had won four gold medals at the 1936 Olympic Games.

Wilma returned to Tennessee State University, where she completed her Bachelor of Education (BEd) Degree. Wilma graduated with her university award in 1963. After the completion of Wilma's university studies, she re-married, this time with her high school boyfriend, Robert Eldridge. In addition to the one girl named Yolanda, they had prior to their marriage, the married couple also went on to have three more children, a daughter named Djuanna, and two sons named Robert Jr., and Xurry. The couple's marriage lasted almost two decades, however, it ended in divorce in the year 1981.

Wilma's newfound sporting fame and reputation brought her unprecedented global influence. In the year 1963, the United States Department of State requested Wilma become a 'Goodwill Ambassador' to the Friendship Games held in Dakar, Senegal. Furthermore, Wilma also visited other countries across Africa, including Ghana, Guinea, Mali, and Upper Volta, where she attended sporting events, visited schools, and made guest appearances on television shows and radio broadcasts.

In 1977, Wilma's autobiography, *Wilma: The Story of Wilma Rudolph* was published. Wilma's autobiography was written with prominent author, Martin Ralbovsky. Throughout Wilma's later years, she became involved in all facets of the modern American society. For example, Wilma was actively engaged with the United States Job Corps Program in Boston, Massachusetts. Furthermore, in the year 1981, Wilma founded the Wilma Rudolph Foundation in Indianapolis, Indiana. The aforementioned Foundation is a not-for-profit organisation that is committed to supporting the training requirements of young American athletes. Last but not least, in 1987, Wilma began to work with DePauw University in Greencastle, Indiana, where she was the Director of the University's Women's Track and Field Program.

On 12 November 1994, Wilma passed away due to a brain tumour in Brentwood, Tennessee, the United States of America. Wilma was 54 years old at the time of her death. Wilma was buried at the Edgefield Missionary Baptist Church in the City of Clarksville, Tennessee. On 17 November 1994, a memorial service was held in Wilma's honour at the Tennessee State University's Kean Hall. In addition, the Tennessee State Flag was flown at half-mast across the State, in proud acknowledgement of Wilma's matchless contribution to American athletics, and the greater World of Sport.

Furthermore, Wilma's sporting accomplishments and positive contribution to the American society, earnt her countless awards and accolades throughout her lifetime and beyond. Some of Wilma's awards and honours include: in 1974, Wilma was inducted into the United States National Track and Field Hall of Fame, in 1980, Wilma was admitted to the International Sports Hall of Fame, in 1983, Wilma was admitted to the United States Olympic Hall of Fame, in 1990, Wilma became the first African American woman to receive the National Collegiate Athletic Association's Silver Anniversary Award, and in 1994, Wilma was made a member of the United States National Women's Hall of Fame. Last but not least, in 2004, the United States Postal Service issued a U.S. 23-cent commemorative postage stamp to honour Wilma Rudolph.

Considered in its historical context, Wilma's profound story is unlike any other. Not only did Wilma overcome a childhood riddled with diseases and several medical conditions, however, she also succeeded in a racially segregated American society. An American society, which at the time, did not voluntarily offer public resources and State funding, high personal income, respectable and well-paid employment opportunities, private wealth, and a quality education to the African American people. In addition, to the factor of race, there were the notable factors of sex, colour, ethnicity, and gender that Wilma had to confront in her sporting journey. Wilma's sporting achievements have truly made it all the more possible for the next generation, and the many generations yet to come, to not only aspire, but also to *accomplish* the greatest of personal sporting ambitions.

Věra Čáslavská (1942-2016)

Věra Čáslavská was born during the course of *World War II (1939-1945)* on 3 May 1942 in Prague, Czechia. Věra's father managed a local grocery shop. Věra's mother was a housewife, who also assisted her husband to manage the grocery shop. Věra spent her childhood years in the Karlin District of Prague, she came from an underprivileged family. Furthermore, Věra had two sisters, named Eva and Hana, and one brother, named Vašek. From a young age, Věra and her two sisters received dance lessons and language classes.

When Věra was seven years old, she became involved in the sport of figure skating. As a child prodigy, Věra's remarkable aptitude and sporting talent won her the Youth Figure Skating Championship in Prague. When Věra was fifteen years old, she gained a newfound interest in gymnastics. Thereafter, Věra was trained under the tutelage of world-renowned Czechoslovakia female gymnast, Eva Bosáková (1931-1991). Věra was a naturally talented and gifted gymnast. In the year 1958, at the young age of sixteen, Věra made her debut at the World Artistic Gymnastics Championships held in Moscow, the Union of Soviet Socialist Republics. Věra's incredible gymnastics performance won her a silver team medal. In 1959, Věra capitalised on her debut experience, and she excelled at the European Women's Artistic Gymnastics Championships, where she won a gold medal for her incredible Vault performance, and she also secured a silver medal on the Balance Beam Event.

Věra progressed from strength-to-strength in her chosen sport of gymnastics. At the 1960 Olympic Games held in Rome, Italy, Věra was a member of the Czechoslovak Gymnastics Team, and she won a silver team medal. During Věra's first Olympic Games, she also participated in several other Gymnastics Events, including the Balance Beam, Floor Exercises, Horse Vault, and Uneven Bars. Following the 1960 Olympic Games, Věra participated in the 1962 Artistic Gymnastics World Championships held in Prague, Czechoslovakia. Věra's individual and team performances at the 1962 World Championships earnt her a total of four medals! Věra's 1962 medal tally included, one gold in the Vault, two silver across the Team All-Round and Individual All-Round, and one bronze in the Floor Exercise.

Věra's next major sporting contest was the 1964 Olympic Games held in Tokyo, Japan. Věra competed in six Artistic Gymnastics Competitions at the 1964 Olympic Games. Věra's performance was second to none, she managed to win three gold medals across the Women's Balance Beam, Horse Vault, and Individual All-Round Competitions. Věra also secured the silver medal in the Team All-Round Event. The remaining two events in which Věra participated were the Uneven Bars and Floor Exercise, and she managed to secure fifth and sixth place, respectively. Thereafter, Věra continued to compete professionally in World Championships across Europe, namely, the 1965 European Women's Artistic Gymnastics Championships held in Sofia, Bulgaria, and the 1967 European Women's Artistic Gymnastics Championships held in Amsterdam, the Netherlands.

Věra's last Olympics performance was at the 1968 Olympic Games held in Mexico City, Mexico. Věra saved her best gymnastics performance for last. However, Věra's professional training and final preparation for the 1968 Olympic Games was not without civil disturbance and political unrest. Beginning in January of 1968, *the Prague Spring* was taking place, it was a protest movement that demanded the immediate introduction of political reforms in Věra's home country (Czechoslovakia). Věra did not steer clear of the political discourse, and she was a strong supporter of the *Prague Spring* movement. Not to mention, Věra was also publicly against the Soviet Union's 'occupation' of her home country. For example, consider that Věra had signed *The Two Thousand Words Manifesto* authored by Czechoslovakian progressive writer, political activist, and journalist, Ludvik Vaculík (1926-2015). The aforesaid Manifesto was a political document, which demanded democracy as the favoured political system in Czechoslovakia.

On 20 August 1968, the Soviet Union utilised *the Warsaw Pact of 1955* to mount an invasion of Czechoslovakia. The Soviet Union's use of military force intended to deter the progression of democratic and liberal political reforms, and also provide full Soviet support to the loyal communist political leaders in the Country. Notwithstanding the disturbing geopolitical events of Europe, Věra went to Mexico City and she competed in six Artistic Gymnastics Events, where she won a record four gold and two silver medals! Věra secured gold in the Women's Floor Exercise, Horse Vault, Individual All-Round, and Uneven Bars. In addition, Věra managed to attain second place in both the Women's Balance Beam and the Team All-Round Event, which earnt her two silver medals. Věra's memorable and remarkable performance at the 1968 Olympics earnt her the Czechoslovakia's 'Sportsperson of the Year' Award in the same year.

Also in the year 1968, Věra married Czech middle-distance runner, Josef Odložil (1938-1993). Věra and Josef's wedding ceremony took place at the Mexico City Cathedral in Mexico. The married couple had two children, a son named Martin, and a daughter named Radka. Unfortunately, Věra and Josef divorced in 1987. Věra also suffered from bouts of depression for quite some time after their divorce, and also following the tragic death of her former husband at the hands of their son, Martin, in a violent altercation in 1993. Consequently, Věra withdrew from public life and major social events, however, she went on to conquer her depression and make a full recovery in her later years.

Unfortunately, the ideological divide of *the Cold War* politics practically forced Věra into early retirement. In addition, Věra was also denied permission to travel abroad, and she was not allowed to participate in sporting events in Czechoslovakia or in foreign countries. In effect, Věra became a 'political prisoner' in her own Country due to the overbearing influence of the Soviet Union. A much-needed change in fortune arrived for Věra with the initiation of *the Velvet Revolution* (also known as *the Gentle Revolution*) in November of 1989, and the formal dissolution of the Soviet Union in 1991. Now Věra's standing and reputation finally began to take a positive orientation in her home Country. Subsequently, Věra went on to become an Advisor on Sports Affairs to Czechoslovakia's President, Václav Havel (1936-2011), and she was also appointed Honorary President of the Czech-Japan Association. In Věra's later years, she was elected President of the Czech Olympic Committee. Not to mention, in the year 1995, Věra was appointed to the International Olympic Committee (IOC) Membership Committee.

On 30 August 2016, Věra passed away from pancreatic cancer in Prague, the Czech Republic. Věra was 74 years old at the time of her death. Věra was presented with a number of awards and prizes for her sporting prowess and grand achievements in gymnastics, both during her lifetime and beyond. Some of Věra's prized accolades include, recipient of the 1989 *Pierre de Coubertin* International Fair Play Trophy presented by *the United Nations Educational, Scientific, and Cultural Organisation* (UNESCO). Not to mention, Věra's 1991 induction into the International Women's Sports Hall of Fame. Furthermore, Věra was the recipient of the 1995 Czech Republic's Medal of Merit. In addition, consider Věra's 1998 induction into the International Gymnastics Hall of Fame. Last but not least, in 2010, Věra was awarded the Japanese Order of the Rising Sun (Third Class).

Patricia Susan Summitt (1952-2016)

Patricia Susan Summitt was born on 14 June 1952 in Clarksville, Tennessee, the United States of America. Patricia's father was Richard Head, and her mother was Hazel Albright Head. Patricia was raised on a Montgomery Country Dairy Farm, and she completed endless chores on the family farm, which was part and parcel of her childhood experience. Working on the family farm instilled in Patricia admirable values such as discipline, perseverance, conscientiousness, and diligence.

Patricia's father, Richard, often made Patricia take personal responsibility and initiative in managing operational activities associated with the dairy farm. Patricia had four siblings, a younger sister named Linda, and three older brothers named Charles, Kenneth, and Tommy. Patricia's time as a child, spent in the company of her three brothers, shaped her into a more assertive, confident, driven, and authoritative person. These positive attributes assisted Patricia's future development in the team sport of basketball. Initially, Patricia attended Roosevelt Elementary School. Thereafter, Patricia was educated at Cheatham County High School in Ashland City, where she was part of the School Basketball Team.

Following the completion of high school, Patricia matriculated at the University of Tennessee in Tennessee. At university, Patricia's love for team sports truly flourished. Patricia was a member of the University Basketball Team, known as the Tennessee Martin University Skyhawks. In addition, Patricia studied a Bachelor of Physical Education at university, which she later complemented with a Master's Degree in Physical Education in 1976. The presence of sex discrimination made university and sports life an inequitable playing field. Despite Patricia's natural talent as an athlete, she was not awarded an athletic scholarship, however, Patricia's parents whole-heartedly supported their daughter's sporting commitments and university study endeavours.

Patricia's first-rate performance on the University of Tennessee Basketball Team merited her a place in the 1976 Summer Olympics held in Montréal, Québec, Canada. At the Olympic Games, Patricia was Co-captain of the United States Women's National Basketball Team, which won the silver medal. At twenty-four years of age, Patricia was the oldest member on the National Basketball Team, however, age proved no barrier to her sporting success. In fact, Patricia's leadership and life experience added immense value to the team of younger female basketball players. Patricia's presence imparted a sense of confidence to her team members. Not to mention, Patricia enhanced the team morale, and she also provided invaluable guidance to her fellow team members on the basketball court.

During and following Patricia's stellar career in Women's Basketball, she was also a Professional Women's Basketball Coach. From 1974 until 2012, Patricia was the Head Coach of the University of Tennessee Lady Volunteers Basketball Team (commonly known as the Lady Vols). During Patricia's tenure, the Lady Vols' Basketball Team achieved respectable performance statistics, including victory in eight National Collegiate Athletic Association (NCAA) Championships, wins in sixteen South-Eastern

Conference Regular Season Titles, and victory in sixteen South-Eastern Conference Tournament Championships.

In addition, under Patricia's coaching and leadership, the Lady Vols proceeded to the National Collegiate Athletic Association's Women's Basketball 'Final Four' on eighteen separate occasions. Furthermore, during the seasoned tenure of Patricia being the Head Coach of the Lady Vols', this Women's Basketball Team secured a record 1,098 Career Wins. That is more victories than any other Division I College Basketball Coach, regardless be it Men's or Women's Basketball, in the history of the National Collegiate Athletic Association. Patricia's winning record held until 2020, when it was superseded by American basketball coach, Tara Ann VanDerveer, who represented Stanford University's Women's Basketball Team.

In 1980, Patricia married a bank executive named Ross Barnes Summitt. The married couple had one son named Tyler. Regrettably, Patricia and Ross' marriage ended in divorce in the year 2007. Beyond Patricia's notable achievements on the sporting field, she also co-authored two motivational books with American sports columnist and writer, Sally Jenkins, namely, *Raise the Roof*, and *Sum it Up (1,098 Victories, a Couple of Irrelevant Losses, and a Life in Perspective)*. The two aforesaid books detail Patricia's personal stories, struggles, accomplishments, and life experiences. Patricia's books are useful far beyond the sporting World of Basketball, and they contain some invaluable life lessons. In sum, Patricia's self-help books can assist any person to create a whole and fulfilling life.

Arguably, Patricia's greatest coaching accomplishment was leading the United States Women's National Basketball Team to a decisive victory. Under Patricia's stewardship the Women's National Basketball Team won gold at the 1984 Olympic Games held in Los Angeles, California, the United

States of America. In the year 2012, after a seasoned and successful career as a first-rate coach of Women's Basketball, Patricia retired from coaching the game that she most loved. Thereafter, Patricia secured the position of 'Head Coach Emeritus' to continue to indirectly support the Lady Vols.

On 28 June 2016, Patricia passed away after a long battle with Alzheimer's disease. Patricia was 64 years old at the time of her death. Patricia's outsized national contribution to Women's Basketball has been honoured throughout the United States of America, both during her life time and beyond. In 1990, Patricia was inducted into the International Women's Sports Hall of Fame. Furthermore, in 1999, Patricia was inducted into the U.S. Women's Basketball Hall of Fame. Not to mention, in the year 2000, Patricia was declared the Naismith Women's College Coach of the Century.

In addition, in 2011, Patricia was inducted into the Tennessee Women's Hall of Fame. Subsequently, in the year 2012, Patricia was awarded the Presidential Medal of Freedom by the U.S. President, Barack Obama (r. 2009-2017). Last but not least, in Patricia's memory and honour 'the Pat Summitt Clinic' was opened in January of 2017 at the University of Tennessee Medical Centre. The newfound Clinic provides dedicated medical care and treatment options for patients suffering from Alzheimer's disease. The Pat Summitt Clinic also promotes scientific research, offers educational programs, and provides psychological support to patients and their families.

Florence Delorez Griffith Joyner (1959-1998)

Florence Delorez Griffith Joyner was born on 21 December 1959 in Los Angeles, California, the United States of America. Florence's father was an electrician named Robert Griffith. Florence's mother was a seamstress and teacher named Florence Scott Griffith. When Florence was still a young child, her parents separated. Thereafter, Florence was raised by her mother in a public housing project known as the Jordan Downs Housing Project which was situated in an impoverished and underprivileged area, namely, the Watts Neighbourhood in Los Angeles. In addition, Florence had ten siblings in her family. Most notably, from the young age of seven, Florence was actively involved in track and field sporting activities.

As a child, Florence participated in outdoor sports with her brothers, which helped her to develop a competitive mindset. Not to mention, at the youthful age of seven, Florence chased jackrabbits to practice her running, and also to improve her speed and agility. Florence joined the Sugar Ray Robinson Youth Foundation to participate in sports, such as basketball, football, track and field, and volleyball. Florence's passion for running was all too evident from her childhood years. At fourteen, and again at fifteen years of age, Florence went on to win the Jesse Owens National Youth Games. In the year 1978, Florence completed her schooling at Jordan High School in Los Angeles. Florence's school sporting performance was exceptional, and she established school records in the Long Jump and Sprint events.

After high school, Florence briefly attended California State University (CSU) in Northridge, Los Angeles, however, she withdrew due to financial difficulties. During Florene's short tenure at CSU, she was a member of the University's Track and Field Team, where she was trained by American track coach, Bob Kersee. Thereafter, Florence worked as a Bank Teller to financially support her family, before she returned to her university studies. To Florence's great benefit, Bob had secured a new position as Assistant Coach at the University of California, Los Angeles (UCLA). Not to mention, Bob was very thoughtful in assisting Florence to secure financial aid for her to enrol at the UCLA in 1980.

Setting aside Florence's university studies at the UCLA, she focused her time, effort, and energy on the upcoming 1980 Olympic Games to be held in Moscow, the Union of Soviet Socialist Republics. Unfortunately, Florence was unsuccessful in the Qualifying Round of the Women's 200-metres Race at the United States Olympic Trials for the forthcoming 1980 Olympic Games. Notwithstanding Florence not securing her place amongst the best U.S. track and field athletes that qualified into the U.S Olympic Games Team, the United States formally boycotted the 1980 Olympics in a diplomatic protest of the Soviet Union's invasion of Afghanistan in 1979. However, all was not lost at the 1980 U.S. Olympic Trials, for Florence met her future husband and coach, American track and field athlete, Al Joyner.

While Florence continued to train to the best of her ability in track and field, she also went on to complete her studies at the UCLA. While Florence completed her Bachelor's Degree, she also participated in the National Track and Field Competitions. Most notably, in 1982, Florence won the Women's 200-metres Sprint at the National Collegiate Athletic Association (NCAA) Championships in a respectable time of 22.39 seconds. In addition, in 1983, Florence also secured the NCAA title in the Women's 400-metres Race in a commendable time of 50.94 seconds. Beyond Florence's impressive sporting achievements, in the year 1983, she also graduated with a Bachelor of Psychology Degree from the University of California, Los Angeles.

The next major International Sporting Event was the 1984 Olympic Games in Los Angeles, the United States. This time Florence qualified in the Women's 200-metres Race at the United States Olympic Trials. Florence's performance was exemplary at the 1984 Olympics, which were held in her home country. Most notably, Florence secured a silver medal for her strong performance in the Women's 200-metres Race. Florence was somewhat disappointed with claiming silver at the 1984 Olympics, and she temporarily withdrew from Track and Field Sporting Competitions. In 1987, Florence set her mind to becoming the best athlete that she could become, and she re-commenced her elite athlete training program. In addition, in the year 1987, Florence married her track and field coach, Al Joyner, who secured a gold medal at the 1984 Olympic Games in the Men's Triple Jump Event.

Thereafter, Florence went on to participate in the 1987 Second World Championships in Athletics which were held in Rome, Italy. Florence competed in the Women's 200-metres Sprint, where she won a silver medal for her admirable race time of 21.96 seconds. Additionally, Florence was also part of the Women's 4 x 100-metre Relay Race Event. The strong U.S. Women's Team performance included Florence's three American team members, Alice Regina Brown, Diane Williams, and Pam Marshall. The U.S. Team secured a gold medal victory, in a team-effort record time of 41.58 seconds.

Florence's best track and field performance was at her last major International Sporting Competition, namely, the 1988 Olympic Games held in Seoul, South Korea. In the lead up to the 1988 Olympics, Florence continued to be trained by her old-time university coach, Bob Kersee, as well as her husband and Olympic gold medallist in Triple Jump, Al Joyner. However, following the U.S. Olympic Trials, Florence parted ways with her long-time track and field coach, Bob Kersee. Thereafter, Florence trained full-time with her husband, Al Joyner. In effect, Al Joyner assumed the personal and professional responsibility of preparing Florence for the Olympic Track and Field Sporting Events held in Seoul.

Florence's sporting accomplishments at the 1988 Olympic Games were her most astonishing yet. In fact, Florence succeeded in winning three gold medals, and one silver medal for her truly brilliant Olympics performance! Florence competed in two individual Olympic Events, namely, the Women's 100-metres Sprint winning gold, and the Women's 200-metres Sprint also winning gold. In addition, Florence competed in two team Olympic Events, that is the Women's 4 x 100-metre Relay Race Event winning gold, and the Women's 4 x 400-metre Relay Race Event winning silver. Most notably, in the Women's 100-metres Sprint, Florence completed the race in a World Record time of 10.54 seconds! Not to mention, in the Women's 200-metres Sprint, Florence established a new World Record time of 21.34 seconds!

In the year 1989, Florence decided to formally retire from Professional Track and Field Competition. Florence's life priorities also started to change at this time. Most importantly, Florence and Al decided to start a family together. The married couple welcomed their first baby daughter named Mary Ruth Joyner on 15 November 1990. There was some controversy that Florence retired allegedly due to the use of banned sports performance enhancing substances, however, completed drug tests never found a positive result to substantiate such unfounded claims. Florence did not proceed to compete in the 1996 Olympic Games held in Atlanta, Georgia, the United States, this was due to an Achilles tendon injury.

On 21 September 1998, Florence tragically passed away in her sleep in Mission Viejo, California. Florence was only thirty-eight years old at the time of her death. Florence's cause of death was a severe epileptic seizure, she had suffered from a cavernous haemangioma (also known as cerebral cavernous malformation). Florence had a recorded medical history of seizures, and there was nothing suspicious about her untimely death. Florence was buried at El Toro Memorial Park in Lake Forest, California, the United States of America.

Florence's track and field performances, and her unforgettable sporting achievements have been honoured throughout her lifetime and beyond. For example, consider in 1988, Florence was the recipient of the Sullivan Award. Furthermore, in 1995, Florence was inducted into the United States' Track and Field Hall of Fame. Last but not least, in the year 2000, the 102nd Street School in Los Angeles was renamed the Florence Griffith Joyner Elementary School.

CONCLUSION

The Struggle of Women: Major Female Figures throughout World History has examined some of the greatest women in human history. This book investigatec the remarkable achievements of a number of women across fields and professions as diverse as philosophy, religion, science, medicine, politics, law, and sport. Of course, women have contributed to society and the human civilisation, far beyond these several domains, and the reader is encouraged to explore the invaluable contribution of women in other facets of the ancient and modern world.

In presenting a urıversal and representative view of women, this book has considered significant women across a number of continents, cultures, and countries, including, Australia, Canada, Czechoslovakia, Egypt, France, Germany, India, Ireland, Italy, the Netherlands New Zealand, North Macedonia, Norway, Peru, Poland, Romania, Russia, Spain, Sri Lanka, Sweden, the Union of Soviet Socialist Republics, the United Kingdom, and the United States of America. This is not to infer, that significant women from other equally important countries, that were not explored here, did not make a lasting contribution to humanity, only that it was beyond the limited scope of this book.

For countless centuries the role of women has been defined by corsets, customs, and conventions. Historically, women have not been able to freely exercise their agency, autonomy, and action in a truly independent manner, however, this book has illustrated that women can and do achieve world-class success in their chosen field. With respect to the significant women that this book has explored, what has made their personal story truly inspirational is the overcoming of entrenched barriers, rigid ideologies, socio-economic and political inequality, racial prejudice, sexist power dynamics, and the male-dominated hierarchical structures found in powerful institutions of the State.

Furthermore, historically speaking, women have also been defined by behavioural, social, religious, economic, and cultural expectations of gender roles. In addition, women have been subjected to discrimination in national laws that functioned to undermine and disable their full participation in the civil society. Not to mention, women continue to confront the common place prejudice and systematic bias in seeking to challenge the status quo of what it means to be a woman in the contemporary world.

From the outset, the greater purpose of this book was a very humble one, and that was to introduce select women who have made important contributions in the history of the human civilisation. That purpose has been fulfilled. This book has delineated some of the significant female figures that are to be found in the ever-evolving contours of understanding the invaluable contribution of women in both the ancient and modern world.

As more research and evidence comes to light, a better understanding shall evolve about the underrepresented role that women have performed, and continue to perform in our world. Indeed, much more remains to be understood, learned, and changed, for the creation of an

Ideal World, based on the universal principles of equality, freedom, justice, the rule of law, fairness, human dignity, liberty, equity, and peace.

BIBLIOGRAPHY

Acker, J. (2006). Inequality Regimes: Gender, Class, and Race in Organisations. *Gender and Society*. Volume 21, No. 4, (August 2006), pp. 441-464.

Adams, J. (2014). *Women and the Vote: A World History*. Oxford: Oxford University Press.

Adams, K. H., and Keene, M. L. (2007). *Alice Paul and the American Suffrage Campaign*. Urbana: University of Illinois Press.

Adams, S. L. (2014). *Mad Mothers, Bad Mothers, and What a 'Good' Mother Would Do. The Ethics of Ambivalence*. New York: Columbia University Press.

Agrippa, H. C. (Rabil, A., Ed. and Trans.) (1996). *Declamation on the Nobility and Pre-eminence of the Female Sex*. Chicago: The University of Chicago Press.

Aiken, S. H. (1990). *Isak Dinesen and the Engendering of Narrative* Chicago: University of Chicago Press.

Aitken, J. (2013). *Margaret Thatcher: Power and Personality*. London: Bloomsbury.

Alexander, A. L. (2019). *Princess of the Hither Isles. A Black Suffragist's Story from the Jim Crow South*. New Haven, Connecticut: Yale University Press.

Allen, J. A. (2009). *The Feminism of Charlotte Perkins Gilman. Sexualities, Histories, Progressivism*. Chicago: University of Chicago Press.

Anderson, K. (1996). *After Suffrage: Women in Partisan and Electoral Politics before the New Deal.* Chicago: University of Chicago Press.

Anderson, K. (1997). *Changing Woman: A History of Racial Ethnic Women in Modern America*. Oxford: Oxford University Press.

Anishanslin, Z. (2017). *Portrait of a Woman in Silk. Hidden Histories of the British Atlantic World.* New Haven, Connecticut: Yale University Press.

Ariail, C. M. (2020). *Passing the Baton: Black Women Track Stars and American Identity*. Urbana: University of Illinois Press.

Arjava, A. (1998). *Women and Law in Late Antiquity*. Oxford: Clarendon Press.

Azaransky, S. (2011). *The Dream is Freedom. Pauli Murray and American Democratic Faith*. Oxford: Oxford University Press.

Backscheider, P. R. (2007). *Eighteenth-Century Women Poets and Their Poetry. Inventing Agency, Inventing Genre*. Baltimore: Johns Hopkins University Press.

Backscheider, P. R. (2021). *Women in Wartime. Theatrical Representations in the Long Eighteenth Century*. Baltimore: Johns Hopkins University Press.

Baker, J. H. (2002). *Votes for Women: The Struggle for Suffrage Revisited*. Oxford: Oxford University Press.

Balsdon, J. P. V. D. (1962). *Roman Women: Their History and Habits*. London: Bodley Head.

Banner, L. W. (1980). *Elizabeth Cady Stanton: A Radical for Woman's Rights*. Boston: Little, Brown, and Company.

Bannet, E. T. (2000). *The Domestic Revolution. Enlightenment Feminisms and the Novel*. Baltimore: Johns Hopkins University Press.

Barry, K. (2020). *Susan B. Anthony: A Biography*. New York: New York University Press.

Bauer, N. (2001). *Simone de Beauvoir, Philosophy, and Feminism*. New York: Columbia University Press.

Baweja, P. (2021). *A Philosophical Treatise of Reality: Volume One*. Melbourne: Paul Baweja.

Baweja, P. (2021). *A Philosophical Treatise of Reality: Volume Two*. Melbourne: Paul Baweja.

Baweja, P. (2021). *A Philosophical Treatise of Reality: Volume Three*. Melbourne: Paul Baweja.

Baweja, P. (2021). *A Philosophical Treatise of Reality: Volume Four* Melbourne: Paul Baweja.

Beattie, C. (2007). *Medieval Single Women. The Politics of Social Classification in Late Medieval England.* Oxford: Oxford University Press.

Bendroth, M. L. (1996). *Fundamentalism and Gender, 1875 to the Present*. New Haven, Connecticut: Yale University Press.

Berkovitch, N. (2002). *From Motherhood to Citizenship. Women's Rights and International Organisations*. Baltimore: Johns Hopkins University Press.

Berry, D. R., and Gross, K. N. (2020). *A Black Women's History of the United States*. Boston: Beacon Press.

Bloch, R. H. (1991). *Medieval Misogyny and the Invention of Western Romantic Love*. Chicago: University of Chicago Press.

Boddy, J. (2007). *Civilising Women. British Crusades in Colonial Sudan*. Princeton, New Jersey: Princeton University Press.

Bolzendahl, C. (2014). Opportunities and Expectations: The Gendered Organisation of Legislative Committees in Germany, Sweden, and the United States. *Gender and Society*. Volume 28, No. 6, (December 2014), pp. 847-876.

Booth, A. (2004). *How to Make It as a Woman. Collective Biographical History from Victoria to the Present.* Chicago: University of Chicago Press.

Bornstein, D., and Rusconi, R. (Eds.) (Schneider, M. J., Trans.)   (1996). - *Women and Religion in Medieval and Renaissance Italy.* Chicago: University of Chicago Press.

Botting, E. H. (2016). *Wollstonecraft, Mill, and Women's Human Rights.* New Haven: Yale University Press.

Boyd, A. E. (Ed.) (2009). *Wielding the Pen. Writings on Authorship by American Women of the Nineteenth Century.* Baltimore: Johns Hopkins University Press.

Boyd, A. E. (2010). *Writing for Immortality. Women and the Emergence of High Literary Culture in America.* Baltimore: Johns Hopkins University Press.

Brand, L. A. (1998). *Women, the State, and Political Liberalisation. Middle Eastern and North African Experiences.* New York: Columbia University Press.

Braude, A. (1999). *Women and American Religion.* Oxford: Oxford University Press.

Broad, J. (Ed.) (2019). *Women Philosophers of Seventeenth-Century England. Selected Correspondence.* Oxford: Oxford University Press.

Brody, M. (2004). *Victoria Woodhull. Free Spirit for Women's Rights*. Oxford: Oxford University Press.

Brown, N. E. (2014). *Sisters in the Statehouse. Black Women and Legislative Decision Making.* Oxford: Oxford University Press.

Brown, P. (2008). *The Body and Society. Men, Women, and Sexual Renunciation in Early Christianity*. New York: Columbia University Press.

Buechler, S. M. (1990). *Women's Movements in the United States.* New Brunswick, New Jersey: Rutgers University Press.

Bush, J. (2007). *Women Against the Vote. Female Anti-Suffragism in Britain*. Oxford: Oxford University Press.

Cahill, C. D. (2021). *Recasting the Vote: How Women of Colour Transformed the Suffrage Movement*. Chapel Hill: University of North Carolina Press.

Caine, B. (1993). *Victorian Feminists*. Oxford: Oxford University Press.

Caine, B. (1997). *English Feminism, 1780-1980*. Oxford: Oxford University Press.

Campbell, P. (1993). *No Going Back. Women as University Students*. Halifax: Fernwood Publishing.

Catano, J. V., and Novak, D. A. (2011). *Masculinity Lessons. Rethinking Men's and Women's Studies*. Baltimore: Johns Hopkins University Press.

Catt, C. C., and Shuler, N. R. (2020). *Woman Suffrage and Politics: The Inner Story of the Suffrage Movement*. New York: Dover Publications.

Celani, D. P. (1996). *The Illusion of Love. Why the Battered Woman Returns to Her Abuser*. New York: Columbia University Press.

Cereta, L. (Robin, D., Ed. and Trans.) (1997). *Collected Letters of a Renaissance Feminist*. Chicago: University of Chicago Press.

Chapman, M. (2017). *Making Noise, Making News. Suffrage Print Culture and U.S. Modernism*. Oxford: Oxford University Press.

Chojnacka, M. (2001). *Working Women of Early Modern Venice*. Baltimore: Johns Hopkins University Press.

Christ, C. P., and Plaskow, J. (2017). Two Views of Divinity in the World: Conversations in Embodied Theology. *Journal of Feminist Studies in Religion*. Volume 33, Number 2, Fall 2017, pp. 97-103.

Clark, G. (1994). *Women in Late Antiquity. Pagan and Christian Lifestyles*. Oxford: Oxford University Press.

Clarke, D. (2007). *Driving Women. Fiction and Automobile Culture in Twentieth-Century America*. Baltimore: Johns Hopkins University Press.

Clemens, E. S. (1993). Organisational Repertoires and Institutional Change: Women's Groups and the Transformation of U.S. Politics, 1890-1920. *American Journal of Sociology*. Volume 98, No. 4, pp. 755-798.

Clifford, G. J. (2016). *Those Good Gertrudes. A Social History of Women Teachers in America.* Baltimore: Johns Hopkins University Press.

Coakley, J. W. (2006). *Women, Men, and Spiritual Power. Female Saints and their Male Collaborators*. New York: Columbia University Press.

Cobb, L. S. (2008). *Dying to Be Men. Gender and Language in Early Christian Martyr Texts*. New York: Columbia University Press.

Coburn, J. (2021). "Basically Feminist": Women Strike for Peace, Maternal Peace Activism, and Memory of the Women's Peace Movement. *Journal of Women's History.* Volume 33, Number 2, pp. 136-162.

Cook, S. J. (2007). *Working Women, Literary Ladies. The Industrial Revolution and Female Aspiration*. Oxford: Oxford University Press.

Cott, N. F. (1977). *The Bonds of Womanhood: Woman's Sphere in New England, 1780-1835*. New Haven, Connecticut: Yale University Press.

Cott, N. F. (1989). *The Grounding of Modern Feminism*. New Haven, Connecticut: Yale University Press.

Cox, V. (2008). *Women's Writing in Italy, 1400-1650*. Baltimore: Johns Hopkins University Press.

Cox, V. (2011). *The Prodigious Muse. Women's Writing in Counter-Reformation Italy*. Baltimore: Johns Hopkins University Press.

Creager, A. N. H., Lunbeck, E., and Schiebinger, L. (Eds.) (2001). *Feminism in Twentieth-Century Science, Technology, and Medicine.* Chicago: University of Chicago Press.

Curtin, J. (2012). Carol Bacchi and Joan Eveline. Mainstreaming Politics: Gendering Practices and Feminist Theory. *International Feminist Journal of Politics*. Volume 14, Issue 1, pp. 174-176.

D'Antonio, P. (2010). *American Nursing. A History of Knowledge, Authority, and the Meaning of Work*. Baltimore: Johns Hopkins University Press.

Darwin, H. (2018). Redoing Gender, Redoing Religion. *Gender and Society*. Volume 32, No. 3, (June 2018), pp. 348-370.

Davey, J. (2019). *Mary Countess of Derby and the Politics of Victorian Britain*. Oxford: Oxford University Press.

Davis, A. Y. (2019). *Women, Race, and Class*. London: Penguin Books.

De Beauvoir, S. (2006). *The Women Destroyed.* London: Harper Perennial Modern Classics.

De Beauvoir, S. (2011). *The Second Sex.* New York: Vintage Books.

Delap, L. (2020). *Feminisms: A Global History*. Chicago: University of Chicago Press.

Deliovsky, K. (2010). *White Femininity. Race, Gender, and Power*. Halifax: Fernwood Publishing.

Denlinger, E. (2005). *Before Victoria. Extraordinary Women of the British Romantic Era*. New York: Columbia University Press.

Deutsch, S. (2000). *Women and the City. Gender, Power, and Space in Boston, 1870-1940*. Oxford: Oxford University Press.

Dolan, K. (2014). *When Does Gender Matter? Women Candidates and Gender Stereotypes in American Elections*. Oxford: Oxford University Press.

Drachman, V. G. (2001). *Sisters in Law. Women Lawyers in Modern American History.* Cambridge, Massachusetts: Harvard University Press.

Duby, G. (Dunnett, J., Trans.) (1994). *Love and Marriage in the Middle Ages*. Chicago: University of Chicago Press.

Dudden, F. E. (2014). *Fighting Chance. The Struggle over Woman Suffrage and Black Suffrage in Reconstruction America*. Oxford: Oxford University Press.

Dudden, F. E. (2019). Women's Rights Advocates and Abortion Laws. - *Journal of Women's History.* Volume 31, No. 3, pp. 102-123.

Dumenil, L. (2019). *American Working Women in World War II. A Brief History with Documents.* New York: Bedford Books.

Dunning, B. H. (2019). *The Oxford Handbook of New Testament, Gender, and Sexuality.* Oxford: Oxford University Press.

Dzielska, M. (Lyra, F., Trans.) (1996). *Hypatia of Alexandria.* Cambridge, Massachusetts: Harvard University Press.

Eby, C. V. (2014). *Until Choice Do Us Part: Marriage Reform in the Progressive Era.* Chicago: University of Chicago Press.

Elshtain, J. B. (1981). *Public Man, Private Women. Women in Social and Political Thought.* Princeton, New Jersey: Princeton University Press.

Evans, M. (2011). Doing gender: Gender and women's studies in the twenty-first century. *Women's Studies International Forum.* Volume 34, Issue 6, (Nov-Dec 2011), pp. 603-610.

Felski, R. (2003). *Literature after Feminism.* Chicago: University of Chicago Press.

Ferguson, L. (2014). This is our Gender Person: The Messy Business of Working as a Gender Expert in International Development. *International Feminist Journal of Politics.* Volume 17, Issue 3, pp. 380-397.

Fisher, K. (2006). *Birth Control, Sex, and Marriage in Britain 1918-1960.* Oxford: Oxford University Press.

Flanagan, M. A. (2002). *Seeing with Their Hearts. Chicago Women and the Vision of the Good City, 1871-1933.* Princeton, New Jersey: Princeton University Press.

Flemming, R. (2001). *Medicine and the Making of Roman Women. Gender, Nature, and Authority from Celsus to Galen.* Oxford: Oxford University Press.

Flexner, E. (1959). *Century of Struggle: The Woman's Rights Movement in the United States*. Cambridge, Massachusetts: Harvard University Press.

Ford, L. E. (2017). *Women and Politics: The Pursuit of Equality*. New York: Routledge Publication.

Foster, A. E. (2011). *Integrating Women into the Astronaut Corps. Politics and Logistics at NASA, 1972-2004*. Baltimore: Johns Hopkins University Press.

Fraiman, S. (1993). *Unbecoming Women. British Women Writers and the Novel of Development*. New York: Columbia University Press.

Frank, K. (2007). *Indira: The Life of Indira Nehru Gandhi*. London: Harper Perennial.

Fraser, A. (1988). *The Warrior Queens*. New York: Alfred A. Knopf.

Fredman, S. (1997). *Women and the Law*. Oxford: Oxford University Press.

Freeman, M. A., Chinkin, C., and Rudolf, B. (2013). *UN Convention on the Elimination of All Forms of Discrimination Against Women. A Commentary*. Oxford: Oxford University Press.

Friedan, B. (2010). *The Feminine Mystique*. London: Penguin Books.

Gaddini, K. (2022). *The Struggle to Stay. Why Single Evangelical Women are Leaving the Church*. New York: Columbia University Press.

Gallman, J. M. (2006). *America's Joan of Arc. The Life of Anna Elizabeth Dickinson*. Oxford: Oxford University Press.

Garcia, M. (2021). *We Are Not Born Submissive: How Patriarchy Shapes Women's Lives*. Princeton, New Jersey: Princeton University Press.

Gates, B. T. (1999). *Kindred Nature: Victorian and Edwardian Women Embrace the Living World*. Chicago: University of Chicago Press.

Gay, R. (2014). *Bad Feminist: Essays*. New York: Harper Collins.

Geary, P. J. (2006). *Women at the Beginning. Origin Myths from the Amazons to the Virgin Mary.* Princeton, New Jersey: Princeton University Press.

Gelbart, N. R. (2021). *Minerva's French Sisters. Women of Science in Enlightenment France*. New Haven, Connecticut: Yale University Press.

Gelles, E. B. (Ed.) (2004). *The Letters of Abigaill Levy Franks, 1733-1748.* New Haven, Connecticut: Yale University Press.

Giddings, P. J. (2009). *Ida: A Sword Among Lions: Ida B. Wells and the Campaign Against Lynching.* New York: Amistad.

Gidlow, L. (2020). More Than Double: African American Women and the Rise of a "Women's Vote". *Journal of Women's History*. Volume 32, Issue 1, pp. 52-61.

Ginsburg, R. B. (2016). *My Own Words*. New York: Simon and Schuster.

Ginsburg, R.B., and Tyler, A. L. (2021). *Justice, Justice Thou Shalt Pursue. A Life's Work Fighting for a More Perfect Union*. California: University of California Press.

Gleadle, K. (2009). *Borderline Citizens. Women, Gender, and Political Culture in Britain, 1815-1867*. Oxford: Oxford University Press.

Glenn, S. A. (2002). *Female Spectacle. The Theatrical Roots of Modern Feminism*. Cambridge, Massachusetts: Harvard University Press.

Glover, L. (2020). *Eliza Lucas Pinckney. An Independent Woman in the Age of Revolution.* New Haven, Connecticut: Yale University Press.

Gold, P. S. (1985). *The Lady and the Virgin: Image, Attitude, and Experience in Twelfth-Century France.* Chicago: University of Chicago Press.

Good, C. A. (2015). *Founding Friendships: Friendships between Men and Women in the Early American Republic*. Oxford: Oxford University Press.

Goodier, S., and Pastorello, K. (2017). *Women Will Vote. Winning Suffrage in New York State*. Ithaca, New York: Cornell University Press.

Goodlad, L. M. E. (2004). *Victorian Literature and the Victorian State. Character and Governance in a Liberal Society.*Baltimore: Johns Hopkins University Press.

Gordon, L. (2019). *Outsiders. Five Women Writers Who Changed the World*. Baltimore: Johns Hopkins University Press.

Gornick, V. (2005). *The Solitude of Self: Thinking about Elizabeth Cady Stanton*. New York: Farrar, Strauss, and Giroux.

Grayzel, S. R., and Proctor, T. M. (2017). *Gender and the Great War.*Oxford: Oxford University Press.

Griffith, E. (1984). *In Her Own Right: The Life of Elizabeth Cady Stanton*. New York: Oxford University Press.

Gudmundsdottir, A. (2010). *Meeting God on the Cross. Christ, the Cross, and the Feminist Critique.* Oxford: Oxford University Press.

Hagelin, S., and Silverman, G. (2022). *The New Female Antihero: The Disruptive Women of Twenty-First-Century U.S. Television*. Chicago: University of Chicago Press.

Haliczer, S. (1996). *Sexuality in the Confessional. A Sacrament Profaned*. Oxford: Oxford University Press.

Hamlin, K. A. (2014). *From Eve to Evolution. Darwin, Science, and Women's Rights in Gilded Age America*. Chicago: University of Chicago Press.

Hamori, E. J. (2015). *Women's Divination in Biblical Literature. Prophecy, Necromancy, and Other Arts of Knowledge.*New Haven, Connecticut: Yale University Press.

Hanawalt, B. A. (2007). *The Wealth of Wives. Women, Law, and Economy in Late Medieval London.* Oxford: Oxford University Press.

Harding, S., and O'Barr, J. F. (1987). *Sex and Scientific Inquiry*. Chicago: University of Chicago Press.

Harris, J. (Ed.) (2003). *Civil Society in British History. Ideas, Identities, Institutions*. Oxford: Oxford University Press.

Harris-Perry, M. V. (2013). *Sister Citizen. Shame, Stereotypes, and Black Women in America*. New Haven, Connecticut: Yale University Press.

Harrison, B. (1987). *Prudent Revolutionaries. Portraits of British Feminists between the Wars*. Oxford: Oxford University Press.

Harvey, K. (2012). *The Little Republic. Masculinity and Domestic Authority in Eighteenth-Century Britain.* Oxford: Oxford University Press.

Held, V. (1993). *Feminist Morality: Transforming Culture, Society, and Politics*. Chicago: University of Chicago Press.

Herrin, J. (2002). *Women in Purple. Rulers of Medieval Byzantium*. Princeton, New Jersey: Princeton University Press.

Herring, J. (2017). Sue Westwood: Ageing, Gender, and Society: Equality in Late Life. *Feminist Legal Studies*. Volume 26, Issue 1, pp. 109-111.

Hewitt, N. A. (1988). *Women's Activism and Social Change. Rochester, New York, 1822-1872.* Ithaca, New York: Cornell University Press.

Hilden, P. (1986). *Working Women and Socialist Politics in France 1880-1914. A Regional Study*. Oxford: Clarendon Press.

Hinton, J. (2002). *Women, Social Leadership, and the Second World War*. Oxford: Oxford University Press.

Hirshman, L. (2015). *Sisters in Law: How Sandra Day O'Connor and Ruth Bader Ginsburg Went to the Supreme Court and Changed the World*. New York: Harper Collins.

Hogan, K. (2001). *Women Take Care. Gender, Race, and the Culture of AIDS*. Ithaca, New York: Cornell University Press.

Hogan, L. S. (2008). A Time for Silence: William Lloyd Garrison and the "Woman Question" at the 1840 World Anti-Slavery Convention. *Gender Issues*. Volume 25, Issue 2, pp. 63-79.

Hollings, C., Martin, U., and Rice, A. (2018). *Ada Lovelace: The Making of a Computer Scientist.* Oxford: Bodleian Library Publishing.

Holmes, M. (2017). *Working for the Common Good. Canadian Women Politicians.* Halifax: Fernwood Publishing.

Homans, M. (1998). *Royal Representations. Queen Victoria and British Culture, 1837-1876.* Chicago: University of Chicago Press.

Houts, E. v. (2019). *Married Life in the Middle Ages, 900-1300.* Oxford: Oxford University Press.

Howell, M. C. (1986). *Women, Production, and Patriarchy in Late Medieval Cities.* Chicago: University of Chicago Press.

Hunt, M. E. (2020). The Power of Silence in the Work of Justice: Feminist Catholicism in Action. *Journal of Feminist Studies in Religion.* Volume 36, Number 1, (Spring 2020), pp. 99-111.

Hunter, J. (2002). *How Young Ladies Became Girls. The Victorian Origins of American Girlhood.* New Haven, Connecticut: Yale University Press.

Hylen, S. E. (2018). *Women in the New Testament World.* Oxford: Oxford University Press.

Inglehart, R., and Norris, P. (2003). *Rising Tide: Gender Equality and Cultural Change Around the World.* Cambridge: Cambridge University Press.

Jackson, R. M. (2010). *Destined for Equality. The Inevitable Rise of Women's Status.* Cambridge, Massachusetts: Harvard University Press.

Jacob, S. (2021). A Postcolonial, Indian Feminist Response to Mary, Mother of Martyrs. *Journal of Feminist Studies in Religion.* Volume 37, Issue 1, pp. 159-165.

Jacobson, D. (2013). *Of Virgins and Martyrs. Women and Sexuality in Global Conflict.* Baltimore: Johns Hopkins University Press.

Jalland, P. (1986). *Women, Marriage, and Politics 1860-1914.* Oxford: Oxford University Press.

Jardins, J. D. (2010). *The Madame Curie Complex: The Hidden History of Women in Science*. New York: The Feminist Press at the City University of New York.

Jeansonne, G. (1996). *Women of the Far Right*. Chicago: University of Chicago Press.

Jensen, J. M. (1988). *Loosening the Bonds. Mid-Atlantic Farm Women, 1750-1850*. New Haven, Connecticut: Yale University Press.

Johnson, J. M. (2015). Following the Money: Wealthy Women, Feminism, and the American Suffrage Movement. *Journal of Women's History*. Volume 27, Issue 4, pp. 62-87.

Johnson, P. D. (1991). *Equal in Monastic Profession: Religious Women in Medieval France*. Chicago: University of Chicago Press.

Jolly, M. (2008). *In Love and Struggle. Letters in Contemporary Feminism*. New York: Columbia University Press.

Kennedy, V. L. (2012). *Born Southern. Childbirth, Motherhood, and Social Networks in the Old South*. Baltimore: Johns Hopkins University Press.

Kent, S. K. (2021) *Gender: A World History*. Oxford: Oxford University Press.

Kerrison, C. (2015). *Claiming the Pen. Women and Intellectual Life in the Early American South*. Ithaca, New York: Cornell University Press.

Klapisch-Zuber, C. (Cochrane, L. G., Trans.) (1985). *Women, Family, and Ritual in Renaissance Italy*. Chicago: University of Chicago Press.

Knop, K. (2004). *Gender and Human Rights*. Oxford: Oxford University Press.

Kraditor, A. S. (1981). *The Ideas of the Woman Suffrage Movement, 1890-1920*. New York: W. W. Norton and Company.

Lake, J. (2016). *The Face That Launched a Thousand Lawsuits. The American Women Who Forged a Right to Privacy*. New Haven, Connecticut: Yale University Press.

Landes, J. B. (1988). *Women and the Public Sphere in the Age of the French Revolution*. Ithaca, New York: Cornell University Press.

Langbauer, L. (2018). *Women and Romance. The Consolations of Gender in the English Novel*. Ithaca, New York: Cornell University Press.

Langland, E., and Gove, W. (Eds.) (1984). *A Feminist Perspective in the Academy: The Difference it Makes.* Chicago: University of Chicago Press.

Lansbury, J. H. (2014). *A Spectacular Leap: Black Women Athletes in Twentieth-Century America.* Fayetteville: University of Arkansas Press.

Leeb, C. (2017). *Power and Feminist Agency in Capitalism. Toward a New Theory of the Political Subject*. Oxford: Oxford University Press.

Lerner, G. (1987). *The Creation of Patriarchy*. Oxford: Oxford University Press.

Lerner, G. (Ed.) (1992). *Black Women in White America: A Documentary History*. New York: Vintage Books.

Lerner, G. (1993). *The Creation of Feminist Consciousness: From the Middle Ages to Eighteen-Seventy.* New York: Oxford University Press.

Lindley, S. H. (1996). *You have Stept out of your Place. A History of Women and Religion in America*. Louisville: Westminster John Knox Press.

Lorber, J. (1995). *Paradoxes of Gender*. New Haven, Connecticut: Yale University Press.

Lovenduski, J. (2008). State Feminism and Women's Movements. *West European Politics.* Volume 31, No. 1, pp. 169-194.

Lowe, M. A. (2005). *Looking Good. College Women and Body Image, 1875-1930*. Baltimore: Johns Hopkins University Press.

MacLean, N. (2008). *The American Women's Movement, 1945-2000. A Brief History with Documents.* New York: Bedford Books.

Macy, G. (2012). *The Hidden History of Women's Ordination. Female Clergy in the Medieval West*. Oxford: Oxford University Press.

Maddox, B. (2003). *Rosalind Franklin: The Dark Lady of DNA*. New York: Harper Collins.

Mandell, D. R. (2011). *Tribe, Race, History. Native Americans in Southern New England, 1780-1880*. Baltimore: Johns Hopkins University Press.

Manne, K. (2017). *Down Girl: The Logic of Misogyny*. Oxford: Oxford University Press.

Marcus, S. (2007). *Between Women. Friendship, Desire, and Marriage in Victorian England.* Princeton, New Jersey: Princeton University Press.

Markel, H. (2021). *The Secret of Life: Rosalind Franklin, James Watson, Francis Crick, and the Discovery of DNA Double Helix*. New York: W. W. Norton and Company.

Martin, M. (2009). *Selling Beauty. Cosmetics, Commerce, and French Society, 1750-1830.* Baltimore: Johns Hopkins University Press.

Massie, R. K. (2012). *Catherine the Great: Portrait of a Woman*. New York: Random House Trade.

Matthews, G. (1994). *The Rise of Public Woman. Woman's Power and Woman's Place in the United States, 1630-1970.* Oxford: Oxford University Press.

Mayeri, S. (2014). *Reasoning from Race: Feminism, Law, and the Civil Rights Revolution*. Cambridge, Massachusetts: Harvard University Press.

Mayhall, L. E. N. (2003). *The Militant Suffrage Movement. Citizenship and Resistance in Britain, 1860-1930*. Oxford: Oxford University Press.

McCurry, S. (2019). *Women's War. Fighting and Surviving the American Civil War.* Cambridge, Massachusetts: Harvard University Press.

McGrayne, S. B. (2001). *Nobel Prize Women in Science: Their Lives, Struggles, and Momentous Discoveries*. Washington, DC: Joseph Henry Press.

McIntosh, J. L. (2008). *From Heads of Household to Heads of State. The Preaccession Households of Mary and Elizabeth Tudor*. New York: Columbia University Press.

McKenna, K. (2018). *No Choice. The 30-Year Fight for Abortion on Prince Edward Island*. Halifax: Fernwood Publishing.

McMillen, S. G. (2015). *Lucy Stone: An Unapologetic Life*. Oxford: Oxford University Press.

McMillen, S. G. (2009). *Seneca Falls and the Origins of the Women's Rights Movement*. Oxford: Oxford University Press.

Milam, E. L. (2011). *Looking for a Few Good Males. Female Choice in Evolutionary Biology.* Baltimore: Johns Hopkins University Press.

Miles, R. (1990). *The Women's History of the World*. New York: Harper and Row.

Moghadam, V. M. (2005). *Globalising Women. Transnational Feminist Networks*. Baltimore: Johns Hopkins University Press.

Moi, T. (2009). *Simone De Beauvoir. The Making of an Intellectual Woman*. Oxford: Oxford University Press.

Moon, H. (2008). Women Priests. Radical Change or More of the Same? - *Journal of Feminist Studies in Religion*. Volume 24, Issue 2, pp. 115-134.

Moore, D. (2020). *What Stars Are Made Of. The Life of Cecilia Payne-Gaposchkin*. Cambridge, Massachusetts: Harvard University Press.

Morantz-Sanchez, R. (2000). *Conduct Unbecoming a Woman. Medicine on Trial in Turn-of-the-Century Brooklyn.* Oxford: Oxford University Press.

More, E. S. (2001). *Restoring the Balance. Women Physicians and the Profession of Medicine, 1850-1995*. Cambridge, Massachusetts: Harvard University Press.

More, E. S., Fee, E., and Parry, M. (Eds.) (2008). *Women Physicians and the Cultures of Medicine*. Baltimore: Johns Hopkins University Press.

Morris, M. (2015). *Sex, Money, and Personal Character in Eighteenth-Century British Politics*. New Haven, Connecticut: Yale University Press.

Muir, E. G. (2019). *A Women's History of the Christian Church: Two Thousand Years of Female Leadership*. Toronto: University of Toronto Press.

Nadasen, P. (2002). Expanding the Boundaries of the Women's Movement: Black Feminism and the Struggle for Welfare Rights. *Feminist Studies*. Volume 28, Issue 2, pp. 270-301.

Nagel, P. C. (1999). *The Adams Women. Abigail and Louisa Adams, Their Sisters and Daughters.* Cambridge, Massachusetts: Harvard University Press.

Najar, M. (2007). *Evangelising the South. A Social History of Church and State in Early America.* Oxford: Oxford University Press.

Nelson, F. (2009). *In the Other Room. Entering the Culture of Motherhood.* Halifax: Fernwood Publishing.

Nimura, J. P. (2021). *The Doctors Blackwell: How Two Pioneering Sisters Brought Medicine to Women and Women to Medicine.* New York: W. W. Norton and Company.

Norton, M. B. (2014). *Separated by Their Sex. Women in Public and Private in the Colonial Atlantic World.* Ithaca, New York: Cornell University Press.

Nussbaum, M. C. (1999). *Sex and Social Justice*. Oxford: Oxford University Press.

Nystrom, J. A. (2015). *New Orleans after the Civil War. Race, Politics, and a New Birth of Freedom.* Baltimore: Johns Hopkins University Press.

Ogilvie, S. (2003). *A Bitter Living. Women, Markets, and Social Capital in Early Modern Germany.* Oxford: Oxford University Press.

Okin, S. M. (2013). *Women in Western Political Thought*. Princeton, New Jersey: Princeton University Press.

Orgad, S. (2019). *Heading Home. Motherhood, Work, and the Failed Promise of Equality.* New York: Columbia University Press.

Orser, B., and Elliott, C. (2015). *Feminine Capital: Unlocking the Power of Women Entrepreneurs.* Stanford, California: Stanford University Press.

Park, K. (2006). *Secrets of Women. Gender, Generation, and the Origins of Human Dissection*. New York: Zone Books.

Peck, L. L. (2018). *Women of Fortune: Money, Marriage, and Murder in Early Modern England*. Cambridge: Cambridge University Press.

Phillippy, P. (2005). *Painting Women. Cosmetics, Canvases, and Early Modern Culture*. Baltimore: Johns Hopkins University Press.

Phoenix, K. (2021). *Gender Rules: Identity and Empire in Historical Perspective*. Oxford: Oxford University Press.

Poulos, M. (2009). *Arms and the Woman. Just Warriors and Greek Feminist Identity*. New York: Columbia University Press.

Pugh, M. (2002). *The March of the Women. A Revisionist Analysis of the Campaign for Women's Suffrage, 1866-1914*. Oxford: Oxford University Press.

Purvis, J. (2002). *Emmeline Pankhurst: A Biography*. London: Routledge Publication.

Purvis, J., and Hannam, J. (Eds.). (2021). *The British Women's Suffrage Campaign: National and International Perspectives*. New York: Routledge Publication.

Purvis, J., and Holton, S. S. (Eds.) (2000). *Votes for Women*. London: Routledge Publication.

Rhode, D. L. (2014). *What Women Want: An Agenda for the Women's Movement*. Oxford: Oxford University Press.

Renn, K. A. (2014). *Women's Colleges and Universities in a Global Context*. Baltimore: Johns Hopkins University Press.

Rhoton, L. A. (2011). Distancing as a Gendered Barrier: Understanding Women Scientists' Gender Practices. *Gender and Society*. Volume 25, No. 6, (December 2011), pp. 696-716.

Richards, J. (2020). *The Fury Archives. Female Citizenship, Human Rights, and the International Avant-Gardes*. New York: Columbia University Press.

Ridgeway, C. L. (2008). Framed Before We Know It: How Gender Shapes Social Relations. *Gender and Society*. Volume 23, No. 2, (April 2009), pp. 145-160.

Rivers, C., and Barnett, R. C. (2013). *The Truth About Girls and Boys. Challenging Toxic Stereotypes About Our Children.* New York: Columbia University Press.

Robinson, A. (2002). *The Life and Work of Jane Ellen Harrison*. Oxford: Oxford University Press.

Robnett, B. (1999). *How Long? How Long? African American Women in the Struggle for Civil Rights.* Oxford: Oxford University Press.

Ronald, S. (2012). *Heretic Queen: Queen Elizabeth I and the Wars of Religion*. New York: St. Martin's Press.

Rose, D. (2018). *Citizens By Degree: Higher Education Policy and the Changing Gender Dynamics of American Citizenship*. Oxford: Oxford University Press.

Rose, M. B. (2002). *Gender and Heroism in Early Modern English Literature*. Chicago: University of Chicago Press.

Rosen, J. (2019). *Conversations with RBG: Ruth Bader Ginsburg on Life, Love, Liberty, and Law.* New York: Henry Holt and Company.

Rosenberg, R. (1983). *Beyond Separate Spheres. Intellectual Roots of Modern Feminism*. New Haven, Connecticut: Yale University Press.

Rosenberg, R. (2004). *Changing the Subject. How the Women of Columbia Shaped the Way We Think about Sex and Politics*. New York: Columbia University Press.

Rupp, L. J. (1978). *Mobilizing Women for War. German and American Propaganda, 1939-1945*. Princeton, New Jersey: Princeton University Press.

Rupp, L. J. (1998). *Worlds of Women. The Making of an International Women's Movement*. Princeton, New Jersey: Princeton University Press.

Ryan, K. A. (2014). *Regulating Passion. Sexuality and Patriarchal Rule in Massachusetts, 1700-1830*. Oxford: Oxford University Press.

Ryan, M. P. (1992). *Women in Public. Between Banners and Ballots, 1825-1880*. Baltimore: Johns Hopkins University Press.

Sailes, G. A. (Ed.) (1998). *African Americans in Sport*. New York: Routledge Publication.

Salerno, B. A. (2008). *Sister Societies. Women's Antislavery Organisations in Antebellum America.* DeKalb: Northern Illinois University Press.

Sangari, K. (2020). *Politics of the Possible. Essays on Gender, History, Narratives, Colonial English.* New Delhi: Tulika Books.

Sayre, A. (2000). *Rosalind Franklin and DNA*. New York: W. W. Norton and Company.

Schneider, E. M. (2002). *Battered Women and Feminist Law-making*. New Haven: Yale University Press.

Scott, A. M. (Ed.) (1994). *Gender Segregation and Social Change. Men and Women in Changing Labour Markets*. Oxford: Oxford University Press.

Siegel, M. L. (2020). *Peace on Our Terms. The Global Battle for Women's Rights After the First World War*. New York: Columbia University Press.

Sigerman, H. (2001). *Elizabeth Cady Stanton. The Right is Ours*. Oxford: Oxford University Press.

Simmons, C. (2012). *Making Marriage Modern. Women's Sexuality from the Progressive Era to World War II.* Oxford: Oxford University Press.

Sklar, K. K. (1997). *Florence Kelley and the Nation's Work. The Rise of Women's Political Culture, 1830-1900.* New Haven, Connecticut: Yale University Press.

Sklar, K. K. (2019). *Women's Rights Emerges within the Anti-Slavery Movement, 1830-1870. A Brief History with Documents.* New York: Bedford Books.

Small, H. (1999). *Florence Nightingale: Avenging Angel.* New York: Palgrave Macmillan.

Small, H. (2019). *A Brief History of Florence Nightingale: and Her Real Legacy, a Revolution in Public Health.* London: Robinson.

Smiet, K. (2015). Post / secular truths: Sojourner Truth and the intersections of gender, race, and religion. *European Journal of Women's Studies.* Volume 22, No. 1, pp. 7-21.

Smith, R. J. D. (2018). *Excessive Saints. Gender, Narrative, and Theological Invention in Thomas of Cantimpré's Mystical Hagiographies.* New York: Columbia University Press.

Sneider, A. L. (2007). *Suffragists in an Imperial Age. U.S. Expansion and the Woman Question, 1870-1929.* Oxford: Oxford University Press.

Søland, B. (2000). *Becoming Modern. Young Women and the Reconstruction of Womanhood in the 1920's.* Princeton, New Jersey: Princeton University Press.

Solomon, B. M. (1986). *In the Company of Educated Women.* New Haven, Connecticut: Yale University Press.

Spain, D. (2016). *Constructive Feminism. Women's Spaces and Women's Rights in the American City.* Ithaca, New York: Cornell University Press.

Spear, J. M. (2014). *Race, Sex, and Social Order in Early New Orleans.* Baltimore: Johns Hopkins University Press.

Spiers, E. (2018). *Pop-Feminist Narratives. The Female Subject under Neoliberalism in North America, Britain, and Germany*. Oxford: Oxford University Press.

Steans, J. (2007). Debating women's human rights as a universal feminist project: defencing women's human rights as a political tool. - *Review of International Studies*. Volume 33, Issue 1, pp. 11-27.

Steele, V. (1985). *Fashion and Eroticism: Ideals of Feminine Beauty from the Victorian Era to the Jazz Age*. New York: Oxford University Press.

Stites, R. (1978). *The Women's Liberation Movement in Russia. Feminism, Nihilism, and Bolshevism, 1860-1930*. Princeton, New Jersey: Princeton University Press.

Styles, J., and Vickery, A. (Eds.) (2007). *Gender, Taste, and Material Culture in Britain and North America, 1700-1830*. New Haven, Connecticut: Yale University Press.

Sullivan, K. S. (2007). *Constitutional Context. Women and Rights Discourse in Nineteenth-Century America.* Baltimore: Johns Hopkins University Press.

Swift, H. J. (2008). *Gender, Writing, and Performance. Men Defending Women in Late Medieval France.* Oxford: Oxford University Press.

Swinth, K. (2018). *Feminism's Forgotten Fight. The Unfinished Struggle for Work and Family*. Cambridge, Massachusetts: Harvard University Press.

Symons, D. (1981). *The Evolution of Human Sexuality*. Oxford: Oxford University Press.

Talbot, A-M. (Ed.) (1996). *Holy Women of Byzantium. Ten Saints' Lives in English Translation.* Cambridge, Massachusetts: Harvard University Press.

Taylor, V. (1999). Gender and Social Movements: Gender Processes in Women's Self-Help Movements. *Gender and Society*. Volume 13, No. 1, (February 1999), pp. 8-33.

Teele, D. L. (2020). *Forging the Franchise: The Political Origins of the Women's Vote*. Princeton, New Jersey: Princeton University Press.

Terrell, M. C. (2020). *A Coloured Woman in a White World*. Lanham: Rowman and Littlefield Publishers.

Thompson, M. S. (2014). Sisters' History is Women's History: The American Context. *Journal of Women's History*. Volume 26, No. 4, pp. 182-190.

Tomaselli, S. (2021). *Wollstonecraft: Philosophy, Passion, and Politics*. Princeton, New Jersey: Princeton University Press.

Towns, A. E. (2010). *Women and States: Norms and Hierarchies in International Society.* Cambridge: Cambridge University Press.

Tungohan, E. (2017). The Transformative and Radical Feminism of Grassroots Migrant Women's Movement(s) in Canada. *Canadian Journal of Political Science*. Volume 50, Issue 2, pp. 479-494.

Tyson, S. (2018). *Where are the Women? Why Expanding the Archive Makes Philosophy Better.* New York: Columbia University Press.

Valdini, M. E. (2019). *The Inclusion Calculation. Why Men Appropriate Women's Representation*. Oxford: Oxford University Press.

Venarde, B. L. (1999). *Women's Monasticism and Medieval Society. Nunneries in France and England, 890-1215.* Ithaca, New York: Cornell University Press.

Vetter, L. P. (2021). Elizabeth Cady Stanton and Lucretia Mott: radical 'co-adjutors' in the American women's rights movement. *British Journal for the History of Philosophy*. Volume 29, No. 2, pp. 244-258.

Vickery, A. (2003). *The Gentleman's Daughter. Women's Lives in Georgian England*. New Haven, Connecticut: Yale University Press.

Waggenspack, B. (1989). *The Search for Self-Sovereignty: The Oratory of Elizabeth Cady Stanton*. New York: Greenwood Press.

Walker, M. U. (2007). *Moral Understandings. A Feminist Study in Ethics*. Oxford: Oxford University Press.

Walton, M. (2015). *A Woman's Crusade: Alice Paul and the Battle for the Ballot*. New York: St. Martin's Griffin.

Ware, S. (1987). *Beyond Suffrage. Women in the New Deal*. Cambridge, Massachusetts: Harvard University Press.

Ware, S. (2019). *Why They Marched: Untold Stories of the Women Who Fought for the Right to Vote*. Cambridge, Massachusetts: Harvard University Press.

Watts, E. J. (2019). *Hypatia: The Life and Legend of an Ancient Philosopher*. Oxford: Oxford University Press.

Weinbrot, H. D. (2013). *Literature, Religion, and the Evolution of Culture, 1660-1780*. Baltimore: Johns Hopkins University Press.

Weiss, E. (2019). *The Woman's Hour: The Great Fight to Win the Vote*. New York: Penguin Books.

Weiss, P. (2014). Declaring Sexual Equality: Documents from Around the Globe. *Feminist Formations*. Volume 26, Issue 3, (Winter 2014), pp. 147-166.

Weitekamp, M. A. (2005). *Right Stuff, Wrong Sex. America's First Women in Space Program*. Baltimore: Johns Hopkins University Press.

Wellman, J. (1991). The Seneca Falls Women's Rights Convention: A Study of Social Networks. *Journal of Women's History*. Volume 3, No. 1, pp. 9-37.

Wellman, J. (2004). *The Road to Seneca Falls: Elizabeth Cady Stanton and the First Woman's Rights Convention*. Urbana: University of Illinois Press.

Wellman, K. (2013). *Queens and Mistresses of Renaissance France*. New Haven, Connecticut: Yale University Press.

Westbrook, L., and Saperstein, A. (2015). New Categories are not Enough: Rethinking the Measurement of Sex and Gender in Social Surveys. *Gender and Society*. Volume 29, No. 4, (August 2015), pp. 534-560.

Wheeler, L. A. (2007). *Against Obscenity. Reform and the Politics of Womanhood in America, 1873-1935.* Baltimore: Johns Hopkins University Press.

Williams, D. T. (2022). *The Capital of Free Women. Race, Legitimacy, and Liberty in Colonial Mexico*. New Haven, Connecticut: Yale University Press.

Winkle-Wagner, R. (2009). *The Unchosen Me. Race, Gender, and Identity among Black Women in College*. Baltimore: Johns Hopkins University Press.

Wiseman, S. (2007). *Conspiracy and Virtue. Women, Writing, and Politics in Seventeenth-Century England.* Oxford: Oxford University Press.

Wolbrecht, C. (2000). *The Politics of Women's Rights. Parties, Positions, and Change*. Princeton, New Jersey: Princeton University Press.

Wollstonecraft, M. (2020). *A Vindication of the Rights of Woman*. London: Penguin Books.

Woollacott, A. (2001). *To Try Her Fortune in London. Australian Women, Colonialism, and Modernity*. Oxford: Oxford University Press.

Zahniser, J. D., and Fry, A. R. (2014). *Alice Paul: Claiming Power*. New York: Oxford University Press.

Ziarek, E. (2001). *An Ethics of Dissensus*. Stanford, California: Stanford University Press.

Ziarek, E. (2005). *The Rhetoric of Failure*. New York: State University of New York Press.

Ziarek, E. (2012). *Feminist Aesthetics and the Politics of Modernism.* New York: Columbia University Press.

Zinsser, J. P. (Ed.) (2005). *Men, Women, and the Birthing of Modern Science.* DeKalb: Northern Illinois University Press.

Zippel, K. (2017). *Women in Global Science. Advancing Academic Careers through International Collaboration*. Stanford, California: Stanford University Press.